The Scholar and the State

# The Scholar and the State

*Fiction as Political Discourse
in Late Imperial China*

LIANGYAN GE

UNIVERSITY *of* WASHINGTON PRESS ✻ SEATTLE *&* LONDON

Publication of this book was made possible in part by grants from the Chiang Ching-kuo Foundation for International Scholarly Exchange and from the James P. Geiss Foundation, a nonprofit foundation that sponsors research on China's Ming dynasty (1368–1644).

© 2015 by the University of Washington Press
Printed and bound in the United States of America
Composed in Minion Pro, typeface designed by Robert Slimbach
18  17  16  15    5  4  3  2  1

All rights reserved. No part of this publication may be reproduced or transmitted in any form or by any means, electronic or mechanical, including photocopy, recording, or any information storage or retrieval system, without permission in writing from the publisher.

University of Washington Press
www.washington.edu/uwpress

Library of Congress Cataloging-in-Publication Data

Ge, Liangyan.
The scholar and the state :
fiction as political discourse in late imperial China /
Liangyan Ge.
    pages   cm
Includes bibliographical references and index.
ISBN 978-0-295-99417-8 (hardcover : acid-free paper)
1. Chinese fiction—History and criticism.
2. Literature and society—China.
3. Scholars—China—History.
4. China—Intellectual life.
I. Title.
PL2415.G4   2015
895.13009—dc23           2014007526

The paper used in this publication is acid-free and meets the minimum requirements of American National Standard for Information Sciences—Permanence of Paper for Printed Library Materials, ANSI Z39.48-1984.∞

To all my teachers,
from elementary school to graduate school
and beyond

# Contents

Acknowledgments ix
A Note on Chinese Romanization xi

**Introduction 3**

**1. A Rugged Partnership**
The Intellectual Elite and the Imperial State 16

**2. *Romance of the Three Kingdoms***
The Mencian View of Political Sovereignty 34

**3. The Scholar-Lover in Erotic Fiction**
A Power Game of Selection 67

**4. *The Scholars***
Trudging Out of a Textual Swamp 98

5. The Stone in *Dream of the Red Chamber*
Unfit to Repair the Azure Sky  136

**Coda**
Out of the Imperial Shadow  170

Notes  181
Glossary of Chinese Characters  229
Selected Bibliography  247
Index  267

# Acknowledgments

For the research and writing that have resulted in this book, I received generous financial support from the Chiang Ching-kuo Foundation in the form of a research grant. I also benefited from a research travel grant from the University of Notre Dame's Institute for Scholarship in Liberal Arts, which enabled me to visit some of the major libraries in China, including the National Library in Beijing and the Municipal Library of Shanghai. I am grateful to the College of Arts and Letters and the Department of East Asian Languages and Cultures at University of Notre Dame for granting me a one-year research leave and a one-semester research leave, which greatly facilitated this book project.

I am deeply indebted to many individuals for their help throughout the entire course or at different stages of the project. Eugene Eoyang, as always, has been a major source of inspiration for me. At an early stage of the project I received advice from Benjamin Elman, which proved immensely valuable. Several other scholars—including Robert Hegel, Anthony Yu (even in his retirement!), Victor Mair, David Rolston, Vibeke Børdahl, Martin Huang, Patricia Sieber, Paul Jakov Smith, Anne E. McLaren, Margaret Wan, Ming Dong Gu, Sheldon Hsiao-peng Lu, Guo Yingde, Xin Ying, Shi Yaohua, and Han Jiegen, among others—either shared with me their views on the project or offered comments and suggestions on my manuscript or portions of it. To them, I am deeply grateful.

I am also thankful to my colleagues and students at University of Notre Dame, who have made teaching and research such a joy for me. Special thanks are due to the staff of Notre Dame's Hesburgh Library, especially Hye-jin Juhn, for indulging my numerous requests for interlibrary loans of books and articles.

Let me thank my wife, Yongqing, who has spared me most of the household chores throughout the years, which made this book project considerably less daunting to me. Thanks are also due to my daughter Sherry and her husband Vijay, who, as medical students, have become my best-trusted health advisers and a major source of encouragement. I am also grateful to my numerous friends in China, the United States, and elsewhere, whose telephone calls and email messages have added so much joy and comfort to my life.

Two anonymous reviewers with the University of Washington Press read my manuscript meticulously and offered many insightful comments and suggestions for revision. To them, I am profoundly indebted. Needless to say, any remaining errors and shortcomings in this book are mine. I am also deeply thankful to the editors at the University of Washington Press, especially Executive Editor Lorri Hagman, who have been instrumental in bringing this work to print.

If this book can be considered any kind of achievement, I owe it to the teachers who guided my intellectual development, from elementary school to graduate school. Even after I became a college professor, I continued to benefit from my teachers, even though I did not formally take a course with some of them. To all my teachers, this book is dedicated, with enduring respect and gratitude.

# A Note on Chinese Romanization

In this book the pinyin system is used for Chinese romanization. For citations from sources where the Wade-Giles system is used, all Chinese names and terms in the text have been converted to pinyin for the sake of consistency. The Wade-Giles romanization for titles of books and articles, however, remains unchanged. I thank the original authors for their understanding.

The Scholar and the State

# Introduction

"What is the political stance of this work?" "What is the writer's relationship to political power? Is the writer an insider [*tizhinei*] or an outsider [*tizhiwai*]?" These are questions that critics of modern Chinese fiction regularly ask. In comparison, such an emphasis on politics is much less common in the field of late imperial Chinese vernacular fiction, where interpretation is usually conducted in the framework of a school of thinking, most often Confucianism, and sometimes Daoism or Buddhism.[1] That, of course, does not mean Chinese fiction was impervious to political reading before it entered the modern age. Premodern Chinese vernacular fiction was deeply embedded in a complex network of power relations, which inevitably instilled political meanings into it. Adopting an interdisciplinary approach and drawing on sociopolitical history, intellectual thinking, and literary studies, this book offers a reading of a number of works of vernacular fiction from the Ming (1368–1644) and Qing (1644–1911) periods in terms of the relationship between the intellectual elite and the imperial power.

On a personal level, a writer of Chinese vernacular fiction was typically someone who was disgruntled and resentful. His bitterness, according to many traditional critics, was usually rooted in his failure in the civil service examinations, which could in turn serve as a motivation for his fiction writing. The author of one of the prefatory pieces to the Rongyutang edition of *Water Margin* (Shuihu zhuan; also translated as *Outlaws of the Marsh*), allegedly Li Zhi (1527–1602), calls the novel a work for "venting indignation" (*fafen*). And the reason for the ire, as suggested in the slightly oblique language here, was the unfairness in the imperial state's system for selecting officials: "Nowadays, less virtuous persons dominate more virtuous ones, and the less worthy dominate the worthier. And that is the rule. If a less worthy person is the dominator and a worthier one is dominated, how can the latter be submissive without feeling humiliated? This is like a weaker person being the captor while a stronger one is the captive. How can the latter allow himself to be captured without trying to escape?"[2]

The late Ming critic Yang Minglang assumes a similar vein in his preface to *Registers of Heroes* (Yingxiong pu), a combination of the simplified versions (*jianben*) of both *Romance of the Three Kingdoms* (Sanguo yanyi) and *Water Margin*. He asks in the preface: "Under the chilly mists and the cold moon, or amid the bitter winds and miserable rain, wouldn't there be heroes and people of outstanding talent joining each other in chanting the stirring strains, to pour out their grievances and indignation?" The grievance over the system of official selection is only thinly veiled: "Those who are sovereigns must read this book; once they have read it, the heroes will be on the sides of the throne. Those who are prime ministers must read this book; once they have read it, the heroes will be in the imperial court."[3] Likewise, in his preface to the 1658 edition of his novel *Ping Shan Leng Yan*, the pseudonymous author Tianhuazang Zhuren (Owner of the Depository of Heavenly Flowers) laments over his wasted abilities: "Facing the spring flowers and autumn moon, one cannot help being moved to tears: what is the use of my talent?" Fiction writing was thus a vent for his pent-up emotions: "One cannot do anything but project in fiction the illusory grandeur of his career.... All that is delightful and wonderful on the page is actually what he wanted to cry and weep for in life."[4]

For many fiction writers, failure in the examinations was the most emotional setback of their personal lives. It reshaped their literary imagination and left an indelible imprint on their writings. Indeed, the topic of the examinations is ubiquitous in Chinese vernacular fiction. Among the short stories in Feng Menglong's (1574–1645) three anthologies of vernacular tales known as *San yan*, those that deal directly with the examinations count for over forty percent.[5] The situation is similar with novels. In many works the topic is prominent in the foreground of the narrative;

in others, it lurks beneath the surface. One example is *Journey to the West* (Xiyou ji), a novel in which most of the characters are ostensibly supernatural beings. Through many years of diligent learning, the monkey Sun Wukong acquires magic powers unrivaled in the heavenly court, but is denied any official position above that of stable manager. Enraged with this insult and belittlement, the monkey takes revenge by wreaking havoc in heaven.

Such veiled lampoons of the perceived unfairness in official selection are also seen in *Water Margin,* where a group of aspirant warriors are forced to become bandits. They then prove their superior worth by repeatedly defeating the government forces headed by imperially appointed commanders. The warriors in the novel who become *marginalized*—as the title of the novel suggests—intriguingly parallel the historical compilers of the novel who drifted into a *marginalized* cultural zone.

Traditional Chinese fiction commentators have considered vernacular fiction a channel for venting personal grievances and frustration, despite questions of authorship in some cases and inadequate biographical information in others. However, failure to enter officialdom was more the rule than the exception for the literati in late imperial China, and what might appear to be a particular scholar's personal setback was actually a misfortune shared by thousands of his peers. So even without comprehensive biographical information, we can presume that this disposition would have been shared by the vast majority of the literati.

This collective approach is appropriate to the subject. The form of Chinese vernacular fiction, like that of the Western novel, is predominantly biographical, which gives shape to otherwise infinite and discrete material from social reality. The narrated life of the central character serves the purpose of elucidating his relationship with the "world of ideals," which, in Georg Lukacs's words, "stands above him" but at the same time is "realized only through his existence within that individual and his lived experience."[6] The central character thus becomes a "problematic individual," and everything in the fictional world has to go through him to receive a "unified articulation." He should therefore be considered an embodiment of a certain type of problematic in social life, rather than merely a surrogate of the author as an individual person. Indeed, as a central theme in Chinese vernacular fiction, government service is associated with communal and transpersonal imagery conglomerated and preserved throughout the experiences of generations of literati, akin to the Jungian notion of the collective unconscious. Fundamental patterns and forms in the fictional presentation of the literati experience are thus not so much personal as, to follow the Jungian terminology again, archetypal.

Consequently, the fictional voice about official selection and government service is depersonalized, but depersonalization is only the first step in historicizing it. We may consider fiction as a reflection of the historical environment in which it was born. To do so is certainly useful, yet ultimately it may prove to discount the efficacy of literature. To consider fiction purely as a product of history is to treat history as a finished process prior to literary creation. In that view, literature is seen as a mere derivative, conceived and nurtured within the parent body of social history. This hierarchy of history over literature is a far cry from the Aristotelian view that poetry, "more concerned with the universal," is "more philosophical and more significant than history," which is "more with the individual."[7] Modern historical criticism has taken a different understanding of the relationship of literature to history. Instead of treating literature simply as determined by history, some consider literary practices as political forces that participate in the dialectic process of history.[8] Others refuse to treat history as a mimetic reenacting of events that have taken place in the external world. Instead, they look at history, like literature, as a discursive practice. For them, history is not a completed story of the past but an open-ended process of getting to know the world, a world that is constantly joined by history writing itself.[9] In that sense, literary works are no less historical documents than history, as literature, like writing of history, attempts simultaneously to know the world and to participate in it. Citing approvingly Herder's notion of "the mutual embeddedness of art and history," some scholars of New Historicism argue that poetry "is not the path to a transhistorical truth . . . but the key to particular historically embedded social and psychological formations."[10] As a literary work is no longer seen as a mirror passively reflecting reality but an active player in social life, it is as much an event in history as a representation of it: "If an entire culture is regarded as a text, then everything is at least potentially in play both at the level of representation and at the level of event. Indeed, it becomes increasingly difficult to maintain a clear, unambiguous boundary between what is representation and what is event. At the very least, the drawing or maintaining of that boundary is itself an event."[11]

This book is an attempt to historicize Chinese vernacular fiction as a representation of as well as a participant in the sociopolitical reality of the time. It focuses on political discourse in the fictional texts, which are heavily informed by both the engagement and the tension between the interests of the intellectual elite and those of the imperial power (often referred to as *shi* 勢) during the late dynasties.¹² Imperial power refers to the political authority centered on the throne, but it is always a larger notion than the emperor as a person. In Chinese dynastic history there were rulers who were too weak or too young to fully exercise the imperial authority. In those cases, imperial power, completely or partially, fell into the hands of strong men (or, in some cases, women) close to the power center. Even a capable emperor would need assistance from his aides, many of whom were scholar-bureaucrats. Their dual status as both scholars and officials underscores the fact that imperial power and the intellectual elite were not completely discrete categories.

Nor was the intellectual elite, whose members were often known as *shi* 士 or *shidafu*, a homogeneous social group. Between these two terms, *shi* may be of earlier origin, with a broader semantic range: originally it referred simply to a male adult, typically one of the lowest rank of nobility, before it came to be used in pre-Qin times (prior to 221 BCE) to indicate an office holder. In the latter sense, it became largely synonymous with *shidafu*.¹³ In the context of the late imperial times, both *shi* and *shidafu* refer to intellectuals in general, in and out of civil officialdom. According to the dictionary *Sea of Words* (Cihai), *shidafu* was a term for bureaucrats in "ancient times" (*gushi*) but came to refer to respected scholars in general in "premodern periods" (*jiushi*).¹⁴ The semantic shift itself reflects a historical change in the formation of the intellectual elite that may have started prior to late imperial times. A modern historian has informed us that in the Northern Song period (960–1126) "those who called themselves *shi* still thought of themselves as people who served in government"; by the end of the Southern Song (1127–1279), however, there were as many as 450,000 examination candidates and a mere 20,000 officials.¹⁵ That change continued throughout the Ming and Qing periods. While the number of the examination candidates increased steadily, the overwhelming majority of them ended up receiving no official appointments.

As the *shi* gradually evolved from a social group almost identical with civil bureaucracy into one preponderantly outside officialdom, they drifted increasingly away from the gravity of political power. To be sure, the literati and the political authorities were never completely at odds with each other. The fact that the imperial state continued to recruit scholars to replenish civil officialdom was sufficient evidence for their interdependence. Furthermore, to maintain order in local communities, especially beneath the county level, the imperial government relied heavily on the local gentry, mostly literati.[16] However, the authoritarian rule of the imperium and its seizure of the moral primacy from the *daotong*, or the lineage of orthodox learning, significantly reshaped its relationship to the literati.[17] Despite the complexities and possible ambiguities in the relationship, macrocosmically one may consider the literati and imperial state as two distinct and interacting social forces. Even in some cases of scholar-bureaucrats, their official status may not necessarily have prevented them from being considered members of the intellectual elite. In fact, because of their proximity to the center of political power, their stories might reflect the *shi* (intellectual elite)—*shi* (state power) relationship most clearly.

In Western scholarship on premodern Chinese literature and culture, the word "literati" has been treated as the standard English equivalent of *shi* or *shidafu*. This book follows that practice. However, "literati," which literally means "men of letters" (*wenren*), may not always do full justice to *shi* or *shidafu*, who were not only culturally elites but could also be social and political activists. As Tu Wei-ming puts it, "The priestly function and philosophical role in both the public image and the self-definition of the Confucian scholar compels us to characterize him not only as a 'literatus' but also as an 'intellectual.'"[18] In view of such semantic nuances, this book will also use terms such as "intellectuals" and "scholars," which are considered generally interchangeable with but specifically complementary to the term "literati."

Obviously, the match between the literati and the imperial state was never one of two equals. Most often the state was on the offensive, forcing the literati to protect or negotiate for their own interests. In Antonio Gramsci's words, "state = political society + civil society, in other words hegemony protected by the armor of coercion."[19] Yet the "cultural hegemony" of the imperial state is not to be considered here purely an external threat to the literati. Michel Foucault proposes that power should always be regarded as a relationship, as power would cease to be power if it meets no resistance: "I would like to suggest another way to go further toward a new economy of power relations.... It consists in taking the forms of resistance against different forms of power as a starting point. To use another metaphor, it consists in using this resistance as a chemical catalyst so as to bring to light power relations, locate their position, find out their point of application and the methods used."[20]

In a sense, Chinese imperial power could not be simply *possessed* by the throne or the state, because it could never exist as an entity or structure external to the social nexus. It would not become realized until it went into connection, collision, or confrontation with other social forces. Imperial power not only subjected Chinese literati to passivity but also spurred them to new actions. What defines that power relationship, to borrow from Foucault again, is "a mode of action that does not act directly and immediately on others" but "acts upon their actions: an action upon action, on possible or actual future or present actions."[21] Indeed, while relying heavily on intellectual elites for the civil administration of the empire, imperial power also had to control them and thwart their desires and aspirations. Such "antagonism of strategies" was, perhaps more than other social relations, responsible for the particular type of cultural order in imperial China. What happened between the state and the literati was therefore not only a struggle over domination but also a catalysis generating new cultural phenomena and meanings.

The system of civil service examinations was, beyond any doubt, the most important interface between the literati and the state. Back in the Tang period (618–907), Emperor Taizong (r. 627–49) once made this outcry of joy at the sight of a long file of successful candidates of the metropolitan examinations: "All heroes of the empire have now entered my fold."[22] Surely there was good reason for the emperor's exultation. If he indeed had all men of talent under his control, he would not only be able to replenish civil officialdom but also leave little opportunity for political opposition. The emperor's exclamation summarizes the nature of the examination system, a sociopolitical institution he himself helped to develop.[23] For over a thousand years since its genesis during the Sui dynasty (589–618), the examination system served as the imperial state's primary avenue for selecting civil officials and was the most important means for political and ideological control of the literati. Starting in the Yuan period (1279–1368), when the government adopted the Cheng-Zhu school of learning as the core of the examination curriculum, the literati's intellectual lives were "constricted into a system of concepts, arguments, and beliefs endorsed by the state for larger political purposes."[24] In the meantime, as an official appointment usually brought about enormous social prestige and abundant economic benefits, success in the examinations became for many scholars the ultimate goal of education. The examination system thus became a realm where "imperial dynasties, gentry-literati elites, and classical studies were tightly intertwined," and when the institution was finally abolished in the early twentieth century, they all fell with it.[25]

One of the "larger political purposes" of imperial power with the examination system was its appropriation of the *dao* learning (*daoxue*). The rulers—especially emperors Hongwu (r. 1368–98) and Yongle (r. 1403–24) of the Ming and emperors Kangxi (r. 1662–1722), Yongzheng (r. 1723–35), and Qianlong (r. 1736–95) of the Qing—played the roles of both apostle of *dao* learning and sponsor of massive literary projects. By doing so they made themselves appear like "sage-kings," boasting supreme authority in both state politics and moral and intellectual matters. Indeed, much more than the pristine form of Confucianism represented by Confucius and Mencius, the Cheng-Zhu school of thinking was, from its inception, a product of the power relations between the *daotong* and the *zhengtong*, or the lineage of political power. Yet the Ming and Qing rulers further tightened their ideological grip, often through their tampering with the Confucian canon and manipulation of the examination curriculum. The state's appropriation of the *daotong* in late imperial China may be considered a good example of the symbiotic dynamic between power and knowledge. On the one hand, the Confucian orthodoxy exerted some influence on political power; on the other hand, the imperial state constantly attempted to reshape *dao* learning into a form of knowledge that could best serve its own purposes. In that sense, the Cheng-Zhu school of thought, as the state ideology and the criterion for official selection, should be considered a discourse fashioned by the joint forces of both political power and academic learning.

Confucianism, in both its pristine version and the Cheng-Zhu formulation, was a system of thinking with a strong emphasis on moral cultivation and perfection on both personal and communal levels. With their moral and intellectual superiority, leading figures in the *daotong* tradition such as Confucius and Mencius did not serve society as princes or administrators but primarily as teachers. The Confucian practice of moralizing people's day-to-day conduct, like the Christian church's guidance of its members to salvation, was akin to a shepherd's care for his flock. Indeed, in its role of moral stewardship for the people and its rivalry and competition with political power, the authority of the *daotong* was not unlike "an old power technique that originated in Christian institution," which Foucault calls the "pastoral power."[26] Yu Yingshi has noted that the bifurcation of the *zhengtong* and the *daotong* in Chinese history was "not totally incomparable to that of the state and the church in the West," even though "anything resembling the church-state confrontation in the West never truly took place in China."[27] Foucault argues that, while the "ecclesiastical institutionalization" of the pastoral power "has ceased or at least lost its vitality since the eighteenth century," its function became integrated into modern Western state power, which is "both an individualizing and totalizing form of power."[28] Even though Foucault asserts that this "tricky combination" was never seen before in the history of human societies, not "even in the old Chinese society,"[29] a remarkable parallel is discernible between the modern Western state's adoption of the pastoral power and the state's appropriation of the *daotong* in late imperial China. By adopting pastoral power, modern Western state started to use a particular set of techniques and rationalities that had originally belonged to the church in order to "govern or guide people's conduct as individual members of a population."[30] Quite similarly, the state in late imperial China seized from the *daotong* the moral guardianship of its people, especially through the regime of the examinations and the education system closely geared to official selection.

The literati's frustration was thus twofold, as they were largely displaced from both their traditional profession of civil officialdom and their traditional role of moral leadership. In their power relationship with the imperial state, they were obviously at a great disadvantage. Yet, if a power relationship is a field of interactions, as Foucault insists, Chinese vernacular fiction, or at least a significant part of it, may be considered the literati's "action" upon the "action" of the state. Indeed, the popular perception of vernacular fiction as an unofficial and unorthodox discourse—suggested in such epithets as "wild" (*ye*) and "extra" (*wai*) that frequently appear in fiction titles—always cast on it a coloring of unruliness and intractability. Of course, under the threat of literary inquisition few writers would be blatantly seditious or even publicly repudiate the tenet of political loyalty.

Consequently, fictional expressions of political discontent and disillusionment are for the most part subtle and covert.

As the imperial state became the predominant voice in the public discourse of ethics and morality, the speech rights for the literati were diminished. It has been suggested that the literati in late imperial China found themselves "in a state of collective aphasia."[31] Under such circumstances, they found an alternative discourse in *xiaoshuo*, supposedly an insignificant discourse on trifle matters, as the term *xiaoshuo*, literally "small talk," suggests. The bifurcation of these two different discourses may shed light on some salient features of Chinese vernacular fiction. For instance, the fictional indulgence in *qing* as private and personal feelings might be, among other things, a counterweight to the neo-Confucian emphasis on *li* as truth in the public sphere. For fiction writers, the retreat from public discourse was therefore not really a retreat in defeat. By earning their speech rights in "small talk," they quickly turned it into a platform on "big" issues; by seemingly pulling themselves away from politics, they found a way to reenter it.

Yet exclusive focus on concrete historical happenings in the immediate context of a literary work may result in seeing the tree while losing sight of the forest. Historicism with no vision is, in Hayden White's formulation, "a timid historicism."[32] This book aims to render fictional works intelligible in terms of their synchronic as well as diachronic meanings. For that purpose, they are viewed not merely in the context of a particular historical period—namely, late imperial dynasties—but also in the sequenced and layered history of the relationship between the intellectuals and the state since the early times of imperial China. In this more teleological approach, these works in Chinese vernacular fiction are to be considered a late chapter in a master narrative of that intricate relationship. Toward that end, chapter 1 offers a brief survey of the evolution of the *shi* (士)-*shi* (勢) relationship throughout Chinese imperial history. In particular, it discusses the implication of the literati's alienation from their traditional identity as office-holders and the political authorities' appropriation of the *daotong* in late imperial times, and considers the literati's power relationship with the state a crucial factor for the general intellectual climate. In short, this chapter brings out the contours of the sociopolitical landscape for Chinese vernacular fiction.

Considering works of fiction as political acts and events, one may realize that some of them could have been catapulted into existence by a certain political situation. A case in point is *Romance of the Three Kingdoms* (hereafter *Three Kingdoms*), which will be discussed in chapter 2. The depiction of the ruler-minister and ruler-subject relationships in this historical novel demonstrates a strong affinity to the Mencian ideal of political sovereignty, which advocates reciprocity and interdependence between the ruler and the ruled and between political power and intellectual talent. This chapter offers a review of the authoritarian rule by the founding emperors of the Ming, Hongwu (Zhu Yuanzhang) and Yongle (Zhu Di), especially their suppression of the Confucian classic *Mencius* (Mengzi) and manipulation of the examination curriculum. The unswerving adherence to the Mencian view in *Three Kingdoms*, whose earliest textual exemplar may be dated to the early decades of the Ming, may be seen as a political statement by the literati. While the novelist clearly had to maintain a certain degree of allegiance to historical sources, the manners in which he selected and revised historical information signals a political stance against absolute imperial dominance, which becomes clear when viewed against the background of early Ming politics.

As one sees in *Three Kingdoms*, a man of talent in the Three Kingdoms period was in an advantageous position to select his political master. The literati in late imperial times no longer had that luxury, when highly centralized imperial power became the sole employer of talent and intelligence. Chapter 3 examines similarities between the selection of scholars for civil bureaucracy and the selection of women for the palace staff and imperial harem in late imperial China. Taking advantage of the affinities between these processes, late Ming and early Qing fictional eroticism frequently employs the civil service examinations as a metaphor for the selection of women in sexual escapades. A number of seventeenth-century erotic narratives are relevant here, including Li Yu's (1611–80) *The Carnal Prayer Mat* (Rou putuan), allowing us to read the narrated eroticism hinged upon the examination metaphor as satire and parody of the imperial state as the ultimate selector from the human resources empire-wide.

If the seventeenth-century writers of fictional eroticism turned official selection into the butt of bawdy jokes, the eighteenth-century novelist Wu Jingzi (1701–54) assumed a more somber approach in his masterwork *The Scholars* (Rulin waishi), which presents a panoramic picture of moral ills. Chapter 4 shows how the seemingly episodic narrative structure in *The

*Scholars* veils a consistent thematic thread involving the literati's struggle to break out of the capsule of texts in which the state has entrapped them. As spiritual heirs to Wang Mian, with whom the novel begins, the four "extraordinary figures" (*qiren*) at the conclusion of the novel herald a new generation of educated men who are able to extricate themselves from the servitude to the imperial state. *The Scholars* thus presents an account of the literati's wrestling with political power and their shift from serving the state toward serving the society.

In a sense, the four "extraordinary figures" at the end of *The Scholars* herald the advent of another such figure, namely Jia Baoyu in the slightly later novel *Dream of the Red Chamber* (Honglou meng). Taking the reflexive nature of the novel as the premise, chapter 5 examines Jia Baoyu's strong aversion to a bureaucratic career and his status as the destined maker of the "Story of the Stone" (Shitou ji), the narrative text about his mundane experience that is eventually to be inscribed on the supernatural rock. The narrative account of the Stone-*baoyu* (the jade)-Baoyu trinity may be seen as a dramatic recuperation of the story of the fictionalized novelist in the prefatory piece titled "Fanli" (literally, statement of general principles), especially his conversion to fiction writing. *Dream of the Red Chamber*, in this light, can be read as a fiction about a young scholar's rethinking of the literati's long-standing political commitment to government service and all the complications surrounding his independent vocational decision.

Given the enormous corpus of Chinese vernacular fiction, the works to be discussed here are intended to be only illustrative. While the fiction writers may not have been fully aware of their historical roles, they were, after all, prepared by the ideological conditions of their times. Individual works are thus not isolated and discrete artifacts but *paroles* in the larger system of *langue*, that is, individual utterances in a collective discourse of the literati. Indeed, one may discern an attempt in Chinese vernacular fiction, even though often repressed as a "political unconscious," to redefine the literati's group identity and reassess their place in the changed power structure. In particular, Chinese vernacular fiction represents a relentless effort to destabilize the value system of the day, or the symbolic order that the state helped to sustain and bolster with the moral teachings that it had appropriated from the *daotong*, especially the teaching on government service. In doing so, the genre heralds the intellectuals' social and cultural roles in a new age. To that extent, late imperial Chinese vernacular fiction "must be read as a symbolic meditation on the destiny of community."[33]

Many works of Chinese vernacular fiction are known for their remarkable polysemy and multifariousness. They can be contextualized in multiple ways with different configurations of cultural forces of the time—the burgeoning commercial economy, rising urban culture, the booming print and publishing industry, spreading literacy, the evolving aesthetic tastes, the interfusion between elite culture and popular culture—resulting in virtually inexhaustible interpretational possibilities. The purpose of this book is a modest one, namely, to call further attention to a way of reading Chinese vernacular fiction that has not been adequately discussed. The political reading presented here complements other readings but does not aim to supersede them.

All of the works discussed here were written before the end of the eighteenth century. There is a reason for not including later works. With the intrusion of the Western powers—an intrusion that had cultural, economic, and military consequences—Qing China became significantly different in the nineteenth century. The addition of the West as a new player thoroughly changed the political landscape of the country. For that reason, nineteenth-century Chinese fiction falls out of the scope of the present book, and should be the topic for another study.

CHAPTER 1

# A Rugged Partnership

*The Intellectual Elite and the Imperial State*

Let us begin with a doggerel titled "Exhortation to Studies" (Quan xue wen), allegedly composed by Emperor Zhenzong of the Song (r. 998–1022):

> To enrich one's family, no need to acquire good farmlands,
> In books there are thousands of bushels of grains.
> To have a comfortable home, no need to pile up bricks,
> In books there are houses made of gold.
> Don't worry that you have no retinue when you travel,
> In books there are carriages lined up for you.
> Don't complain there is no matchmaker to find you a wife,
> In books there are jade-like beauties.[1]

No doubt, the prospect of dramatic upward mobility presented so seductively here could be a powerful motivation for education and for the literati's participation in the triennial cycle of examinations. However, in their relationship to the state power, Chinese intellectual elites had other things at stake, things that were more important than "houses made of gold" or "jade-like beauties."

## CHINESE INTELLECTUALS AND GOVERNMENT SERVICE

Since the ancient times, Chinese intellectuals, or the *shi*, had always considered themselves the mainstay in the learning of the *dao*, the principle that was supposed to be the governing force of all relations in society as well as in the cosmos. Idealistically, adherence to the *dao* was their ultimate commitment, transcending all materialistic pursuits. For Confucius, that commitment was the distinguishing quality of a "superior man" (*junzi*): "The superior man seeks the *dao* and is indifferent to food . . . and the superior man is concerned about [the lack] of the *dao* and not about his poverty." A *shi* should uphold the *dao* for its own sake, and not for any egoistic considerations: "A man can promote the *dao* which he follows, but the *dao* cannot promote the man."² Mencius took over that idea from Confucius and further elaborated it: "When there is the *dao* in the world, one follows the *dao* all his life; when there is a lack of the *dao* in the world, one lays down his life for the *dao*."³

In the Confucian imagination, the halcyon era of antiquity under the rule of the legendary sage-kings remained the ultimate model for later historical periods to emulate. The social harmony in that lost golden age was seen as based on a seamless unity between the *dao* and political power, or *shi* 勢. "Wise kings in antiquity," as Mencius observed, "devoted themselves to goodness, forgetting their own exalted positions" (*hao shan er wang shi*).⁴ The Mencian words were echoed by the early Qing scholar Wan Sida (1633–83): "Yao, Shun, Yu, Tang, King Wen, and King Wu were all scholars who became rulers" (*ru er jun zhe*). According to Wan, that was the reason that "in those times the lineage of the *dao* learning was highly esteemed, society was harmonious, people were warm-hearted and honest, and there was nobody who would undermine the *dao*."⁵ That happy union between the *dao* and political power, however, did not last forever. In Confucius' own time, the Spring and Autumn period (841–476 BCE), "rituals corrupted and music crumpled" (*lihuai yuebeng*). Paradoxically, however, it was precisely this disruption and disintegration of cultural order that was responsible for what Yu Yingshi has called a historical "breakthrough" (*tupo*), for it catalyzed the formation of the *shi* as a new and self-conscious social group.⁶ As the era of the sage-kings had long passed, the intellectuals, in defending and advocating the *dao*, could no longer take support from the political powers for granted. That was the beginning of the bifurcation of the two traditions: the *daotong* (lineage of *dao* learning) and the *zhengtong* (lineage of state power). The *daotong*, as Fei Xiaotong has informed us, was "a crucial notion in traditional literati's political consciousness."[7] As a tradition to be passed on from one generation to the next, it had endowed the Confucian project of establishing a moral order on the *dao* with a teleological meaning, which in turn became associated with the Confucians' sense of historical responsibility: "A *shi* should not be without a broad mind and vigorous endurance. His burden is heavy and his course is long. He takes perfect virtue as his responsibility—isn't that burden heavy? He never ends it until his death—isn't that course long?"[8]

That Confucian sense of social obligation easily translated into a desire to participate in governance. The *daotong*, therefore, was never insulated from the *zhengtong*. Rather, the Confucian intellectuals were clearly aware that they would not be able to realize their ideal of perfect moral order simply by working in closed studios. Considering themselves both morally and intellectually superior, they were eager to demonstrate their worth by running state affairs: "When a country is well-governed, poverty and ignominy are things to be ashamed of. When a country is ill-governed, opulence and decency are things to be ashamed of."[9]

For many centuries, the *shi* were indeed the most qualified candidates for official positions. Their moral, political, and administrative aspirations were well registered in the celebrated Confucian tenet, "internal sageliness and external kingliness" (*nei sheng wai wang*).[10] The relationship between *nei sheng* and *wai wang* was best expounded in *The Great Learning* (Daxue): "The ancients who wished to illustrate illustrious virtue throughout the kingdom first ordered well their own States. Wishing to order well their States, they first regulated well their families. Wishing to regulate their families, they first cultivated their persons.... Their persons being cultivated, their families were regulated. Their families being regulated, their states were rightly governed. Their states being rightly governed, the whole kingdom was made tranquil and happy."[11]

To the Confucians, self-cultivation and participation in governance were thus not only in a seamless continuum but also complementary to each other. "In obscurity a man makes perfect his own person," as Mencius exhorted, "but in prominence he makes perfect the whole Empire as well."[12] Yet a true Confucian scholar would never be content with making perfect only his own person. As suggested in the progressive order in the passage from *The Great Learning*, moral cultivation of the self was considered not an end in itself but the premise for the larger moral project, namely, making perfect "the whole empire." Believing in the perfectibility not only of their individual selves but also of the Chinese civilization at large, Confucian intellectuals found it impossible to detach themselves from governance and secular politics. Tu Wei-ming has put it most astutely: "Had they been offered a comparable choice of rendering to Caesar what is Caesar's and to God what is God's in which the kings minded political business and the Confucians were allowed to devote themselves wholly to cultural matters, they would have had to reject it."[13]

Ever since the *shi* became a self-conscious social group, they had always considered government service crucial for their moral project of "making perfect the whole empire." "The four classes of commoners—scholars, farmers, craftsmen, and merchants—have their respective occupations. Scholars are the ones who study in order to take up official positions" (*xue yi ju wei yue shi*).[14] In the eyes of many Confucian intellectuals, it was their heavenly endowed birthright to be civil officials. "One who studies well should become an official" (*xue er you ze shi*), as Confucius himself said tersely.[15] "A *shi* losing his official position," observed Mencius, "is like a feudal lord losing his state. . . . A *shi* taking office is like a farmer cultivating his land."[16] By saying so, Mencius considered office-holding simply a defining attribute of a scholar. Xunzi, on his part, used the term "gentlemen" (*junzi*) to refer to scholars. Despite all the differences between them, Xunzi's view of the intellectual's social role was quite similar to Mencius'. According to Xunzi, the "gentlemen" should be the ones in charge of social matters: "Heaven and Earth gave birth to the gentlemen, and the gentlemen are the ones to manage the matters between Heaven and Earth."[17] For the literati, to be bolted out of officialdom was thus not merely to be deprived of the vocational choice that they had been taught they were destined to take. More importantly, it would signify the shattering of a moral and political ideal that they had cherished for centuries as a social group.

## THE LITERATI'S DECLINING SOCIAL STATUS

Throughout Chinese imperial history, the intellectuals' participation in governance necessarily meant some kind of collaboration between the forces representing those two traditions, the *daotong* and the *zhengtong*. For a considerably long period, Chinese rulers were generally willing to accept and respect the collective status of the *shi* as the upholder of the *daotong*. To exploit their intellectual and moral resources, rulers even had to treat some of the *shi* as mentors (*shi*) or friends (*you*). Duke Huan of the Qi (r. 685–643 BCE), for instance, was fully aware that he would not be able to govern effectually without the help of men of intelligence and talent. When Bao Shuya recommended Guan Zhong (d. 645 BCE), who had once almost killed Duke Huan on the battlefield, the duke paid respect to his future adviser profusely by having Guan Zhong "perfumed thrice and bathed thrice" before he went a long way to meet him in person.[18]

Indeed, the civil service from the *shi* was often the most crucial buttress for political sovereignty. The king of the Qin, Ying Zheng (r. 246–210 BCE), would not have become the First Emperor of a unified China without the counsel of his top advisers, especially Han Fei (d. 233 BCE) and Li Si (d. 208 BCE). For Liu Bang, the founding emperor of the Han (r. 206–195 BCE), it was the court ritual and music instituted by the scholars such as Shusun Tong (fl. 206 BCE) that helped establish his dignity as monarch.[19] However, even when many of them served prominently in civil bureaucracy, the *shi* were never truly share-holders of the state power, which belonged ultimately to the throne. Confucius remained no more than a "commoner king" (*suwang*) despite all the dazzling titles that the rulers of successive dynasties bestowed on him, and his followers in all subsequent historical periods were often among the earliest to defend the throne against any possible usurpers.

In general, the *daotong* in the pre-Qin times managed to hold its own in its interaction with the *zhengtong*, as the state power consistently found itself in need of the support from the *shi* both morally and intellectually. That situation, however, started to change during the Qin (221–206 BCE). After its unification of China, the suddenly exalted power of the imperial state found a most intense expression in the First Emperor's decision in 213 BCE to "burn books and bury scholars alive" (*fenshu kengru*), which was tantamount to a blitzkrieg on the *daotong*. The situation of course changed considerably during the Han. Soon after taking the throne, Liu Bang was wise enough to realize that, while he had won the empire by fighting on horseback, he would not be able to rule the empire on horseback as well.[20] He issued an edict where he appeared—following the examples of King Wen of the Zhou and Duke Huan of the Qi—a sincere and eager seeker for talent: "No kings were more prominent than King Wen of the Zhou; and no lords were more prominent than Duke Huan of the Qi. Both were successful because of the assistance from men of abilities.... Those among the men of virtue and ability who are willing to follow me— I can make them prominent and esteemed. I hereby make this intention of mine known to the entire empire."[21]

During his long reign, Emperor Wu of the Han (r. 140–88 BCE) issued several edicts calling on officials at different levels to recommend men of virtue and talent—*xianliang fangzheng*, as they were called—to replenish the bureaucratic ranks. Adopting the proposal by Dong Zhongshu (179–104 BCE), himself a product of the *xianliang fangzheng* selection, Emperor Wu endorsed Confucianism as the orthodox ideology of the empire, and knowledge of the Confucian classics, especially *Chunqiu* and *Gongyang*, became a criterion in official selection.[22] Despite such policy changes on the part of the imperial state, however, Chinese *shi* by then had irrevocably lost the autonomous standing they had once enjoyed. As the *daotong* was no longer in a position to counterpoise the *zhengtong*, intellectuals could no longer be mentors or friends to the rulers, instead becoming merely servants to their imperial master. This passage by Dongfang Shuo (154–93 BCE) perhaps best describes the general conditions of Chinese *shi* throughout post-Qin times: "When lifted they are as lofty as above the clouds, and when suppressed they are as lowly as at the bottom of an abyss. When consulted they are like tigers, and when neglected they are like rats."[23]

Indeed, Dongfang Shuo's own dual status as an erudite scholar-writer and a court jester (*nongchen*) functioning as no more than a plaything for the emperor epitomizes the situation of Chinese *shi* under imperial rule. Yet Dongfang Shuo did not actually live in the worst of times from the intellectuals' perspective. In a sense, one may consider the history of imperial China as a process of sustained intensification of state power, which culminated in the Ming and Qing periods. Wu Han's description of the changes in court etiquette vividly reflects the shift in the balance of power between the ruler and the intellectual elite. According to Wu, top scholar-officials sat with the emperor during the Tang; they stood in front of the seated emperor during the Song; but they had to prostrate themselves and kowtow to the emperor during the Ming and Qing.[24]

In particular, scholars have noted a significant change in court politics from the Song to the Ming.²⁵ Whether the Northern Song scholar-official Wen Yanbo's (1006–97) famous statement that the emperor "rules the empire along with the literati" (*yu shidafu zhi tianxia*) reflects faithfully the political culture of the day or just his wishful thinking, it may be said that Song literati enjoyed a relatively stable relationship with the throne.²⁶ Throughout the Northern and Southern Song, rarely were courtiers put to death or subjected to severe physical torture.²⁷ The relatively relaxed political atmosphere was conducive to what Yu Yingshi calls Song literati's "political subject consciousness" (*zhengzhi zhuti yishi*).²⁸ In contrast, Ming rulers were notorious for their brutal killing and various forms of persecution of civil officials. Shen Defu's (1578–1642) *Wanli yehuobian* offers detailed accounts of the appalling disgrace of the wives and daughters of executed officials and the horrendous sufferings of those who survived the cruel penalties of "flogging at court" (*tingzhang*) or "standing pilloried in public" (*lijia*).²⁹ As an extremely humiliating and often fatal punishment, "flogging at court" had been used only sporadically during the Tang, but it became instituted in the Ming as a standard penalty for civil officials. The morbid relationship between the throne and civil bureaucracy during the Ming is summarized by Liu Zongzhou (1578–1645): "The emperor was increasingly suspicious of the ministers and treated them as slaves, and the ministers were increasingly fearful of the emperor and maintained a distance from him as remote as that between the states of the Qin and the Yue."³⁰ Such alienation and mistrust between the *shi* 士 and the *shi* 勢, as some scholars argue, may have contributed more to the eventual demise of the dynasty than either the peasant rebellions or the Manchu military threat.³¹

## THE IMPERIAL POWER'S APPROPRIATION OF THE *DAOTONG*

If the transmission of the *dao* learning and state power had been two lineages more or less separate in previous periods, they seemed to converge during the Ming and Qing. The rulers' absolute political power gave them the unchallenged authority not only in government affairs but in moral and intellectual matters as well. They could interpret, select, and even censor the canonical writings and commentaries in whatever ways would promote their rule, as exemplified by Zhu Yuanzhang's suppression and then expurgation of *Mencius* (Mengzi), one of the most studied and revered works in the Confucian canon. By usurping the moral and ideological authority of the *daotong*, the rulers anointed themselves as new "sage-kings." Take the Yongle emperor Zhu Di for example. He completed in 1409, with the help of the Hanlin academicians, a work titled *Laws of the Mind in the Sages' Learning* (Shengxue xinfa). While the four-volume work was first presented to the crowned prince as part of his educational curriculum, it was actually intended for all literati across the empire to follow, as it covered virtually every aspect of the moral philosophy in the Cheng-Zhu learning.[32] A few years later, under Zhu Di's auspices, a collection of commentaries on the Four Books and Five Classics, titled *Wujing Sishu daquan*, was compiled, followed by a compendium in the *dao* learning with the title *Complete Collection of Writings on Nature and Principle* (Xingli daquan). These works remained the core of the examination curriculum throughout the Ming dynasty despite occasional challenges from scholars.[33] Liang Qichao (1873–1929) went so far as to suggest that "they were almost the only books that many Ming literati ever read."[34] By initiating such projects and deciding on the selection of classical commentaries, Zhu Di made himself appear not only as a faithful apostle of the Chen-Zhu doctrine but also as the one to reauthorize it as cultural and philosophic orthodoxy. Meanwhile, to put an imperial imprint on the nation's literary and intellectual legacy, the emperor sponsored the colossal encyclopedic project that resulted in the compilation of the *Great Compendium of the Yongle* (Yongle dadian). It was to be rivaled in scale only by the *Complete Collection of the Four Treasuries* (Siku quanshu), a similar project under the auspices of Emperor Qianlong three centuries later.

In general, the relationship between the Han literati and the Manchu state during the High Qing period—roughly from the mid-seventeenth century to the end of the eighteenth—was more subtle and complex. In the early Qing, it was particularly complicated by the ethnical sentiments of Ming loyalists who refused to serve under the new regime.[35] The anti-Manchu feelings, however, started to wane as Emperor Kangxi, reversing the hard-line policies of the Oboi regency (1661–69), adopted a more conciliatory and mollifying attitude toward the Han literati, especially those from the Jiangnan (Lower Yangzi) region.[36] His most successful initiative to recruit the service of Han scholars was the special *boxue hongci* (literally, broad learning and grand words) examination in 1678. While it was boycotted by the most prominent Ming loyalists including Gu Yanwu (1613–82) and Huang Zongxi (1610–95), the emperor did manage to win over several important scholars of the day with his magnanimous treatment of the candidates.[37]

In the meantime, Qing rulers continued to uphold Confucianism as the state ideology and maintained the status of neo-Confucianism as the foundation of the examination curriculum. In 1657, Emperor Shunzhi (r. 1644–61) decreed to dedicate to Confucius the honorific title of "Supremely Consecrated Master" (*zhisheng xianshi*), exactly the same title as dedicated by Emperor Jiajing (r. 1522–66) of the Ming.[38] Emperor Kangxi even traveled to the Confucian Temple in Qufu to pay tribute to Confucius in person.[39] Under Kangxi's auspices, several new editions of Confucian classics were published, including *Comprehensive Elucidations on the Book of Changes* (Zhouyi zhezhong), *Collection of Commentaries on the Book of Poetry* (Shijing chuanshuo huizuan), and *Collection of Commentaries on Spring and Autumn* (Chunqiu chuanshuo huizuan). A series of works that highlight the Cheng-Zhu learning were compiled in the final decade of Kangxi's reign, including *Complete Works of Master Zhu* (Zhuzi quanshu) and *Essential Meanings of the Works on Human Nature and Principle* (Xingli jingyi), a long series of book projects comparable to the one during the Yongle reign of the Ming.

Despite the differences between them, Qing rulers obviously learned something from their Ming predecessors in their treatment of the literati. As a harsh means of political control, the literary inquisition (*wenziyu*) under Kangxi, Yongzheng, and Qianlong is well documented.[40] Apart from that, many Qing measures to keep the literati on a tight rein were actually inherited from the Ming. For instance, following the suit of Zhu Yuanzhang who had a whole set of conduct codes for students inscribed on a horizontal stele (*wobei*) in the Imperial Academy (Guozijian), Emperor Shunzhi of the Qing installed a horizontal stele of his own as a stern warning to the students.[41] Like Zhu Yuanzhang's *Grand Announcement* (Dagao) and *Sacred Edict in Six Maxims* (Shengyu liuyan), tracts of moral and legal admonitions to the literati empire-wide, Emperor Kangxi issued his *Sacred Edict* (Shengyu) in 1670, on the basis of which Emperor Yongzheng decreed his *Sacred Edict for General Admonitions* (Shengyu guangxun) in 1724. Both tracts, like their Ming precedents, were to be used in "local examinations and moral lectures by local officials."[42]

Ironically, Qing rulers' emulation of the Ming practice helped change many Han literati's early perception of the Manchu regime as one of foreign conquerors who would rupture Chinese cultural tradition. It helped create an impression that the Manchu rule was an extension of the Ming and thus rendered meaningless any lingering nostalgic attachment to the toppled dynasty. To be sure, anti-Manchu sentiments died hard in certain circles, but generally speaking the relationship of Han literati to Qing rulers, starting perhaps in the late years of Kangxi's reign, became more political than ethnical. More importantly, following their Ming examples, Qing rulers, especially Kangxi, successfully established themselves as the new standard bearers of the *daotong* tradition. Li Guangdi (1642–1718), Grand Counselor (Daxueshi) under Kangxi and a prominent Confucian scholar of the day, was perceptive enough to understand the significance of his imperial master's patronage of the *dao* learning: "From Master Zhu to His Majesty on the throne, it has been another five hundred years. It corresponds to the expected time span for the advent of a kingly ruler to embody the sages' teachings.... Our respected Emperor has received the mandate of Heaven to carry on the lineage of the *dao* in order to enhance it into a grand scheme (*yi yi yu dayou*)."[43] Kangxi was said to be the one who had taken over the torch of the *daotong* from Zhu Xi (1130–1200). For the emperor, political power and moral and intellectual authority had become one, as he declared: "The corpus of the ancient sages' words admonishes people of thousands of generations. This is *daotong,* and this is *zhitong* [lineage of political state] as well" (*Daotong zai shi, zhitong yi zai shi yi*).[44]

What Li Guangdi said about Emperor Kangxi was echoed decades later by a less prominent but by no means less known scholar, Zeng Jing (1679–1735), who was imprisoned, and later executed, for attempting to incite a rebellion against Emperor Yongzheng.[45] Whether or not he was sincere in his statement of repentance, Zeng said precisely what Yongzheng wanted to hear from the literati across the empire:

> Emperor Shengzu's [i.e., Kangxi] mind was Heaven's mind, and Emperor Shengzu's virtues were Heaven's virtues. Therefore all matters in governance and all conventions from our ancestors must be subjected to Emperor Shengzu's criteria.... In recent years there have been prominent achievements both in warfare and in peace and repeated advents of auspicious auguries. The yin and the yang mingle in perfect harmony, and the

people live in comfort and abundance. The Four Seas have become a realm of bliss, and the Myriad Names are sharing prosperity and happiness. That is indeed because His Majesty's virtues match those of the Two Sovereigns and Three Kings. It is therefore beyond any doubt that his reign is just as successful as those of Yu, Xia, Shang, and Zhou.[46]

Indeed history was believed to have come full circle, as these Qing rulers made themselves revered as second coming of the sage-kings of antiquity. From the Manchu rulers' perspective, to further Confucianize the imperial state was the most effective measure to legitimize their regime and to moralize the social life. In the eyes of the intellectual gentry, however, it was blatant usurpation of the moral supremacy from the *daotong*, of which they had been spokesmen for centuries. What happened between Emperor Yongzheng and the licentiate Zeng Jing, despite its ethnical overtone, was primarily a political battle.[47] In a way, it may be considered an epitome of the intellectual elite's relationship to state power in the late imperial times: when the literati were losing their moral and intellectual primacy to political authorities, it became imperative for them to make adjustments to their agenda.

## THE LITERATI'S REFOCUSING FROM STATE TO SOCIETY

One central idea on the agenda of the *daotong* had been that of *dejun xingdao*, or gaining the support from the ruler in practicing the *dao*. Obviously, within the political structure of imperial China, *dejun xingdao* represented the Confucians' best chance to tame the beast of imperial power and make it cooperative to the Confucian project. It could be an expeditious channel for the Confucians to reach the goal of *wai wang*, or external kingliness. To that extent, it summarizes much of the moral and political meanings of the literati's government service. In Chinese history, Zhuge Liang (181–234), prime minister of the state of Shu during the Three Kingdoms period (220–80), was often considered paradigmatic of a civil official winning wholehearted support from his imperial master.[48] Also considered exemplary was the political alliance between the Northern Song reformer Wang Anshi (1021–86) and Emperor Shenzong (r. 1068–85), which was indicative of the generally constructive dynamic between the literati and the imperial power of the time.[49]

The closest Ming counterpart to Wang Anshi was perhaps Zhang Juzheng (1525–82), the de facto prime minister during the early years of the Wanli reign (1573–1619). More than anyone else, he was responsible for a brief period of prosperity in the empire. Just like Wang Anshi, who was acclaimed by Emperor Shenzong as his "mentor and minister" (*shichen*), Zhang Juzheng served as both teacher and chief adviser to his young emperor, ironically another Emperor Shenzong.[50] As was symptomatic of the much altered political culture of the Ming, however, the imperial pupil changed color soon after Zhang's death and almost had his former teacher's body disinterred and whipped.[51] Yet, at least during Zhang's lifetime, the emperor was too young and too inexperienced to be a harsh master. To that extent, Zhang was actually much more fortunate than many other scholar-officials in late imperial times.

One prominent example of those less fortunate scholar-officials was Wang Yangming (1472–1528), founder of the so-called school of Wang Learning (*Wang xue*) that had a pervasive influence on many literati of the late Ming and Qing. In 1506 Wang memorialized the newly inaugurated Emperor Wuzong (r. 1506–21), appealing for leniency on behalf of some of his colleagues who had affronted the powerful eunuch Liu Jin. As a result, he was flogged at court and then banished to a remote post in Longchang, Guizhou. This brutal punishment may have been the catalyst for the transmutation of Wang's thinking. Realizing that it was now completely impossible for the literati to "gain the support of the ruler in practicing the *dao*," Wang turned in a new direction. As Yu Yingshi puts it, Wang's new theory about *liangzhi*, innate knowledge in everyone's mind, "marks an epoch-making change in Confucian political concepts," because it led to "the notion of *juemin xingdao* [awakening the people to practice the *dao*]."[52] Clearly, from *dejun xingdao* to *juemin xingdao* it was a political and intellectual reorientation for the literati, or a shift of focus from the ruler to the people and from the imperial state to the rest of the society at large.

A similar change was reflected in the general perception of government service. Many members of the intellectual gentry gave up the idealistic view of participating in governance as a vehicle for their ultimate moral fulfillment. In the early Ming, for instance, some scholars tried hard to evade official appointments, which prompted Zhu Yuanzhang to institute the penal code against "the literati within the boundaries of the empire who refuse to be employed by the sovereign" (*Huanzhong shidafu buwei jun yong*).⁵³ In the early Qing, there were of course many instances of boycotting government service, which were perhaps no less political than ethnic in nature. As the *daotong* was declining and its ethical and intellectual supremacy seized by the imperial state, government service lost much of its moral luster. To be sure, there was no lack of examination candidates competing for the limited number of vacancies in officialdom, but what remained as a major motivation for office seeking was the prospect of earthly remunerations. As Wang Yangming complained angrily in his letter to a friend, "In recent times the so-called ethics has come to mean no more than official rank, and the so-called official rank no more than wealth and privilege."⁵⁴ For many literati, becoming an official or remaining a commoner was just a banal choice between two different ways of livelihood. In Fei Xiaotong's pungent words, it was a choice between "breaking one's backbone" (from bowing obsequiously to people in higher power) and "breaking one's arms" (from laboring arduously and painstakingly).⁵⁵

Without downplaying the importance of the intrinsic reasons within the intellectual movements themselves, one may consider the changed *shi* (士)-*shi* (勢) relationship the most crucial external factor for intellectual developments in late imperial China. William T. de Bary has cautioned us that one should view the "seeming introversion of Ming thought and its apparent quietistic tendency" against the adversities in the sociopolitical environment: "Nothing was more real and practical for the thinker and scholar in that age than the preservation of his life, his integrity, and his fidelity to essential Confucian values in the face of such overwhelming odds."⁵⁶ Realizing that the days of *dejun xingdao* were irrevocably gone, many literati started turning away from the state power, if not blatantly in action then at least in thought. An immediate corollary was what de Bary terms a trend of "individualism" in late Ming thought.⁵⁷ Among Wang Yangming's followers in the so-called Taizhou school, Wang Gen's (1483–1541) famous personal idiosyncrasy, He Xinyin's (1517–79) uninhibited formulations of individual desires, and Li Zhi's (1527–1602) defiant iconoclasm can perhaps all be considered expressions of a pervasive sense of disillusionment. Indeed Wang Gen never sought an official appointment, He Xinyin renounced any further attempt in the examinations after winning a *juren* degree, and Li Zhi voluntarily resigned from official service into a private life of study and contemplation.

Scholars who did not consider themselves Wang Yangming's followers also reacted to the clampdown of imperial power, and some of them were even more vehement and vocal. Among them, Lü Kun (1536–1618) boldly argued for a higher authority of the moral and intellectual tradition, which he called *li*, over the imperial state.[58] During the Ming-Qing transition, Gu Yanwu fiercely assailed the examination system, especially the rigid *bagu* essay format. In the meantime, he drew a distinction between *guo* (state) and *tianxia* (nation, society, or civilization); by doing so he powerfully challenged the traditional view of political sovereignty that equated the emperor with the empire.[59] In a similar vein, Huang Zongxi made a pungent accusation against the autocratic monarchy system: "[The emperors] thought that all powers in the empire were derived from them, and therefore they felt justified to monopolize all the advantages in the empire to themselves and impose all the disadvantages upon others. To deter the people in the empire from being selfish, they made their revered private interests the public cause of the empire. Once it started that way it never stopped, and as time went on it came to be taken for granted. They regarded the empire as an enormous piece of property to be handed down to their sons and grandsons."[60]

An equally scathing critic of the imperial power was the early Qing scholar Tang Zhen (1630–1704), who had the courage to call "all the rulers since the Qin" "thieves." According to Tang, "Rulers alone were responsible for all the chaos in the empire" (*luan tianxia zhe wei jun*), and for that reason their power should be limited.[61] It is of course debatable whether such vehement condemnations of imperial power were fully justified. After all, if rulers were to blame for any chaos in the empire, they should deserve some credit for social stability and prosperity as well. However, the voices from Gu Yanwu, Huang Zongxi, Tang Zhen, and others clearly signaled a growing mistrust of state power and an increasing awareness of the distinction between serving the nation and society and serving the imperial state, despite all the subtle connections between those two types of service.

Consistent with their call to differentiate the emperor from the empire, Gu Yanwu advocated "management of the nation and pragmatic application of knowledge" (*jingshi zhiyong*), and Huang Zongxi brought up the slogan "administer the empire to benefit the people" (*zhi tianxia wei min yong*). They were certainly not isolated proponents of useful and practical knowledge. The late Ming already witnessed the launching of an intellectual trend of turning away from abstract textual scholarship associated with the examinations toward forms of learning that were more practical and useful to society and the people. Several scholars made major contributions in different disciplines: Li Shizhen (1518–93) in medicine, Xu Guangqi (1562–1633) in agronomy and astronomy, Xu Xiake (1586–1641) in geography, and Song Yingxing (1587–?) in technography, to name only a few most prominent examples. During the Ming-Qing transition, Fang Yizhi (1611–71) distinguished himself as a scholar of remarkable versatility, leaving his imprints in various disciplines ranging from philology and literature to geometry and physics. For him, the Confucian concept of *gewu,* or "investigation of things," was not such an abstract notion as glossed by the Cheng brothers and Zhu Xi; nor did it mean an effort in one's mind as Wang Yangming understood it. Rather, it meant concrete and detailed studies of physical objects in the external world, including the cosmos itself.[62] This reinterpretation represented a conscious effort to channel scholarly attention from the neo-Confucian "pure talk" (*qingtan*) to tangible subjects in natural sciences.

Such a spurt of intellectual interests in "learning of substance" (*shixue*) paved the path for the advent of the so-called Yan-Li School in the early Qing, represented by Yan Yuan (1635–1704) and his student Li Gong (1659–1733). For Yan Yuan, true knowledge lied only in practice, and "the superficial words are more disastrous than burning books and burying scholars alive."[63] The indulgence in empty words, as Li Gong saw it, was a major reason for the downfall of the Ming: "There were no capable ministers in court and no down-to-earth officials within the empire. Sitting in the commander's headquarters and commentating on *The Chronicle of Zuo* [Zuo zhuan], composing poems and delivering orations when the enemy troops were approaching the city—such were the practices shared by senior officials. They dismissed achievements in practical matters as trifles, and gasped for breath from writing books day and night, calling them works to pass down to posterity. As result, river dikes were broken and fish were mashed, and people were plunged into misery and sufferings."[64]

When Yan and Li condemned empty words and advocated learning of substance, they pointed the spearhead directly at the teaching of the Cheng-Zhu school, which they considered deviating from the pristine

Confucianism. Yan Yuan made it clear in his characteristically inflammatory words: "The 'nature' [*xing*] that the Song scholars [*Song ru*] talked about was not the same as what Mencius meant, and the Song scholars' *dao* was not the same *dao* as upheld by Yao, Shun, the Duke of Zhou, and Confucius.... Only by eliminating one tenth of Cheng and Zhu does one become able to understand one tenth of Confucius and Mencius."[65] Since the Cheng-Zhu learning was endorsed by the imperial power as the state ideology and adopted as the kernel of the examination curriculum, the assault from Yan and Li on neo-Confucianism carried tremendous political ramifications.

Separate from but also related to the intellectual interest in "learning of substance" was the enduring movement of Evidential Studies (*kaojuxue*). The history of the movement can be traced all the way to the mid-late Ming, when scholars such as Yang Shen (1488–1559), Gui Youguang (1506–71), and Jiao Hong (1540–1620) looked up to the Tang and Song times for models in classic scholarship. In the early Qing, the movement received an impetus from such prominent figures as Gu Yanwu and Yan Ruoqu (1638–1704), whose meticulous studies in philology and classic exegesis exemplified the spirit of intellectual empiricism. Yet evidential scholarship did not reach its full swing until around the mid-eighteenth century, when it assumed the status as the mainstream methodology in academic studies. As representatives of the renewed fascination in textual studies, Hui Dong (1696–1758), Dai Zhen (1724–77), Duan Yucai (1735–1815), Wang Yinzhi (1766–1834), Qian Daxi (1728–1804), and Wang Niansun (1744–1832) achieved a great deal in systemizing, authenticating, and annotating an enormous corpus of classic texts.[66]

The so-called Qian-Jia Han learning (*Han xue*), by which the movement of Evidential Studies that flourished during the Qianlong and early Jiaqing reigns (1796–1820) is often referred to, was therefore the acceleration of an intellectual trend that had started much earlier. Externally, it has often been associated with the literati's evasion of literary inquisition from the imperial government, as the literati felt, in Liang Qichao's words, "the literary net was excessively tight" (*wenwang tai mi*).[67] More recent studies by Chinese scholars have called that view into question. "The achievements of the Qian-Jia evidential scholarship," argues Guo Kangsong, "were not so much because of the literary inquisition as because of the intellectual development within the evidential scholarship itself."[68] To be sure, literary inquisition certainly was not the only means for the Qing government's political and ideological repression. A more pervasive measure was the state's monopoly of the established official discourse of the Cheng-Zhu orthodox learning. "Qing court," as the modern Chinese historian and philosopher Qian Mu has observed, "venerated the Cheng-Zhu school in order to shackle everyone across the entire empire."[69] As the sanctified and ossified official discourse, neo-Confucianism was jealously shielded by the political authorities and perpetuated in the examination system. As there was little room for the literati to participate in that discourse, they needed different arenas for their talent and knowledge. Textual research promised to be one such arena, especially since the government might consider it a useful red herring for the literati's intellectual curiosity. Yet the innocuous and apolitical nature of Evidential Studies was more apparent than real. With their high regard for Han scholars such as Xu Shen (58–149), Ma Rong (79–166), Zheng Xuan (127–200), and Jia Kui (174–228) and their criticism of Song scholars, especially the Cheng brothers and Zhu Xi, the evidential scholars expressed a strong mistrust of the neo-Confucian metaphysical speculations. That academic query, in the meantime, cast serious doubt on the political authorities that privileged and valorized the Cheng-Zhu learning as the official ideology.

## THE POLITICAL SETTING FOR CHINESE VERNACULAR FICTION

As the brief survey in this chapter demonstrates, the relationship to the state power was always crucial to the aspirations of Chinese literati as a social group. And the evolution of that relationship was always a pressing reason for literati to adjust their expectations and redefine their roles in society and culture. The Confucian intellectuals' participation in government service was closely associated with their ideal of building a moral order on the *dao,* and their cooperation with the state seemed the most feasible avenue for the realization of that ideal. In general terms, however, there was a growing sense of disillusionment with imperial power among intellectuals, which reached a new height in the late dynasties. Accompanying that disillusionment was a trend in intellectual thinking that attempted to distinguish service to the state from service to society and the people. Along with that distinction emerged a new understanding of the Confucian concept of participation in social affairs.

Thus, Chinese vernacular fiction came into existence at a historical moment: diachronically, the agelong partnership between the *daotong* and the *zhengtong* had entered its final stage; synchronically, the bond between the literati and the imperial state became very complex and far-reaching. How do the fictional works produced in this setting fit in the larger picture of the *daotong-zhengtong* contention? How can they be considered the literati's efforts to negotiate with the value system sustained by political power? And how can they be interpreted as reflections of the literati's rethinking of their identity and historical mission? These are the questions to be addressed in the following chapters.

CHAPTER 2

# *Romance of the Three Kingdoms*

## *The Mencian View of Political Sovereignty*

It is by no means coincidental that *Romance of the Three Kingdoms,* the earliest of the "four masterworks" of Ming fiction, is a historical novel. To be sure, its claim to be a "popular explication" (*yanyi*) of an official history, as its title indicates, may have put a tether on the author's imagination. Whether Zhang Xuecheng's (1738–1801) famous assertion that the novel is "seventy percent facts and thirty percent fabrications" (*qifen shishi sanfen xugou*) is accurate or not, the novelist had to maintain at least a nominal allegiance to history.[1] Nevertheless, the novel is heavily selective in its representation and elaboration of the materials from different sources, which may suggest a keen interest not merely in history per se but in using history to allude to the present.[2] "Fiction can reflect popular political attitudes," as a Western sinologist commented when discussing popular political thoughts reflected in *Romance of the Three Kingdoms,* "especially when, like this novel, it is political in its conception, and also very popular."[3] According to another Western scholar, the historical personages and past events in Ming historical fiction are inextricably related to politics, and the novelist's interest in the historical subject may therefore reflect a concern about the sociopolitical situation of his own time.[4] That view on Ming historical fiction in general is pertinent to *Romance of the Three Kingdoms* in particular. An official history such as *Chronicle of the Three Kingdoms* (Sanguo zhi) seldom provided sufficient details of historical events, which became an opportunity for the novelist. He could flesh out the sketchy recording in official history with information selected from many other sources, not merely to make the narrative a better story but also instill in it a particular type of ethical and political persuasions.[5]

What ethical and political persuasions does one see in *Romance of the Three Kingdoms*? And in what ways can the interests reflected in this historical novel be related to the sociopolitical climate in the historical period of its composition? While the earliest known edition of the novel was dated to the early sixteenth century, its manuscript prototype was composed much earlier, most likely in the early decades of the Ming. Most relevant to the discussion here are the early Ming rulers' harsh treatment of the literati and their manipulation of the curriculum of the civil service examinations, epitomized in Zhu Yuanzhang's suppression and expurgation of *Mencius*, a classic that advocates a type of sovereign–subject relationship vastly different from the emperor's political absolutism. In *Romance of the Three Kingdoms*, Liu Bei, the leader of Shu, is presented as a ruler who wins support from the common people with his compassion and loyalty from his ministers and captains with his fraternal love. The novel also features a plethora of men of talent, with Zhuge Liang, Liu Bei's wise adviser and capable prime minister, as their ultimate representative. Against the background of the sociopolitical life of the early Ming, the coupling of a "benevolent ruler" and a man of great talent in the novel may be considered a literary expression of the Mencian view of political sovereignty when *Mencius* was censored and when the intensity of imperial rule reached an unprecedented level in Chinese history. Precisely because of the painful absence of a reciprocal ruler-subject relationship in reality, a novelistic simulacrum became all the more appealing to the intellectual gentry, who had long been nurtured by the Mencian teaching both morally and politically.

## ROMANCE OF THE THREE KINGDOMS AND THE EARLY MING DECADES

The earliest known edition of *Romance of the Three Kingdoms*, titled *Sanguozhi tongsu yanyi*, features a preface by Jiang Daqi under the pseudonym of Yongyuzi (Mediocre and Slow-Witted Scholar) and another one by Zhang Shangde under the pseudonym of Xiuranzi (Long-Whiskered

Scholar). As these prefaces are dated 1494 and 1522 respectively, that edition could have been published in 1522, possibly following a late fifteenth-century precursor as the 1494 preface might suggest. While no textual exemplars prior to the 1522 edition are extant, it is almost certain that the process of textual evolution had started much earlier. Particularly indicative are some of the interlinear notes on place-names in the 1522 edition, where typically a contemporary place-name is given as a gloss on its ancient and hence more obscure equivalent in the text proper. A number of those contemporary place-names appear in Yuan terms, leading some modern scholars to argue for a Yuan (1279–1368) dating of the text.[6] Yet that argument is compromised by the possibility that such place-names had simply been carried over from preexisting textual sources, especially since some of the notes even contain Song place-names as well.[7] Furthermore, there is evidence that the use of place-names was not stringently regulated during the Ming, as some Yuan place-names that had been officially abolished continued to be used.[8] If the original novelist himself was indeed responsible for these interlinear notes, as most scholars seem to believe, one has to agree that the place-names that came into use the latest are actually more useful for the dating of the text.[9] While it was possible for the writer to use a place-name of an earlier period when his knowledge of the present was interfered by his memory of the past, he was not in a position to use one that was yet to be adopted in the future. Since some of the notes contain Ming place-names, it should be considered a reliable indicator that the composition of the novel could not have been completed at any date earlier than the beginning of the Ming.[10]

*Romance of the Three Kingdoms* is considered to be authored by Luo Guanzhong, to whom several other works of fiction and drama are attributed as well. Despite the disappointingly inadequate information about his life, Luo's historicity has now been generally accepted. Unless new discoveries prove otherwise, his status as the primary—if not the only—writer of *Romance of the Three Kingdoms* seems too well established to be challenged.[11] Among the few Ming sources about Luo Guanzhong's life, a biographic note on Luo in *A Sequel to the Registry of the Ghosts* (Luguibu xubian), a bibliographical work on late Yuan and early Ming popular drama and dramatists, seems most reliable. According to the compiler Jia Zhongming (b. 1343), he had met his friend Luo Guanzhong for the last time in 1364. If Luo had indeed been writing *Romance of the Three*

*Kingdoms* in the late Yuan, Jia should have known and noted it—especially since their final meeting was only four years before the demise of the dynasty. Instead, the compiler, who was particularly generous in commending the playwrights for their literary and cultural accomplishments outside the field of drama, seemed completely unaware of such a project.[12] More importantly, even at the time of his compilation of *A Sequel to the Registry of the Ghosts*, which was no earlier than 1424, Jia still could not associate Luo Guanzhong with any text of *Three Kingdoms*, and lamented in a note that he even did not know how his friend's life had ended.[13] Given the statement in the Jiang Daqi preface—that once the manuscript of the novel was completed literati scholars had "vied with each other to copy it out"—Jia's words can be particularly significant.[14] Since virtually all the extant editions of *Romance of the Three Kingdoms* uniformly acknowledge Luo Guanzhong's authorship, the attribution must have been established early, most likely during the novel's manuscript stage. If such a long manuscript by Luo was in broad circulation at the time, it would be highly unlikely that Jia Zhongming, as such a central figure in the circles of popular literature, should have been unaware of it. That could mean that the circulation and transmission of the manuscript described in the Jiang Daqi preface had not yet taken place by 1424.

As Jia Zhongming's "friend despite a big age gap" (*wangnianjiao*), Luo Guanzhong might have been at least ten years Jia's senior, and would have been at least ninety years old in 1424 if still alive. In fact, Jia simply took Luo's death for granted in his note. On all accounts, Luo's writing career must have ended by then. We do not know whether Luo Guanzhong had completed the writing of the novel during his lifetime. Since the circulation of the manuscript described in the Jiang Daqi preface most likely had not taken place by 1424, it was possible that the manuscript was brought to completion by someone else after that date. However, if we maintain that Luo Guanzhong was the primary writer of *Romance of the Three Kingdoms*, it still seems reasonable to believe that the bulk of the novel had been composed during the early decades of the Ming without completely ruling out the possibility of its initiation in the final few years of the Yuan.[15]

To be sure, nobody knows exactly what the early Ming textual prototype of *Romance of the Three Kingdoms* looked like, yet the relative textual stability among different recensions of the novel can be revealing to us.[16]

Unlike the truly vernacular *Water Margin*, which evolved in proximity to popular orality and incorporated from a variety of oral genres on the levels of both story making and discourse making, *Romance of the Three Kingdoms*, with its multiple textual sources, did not have to rely on a sustained contact with an ongoing oral tradition. As it appears in a mixture of written vernacular (*baihua*) with simplified classical Chinese (*wenyan*), its narrative discourse was less susceptible to the changes in the living language. Where the basic narrative text is concerned, even the pictorial *zhizhuan* editions published by Fujian booksellers in the sixteenth and seventeenth centuries—including *Sanguo zhizhuan*, *Sanguo zhizhuan pinglin*, and others—do not feature major deviations from the 1522 edition. While it was possible, as some modern scholars have suggested, that the *zhizhuan* editions followed a textual exemplar separate from and prior to the 1522 edition,[17] "they cannot be said to comprise a separate textual system" comparable to the "simpler recension" (*jianben*) of *Water Margin*, as Andrew Plaks has judiciously observed.[18] This relative textual stability has an important corollary. While it is obvious that one should not take the 1522 print as a replica of the nonextant Luo Guanzhong prototype,[19] textual changes during the process of manuscript transmission may have been relatively limited, and the essential narrative discourse may have remained largely intact.[20] Since the primary concern here is with the narrative plot rather than details of rhetoric of the novel, the following analysis relies on the 1522 edition as a surrogate for the early Ming text. The discussion of *Romance of the Three Kingdoms* in the rest of this chapter, unless otherwise noted, all pertains to the 1522 edition.

## THE EARLY MING IMPERIAL CENSORSHIP OF *MENCIUS*

Nothing was more symbolic of the early Ming political climate than what happened to *Mencius* (Mengzi), one of the canonized Four Books (*sishu*) of Confucianism and hence a central component of the examination curriculum. As early as 1372, Zhu Yuanzhang became infuriated at the following passage in *Mencius*, which suggests that the loyalty of subjects is not to be taken for granted by the ruler but has to be won with the ruler's compassion and benevolence: "Mencius said to King Xuan of the Qi: 'If a prince [*jun*] treats his subjects [*chen*] as his hands and feet, they will treat him as their belly and heart. If he treats them as his horses and hounds, they will treat him as a stranger. If he treats them as mud and weeds, they will treat him as an enemy.'"[21]

The Mencian teaching here obviously ran counter to Zhu Yuanzhang's intent for absolute sovereign power. As *Mencius* was on every examination candidate's reading list, it could potentially become a threat to Zhu Yuanzhang's political agenda. Denouncing that passage as "improper words by a subject," the emperor adamantly demanded that Mencius be removed from the official pantheon of Confucian sages. Only at the daring remonstrations of the minister of justice Qian Tang and other scholar-officials, did the emperor finally relent and retract that order.[22]

Yet Zhu Yuanzhang's anger against the classic was never soothed, nor was it confined to that particular passage alone. He insisted that all the passages he found objectionable be removed from the classic. After the examinations were reinstated in 1384, Zhu Yuanzhang increasingly felt the need for a censored edition of *Mencius*. Eventually, in 1394, *Expurgated Mencius* (Mengzi jiewen) was published, compiled by Liu Sanwu (1319–1400) and his fellow Hanlin academicians. As many as eighty-five entries in *Mencius* were deleted. Some of them dwell on the view that the legitimacy of the political authority of the ruler should be based on the will of the ruled, and others, like the one cited earlier, advocate mutual respect between a ruler and his ministers or even moral tutelage of just and righteous ministers over their sovereign master.[23] According to the mid-Ming scholar Zhu Yunming (1460–1526), Emperor Hongwu tried to justify the expurgation by describing those removed entries as being out of accord with the times: "Mencius wrote in the Warring States period, and that was the reason his words are sometimes excessively querulous [*yiyang taiguo*]. Today the empire is unified, and therefore students cannot get his intended meaning [*benyi*] but hastily use [his book] in their speeches and actions."[24] Zhu Yuanzhang's publicly expressed wrath against the "Second Sage" (*ya sheng*) in the Confucian tradition and his brazen tampering with a consecrated text spoke volumes of the unbridled power of the throne vis-à-vis the *daotong*, which the intellectual elite had long claimed to represent.

Indeed, Zhu Yuanzhang's phobia of *Mencius*, especially the passages on the ruler-subject relationship, was not surprising. Many such passages could have assumed topical relevance during the early Ming, as the emperor, despite his occasional display of gentleness, often treated the literati like "mud and weeds." Even Song Lian (1310–81), probably the most respected scholar-official of the time, was implicated in the Hu Weiyong (?–1380) case. Only at the persistent remonstrations from his empress did Zhu Yuanzhang spare Song's life; Song, however, died anyway shortly afterward in exile.[25] Another example was what happened during the 1397 metropolitan examination, the last one under the Hongwu reign. The fifty-two candidates who passed the examination turned out to be all from the culturally rich south. Zhu Yuanzhang was suspicious of the partiality of the examiners, Liu Sanwu and Bai Xindao, who were themselves southerners, and appointed Zhang Xin and eleven others as investigators of the case. When the investigators' report reaffirmed the original result of the examination, the infuriated emperor had Bai Xindao, Zhang Xin, and several others executed and Liu Sanwu exiled. After that the emperor himself conducted a reexamination and passed sixty-one candidates, all northerners.[26] Ironically, Liu Sanwu, who had served as Zhu Yuanzhang's pawn in the anti-Mencius campaign only a few years before, became himself a victim of the type of tyranny so fiercely denounced in *Mencius*.

By far the most prestigious school of the early Ming period was Guozijian, the Imperial Academy, which served as the most important base for the production of civil officials.[27] Given such prominence of the school, Zhu Yuanzhang's treatment of the students there can be taken as a measurement of the status of the intellectual gentry at large. In 1382, the emperor issued harsh injunctions regarding the conduct of the students at the academy and had them inscribed on a stone tablet. Any violations of these disciplinary codes could incur a severe beating, banishment to remote frontiers, or even death. Under the superintendent Song Na (d. 1390), deprivation of meals was adopted as a punishment, and every month at least one student either starved to death or hanged himself.[28] Some instructors became concerned. In 1385, one of them, Jin Wenzheng, discussed the matter with the minister of personnel Yu Kai and attempted to make the seventy-five-year-old Song retire, but on hearing of this Zhu Yuanzhang became so enraged that he had Jin, Yu, and several other instructors executed.[29] Even that did not quell all the complaints from the students. In 1394, a student named Yue Lin could not stand the abuse any longer and posted a leaflet of protest. He would have been, according to the regulations set by Zhu Yuanzhang himself, punishable by one hundred strikes of stick flogging followed by exile. But that was not enough to soothe the wrath of the emperor, who instead had the poor student beheaded and the chopped-off head publicly displayed at the top of a pole standing in front of the academy. Furthermore, Zhu Yuanzhang returned to the academy in 1397 to deliver a stern reprimand, in which he threatened that anyone who repeated Yue Lin's offence would be put to death by dismembering (*lingchi*) and that his entire family would be exiled to "the farthest southwest frontiers."[30]

The pole that had carried Yue Lin's chopped-off head stood in front of the Imperial Academy as a warning to the students until 1519, when it was finally removed at the order of Emperor Wuzong (r. 1506–21). By that time, however, the importance of the academy had significantly diminished. Significantly, all the Ming emperors throughout the fifteenth century kept that pole in place. For over one hundred years it remained a symbol of the absolute power of the imperial state and its suffocating dominance over the intellectuals.

Much of Zhu Yuanzhang's cruelty was inherited by Zhu Di. As victor of a bloody civil war, Zhu Di brutally executed dozens of Emperor Jianwen's top civil officials when his coercion for their switch of allegiance was met with defiance and contempt. Among those slain was Fang Xiaoru (1357–1402), who had enjoyed such prestige among the intellectual elite that the monk Daoyan (i.e., Yao Guangxiao, 1335–1418), Zhu Di's top adviser, warned the usurper: "To kill Fang Xiaoru would be to eradicate the seeds of scholarship across the entire empire."[31] When Zhu Di commanded Fang to draft the announcement of his succession to the throne, the prince had the audacity to compare himself to Duke Zhou (Zhou Gong), the legendary brother of King Wu of the Zhou who served devotedly as regent for his nephew, King Cheng (Cheng Wang). Fang steadfastly refused to write the announcement and scornfully berated Zhu Di for the usurpation. The infuriated usurper ruthlessly tortured Fang both physically and mentally for seven days before finally having him dismembered.[32] Ever since Confucius's famous expression of anxiety about not seeing Duke Zhou in his dreams, the duke had been regarded in the Confucian tradition as the ultimate paradigm of the moral and intellectual guidance of the *dao* over secular state power.[33] Zhu Di's forced analogy of his bloody usurpation with Duke Zhou's regency was therefore enormously grotesque.

*Mencius* was censored for over four decades, from 1372, when Zhu Yuanzhang publicly expressed anger over the classic, to 1415, when its complete text was officially reinstated in *Grand Collection of Commentaries on the Four Books* (Sishu daquan). Following the reinstallment of the examinations in 1384, *Mencius* played only a marginal role in official recruitment; after the publication of *Expurgated Mencius* in 1394, "none of the eighty-five entries" excluded from the expurgated version were allowed "to appear in any examination questions or be used as criteria for passing candidates."[34] Even after 1415, those passages were only rarely mentioned in provincial and metropolitan examinations.[35] Unsurprisingly, when *Mencius* was under the imperial censorship, the power of the throne was unchecked. When Zhu Di restored the complete version of *Mencius,* he did so for the same purpose that his father had expurgated it: to utilize the classic for his own political gain. Ironically, the Mencian view against absolute political sovereignty that had once angered Zhu Yuanzhang now became for Zhu Di a much-needed justification for his usurpation. The rehabilitation of the classic, therefore, became just one more example of the throne's manipulation of the Confucian canon and the examination curriculum.

## ROMANCE OF THE THREE KINGDOMS AND THE MENCIAN IDEA OF THE BENEVOLENT RULER

At the core of the Mencian political philosophy—which Benjamin A. Elman calls "an ascending view of political sovereignty" as it stressed the importance of the ruled for the ruler—was the notion of benevolent governance (renzheng).[36] Mencius believed that human nature was innately good.[37] From that premise, he went on to advocate that all people had the natural potential to realize their moral endowment. That sanguine estimate of the average person's moral nature gave rise to the view that the mandate of heaven for a ruler was identical with the mandate from the people: "Heaven sees with the eyes of its people. Heaven hears with the ears of its people."[38] Citing the examples of Jie and Zhou, two tyrannical kings of ancient times, Mencius further dwells on this relationship between the ruler and the ruled:

> It was through losing the people that Jie and Zhou lost the empire, and through losing the people's hearts that they lost their people. There is a way to win the empire; win the people and you will win the empire. There

is a way to win the people; win their hearts and you will win the people. There is a way to win their hearts; amass what they want for them; do not impose what they dislike on them. That is all. The people turn to the benevolent as water flows downwards or as animals head for the wilds. Thus the otter drives the fish to the deep; thus the hawk drives birds to the bushes; and thus Jie and Zhou drove the people to Tang and King Wu. Now if a ruler in the empire is drawn to benevolence, all the feudal lords will drive the people to him. He cannot but be a true king.[39]

In one of the most celebrated dictums by any ancient Chinese thinkers, Mencius summarizes his idea of political sovereignty most succinctly: "The people are of supreme importance; the altars to the gods of earth and grain come next; last comes the ruler" (*Min wei gui, sheji ci zhi, jun wei qing*).[40]

The notion of benevolent governance plays a more prominent role in *Romance of the Three Kingdoms* perhaps than anywhere else in premodern Chinese fiction. Among the rulers of the Three Kingdoms—Cao Cao, Sun Quan, and Liu Bei—only Liu is presented in the novel as a legitimate contender for the Han throne. One reason is, of course, his marginal kinship to the imperial lineage and his honorary title as "Imperial Uncle" (Huangshu). That is indeed the point Zhu Xi makes in the prefatory piece (titled "Fanli") to *Yupi Tongjian gangmu*, where Liu Bei's Shu is regarded as "orthodox rule" (*zhengtong*) while both the Wei and the Wu are denigrated as "illegitimate states" (*jianguo*).[41] It is also the stance Mao Zonggang (1632–1709) assumes at the beginning of his "How to Read *The Romance of the Three Kingdoms*" (Du *Sanguo zhi* fa), where he advocates that imperial lineage, rather than "territorial considerations" (*lun di*), should be the criterion for determining legitimate succession.[42] However, while imperial lineage is certainly an issue in the 1522 edition, it does not occupy such a prominent place as in the Mao Zonggang version.[43] On several occasions in the 1522 edition, this line appears several times in only slight verbal variations: "The Empire does not belong to any one person; it belongs to all the people in the Empire."[44] Significantly, all instances of that line are consistently obliterated in the Mao edition. Another line also frequently recurs in the 1522 edition: "The virtueless should give way to the virtuous" (*wude rang youde*). Any ruler can lose the mandate of heaven if he strays from the appropriate path, and in that case he deserves to be replaced by someone morally superior, whether or not he is a member of the imperial clan. "Everyone," as Lu Su says to Sun Quan, "can become a Yao or a Shun," citing the names of the legendary kings in the antiquity to whom the throne was abdicated because of their exemplary virtues (*SGZTSYY*, 2:951). Evidently, the 1522 edition does not attempt to justify Liu Bei's claim to succession merely with his kinship to the Han imperial lineage.

Although *Romance of the Three Kingdoms* is not completely consistent in its depiction of Liu Bei, it presents him as a benevolent and righteous ruler. In that regard, it is not only radically different from the official history *Chronicle of the Three Kingdoms*, where Liu Bei is not considered a legitimate contender for the throne, but also a far cry from *Popular Stories of the Three Kingdoms* (*Sanguozhi pinghua*), the narrative text from the popular Three Kingdom cycles. Episodes that exemplify Liu Bei's righteous behavior, regardless of their origins, become amplified and elaborated in the novel. For instance, Liu's persistent declinations to take over Xuzhou (from his friend Tao Qian) and Jingzhou (from his clansman Liu Biao), mentioned only cursorily in *Chronicle of the Three Kingdoms* and completely absent from *Popular Stories of the Three Kingdoms*, become two lengthy narrative stretches in the novel fleshed out with all details. Meanwhile, narrative details that could potentially compromise Liu Bei's character are consistently removed or modified. One early example is the whipping of the inspector (*duyou*) after Liu Bei is made a local magistrate in the county of Anxi (*SGZTSYY*, chap. 2). In *Chronicle*, it is Liu who ties up and thrashes the arrogant inspector. In *Popular Stories*, Zhang Fei kills a prefect and then beats the inspector to death in Liu's presence. In the novel, however, Zhang Fei is the one who beats the inspector without Liu's knowledge, and Liu then restrains the impetuous Zhang from killing the inspector. Furthermore, in *Popular Stories* Liu Bei and his sworn brothers become bandit chieftains in the Taihang Mountains after Zhang Fei's rampage. In the novel, however, they never become bandits, only hiding briefly at the place of one of Liu Bei's kinsmen in Daizhou (*SGZTSYY*, chap. 2).

Several other episodes in the novel contribute to this elevated version of Liu Bei. He avoids "the slightest disturbance to the local people" when he is a county official in Anxi (*SGZTSYY*, 1:48). People line up on the streets in Xuzhou, entreating him to become their prefect (*SGZTSYY*, 1:651). And he successfully reforms the political administration as the magistrate of Xinye, "to the delight of soldiers and civilians alike" (*SGZTSYY*, 2:1103). Of particular interest is Liu Bei's retreat from Cao Cao's ferocious offense before the Red Cliffs battle, when thousands of the residents in the counties of Xinye and Fancheng flee along with Liu's troops. The flocks of refugees become an encumbrance for the exodus while Cao Cao's forces are getting closer, but Liu refuses to abandon the civilians. Of that incident *Chronicle of the Three Kingdoms* offers a very brief account: "Someone said to the Previous Master [*xianzhu*]: 'We should move quickly to secure Jiangling. While we have many people now, most of them are not soldiers. If Cao's forces arrive, what can we do?' The Previous Master replied: 'The foundation for any great cause is always the people. Now that they have been following me, how can I bear to abandon them?'"[45] The narration in *Popular Stories of the Three Kingdoms* is even sketchier. Despite the generally pro-Shu stance in the popular narrative, Liu Bei's attitude toward the refugees is noncommittal at best: "The Counselor [*junshi*] spoke to the Imperial Uncle: 'Cao's troops are getting closer. If we still take care of the civilians, what can we do if Cao arrives?' Xuande [i.e., Liu Bei] didn't say anything in reply."[46]

In the novel, however, this episode becomes significantly amplified with vivid details about the interaction between Liu Bei and his civilian followers:

> The people of the two counties, old and young, cried out in unison: "We will follow Lord Liu till the end of our lives." That same day, amid weeps and tears, the exodus began.... Chased by Cao Cao's forces, the civilians from Xinye and Fancheng, supporting the elders and carrying the babies, bringing along sons and daughters, crossed the river like rolling waves. Bitter cries rang out on both shores ceaselessly. Standing on his boat, Xuande was deeply saddened: "These common folk have all been made to suffer this disaster for my sake. What is left for me to drag out this existence for?" So saying, he attempted to throw himself into the water, but was restrained by those around him. Everyone that heard him was moved to tears. After reaching the south shore, Xuande looked back to those on the other side who were still waiting tearfully to cross the river. He immediately asked Yunchang to send the boats back in a hurry before he at last mounted the horse.... Kongming said: "... We have such a multitude of

more than one hundred thousand people, but most are civilians and few are soldiers.... Wouldn't it be expedient to leave the people behind for now and go ahead ourselves?" In tears, Xuande replied: "The foundation for any great cause is always the people. Now that they have been following me, how can I bear to abandon them?" Everyone that heard of this incident was deeply moved. (SGZTSYY, 3:1321–28)

This comparison of the different narrative treatments of the same episode illustrates the novelist's effort to accentuate Liu Bei's compassion and benevolence, qualities that the novel further heightens through a contrast of Liu with other warlords. Early in the novel, Dong Zhuo, a potential usurper of the Han throne, plans to move the capital of the empire to Chang'an. When several ministers object to this on the grounds of possible disruption to the ordinary people, Dong replies furiously: "I plan for the empire, and why should I feel sorry for those lowly commoners!" Xun Shuang, one of the ministers, protests: "The people are the foundation for an empire. Only if the foundation is solid will the empire be peaceful." That admonition, however, falls on Dong's deaf ears (SGZTSYY, 1:180).

Cao Cao is portrayed in the novel as being just as ruthless to the common people when provoked. When one of Tao Qian's captains kills Cao's father, the vengeful Cao launches a bloody massacre in Tao's cities (SGZTSYY, 1:321). As for Sun Quan, the novel does not depict him as a scourge to the people, but neither is he presented on any occasion as kind and sympathetic. While Cao Cao once calls himself and Liu Bei the only two "men of aspirations" (*yingxiong*) of the time, the novel presents them more often than not as a pair of antitheses. Summarizing his strategy in confronting and countering Cao Cao, Liu Bei says: "The one who struggles against me like fire against water is Cao Cao. Where Cao is impetuous I am temperate; where he is harsh I am benevolent; where he is cunning I am sincere" (SGZTSYY, 3:1923–34). The novel's depiction of Liu Bei should not always be taken at face value, but in general the "Imperial Uncle" is portrayed as an idealistic ruler of benevolence and righteousness.

## THE RULER AND HIS TREATMENT OF MEN OF TALENT

As mentioned earlier, in Zhu Yuanzhang's *Expurgated Mencius* many Mencian passages on the ruler-minister relationship were obliterated. It is precisely this kind of relationship that takes a central place in *Romance of the Three Kingdoms*. The contention among the three kingdoms for dominance over the empire becomes a competition for men of superior abilities. In the novel, one finds a relentless effort to rewrite history in order to highlight the rulers' recruitment and retention of talents, which is what Mao Zonggang suggests in his *dufa* essay: "There are many histories of former times, but people are especially fond of reading the *Romance of the Three Kingdoms* because there was no other period in which so many talents flourished at the same time."[47]

One example of a ruler incapable of employing and treating talented men properly is Yuan Shao. During much of the early portion of the Jian'an reign (196–219), Yuan is indisputably the strongest of the warlords, boasting the largest army and two of the most formidable warriors of the time, Yan Liang and Wen Chou. Although he has a team of capable advisers, his indecisiveness and suspicion feed the factionalism among them. Ignoring his chief strategist Tian Feng's sensible analysis of the military situation, Yuan rushes to a showdown with Cao Cao at Guandu, and his numerically superior forces are badly defeated. Turning shame into anger, the narrow-minded Yuan then kills Tian Feng in prison, while another of his top aides, Xu You, defects to Cao Cao. Yuan's demise becomes inevitable after he squanders away most of the talent on his side: "The pillars for the North of the River are all broken, / How can Yuan Shao not lose his homeland?" (*SGZTSYY*, 2:997).

In contrast, the leaders of Shu, Wei, and Wu are all remarkably adept in soliciting the service of men of talent, and that is precisely the reason they manage to survive the tangling warfare and establish their respective power bases. Sun Quan may not be a good warrior, but he is superior in "selecting and employing worthy and capable men and enlisting their consistent loyalty from their respective posts" (*juxian renneng, gejin qixin*), as his predecessor and older brother Sun Ce appraises him (*SGZTSYY*, 2:941). Right after Sun Ce's death, Sun Quan hears these words from Zhou Yu, his chief counselor and strategist: "Today men of ambitions are contending with each other. Those who find good men will prosper, and those who don't will perish. Your Lordship must seek the support of brilliant and far-seeing intellects" (*SGZTSYY*, 2:947).

What Zhou Yu says here becomes the guiding motto for Sun Quan. Indeed, his relationship with Zhou Yu himself best exemplifies his successful efforts in using his personal trust and friendship to win unswerving loyalty and dedicated service from talented men. Before the battle at Red Cliffs, Jiang Gan, one of Cao Cao's counselors, volunteers to visit Zhou Yu, trying to persuade Zhou to defect to Cao. Jiang, however, sees the futility of his mission when he hears Zhou Yu describe his relationship with Sun Quan in these words:

> Living as a man of aspirations in this world, I have had the good fortune to serve a lord who appreciates me. In our public capacities we are tied by the amity between a ruler and a minister, and in private we are bonded by the feelings of kinship. What I say, he does; what I propose, he approves. We share with each other all weal and woe. Were the eloquent orators of the old times—Su Qin, Zhang Yi, Lu Jia, and Li Yiji—resurrected to walk the earth again, delivering speeches like rolling streams and wielding their tongues like sharp swords, they would not be able to move me. Let alone any of those pedantic scholars of the present day! (*SGZTSYY*, 3:1475)

What one sees between Sun Quan and Zhou Yu is also seen between Sun and another of his top aides, Lu Su. After the victory at Red Cliffs over Cao Cao, Lu Su goes to join Sun Quan, and the ruler stands by the roadside to welcome the counselor. Afterward Sun quietly asks the overwhelmingly flattered Lu whether his deferential greeting can be taken as sufficient recognition of his meritorious service. Lu first surprises his lord by saying "No," and then delights him with this explanation: "Not until I see your power and virtue prevail throughout the Four Seas and Nine Provinces and Your Highness assume the imperial throne" (*SGZTSYY*, 3:1690).

Like Sun Quan, Cao Cao is also skillful in handling the relationships with his men of abilities. His victory over Yuan Shao, just as he reminisces while paying a visit to Yuan's grave, is primarily because of his superior aptitude in "employing men of intelligence across the land" (*SGZTSYY*, 2:1069). His eagerness to recruit the best talents is clearly demonstrated in his reception of Xu You, Yuan Shao's defecting adviser. At the time Cao is already undressed for bed, but when Xu's arrival is announced, he dashes out—barefoot—to greet Xu, rubbing his hands in excitement and laughing with delight. Once inside the tent, Cao seats Xu and then prostrates himself before his "old friend." Overwhelmed by such warmth and respect, Xu You is immediately convinced that Cao is a different kind of leader from Yuan Shao (*SGZTSYY*, 2:971).

With such eagerness to employ men of intelligence, Cao Cao surrounds himself with a plethora of wise and capable advisers. Among them is Chen Lin, who once wrote a formal denunciation of Cao Cao for Yuan Shao. While that powerful document once irritated Cao profoundly, Cao rejects others' advice to kill Chen when Chen becomes his captive, and puts him on his staff instead in order to make use of his talent. Indeed, these words that the novel cites from the *Chronicle of the Three Kingdoms* on the historical Cao Cao serve as an apt appraisal of the fictional Cao Cao as well: he is able "to recognize men of extraordinary talent and to promote them regardless of their humble origins" (*shiba qicai, buju weijian*) (*SGZTSYY*, 4:2512). Cao is clearly aware that the success of his cause relies more on the wisdom of his counselors than on the prowess of his warriors. Just as his victory over Yuan Shao at Guandu is largely due to Xu You's plan to destroy Yuan's supplies, he believes his defeat at Red Cliffs could have been avoided if Guo Jia, another of his top advisers, had still been alive at the time.

In contrast, however, Cao Cao's attitude toward men of talent is often poisoned by his mistrust and suspicion. Having masterminded the Guandu victory for Cao Cao, Xu You is soon killed by Cao's captain Xu Chu, most likely with Cao's acquiescence.[48] Cao's personal loathing for the defiant spirit of Kong Rong, a brilliant scion of Confucius, eventually prompts him to put Kong to death. Ironically, Kong's final suggestion, if heeded, could have prevented the Red Cliffs debacle for Cao. Yang Xiu, arguably the smartest of Cao's advisers, is executed because he is able to read Cao's innermost thoughts from the slightest inklings. Yang is reckless in parading his endowments in total disregard of the gravity of the situation, but the more fundamental cause for the tragedy is Cao's jealousy of Yang's stupendous genius.[49] An even more typical example is Xun Yu. When Cao Cao needs Xun's service, he calls Xun "my Zifang" (*wu zhi Zifang*), comparing him to Zhang Liang, the wise adviser to the founding emperor of the Han, Liu Bang. After Cao has secured his control of the Central Plain, however, he puts Xun Yu to death for his forthright remonstrations. What happens to Xun Yu happens to his nephew Xun You later. When Cao Cao plans to proclaim himself King of the Wei, Xun You's dissent incurs Cao's wrath, and the fearful Xun soon dies of illness. The final advice of the older Xun to Cao Cao—that "a true gentleman shows his love for others through his virtue" (*Junzi ai ren yi de*)—fails to generate in the perverse leader any love either for himself or for his nephew (*SGZTSYY*, 4:1960).

The tragedy of the Xuns is strikingly similar to that of another man of talent—although of a different type—the "miracle-working physician" Hua Tuo. When Cao Cao suffers a severe headache, he summons the physician. Diagnosing the cause of the pain to be some kind of silting fluid in the head, the physician offers to open Cao's skull with a cleaver after general anesthesia. Suspecting Hua to be an assassin, the enraged ruler sends the physician into prison and has him killed there. By doing so, Cao has himself compared unfavorably with another patient of Hua Tuo's, the Shu general Guan Yu, who lets the physician scrape his bone—with no anesthesia—in the middle of a chess game. But the Hua Tuo–Cao Cao episode is much more significant than just an antithesis to the Guan Yu story: even Hua Tuo fails to understand that Cao Cao is actually more gravely ill than his headache indicates. Despite being "miracle-working" physician, Hua cannot cure the ruler's hopeless disease of unwarranted and obdurate suspicion. Interestingly, the Hua Tuo story in the novel is based on an extensive transformation of its sources in historiography.[50] Unlike those sources, the novel has Cao Cao die of the illness soon after Hua Tuo's death. Ironically, by killing the only physician that could possibly save his life, the patient virtually kills himself.

In general, Cao Cao's treatment of men of talent is blatantly utilitarian. He uses them to promote his cause and he knows well that their service is indispensable. Yet, while he demands their absolute loyalty, he does not offer sincere friendship or camaraderie in return. Instead, he is more interested in Machiavellian manipulation and control. In that respect he is different from Sun Quan and, to an even larger extent, Liu Bei. To steal the capable strategist Xu Shu from Liu Bei, Cao resorts to the abominable trick of detaining Xu's old mother. Taking a forged letter to be an authentic one, Xu Shu hastens to leave Liu Bei in order to save his mother, only to receive a bitter tirade from the old lady for having abandoned a righteous ruler to join a treacherous one. The bitterly disappointed mother subsequently hangs herself, and Xu Shu, although staying with Cao Cao, remains loyal to Liu Bei the rest of his life. During the Red Cliffs battle, Xu Shu is the one that sees through Pang Tong's intention in persuading

Cao Cao to have his boats linked up with chains. Instead of saving Cao's navy from the impending attack with fire, Xu finds an excuse to leave the battlefront.

Xu Shu's enduring allegiance to Liu Bei is by no means surprising. Early in Liu Bei's career, when all his civil officials are no more than "pasty-faced students" (*baimian shusheng*), Liu is anxious to find a better adviser. Then Xu Shu, under the pseudonym of Shan Fu, comes to join him. But before he offers his service, Xu puts Liu to a moral test. As Liu's horse is said to have an ominous potential to ruin its owner, Xu pretends to suggest that Liu give the horse away as a gift. By refusing to put someone else in harm's way, Liu proves himself a humane and virtuous ruler. Xu thus willingly becomes his chief adviser, and soon his skills in directing battles impress friends and foes alike.

When Xu Shu asks for Liu Bei's permission to leave in order to save his mother, several of Liu's men insist that Liu should not let him go. To them, Liu Bei replies: "It would be inhumane for me to use the son while letting the mother be killed. It would be dishonorable for me to hold him against his own will and prevent the son from performing his filial duties. I would rather die than do such an inhumane and dishonorable thing" (*bu wei buren buyi zhi shi*) (SGZTSYY, 2:1165). Liu Bei arranges a farewell dinner for Xu Shu, at which the lord and the counselor face each other and weep bitterly. The prospect of losing his friend to his enemy makes Liu Bei feel as if he were "losing both hands" (*ru shi zuoyoushou*) (SGZTSYY, 2:1165). The next morning, Xu Shu takes his departure, and at this point the novel presents a powerful farewell scene:

> They went for a league without noticing it. "Your Lordship should not take the trouble of escorting me so far," Xu Shu said. "I will travel overnight to see my mother." After Xuande went with him for another league, the officers pleaded him to return. Remaining on horseback, Xuande took Xu Shu's hand, "How sad I am to see you go." So saying, Xuande dried his tears with his sleeve. Xu Shu also wept as he parted from his master. Halting his horse by the edge of the forest, Xuande watched Xu Shu and his small entourage race to the distance. He cried again, before Sun Qian and others came over to console him. "Xu Shu is gone! What will become of me now?" Xuande tried to follow Xu Shu with his tearful eyes, but his view was blocked by a large clump of trees. Pointing to the trees with his

whip, he shouted, "I want all those damn trees cut down!" Sun Qian asked, "Why?" "Because I want to see Xu Shu one more time!" answered the lord. (SGZTSYY, 2:1165–69)

The novel's rendering of the Xu Shu episode is the result of an assiduous and painstaking effort to elaborate on what was a paltry detail in the sources. Apart from his recommendation of Zhuge Liang, the Xu Shu story is completely absent from *Chronicle of the Three Kingdoms*. In *Popular Stories of the Three Kingdoms*, Xu Shu leaves Liu Bei because he feels concerned about his mother's safety, but there is no mention of Cao Cao's custody of her. The farewell scene in *Popular Stories* is narrated in a short paragraph of less than two hundred characters.[51] In *History as Mirror to Aid Governance* (Zizhi tongjian), it is mentioned that Xu's mother was detained by Cao Cao, but there is no mention of Liu Bei's farewell banquet and his subsequent sending-off of Xu Shu.[52] Additionally, no known Three Kingdoms plays from the Yuan and Ming periods are based on the Xu Shu story. The only play that features Xu Shu as a major character is Gao Wenxiu's play *Meeting in Xiangyang* (Xiangyang hui). Part of the play is about Liu Bei's acquisition of Xu Shu's service, but there is nothing about Cao Cao's imprisonment of Xu's mother or Xu's subsequent departure from Liu.

Indeed one may consider Xu Shu a typical literatus who, like thousands of his brethren in imperial China, wishes to achieve fame and success through public service and to leave his name in history. For that end, he needs first to have a "wise ruler" (*mingzhu*) recognize his talent and ability. What he chants while meeting Liu Bei for the first time is akin to the collective voice of the intellectual gentry, not only that of the Three Kingdoms period but of the novelist's own time as well:

Across the land there are worthy men,
Who long for a wise ruler [*mingzhu*] to whom to repair.
The sage lord is seeking worthy men,
Of me, alas, he remains totally unaware.
(SGZTSYY, 2:1138)

The Xu Shu story is particularly significant as it is about one scholar receiving strikingly different treatments from two rulers, both hoping to enlist his service. Indeed, it reminds one of this Mencian passage, a passage that was, unsurprisingly, removed from the classic by Zhu Yuanzhang: "Mencius said, 'Bo Yi would serve only the right prince and befriend only the right man. He would not take his place at the court of an evil man, nor would he converse with him. For him to do so would be like sitting in mud and pitch wearing a court cap and gown.'"[53] Bolstered by numerous other examples in the novel, Xu Shu's experience dramatizes a scholar's relationship with the state power, demonstrating his loyalty and gratitude toward a virtuous and appreciative ruler as well as his renunciation and rejection of an abusing and insolent one.

### ZHUGE LIANG AND OFFICIAL RECRUITMENT

Yet the Xu Shu story is, after all, only a prelude to the advent of Zhuge Liang, by far the brightest star in the galaxy of talents in the novel.[54] Judging from Zhuge Liang's "Memorial for Launching the Expeditions" (*Chushi biao*), Liu Bei's repeated visits to Zhuge's residence in an effort to recruit his service may have been a historical fact.[55] Yet in *Chronicle of the Three Kingdoms* Liu's visits are mentioned only in passing, in one single sentence: "The Previous Lord went to visit Liang, but did not get to see him until the third trip."[56] In *Popular Stories of the Three Kingdoms* the account of the visits remains very brief. In the novel, however, the visits are related in a long stretch of narrative that is clearly one of the most elaborate and memorable episodes of the entire work. According to some historical sources, Zhuge Liang may have presented himself to Liu Bei first before the ruler started his recruiting effort. The novelist, interestingly, completely disregarded those sources, even though they are cited in Pei Songzhi's annotation of *Chronicle of the Three Kingdoms* and therefore conveniently accessible.[57]

After taking departure from Liu Bei, Xu Shu, feeling deeply obliged by the ruler's friendship, goes directly to see Zhuge Liang to notify him of Liu's upcoming visit. Zhuge Liang, seemingly enjoying his life of reclusion too much to enter officialdom, appears to be annoyed and blames Xu Shu for trying to make him "the victim of a sacrifice" (*SGZTSYY*, 2:1174). During Liu Bei's visits in the company of his sworn brothers, the ruler's longing to meet his future adviser is repeatedly thwarted, as he constantly misidentifies people around Zhuge—his friends, brother, and father-in-law—for the Reclining Dragon himself. During the last visit, even though

Zhuge happens to be home, Liu Bei has to wait for hours before the sage wakes from a long nap. In this tortuous episode narrated in lavish detail, Liu Bei seems to be on an almost endless quest for an ever-elusive goal. Of course, this is a familiar narrative ploy to repeatedly postpone the climax and thus tantalize the reader, yet one can better appreciate the merit and significance of this "three visits" episode in an expanded context. Given the fact that Zhuge Liang has been informed by Xu Shu of Liu Bei's imminent visit in advance, his apparent snub to the visiting ruler is obviously premeditated. As Xu Shu had done before him, Zhuge Liang wants to test the lord's sincerity and moral standing. Once again, the positions of a ruler and a scholar in the real world—where a scholar had to pass the examinations before being granted an imperial audience and an official appointment—are turned upside-down in the novel. Historically, Liu Bei may have indeed visited Zhuge Liang three times, but the number of three frequently appears in Chinese vernacular fiction, especially in works with oral or folkloric antecedents.[58] In this "three visits" episode the number happens to be the force that drives the reversal home: while a scholar in reality had to pass examinations at three different levels before entering officialdom, the ruler in the fictional world passes three tests before he finally succeeds in recruiting the man of extraordinary talent.

Zhuge Liang's reluctance to leave reclusion is more apparent than real. While he certainly loves the idyllic life in his native place Longzhong, he has been following affairs of the empire closely. His analyses of the political and military situation for Liu Bei during the latter's final visit cannot be any improvised oration but the result of a careful and thorough study. Despite Zhuge Liang's ostensible aloofness and apathy to his recruiter, the secluded sage has actually been expecting eagerly to be recruited. During his long career as the commander of the Shu forces, Zhuge Liang may sometimes appear like a Daoist wizard, but the young man in the thatched cottage is clearly presented more as a Confucian scholar bidding for his opportunity to enter public service.[59] During Liu Bei's second visit, the ruler mistakes Zhuge Liang's younger brother, Zhuge Jun, for his future counselor. Zhuge Jun chants these lines, which obviously speak of his brother's mind more than his own:

> The phoenix flying ten thousand *li* will roost only on the jade,
> The scholar staying home until a true lord's minister he is made.

Tilling his furrowed fields his destined moment he awaits,
In books and poems his pride and aspirations he places.
The day he meets a wise lord will never be too late,
His fabulous talents will take the world to a better date.
Saving the people from miseries, he will pacify the empire,
Leaving his name in history, to his home he will retire.
(*SGZTSYY*, 2:1197–98)

The difference between the Zhuge Liang in the novel and the Zhuge Liang as a Daoist figure elsewhere in the Three Kingdoms tradition is clearly discernible from some verbal divergences. In the "three visits" episode in the *Popular Stories of the Three Kingdoms*, Zhuge Liang is said to be an "immortal" (*shenxian*). His residence is referred to as *an*, which can mean a thatched hut but also a Daoist sanctuary. The latter is more probable in the text, because his boy servant is referred to as *daotong*, a Daoist novice. In his conversation with Zhuge Liang, Liu Bei addresses him sometimes as *xiansheng* (sir) but more often as *shifu*, a term usually reserved for a religious master.[60] In contrast, the novelistic Zhuge Liang lives in his *caotang*, which means, unequivocally, a thatched cottage. His young servant is referred to as *tongzi*, which means simply "boy." Furthermore, Liu Bei now addresses his host consistently as *xiansheng* and never as *shifu*. There is a similar difference between the novel and the Three Kingdoms variety plays (*zaju*). The anonymous Yuan-edition variety play *Zhuge Liang Attacks [Cao Cao's] Camp in Bowang with Fire* (Zhuge Liang Bowang shaotun) starts with the scene of Zhuge's reception of Liu Bei's third visit. In his self-introducing monologue at the beginning of the scene, Zhuge Liang refers to himself as "this humble Daoist" (*pindao*) and indicates that Reclining Dragon, his sobriquet in the novel, is his "Daoist monastic name" (*daohao*).[61] That format of self-introduction is inherited in Ming Three Kingdoms variety plays and Ming texts of Yuan Three Kingdoms plays that feature Zhuge Liang as a major character, including the Ming version of *Zhuge Liang Attacks [Cao Cao's] Camp in Bowang*. Throughout these plays *pindao* is Zhuge Liang's standard term for self-reference, and all the Shu captains call him sometimes *junshi* (army adviser) but more often *shifu*.[62] In *Romance of the Three Kingdoms*, however, Zhuge Liang refers to himself invariably as Liang, and none of the Shu captains ever address him as *shifu*. Such systematic and sweeping changes of the appellations clearly suggest a conscious effort in the novel to remove part of the Daoist coloration of Zhuge Liang from the popular Three Kingdoms tradition and transform him into a new figure who is fundamentally Confucian. Furthermore, there is even a subtle difference in the description of Zhuge Liang's attire. While there is no such a description in *Popular Stories of the Three Kingdoms,* his costume in the variety plays is invariably a "cloud-rolling hat" (*juanyun guan*) and a "red-cloud crane Daoist gown" (*hongyunhe daopao*). In the novel, however, Zhuge Liang is said to have a "plaited silken band" (*lunjin*) on his head and a "crane cloak" (*he chang*) draped over his shoulders when he receives Liu Bei during Liu's third visit (*SGZTSYY*, 2:1212).

Meanwhile, the novel painstakingly heightens the difference between Zhuge Liang and a pedantic academic. In that regard the most telling moment is Zhuge Liang's debate with the civil officials of Wu when he visits Sun Quan before the Red Cliffs battle. When a Wu official asks him what classics he specializes in, Zhuge Liang seizes the opportunity to set himself apart from "the text-bound pedants" (*xunzhang zhaiju zhi furu*):

> Just think of Yi Yin who tilled the soil in Shen and Jiang Ziya who fished on the Wei River. Just think of men like Zhang Liang and Chen Ping, or Geng Yan and Deng Yu. These worthies of the old times all had the abilities and wisdom to sustain the rule of their kings. But what classics did they specialize in? Do you really think they were like schoolboys spending their days between the writing brush and the ink stone? Do you really think they did nothing but argued with others over trivial textual details and flaunted their compositional skills?[63]

To retort the accusation from another Wu official that he has no genuine learning to justify his prominent position, Zhuge proceeds to dwell on the difference between two kinds of scholars, "scholars of noble character" (*junzi zhi ru*) and "scholars with petty interests" (*xiaoren zhi ru*):

> There are scholars of noble character and scholars with petty interests. The former are righteous and gentle, filial to their parents and loyal to their sovereigns. Looking up they can see the patterns of heaven, and looking down they can understand the principles of earth. Between heaven and earth they benefit myriads of people. Because of their good governance

the empire is as firm as a rock, and because of their achievements their names are written in history. The latter, on the other hand, are those who are engrossed in polishing their words and trivial compositions. When they are young they start to write rhyme-prose, and when they are aged they still bend on the classics. While thousands of words may flow from their writing brushes, in their minds not a single useful idea can be found. (SGZTSYY, 3:1405–6)

One may consider these observations by Zhuge Liang a most incisive commentary on the political institution of official recruitment. Little wonder that Li Yu, who rejected the examination system, readily echoes Zhuge Liang in his marginal comment on *Romance of the Three Kingdoms*: "Most of those who have ruined the world are students of the classics. What is the use of those pedants?"[64] One should remember that this ridicule of the "text-bound" pedants is not as pertinent to the time of the historical Zhuge Liang as to the time the fictional character Zhuge Liang was fashioned. While the status of the Confucian classics was lifted after Confucianism became the state ideology during the reign of Emperor Wu of the Han, the classics were not extensively used as a criterion for official recruitment except for the selection of *boshi dizi*.[65] Nor did the belles-lettres play nearly as significant a role in the official selection of that time as they did in the Tang and Song periods. The major means for selecting officials from among the commoners during the Han and Three Kingdoms periods was the so-called *chaju*, a recommendatory system. While it was supplemented with some kind of examinations, for the most part those examinations did not require rigorous training in the classics.[66] It was in later dynastic periods, especially after the Song, that exegeses and textual learning became almost exclusively the basis for the curriculum of the civil service examinations. This "text-bound" mechanism of talent selection, unsurprisingly, led to the proliferation of "text-bound" scholars. During the Ming, the tendency to equate talent with textual scholarship became compounded by the obsession with a rigid format of examination writing known as the "eight-legged essay" (*bagu wen*), which had evolved from Wang Anshi's *jingyi shi*, the format that the Song prime minister prescribed for the answers to examination questions on the classics.[67] Consequently, many scholars devoted themselves to studying the model eight-legged essays by successful examination candidates in addition to the classics, thus becoming trapped in an even deeper swamp of texts.

Significantly, for Zhuge Liang's debate with the Wu officials, there is no textual source in *Chronicle of the Three Kingdoms, Popular Stories of the Three Kingdoms,* or any extant Yuan or Ming Three Kingdoms variety plays. If the play titles in *A Registry of the Ghosts* and *A Sequel to the Registry of the Ghosts* can serve as indicators, the debate is not likely to have been the subject matter in any of the nonextant Three Kingdoms plays, either. Zhuge Liang's anachronistic denunciation of text-bound pedantry, therefore, was most probably the novelist's invention, a commentary on the official recruitment of his own time that was based exclusively on textual scholarship and a rigid writing style. Yet, what speaks even louder in denouncing the textually centered official selection is Zhuge Liang's superbly successful official career itself as presented in the novel. As a scholar of "noble character" who knows "the patterns of heaven" and "the principles of earth," Zhuge Liang never stoops to the "petty interests" of polishing words in "trivial compositions." His successful official career thus belies any inevitable connection between textual learning and the talent required for officialdom.

Just as the novelist presents Zhuge Liang's talent as of a completely different type from the talent sought in the civil service examinations, he carefully highlights Liu Bei's manner of official recruitment in order to address the concerns about official selection of his own time. In contrast to the early Ming emperors' manipulation of the examination curriculum and intimidation of the examination candidates, Liu Bei insists on recruiting officials in "the proper way," that is, by demonstrating sincerity, respect, and appreciation. After Liu Bei's first visit to Zhuge Liang ends in futility, Zhang Fei suggests that Liu should summon Zhuge instead of making another trip to see him. Liu Bei appeals for more patience from his sworn brother by citing the Mencian line: "To wish to meet a good and wise man while not following the proper way is like wishing him to enter while shutting the door against him" (*SGZTSYY*, 2:1192).[68] After the second visit, when both Guan Yu and Zhang Fei try to dissuade him from going for a third trip, Liu Bei responds by expressing his determination to emulate Duke Huan of the Qi who went to visit a commoner five times before getting to see him (*SGZTSYY*, 2:1207).[69] These allusions here may carry a topical relevance to the early Ming, when Zhu Yuanzhang killed several scholars "who refused to be employed by the sovereign."[70]

The novel's presentation of Liu Bei's humility in recruiting the service of Zhuge Liang may be considered an effort to restore some of the dignity of the literati that had been debased and disgraced by the imperial state. As one recalls, intellectuals upholding their dignity in the face of political power is precisely one of the central ideas in *Mencius*. Mencius himself had this to say of people in power after turning down an invitation from the King of Qi: "They may have their wealth, but I have my benevolence; they may have their exalted rank, but I have my integrity. In what way do I suffer in the comparison?"[71] Scholars, as advocated in *Mencius*, were able to offset their political disadvantage with their moral and intellectual superiority. One example presented in *Mencius* is Zi Si, Confucius's grandson, who is reported to have said this to Duke Miao (Miao Gong): "In point of position, you are the prince and I am your subject. How dare I be friends with you? In point of virtue, it is you who ought to serve me. How can you presume to be friends with me?"[72] Elsewhere, when Mencius was asked about the conditions for the *shi* in the antiquity to take office, the sage is said to have answered:

> "There are three conditions," said Mencius, "under each of which he would take office; equally, there are three conditions under each of which he would relinquish it. First, when he was sent for with the greatest respect, in accordance with the proper rites, and told that his advice would be put into practice, he would go. But when his advice was not put into practice, he would leave, even though the courtesies were still observed. Second, when he was sent for with the greatest respect, in accordance with the proper rites, he would go, though his advice was not put into practice. But he would leave when the courtesies were no longer meticulously observed. Third, when he could no longer afford to eat either in the morning or in the evening, and was so weak from hunger that he could no longer go out of doors, then he could accept charity from the prince who, hearing of his plight, gave to him out of kindness, saying, 'As I have failed, in the first instance, to put into practice the way he taught, and then failed to listen to his advice, it will be to my shame if he dies of hunger in my domain.' But the purpose of this acceptance is merely to ward off starvation."[73]

Despite the probably overgrown technicalities of these "conditions," the Mencian message here is clear: the *shi* deserve respect and appreciation from the ruler before they agree to serve in officialdom. To a significant extent, the novel's presentation of Liu Bei's recruitment of Zhuge Liang illustrates that Mencian view.

LIU BEI AND ZHUGE LIANG:
THE IDEAL RULER–PRIME MINISTER RELATIONSHIP

Liu Bei's humility toward Zhuge Liang does not end with his recruiting effort. After Zhuge Liang becomes his chief strategist, Liu Bei treats Zhuge as his mentor (*yi shili dai zhi*), and compares his relationship to Zhuge to that of a fish to water. The lord and the counselor "eat at the same table and sleep on the same couch, spending all their time discussing the events in the empire" (SGZTSYY, 2:1224). Even the initial doubts by Liu Bei's two sworn brothers about the scholar's ability are dispersed after Zhuge wins the battles at Bowang and Xinye against Cao Cao's numerically superior forces.[74] The young adviser sometimes even appears more like the lord's superior than his aide. Seeing Liu Bei winding a yak's tail into a hat as a pastime, Zhuge Liang gives his master "a stern look" (*zhengse*) and lectures him on the danger of sapping his aspirations by indulging in such frivolous pleasures. The embarrassed lord instantly tosses his toy away and engages his adviser in a discussion of the military situation (SGZTSYY, 2:1264). Later, when Liu Bei stays in Wu for months enchanted by all the sensual pleasures as Sun Quan's new brother-in-law, it is Zhuge's "ruses in brocade bags" (*jinnang miaoji*) entrusted to Zhao Yun that ensure the lord's swift and safe return. Such incidents epitomize the ruler-adviser relationship. As Zhuge Liang consistently serves as the guiding force of the Shu regime, Liu Bei becomes utterly trustful in Zhuge, letting his adviser make decisions for him in many crucial situations. That, however, does not reduce Liu Bei to a mere figurehead. Liu's more accurate appraisal of Ma Su proves him to be a sounder judge of character than his sagacious counselor, whose credulity of Ma's flashy display of knowledge leads to a major military setback at Jieting years later. Yet the Ma Su episode, seemingly damaging to Zhuge Liang's status, is paradoxically reaffirming as well: since Liu Bei has such penetrating eyes for true talent, his complete trust in Zhuge Liang cannot have been misplaced.

The most critical moment in the ruler–prime minister relationship arrives when Liu Bei becomes emotionally overwhelmed by the deaths of Guan Yu and Zhang Fei. To avenge his sworn brothers, Liu Bei impetuously brushes aside Zhuge Liang's remonstration and rushes to lead an expedition against Wu, which the adviser argues is more an ally than a foe. When the judicious ruler is reduced to a devastated and vengeful sworn brother, he quickly loses his sense of judgment. Blindly confident in his numerically superior army, Liu Bei camps all his troops along the wooded bank of the Yangzi River, disregarding the suggestion by his aides to seek advice from Zhuge Liang. When the startled prime minister sends his words, Liu Bei's forces have already fallen victim to an attack with fire, ironically the same kind of assault that Zhuge himself has inflicted so many times on his enemies. However, even in his folly Liu Bei is different from either Yuan Shao or Cao Cao. On his deathbed, the remorseful lord, in tears, admits to his mistake in front of his grief-stricken chief counselor: "How could I have so foolishly rejected your advice and brought this defeat upon myself?" Then the dying lord entrusts Zhuge with the regency for his son and heir, Liu Shan:

> The Previous Emperor continued as he wept, "Your talent is ten times superior to Cao Pi's, and I am sure you will be able to secure the empire and complete our cause. If my heir is worthy of support, support him. If he proves otherwise, please take the throne yourself in Chengdu." Hearing this, Kongming was disconcerted, perspiring profusely. He prostrated himself again and said tearfully, "How can I do otherwise than serve as his right-hand man and remain loyal till the very end of my life?" He knocked his forehead to the floor until his eyes bled.
>   Again the Previous Emperor asked Kongming to sit on his couch. He summoned his sons, Prince Lu Liu Yong and Prince Liang Liu Li, and instructed: "Bear my words in your minds. After I'm gone, I want you and Liu Shan to treat Prime Minister as father. If you show any disrespect, you will be unfilial sons deserving to be eradicated by both men and gods!" Then he said to Kongming, "Please be seated, Prime Minister, and let my sons kowtow to you to acknowledge you as father." The two princes did accordingly, and Kongming said, "Were I to die the cruelest death, I could never return the kindness from Your Majesty." (*SGZTSYY*, 5:2725–26)

While Liu Bei has always cherished Zhuge Liang's service, it takes a colossal blunder on his own part to help him fully appreciate the true value of his chief counselor. This deathbed scene thus marks the culmination of their relationship. Ever since the early days of Zhuge Liang's career, he and his lord have been like brothers. That brotherly bond has developed sometimes as a complement to and sometimes in rivalry with the other set of fraternal relationships, the sworn-brotherhood between Liu Bei and his two top captains, Guan Yu and Zhang Fei. Although there are occasions of moral dilemma such as the one of Guan Yu's release of Cao Cao after the latter's defeat at Red Cliffs, in general Guan and Zhang have faithfully fulfilled their obligations as both friends and subjects. Yet to keep the fraternal devotion merely on a personal level, as Liu Bei does in his expedition against Wu, can only be destructive to the cause of restoring the house of the Han. Significantly, after his attempt to revenge his sworn brothers has led to that disastrous end, Liu Bei is now back, in his last moment of life, attempting to formalize the other brotherly bond by making his chief adviser the surrogate father to his sons. While Zhuge has not shared Liu's vengeful vehemence over the deaths of Guan and Zhang, the brotherhood between the ruler and the prime minister is of a different type, one that is not based on anything like the Peach Garden pledge to die on the same day but on the shared commitment to a common cause.

Liu Bei's request that Zhuge Liang take over the imperial authority when necessary may be akin to the stereotyped scene of Tao Qian's pleading with Liu Bei to take over the prefectship of Xuzhou.[75] Yet, as Liu Bei's proposed transfer of power does not involve merely an official position but the imperial throne itself, it assumes unparalleled magnitude and once again challenges the traditional notion of orthodox rule. Within the novel itself, it contrasts sharply with the two forced abdications at swordpoint: the last Han emperor Liu Xie's handover of the throne to Cao Pi and its almost retributive replay in Cao Huan's relinquishment of power to Sima Yan. In an expanded context, of course, it echoes the time-honored legends of the voluntary transmissions of power among the ancient sage-kings, from Yao to Shun and then from Shun to Yu, a line of succession where virtue and talent took precedence over blood lineage. To be sure, Liu Bei's proposal is only hypothetical. As it turns out, Zhuge Liang, just as he has promised Liu Bei, remains for the rest of his life a prime minister steadfastly loyal to Liu Shan. It is possible, as Mao Zonggang has suggested, that Liu Bei makes that proposal precisely because he is absolutely assured that Zhuge will never turn it into a fact.[76] In that case, the proposal becomes a political tactic. Even if that is the case, it still indicates Liu Bei's staunch confidence in Zhuge Liang's loyalty and devotion. At any rate, the lord's deathbed request to his counselor is an ultimate expression of trust, respect, and appreciation, which secures for his son the continued dedication from the man of unmatched talent and wisdom.

This kind of reciprocal ruler-minister relationship is exactly what is advocated in many of those passages removed from *Mencius*. Liu Bei is depicted as a ruler who treats his chief counselor "as his hands and feet," to borrow the words from that famous Mencian passage. And the counselor, in return, treats his master as his "belly and heart." Indeed the metaphor "hands and feet" frequently recurs in the novel's description of Liu Bei's relationships with his men. When the master sends Xu Shu off, as mentioned earlier, he likens Xu's departure to his "loss of both hands." And, of course, the fraternity between Liu and his two sworn brothers—although warriors rather than scholars—is frequently termed *shouzu zhi qing*, literally, the attachment to others as if they were of the same body as oneself.[77]

It is obvious that the novel's depiction of Liu Bei's relationship to his men becomes all the more potent against the foil of Cao Cao. Even though deviating from his historical counterpart, Cao Cao might have appeared much more realistic to the early audience of the novel. Perhaps it is not far-fetched to say that in the characterization of Cao Cao there are ingredients from Zhu Yuanzhang and Zhu Di. In their treatment of scholar-officials, these early Ming emperors appeared to be a Legalistic antithesis to the Mencian ideal of the benevolent ruler. To that extent they indeed bore some resemblance to the novelistic figure of Cao Cao. Among other things in the novel, the palace physician Ji Ping's defiant denouncement of Cao Cao as traitor and usurper and Cao's brutal tortures of Ji—including cutting off his fingers and tongue before putting him to death and dismembering his body (*SGZTSYY*, 2:757–63)—are strongly reminiscent of what happened between Zhu Di and the Jianwen loyalists, especially Fang Xiaoru.[78] The pro-Shu and anti-Wei stance in *Three Kingdoms*, therefore, may be more than just an inheritance from the novel's antecedents in popular sources or historiographies. The literati sentiments of the novelist's own time could have exerted a shaping influence on the depiction of the major characters.

Throughout Chinese imperial history, prime ministers, or *zaixiang*, were often representative figures of the educated elite, especially since the famous motto by Emperor Taizu of the Song: "It should take a scholar to be a prime minister." (*Zaixiang xiyong dushuren*).[79] As a result, the personal relationship between the emperor and the prime minister could be a barometer of the relationship between the imperial power and the literati. While the official title of the prime minister differed from one dynasty to the next, the man in that position was in most cases the most important aide to the emperor and top administrator of the state. "The empire was not to be governed only by one man," as Huang Zongxi put it, "and official positions were set up to govern it. Officials were, therefore, surrogates of the sovereign."[80] By this observation, Huang Zongxi explains the origin of the institution of civil officialdom, including the position of the prime minister itself. While the emperor always possessed unchallengeable authority, the prime minister, if he was a scholar, could sometimes serve as some kind of a buffer between the throne and civil bureaucracy.

During the thirteen years between the founding of the Ming and Zhu Yuanzhang's annulment of the office of *zaixiang* in 1380, there were as many as twenty-three men who were placed in that position, starting with Xu Da (1332–85). Yet only three of them played any substantial roles, namely, Li Shanchang (1314–90), Wang Guangyang (?–1379), and Hu Weiyong.[81] All three ended up executed by Emperor Hongwu. Li Shanchang lived in his native Dingyuan after his retirement in 1371, but his implication in the Hu Weiyong case led to his execution in 1390. Wang Guangyang was in the office for two years before he was demoted to a local position in the south and then put to death there. Hu Weiyong, who climbed all the way from the position of county magistrate to the very top of bureaucratic hierarchy, was the prime minister from 1373 to 1380, longer than either Li or Wang.

The crimes Hu Weiyong was charged with included "recruiting Japanese pirates" for a possible coup d'état and "acknowledging allegiance in correspondence to the heir apparent of the Yuan," neither of which could be substantiated.[82] Yet Hu's abuse of power and practice of nepotism and bribe-taking had been no secret among the top officials. Several of them, including Xu Da, had memorialized Zhu Yuanzhang about Hu's misdeeds. Even before he appointed Hu the prime minister, the emperor had received counsel from Liu Ji (1311–75), a sagacious scholar and strategist, that Hu was absolutely no material for the top administrative post.[83] Evidently, Zhu Yuanzhang, usually observant and perceptive, was fully aware that Hu was not the right choice. So why did the emperor not only go ahead with the appointment of Hu but also retain him in the position for so long? The most convincing answer is that Zhu Yuanzhang deliberately made Hu the prime minister in order to create a pretext for his eventual abolition of the top civil service position, which proved a crucial step toward his autocracy.[84]

Huang Zongxi considered all the ill governance during much of the Ming period a consequence of the annulment of the position of prime minister.[85] Whether that assessment was accurate or not, it was true that Zhu Yuanzhang's decision had a tremendous impact on Ming political culture. During the rest of the Hongwu years and the entire Yongle reign, the Six Ministries (*liu bu*) reported directly to the emperor, and the so-called Grand Secretariat (*neige*) was little more than a rubber stamp. Without the protection of a prime minister's prominence and prestige, scholar-officials became much more vulnerable to the politically aggressive eunuchs, and consequently the civil bureaucracy was significantly weakened. To be sure, the status of the *neige* was to be raised later in the dynasty, eventually paving the road for the advent of the powerful grand councilor, Zhang Juzheng, who steered the state for about a decade under an adolescent Emperor Wanli. In general, however, the abolition of the prime minister's office further changed the balance of power between the throne and the intellectual elite. If the office of the prime minister as the top scholar-official had served as a symbol of the cooperation between the imperial power and the scholar-gentry, the removal of that symbol institutionalized the throne's monopoly of political power.

It may not have been a mere coincidence that *Romance of the Three Kingdoms*, with its depiction of "a wise ruler and a worthy prime minister" (*mingjun xianxiang*), came into existence at a historical moment that witnessed neither a wise ruler nor a worthy prime minister. Drawing upon the Mencian ideal of political sovereignty, the novel's presentation of the Liu Bei–Zhuge Liang relationship may be best appreciated in the context of the early Ming political situation, including the suppression of *Mencius* and the abolition of the office of the prime minister. It was a time when the literati craved a ruler that would fully appreciate their worth and a powerful and sagacious scholar-official to represent their interests. The fictional depiction of Liu Bei and Zhuge Liang may have been romanticized with an imagination that catered to that yearning.

Indeed, the literati's wish to negotiate with political power in order to regain some of their lost dignity found many literary expressions. In the fourteenth-century popular narrative (*pinghua*) *King Wu's Expedition Against King Zhou* (Wu Wang fa Zhou shu) and the sixteenth-century novel *Creation of the Gods* (Fengshen yanyi), for instance, King Wen of the Zhou has to humble himself in repeated visits to Jiang Ziya before successfully soliciting the service of the wise strategist, an episode that bears remarkable affinity to that of Liu Bei's three visits to Zhuge Liang in *Romance of the Three Kingdoms*. In several of the fifteenth-century chantefables (*cihua*) and late Ming novels that center on the Song judge Bao Zheng, the righteous and resourceful scholar-official is depicted as being able to punish the emperor's kinsmen for their wrongdoings despite intervention from the sovereign himself.[86] Yet nowhere is the literati's yearning for a strengthened position in their interaction with the imperial state more intensely expressed than in *Romance of the Three Kingdoms*. When the emperors of the early Ming wielded absolute political power, the literati sought sanctuary in the fictional world of a historical novel, where they found in the tandem of a wise ruler and a worthy prime minister the best embodiment of the Mencian ideal of political sovereignty.

CHAPTER 3

# The Scholar-Lover in Erotic Fiction

*A Power Game of Selection*

As the imperial state's primary means for the recruitment of civil officials and political and ideological control over the literati, the civil service examinations functioned as the most important contact zone between the *daotong* and the *zhengtong* in late imperial China. What happened in the examinations seemed to embody a partnership that was mutually beneficial: it enabled the state to regularly replenish its bureaucracy with new talent, while it gave the educated elite elevated social status, ample economic gains, and confirmation of their belief in *dao* learning. As Benjamin Elman puts it, the examination system was "a cultural arena within which diverse political and social interests contested each other and were balanced."[1] Indeed, some of the features of the system may have resulted from the negotiations between the interests of the state and those of the literati. In the final analysis, however, the examinations were the lens through which the imperial state scrutinized intellectuals before it selected certain among them according to its own needs. The interaction between the state as an aggressive examiner/selector and scholars as largely passive examinees/selectees vividly reflects the power balance between the *zhengtong* and the *daotong* in late imperial times.

Quite surprisingly, perhaps, one literary representation of this power game of selection in the civil service examinations is in fictional works featuring an erotic scholar-lover, which parody the examinations by

67

using them as a metaphor for the sexual act. Many works in the "scholar-beauty" (*caizi jiaren*) fiction that flourished during the late Ming and early Qing—roughly the seventeenth century—are, to various degrees, erotic in nature.[2] This erotic subgenre typically features a scholar of remarkable talent and a young woman—or in many cases, two or even more—of outstanding beauty. The topics of the examinations and sexual escapades are often parallel and coeval, and the protagonist's status as a scholar and his possession of beautiful women become his two insignias that are equally indispensable and mutually complementary.

Chinese erotic literature, of course, has a history longer than that of the scholar-beauty fiction. Early erotic narratives in classical Chinese (*wenyan*), such as *An Unofficial History of Zhao Feiyan* (Zhao Feiyan waizhuan), *Previously Unrecorded Accounts of the Daye Reign* (Daye shiyi ji), and *An Unofficial History of Yang Taizhen* (Yang Taizhen waizhuan), are typically about a historical emperor and his favorite consort or consorts.[3] The anonymous *Story of the Lord of Perfect Satisfaction* (Ruyijun zhuan), probably written in the fifteenth century, tells of Empress Wu Zetian's (r. 695–704) excessive sexual indulgence with her lover Xue Aocao.[4] A closer precursor to the seventeenth-century erotic scholar-lover is, of course, Ximen Qing in the late sixteenth-century novel *Plum in the Golden Vase* (Jin Ping Mei). To some extent, one may consider the oversexed polygamist and adulterer Ximen a cross between the depraved ruler in the earlier erotic works and the enamored scholar in the scholar-beauty tradition. Indeed, having six wives and numerous mistresses, Ximen bears remarkable resemblances to an emperor surrounded by his harem. At the same time, the novel's presentation of *cai* (wealth), a major source of vice that often functions as Ximen's capital for sexual conquests, may be seen as a parody of *cai* (literary and scholarly latent). At any rate, this unpolished merchant, who is perhaps no more than functionally literate, is no scholar; much less does he have any experience in the civil service examinations. By contrast, the protagonist in the seventeenth-century erotic fiction is usually a young scholar who seeks an examination degree and an official career. By coupling the scholar's sexual experience with his experience in the examinations, these works represent a unique breed of fictional eroticism.

Examined against the sociopolitical context of the time, the rise of the erotic scholar-lover in fiction, with the frequent use of the examinations as a metaphor for his sexual act, may be considered a response to the situation of official selection. By displacing the political setting of the examination system with a sexual setting, fiction writers relocated the scholar to a different framework of power relations. In the meantime, the examination metaphor highlights polarized positions shared by the two situations, the positions of the active and passive players in the power game: the selector and examiner on the one hand and the selectee and examinee on the other. When the scholar transmutes into a virile and potent man often possessing multiple sexual partners, he discards the passive position of the examinee and the selectee and assumes instead the active position of the examiner and the selector. Most important, by juxtaposing the valorized official selection process with the morally questionable sexual selection, this metaphor brings down the examination system from its lofty height and undermines its moral basis. The erotic fiction centered on the scholar-lover thus becomes a subversive parody of the imperial state's selection of scholars.

## THE IDEOLOGICAL SETTING FOR SEVENTEENTH-CENTURY FICTIONAL EROTICISM

It is possible to see the erotic scholar-lover in fiction as a product of the hedonistic literati mores supposedly promoted by the intellectual trend under the sway of the left-wing Taizhou school. Indeed, for Li Zhi (1527–1602), "love for wealth and women" (*haohuo haose*) was among the passions shared and bespoken by all men, and is therefore a "proverbial truth" (*eryan*).[5] Yuan Hongdao (1568–1610), Li Zhi's friend and follower, expressed in a private letter his strong yearning for what he called "five cardinal pleasures" (*wu da kuaihuo*) in human life, with the first pleasure being that of "meeting the best beauties, hearing the best music, tasting the best delicacies, and delivering the best talks in the world."[6] In his famous—or infamous—autoepitaph, Zhang Dai (1597–1679) presented a portrait of himself in the younger years as a sensualist who was fond of "nice houses, pretty girls, good-looking catamites, delicious food, fine steeds, brilliant lanterns, fireworks, theatric performances, and music."[7] No doubt, such manifestos of unbridled individual desires by these influential scholars contributed significantly to the general intellectual and moral environment for fiction writing, as corroborated by what we know about some of the fiction writers' personal lives. One example is Feng Menglong (1574–1646). Having "celebrated liaisons with at least two beautiful and accomplished Suzhou singing girls," Feng was perhaps even more "abandoned to sensual pleasures" and more often "out of bounds of the codes of propriety" than his fellow Wuxian natives of the previous century, Zhu Yunming (1460–1526) and Tang Ying (1470–1523).[8]

However, it is difficult to explain the burst of fictional eroticism centered on the scholar-lover entirely in terms of the newfound candor about sexual desire. After all, libertinism was by no means the predominant ideological discourse of the time, and the influence from the left-wing Taizhou school was usually more than offset by Zhu Xi's orthodox teaching of "preserving the heavenly principle and mortifying human desires" (*cun tianli, mie renyu*). While not a thoroughgoing ethics of asceticism in itself, Zhu Xi's doctrine cast a morally questioning light on sexual passion.[9] Yet the neo-Confucian mistrust of human desires was not the only deterrent to libertinism. In the immediate context of official selection, there was a form of thinking that was largely a hybrid of neo-Confucian moral rigidity and the Daoist and Buddhist ideas of karmic retribution.[10] As the examinations became progressively competitive and the results increasingly unpredictable, it was widely believed that a scholar's moral behavior—and indeed his parents' and ancestors', for that matter—could have a direct bearing on the outcome of his examinations. Under the influence of this conviction, many educated men kept in their households different versions of *gongguoge* (ledgers of merits and demerits), handbooks purported to provide moral guidance for personal behavior and to register one's good and bad deeds, which allegedly would function as the basis for the eventual reward or punishment from heaven.[11] Having originated perhaps as early as the fourth century, these moral manuals became truly popular during the late Ming and early Qing. Since in most cases an educated commoner's chance for upward social mobility hinged on his academic performance, he would be inclined to believe that the highest reward for his accumulated merits would be success in the examinations.

What was supposed to carry a particularly heavy weight on the moral scale was sexual ethics. In the so-called *Ledger of Merits and Demerits Regarding the Ten Precepts* (Shi jie gongguoge) and *Ledger of Merits and Demerits to Warn the World* (Jingshi gongguoge), two moral manuals that were popular during the late sixteenth century, specific numbers of demerits were set for different sexual transgressions.¹² In *Ledger of Merits and Demerits Regarding the Ten Precepts*, for instance, having "lustful thoughts in oneself" would count for ten demerits, any behavior "with the intent to excite lust in women" would count for twenty, and even having a "lewd dream" would result in one demerit. Much harsher penalties for sexual sins were spelled out in *Ledger of Merits and Demerits to Warn the World*: one thousand demerits for "producing erotic books, songs, or pictures," five hundred for "showing preference for one special wife or concubine" (amazingly, the same punishment for burning down someone's house), fifty for each time "sporting with a prostitute or a catamite," and fifty for simply "joking about women."¹³ For a scholar, accumulation of such demerits for sexual misconducts would supposedly lead to the ultimate penalty in the examination hall.

The prevalence of this belief in the connection between a scholar's sexual ethics and his chance in the examinations is corroborated by a large number of anecdotal accounts from different Qing sources, some possibly semifactual while others blatantly fictional.¹⁴ These anecdotes often provide the name of a historical scholar, typically from the Ming or the early Qing, and a specific year for the examination. Despite all the variations in narrative details, the storyline is largely stereotypical, either about sexual abstinence that was rewarded or about licentiousness and lechery that incurred a punishment in the examinations. The temporal gap between the alleged occurrence of the story and the date of the text suggests a period of circulation of rumors about the particular scholar, which in turn testifies to the prevalent attitude toward sexual behavior among the educated elite.

One such anecdote concerns Cao Nai, *zhuangyuan* of 1433. Once, while Cao is serving as a prison warden years before his success in the examinations, he persistently resists the seduction of a beautiful female thief in his custody by repeatedly writing the line *Cao Nai bu ke* on paper slips. Later, during his metropolitan examination (*huishi*), he sees a piece of paper fluttering about in his cell upon which is written the line *Cao Nai bu ke*. The sight inspires him to win the *zhuangyuan* status.¹⁵ Another anecdote is about Wang Maitao, a late Ming scholar from Luanzhou. Wang, according to the story, was once kidnapped by roving bandits. In order to retain Wang as their bookkeeper, the bandits seize a pretty girl and force Wang to take her as his wife. While living with the girl in the same room,

Wang sleeps on a separate bed every night, and eventually escapes with the girl and returns her to her parents. During the provincial examination (*xiangshi*) of 1648, Wang suffers a nose bleed, and the blood stains his examination paper. When the dejected Wang is about to quit the examination, the spirit of the girl's father appears and removes the stains from the paper with a magic touch.[16] In still another anecdote, an early Qing scholar from Zhejiang takes shelter from the rain in an oxcart shed. Seeing a young woman in the same shed, he stands outside under the eave all night, ensuring the woman's safety and avoiding compromising her reputation. Six years later, the scholar takes the provincial examination in 1654. His paper is not passed initially, but each time the chief examiner is about to throw it away, it starts to emit a radiance, finally forcing the examiner to reverse his decision.[17]

While these anecdotes demonstrate reward for sexual prudence, many others show the dire consequences of improper sexual conduct. Zhao Fushan, a provincial scholar (*juren*) from Dengzhou, travels to Beijing for the metropolitan examination in 1655. As he is in a hotel holding a courtesan in his arms, Zhao does not notice that he is next to a statue of the Prince of Wu'an (Wu'an Wang).[18] While Zhao remains in the capital, back at home his father has a dream in which a messenger from the deity declares a postponement of Zhao's success. Zhao indeed fails in the examination that year, and has to study hard for twenty-four more years before he finally wins the *jinshi* status in 1679.[19] Another story is about a provincial scholar in Zhejiang. As his friend covets his neighbor's wife, the scholar tries to help his friend by spreading a rumor about the woman's infidelity. When the neighbor divorces his wife, the scholar offers to write the divorce announcement for him. Afterward, he inadvertently stuffs the draft of the announcement in the hollow shaft of his writing brush. Later, when the scholar takes the metropolitan examination in 1658, the paper in the brush shaft is discovered during the body search. As punishment, he is pilloried and flogged, and then has his status as provincial scholar nullified.[20] In still another case, a talented licentiate from Hanyang has repeatedly failed the provincial examinations. His friend sends for a Daoist master to practice divination for him. The result of the divination shows that the licentiate had been originally destined to become a provincial scholar, but he ruined his fate by seducing a maidservant. On hearing that, the licentiate becomes determined to reform. He compiles a ledger of merits and demerits to warn people against sexual dissolution, and raises money for its publication. In 1696, he finally wins the *juren* status.[21]

The message in these short tales, as in the ledgers of merits and demerits in many scholars' households, helped valorize the moral status of the examination system. According to that message, the acquisition of a civil service degree through the examinations was not only a scholar's ultimate vocational goal but also a sign of moral endorsement from heaven. As the examination system was presented here as a platform for moral judgment, it would appear, almost a priori, morally unassailable in itself. Since it was a mystic force—a deity like the Prince of Wu'an or the law of retribution—that determined the fate of an examination candidate, the institution of official selection, just like its supernatural agents, was elevated above any moral scrutiny. The spiritualistic cloak of these tales and moral manuals thus covered up all the secular filths and institutional defects of the civil service examinations.

Most interesting in these sources is the perception of sexual impropriety as one of the worst symptoms of moral infirmity that a scholar had to overcome before winning a civil service degree. Cai Qizun, *zhuangyuan* of 1670, expressed his sense of moral dilemma in a poem allegedly composed right after he rebuffed a courtesan when he was in the capital for the metropolitan examination:

> The pursuit for fame and success
> And the passion for the breeze and the moon:
> These are what one is obsessed with everyday,
> Again and again they place one's mind in turmoil.
> While one yearns to embrace the verdant and lean against the crimson,
> He cannot let go the green lamp and yellow volumes
> As well as the prestige of the jade hall and golden horse.
> While one wants to rank with the dragons and phoenixes,
> He cannot tear away from the jade faces and flowery smile
> As well as the tender love behind the hibiscus screen.
> How can one have it at both ends—
> To achieve fame and relish amour?[22]

By lamenting not being able to "have it at both ends," Cai places sexual passion and examination success at the opposite ends of an antithetical axis. If a courtesan like Li Wa in the early days of the examination system could hatch a successful examination candidate in her warm and tender embrace, her late Ming and early Qing counterpart was sometimes perceived as an enchantress siphoning a scholar's talent and ruining his chance for a bureaucratic career.[23] From the broad circulation of the moral manuals and the sermonizing anecdotes about sexual ethics, we see a picture notably different from the decadence and dissipation often associated with the sensualist trend that supposedly was all the rage in the late Ming and lingered into the early Qing. It testifies to the complexity and diversity of the ideological situation of the time, with multiple discourses interacting upon and contending with each other. This understanding of the intellectual conditions has important ramifications for the interpretation of the fictional erotic scholar-lover. If the hedonistic thinking was after all not as permeating as it might appear, and if there was actually a powerful discourse policing sexual ethics in the immediate precinct of the examination system, one has good reason to ask whether the creation of the erotic scholar-lover could have been driven by something other than sheer sexual libido.

## TWO SELECTIONS BY THE IMPERIAL POWER

In Li Yu's (1611–80) story "Tower of the Returned Crane" (He gui lou), Emperor Huizong (r. 1101–25) of the Northern Song conducts two processes of selection simultaneously. To reinvigorate his empire, which has been weakened by a prolonged military confrontation with its belligerent northern neighbors, the emperor wishes to replenish the civil bureaucracy with fresh talents, and so issues a decree that all the licentiates across the empire take the examinations that year. At the same time, he wants to recruit women for his harem, and sends eunuchs to all the provinces seeking outstanding beauties. From the examinations, two young men, friends with each other, emerge as the top scholars of the empire, while the search for beauties results in two top candidates, daughters of the same family. The emperor is about to take the girls into his inner palace when one of the ministers daringly remonstrates that the emperor show his virtue of "preferring the worthy over the beautiful" (*yuanse qinxian*); the ruler reluctantly agrees at the last minute to have the sisters married off instead. Under a careful arrangement, the two beautiful young women are married to the two top scholars, with the matching based on the men's respective ranking on the roster of the successful examination candidates.

Li Yu thus presents the selection of scholars for officialdom and the selection of women for the imperial harem as parallel and comparable undertakings. One may find a similar example in *Dream of the Red Chamber*. Jia Baoyu's older sister Yuanchun is selected to be an imperial concubine and Baoyu's female cousin and future wife Xue Baochai arrives in the capital as a candidate in the selection of palace staff, while Baoyu himself is expected to prepare for the official selection in the examinations. It may not be far-fetched to say that Yuanchun's tearful return to visit her family and, later, her forlorn death in the high-walled palace may have contributed to Baoyu's understanding of imperial selection and to his rejection of a bureaucratic career.

Historically, the selection of women and selection of scholars were often almost equally important on a Chinese ruler's agenda. Unlike the civil service examinations, however, the process of selecting palace women has remained relatively obscure. Fortunately, Ji Yun (1724–1805) left us an informative account of a late Ming selection. Following Emperor Xizong's (r. 1621–27) inauguration, the court launched the process of selecting girls to refill the inner palace. Five thousand maidens aged between thirteen and sixteen from all over the empire were assembled in the capital, where they were then divided into dozens of groups. On the first day, the eunuchs gave each girl a preliminary visual assessment, and those who were considered not of the appropriate height or weight were immediately dismissed. On the second day, those who had defects in their facial features, skin, or shoulders and those whose voices were deemed unpleasant were eliminated. On the third day, the eunuchs measured each girl's arms and legs and asked her to walk a few dozen steps in a circle. About one thousand were again sent home for shorter-than-pleasing forearms, bigger-than-desirable toes, or a less-than-elegant gait. The remaining one thousand girls were accepted as palace maids (*gongnü*). Soon after they were admitted to the inner palace, each was taken to a closed room, where an old palace woman felt the girl's breasts by hand, sniffed her armpits, and examined other parts of her body. As a result of this round of examination, three hundred were selected as leaders of the new palace staff. After another month, fifty were chosen to be imperial concubines (*feipin*) based on their temperament and behavior as well the emperor's own observation.

The final round of the selection was a comprehensive test on calligraphy, arithmetic, poetry, and painting. Three candidates emerged as winners, one made the empress and the other two top imperial concubines.[24]

During the Qing, the recruitment of palace maids, known as *xuanxiu*, was conducted every three years from among daughters of the Manchu "banner" (*qiren*) families. Banner leaders and company captains were required to submit to the Department of Revenue (*hubu*) a roster of girls who had reached the age of twelve. On the first day of the selection, each girl was escorted by her relatives to the Shenwu Gate of the Forbidden City, where they waited in line for the girl's turn to be ushered in for the preliminary inspection. The girls who passed it would have their names registered (*jiming*) for the next round of inspection, and those who did not would be allowed to go home to be betrothed or married. If a girl married without first participating in the *xuanxiu* selection, her parents, the leaders of the clan, and the company captains were all to be punished.[25] Girls who had not been inspected would not be allowed to marry even after they reached the age of twenty.[26] Qing emperors, just like their predecessors in earlier dynasties, took it as their birthright to select and collect as many women as they pleased. When Emperor Kangxi lectured his sons on sexual moderation, the father of fifty-six children said this in all seriousness: "I keep only three hundred women around the palace and those who have not served me personally I release when they are thirty years old and send them home to be married."[27]

In the late Qing, the emperor became much more personally involved in the selection of palace maids. The candidates, after entering the inner palace in a file, would stand still at a designated place. Upon the report from the eunuchs, the emperor would arrive in person. Following a "long and deliberate inspection," he would decide on "whom to select and whom to dismiss." The procedure for selecting imperial concubines was more complicated. The candidates who survived the initial sifting would assemble at the Banners Quartermaster's (*baqi lingmiguan*) residence for the second round of selection. Girls from all banners arrived in mule coaches before sunrise. Those who passed the inspection of the banner chiefs became qualified for another round of selection conducted by the Minister of Palace Affairs (*neiwufu dachen*). The final round of selection was in the inner palace, under the supervision of the empress dowager and the emperor himself.[28]

Palace maids had very limited personal freedom, and life for them was often tedious and miserable. Not surprisingly, most parents were reluctant to give their daughters to palace service. For some of the women, however, it could be the first step toward power and prestige. If they were lucky enough to be selected as imperial concubines, they would have a chance to climb the rungs in the elaborate inner-palace hierarchy to become a high-ranking imperial consort (*guifei* or *huangguifei*) or even an empress.[29] With the exception of the empress, the titles for palace women, including the imperial consorts and palace staff, differed from dynasty to dynasty, but the ranking system closely resembled that of civil bureaucracy in general.[30]

The selection of palace women thus entailed multiple rounds of rigorous and meticulous examinations, which indeed makes the process remarkably comparable to that of official selection. An even more significant affinity between these two institutions, however, lies in the candidates' relationship to the imperial power. While talented scholars were recruited to serve the interests of the state, of which the emperor was the supreme representative, beautiful women were selected for palace service or for the carnal gratification of the ruler as man. In both selections, the empire-wide pool to select from was totally at the mercy of the will of the ultimate selector, the emperor. Both processes were usually under the management of the emperor's handpicked agents: top officials in the civil service examinations and trusted eunuchs in the selection of palace women. In either selection, the bias and fraud of the imperial agents could lead to corruption. In the examinations, nepotism and bribery often ran rampant, resulting in elimination of best scholars and selection of mediocre ones.[31] The same thing could happen in the selection of palace women. Thus Wang Zhaojun, the most beautiful woman in the empire, could not be chosen to be an imperial concubine after she became a palace maid. As she and her family refused to bribe the court artist Mao Yanshou, the latter deliberately painted a portrait of her that did not do justice to her beauty. Based on that misrepresentation of her looks, the emperor mistakenly considered her the most dispensable woman in the palace and married her off to the king of the northern "barbarians" as a ransom for peace.[32] This legend of a woman exiled from the palace without having her outstanding beauty recognized can be read as an allegory of talented men rebuffed from civil bureaucracy after being unjustly deemed unworthy by the examiners. That may be a reason for the enduring popularity of the Wang Zhaojun story as subject matter in traditional Chinese literature.[33]

## LITERATI AS IMPERIAL HAREM?

As Li Yu's story "Tower of the Returned Crane" suggests, the parallel between these two selections—of women and scholars—is revealing of the literati's position in the power structure of late imperial Chinese society. Of course, passing the examinations at the provincial and metropolitan levels would bring about covetable honor and prestige to a scholar and his family, and even success in a preliminary examination at the prefectural level (*yuanshi*) would be accepted as an indicator of gentry status. The examinations thus could have an empowering efficacy on the literati. However, if it had always been the dream of Chinese intellectuals to acquire knowledge and abilities in order to "sell them to the kings and princes" (*shouyu diwangjia*), employment in officialdom had become increasingly a "buyer's market" during late imperial times in the wake of more widespread education. In general terms, the balance of power within the apparatus of official selection tilted further in favor of the selector, leaving the scholars in a state of passivity and dispensability not unlike that of the candidates in the selection of women.

Additionally, the comparability of these two selections is akin to a long-standing discursive practice in traditional Chinese culture, the practice of likening the plight of intellectuals to that of women. Qu Yuan's (340?–278? BCE) celebrated trope of "fragrant flowers and beautiful women" (*xiangcao meiren*) is a well-known example.[34] Zou Yang's (2nd century BCE) comparison of the *shi* to palace women is another.[35] During late imperial times, the literati-women analogy became all the more prevalent. In the early Ming, Zhu Yuanzhang summoned the scholar-poet Yang Weizhen (1296–1370) to Nanjing with the intention of placing him in charge of preparing the rituals and music for the new dynasty. Yang, who had served under the Yuan, declined the offer by presenting a poem titled "Ballad of an Old Woman" (Lao kefu yao), in which he compared himself to a widow too old to remarry. Perhaps inspired by Yang's poem, Zhu Yuanzhang, who was unhappy about his civil officials, complained about their ineptitude by saying: "As I see it, even women of the Tang would surpass the scholars today" (*Tang furen you guo jin zhi ruzhe*).[36] Ironically, some Ming scholars themselves would not take issue with the emperor on that disparagement. Shen Defu (1578–1642), for instance, referred to some effeminate scholar-officials of his time sardonically as *ciru,* or "female scholars."³⁷

Likewise, some scholars during the period of Ming-Qing transition expressed an intense anxiety over the literati's debilitation and considered it one of the reasons for the demise of the Ming dynasty. In the meantime, they repeatedly evoked female chastity as a trope for the literati's political loyalty to the toppled Ming house.³⁸ As martyrdom of chaste widows almost became a standard metaphor for the self-sacrifice of Ming loyalists, "Men's stories and women's stories converged to become identical with each other."³⁹ That gender-based political discourse continued to flourish during the High Qing. When the licentiate Zeng Jing attempted to instigate Yue Zhongqi, governor-general of Shaanxi and Gansu, to revolt against Emperor Yongzheng, he could not think of a rhetorical device more effective than the minister-woman analogy. He tried to convince Yue—a descendant of the Southern Song general Yue Fei known for his patriotic devotion and political loyalty—that an official who served the wrong ruler would be like a married woman who lost her chastity to a second man. In his rebuttal, Emperor Yongzheng disputed that Yue Zhongqi would have indeed turned himself into an unchaste woman if he had followed Zeng Jing's seditious advice and rebelled against the Manchu court.⁴⁰ Obviously, the emperor and the licentiate were diametrically opposed to each other on almost everything, but they both agreed that a subject to his ruler was just like a woman to her husband.

Thus, the comparability of the selection of palace women and the selection of civil officials goes much deeper than their similar technical procedures. Both selections operated within similarly lopsided power structures, which warranted the imperial court the unchallengeable privilege as the foremost selector of the nation's human resources. While the emperor would "separate all daughters across the empire from their families for his own pleasure as one man," as Huang Zongxi accused him indignantly, he would also want to put all the most talented scholars across the empire within his fold, as Emperor Taizong of the Tang had once boasted.⁴¹ Indeed the comparability between selection of officials and selection of women—as exemplified particularly by the recruiting of palace women—renders the power relations involved in the civil service examinations meaningfully analogous to those in a sexual act.

## AN EXAMINATION FOR WOMEN

In fictional eroticism centered on the scholar-lover, the protagonist's escapades usually constitute the main body of the narrative, with his examination experience kept in the background. The "scholar" becomes displaced by the "lover," and the scholarly selection by the sexual selection, in an operation of metaphorical substitution. In many works, not only is the man's examination experience intertwined with his sexual experience, but the positions involved in the examinations—the ones of the examiner/selector and the examinee/selectee—also become transplanted into an erotic context. The writer deliberately conflates the process of selecting officials with that of selecting women, and by doing so renders what seems to be an erotic narrative profoundly problematic in meaning.

One case in point here is the relatively obscure twelve-chapter novel *An Examination for Women* (Nükaike zhuan).[42] Set in the Ming period, the novel features a group of courtesans who become candidates in a simulated examination arranged by their scholar-lovers seeking official appointments. It closes the gap between the two selection processes, and the fact that the women being examined and selected here are lowly courtesans only adds to its subversive force. At the outset of the narrative, the male protagonist, a young and brilliant scholar by the name of Yu Mengbai, avows his aspiration to marry a girl with "unequaled talent and matchless beauty in this world."[43] By this announcement he assumes the position of the "selector" and encloses all young women "in this world" in the pool of candidates. With two other young scholars, Yu launches a quest for ideal women, and they meet three beautiful courtesans who are well versed in poetic composition. As a gesture of love, Yu sponsors a simulated examination known as "flower adjudication" (*hua'an*), in which he and his two scholar friends serve as examiners and the three girls and their fellow courtesans are the candidates. As result of the examination, the three beauties win respectively the first, second, and third places. However, as a local ruffian accuses them of "conspiring for a rebellion by secretly setting up spurious government offices," the scholars have to flee, and the three courtesans subsequently set out in search of their scattered lovers.[44] The young men eventually reunite with the courtesans after their successes in the metropolitan examinations.

The literatus-courtesan bond in late imperial China, in addition to being a sexual liaison, could be a companionship based on mutual appreciation and even commiseration.[45] There was indeed good reason for a scholar, especially at a low ebb of his career, to identify with a woman forced into a disdained profession despite her outstanding beauty and talents. In the misfortune of the courtesan, the scholar could see that of his own, and in that sense the liaison became almost an expression of narcissistic self-pity.[46] More interesting in *An Examination for Women*, however, is the juxtaposition of the simulated examination in the brothel with the "real" examinations for the scholars. It should be pointed out that Yu Mengbai's launch of the examination for the courtesans is not an act of impulse. Even before he meets his beloved courtesan, he is already thinking of the comparability between selecting a woman and selecting a scholar in the civil service examinations: "In selecting a girl, beauty is after all of primary importance. It is like grading a piece of writing. A crisp and palatable opening will lead one to mark the lines approvingly with dots and circles, which will promote the merits of the writing."[47]

The simulated examination is, therefore, his premeditated manner of courting, which meticulously models all the formal details in the civil service examinations. The hall for the *hua'an*, just like an examination compound, is heavily guarded at all entrances. Inside the hall, there are several women "officers," each in charge of a specific duty. In addition to a general coordinator (*tidiao guan*), there is a roll caller (*changming guan*), a distributor (*sanjuan guan*) and a collector (*shoujuan guan*) of examination papers, a sealer of the candidates' names on the papers (*mifeng guan*), and two patrol officers (*xunchuo guan*) who keep all candidates under close surveillance.[48] After calling the roll, all the entrances are closed, and all the contestants are requested to write a poem in regulated verse on the topic of "Spring Boudoir" (*chungui*).

Based on the evaluation of the chief examiner Yu Mengbai and his two associates, eighteen poems are passed and ranked. The next day, as all the courtesans wait outside the entrance of the "examination hall," the names of the successful candidates are announced, and the top three winners receive the titles of *zhuangyuan*, *bangyan*, and *tanhua* respectively, exactly the same titles as for the top three graduates from the palace examination. Adorned with golden flowers in their hair and red satin cloaks over their shoulders, they lead the file of new "*jinshi*" in a flashy parade on the street, each riding a white horse with a golden saddle and covered by an ornate parasol. The women finally arrive at the celebratory banquet, where they cluster around their examiners amid all the pompous singing and fanfare.[49] In the meantime, however, the narrator does not forget to remind the reader that all this solemnity is for nothing but a travesty of the real examinations. At the beginning of the examination, all the women candidates have to undergo a thorough body search at the entrance, presumably to prevent them from bringing in any notes. A woman guard reports that one of the courtesans is carrying notes on her. When the guard uncovers the "notes" from their most surreptitious hiding place in the candidate's body and presents them to the superintendent, everyone bursts into embarrassed laughter, as they turn out to be a bloodstained wad of tissues.

Such meticulous, although playful, simulations of the state examinations drive home the analogy between the selection of scholars and the selection of women. The ranking order of the three courtesan winners of the *hua'an*, as it turns out later in the novel, corresponds to that of their scholar lovers in the "real" examinations. Clearly, these two ranking systems take place in the two worlds that do not only parallel each other but also, as a modern scholar has pointed out insightfully, are "ruled by the same logic and arbitrated by the same successful men."[50] Yet scholars take completely different positions in these two worlds. In the real examinations, even the "successful men" were no more than passive examinees and selectees, and had no control over their own fates. Not surprisingly, Yu Mengbai has failed repeatedly in the examinations before he sets up the mock examination for the women. By suspending his experience as an examination candidate and assuming instead the role of an examiner and selector of women, he turns the tables and thoroughly changes his position in the power game. When he confers the title of *zhuangyuan* on the first place winner of the *hua'an*, he not only wins his beloved woman but also gains the empowered status as the selector.

### THE POTENT AND POLYGAMOUS SCHOLAR: *ROMANCE OF THE EMBROIDERED SCREEN* AND *SHADOWS OF THE PEACH BLOSSOMS*

This sexual selector's fantasy is even more piquant in the works that feature a scholar as an oversexed polygamist. One example is the twenty-chapter novel *Romance of the Embroidered Screen* (Xiu ping yuan).[51] The protagonist Zhao Yunke is a young and handsome scholar from Hangzhou. In the opening chapter, Zhao, like the erotic scholar-lover in many other works, is determined to "win the first place in the examinations" and "marry the first-rate beauties under heaven."[52] That declaration establishes the analogous relationship between scholarly pursuit and sexual pursuit. In a series of adventures, he meets four beautiful women one after another, all of whom become his sexual partners. Unlike the unseducible Cao Nai, Zhao is in each case easily captivated. His route of romantic conquests eventually takes him to the capital of the empire, where he wins the status of *zhuangyuan* in the examinations. Obviously, Zhao's sexual escapades incur no penalty for him in the examinations, contrary to the scenarios in those moralizing anecdotes discussed earlier in this chapter. Instead, Zhao's academic success immediately translates into his augmented desirability on the marriage market: a high-ranking official insists on marrying his beautiful daughter to him, an offer he once again finds himself unable to decline. So the scholar who has just been ranked number one among the successful examination candidates now performs another kind of ranking by himself, the ranking of his five wives.

A similar subversive thrust is even more evident in *Shadows of the Peach Blossoms* (Taohua ying), another twenty-chapter novel.[53] Set in the middle of the Ming, the novel is about the young scholar Wei Yuqing who has a series of sexual encounters while pursuing a bureaucratic career through the examinations. After winning his *jinshi* status, Wei is first appointed a county magistrate, then promoted to be a prefect, and finally a governor. While traveling from one office to another, he picks up his women who have been scattered in different places, all of whom become his concubines. The last woman he marries is his principal wife, obviously the biggest prize of his quest and the top-ranked candidate in his sexual selection, and the wedding quite befittingly coincides with the pinnacle of his bureaucratic career. Accounting for his dramatically increased sexual appeal is an itinerant monk's aphrodisiac that enlarges his penis and promotes his virility. Apparently, sexual prowess, replacing scholarly talent, becomes the male protagonist's foremost quality.

As a potent polygamist, Wei Yuqing enjoys a sexual privilege that very few men in late imperial China could possibly have had.[54] Yet the man who had the ultimate sexual privilege was the emperor, as he could select women before any other men. Indeed Wei Yuqing's womenfolk bear a strong resemblance to an imperial harem. The principal wife, who governs the home, looks serious and is ostensibly more interested in homemaking than lovemaking. The concubines, whose ranking is determined by arbitrary rules, are more animated and playful. These depictions tally with what people generally perceive to be the difference between an empress and other imperial consorts.[55] In a metamorphosis of fiction, the scholar Wei Yuqing, who is repeatedly tested in the civil service examinations before he can be selected by the imperial state, becomes a miniaturized version of emperor, the ultimate selector of women.

## LI YU'S STORIES: THE EXAMINATION EROTICIZED

In Li Yu's "Tower of the Returned Crane," as we recall, the two most beautiful girls are finally married to the top two examination candidates. Female beauty becomes a trophy for male talent, and the process of official selection thus changes into one of marital selection. As success in the examinations is reduced to a prelude to the consummation of a sexual union, civil service, which is presumably the purpose of passing the examinations, is simply replaced by a wedding service. A similar maneuver is seen in Li Yu's "Tower of Winning the Contest" (Duo jin lou). A pair of discordant parents promises each of their two daughters to two different men. As the beautiful sisters and four ugly men all appear in court for adjudication, the prefect annuls the mismatches. He then sets an examination for the licentiates in his prefecture and promises to marry the girls to the two highest-ranking candidates who are not married or betrothed. The top two examination essays, as it turns out, are actually written by the same young man. Against the student's initial reluctance, the prefect makes him husband to both sisters. That arrangement of polygamy, which is common in Li Yu's fiction, is justified by the narrator's comment that he is the only candidate with "true talent" (*zhen cai*).[56] Again, female beauty, substituting an official appointment, becomes the true award for male talent. Little wonder that the young scholars in the story "all wished to have Chang'e, the moon goddess, before they even have a chance to snap off a cassia twig."[57]

Li Yu's many other love stories are also replete with references to the examinations. In "Tower for Summer Pleasure" (Xia yi lou), a young scholar, equipped with a telescope, "examines" the girls in the neighborhood from his vantage point on a tower before he "selects" his prospective bride. In "Tower for Stroking Clouds" (Fu yun lou), a group of frivolous youth, during the celebration of the Dragon Boat Festival in Hangzhou, stand at an intersection in the midst of a heavy storm appraising the looks of each passing young women. Hoping the downpour will wash off the women's makeup and reveal their true facial features, these young men call the rain "a godsend opportunity for us to give the examination and select genuine talents."[58] As two beautiful girls pass by, these "examiners" are unanimous in their selection: "Now we have our *zhuangyuan* and *bangyan*, what a pity that we can't find a *tanhua* to round out the top trio! We can only leave the third place unfilled until next year's festival and then hopefully pick up some new talent that we have overlooked."[59]

A similar scene is in "A Male Mother Meng Thrice Changes His Residence" (Nan Mengmu jiaohe sanqian), a story about a young man who castrates himself to repay his same-sex lover and, after the latter's death, brings up his lover's son.[60] In the story, a group of scholars evaluate the looks of teenage boys and rank them in a roster, which they call "register of the examination for beautiful boys" (*meitong kao'an*). "Exactly as in the yellow roster for the palace examinations," the top boys are ranked in three classes (*san jia*), and You Ruilang, the protagonist of the story, is given the title *zhuangyuan* by all the "examiners" unanimously.[61] Evidently, the boys, as substitutes for women, become the sexual examinees and selectees.

Li Yu's "A Widow Sets a Ruse to Get a Bridegroom, and Several Beauties Join Their Efforts to Seize a Talented Scholar" (Guafu sheji zhui xinlang, zhongmei qixin duo caizi), a story collected in *Jade That Is Worth Cities* (Liancheng bi), can be read as a satire of the moralization on sexual asceticism. The protagonist Lü Zaisheng, a handsome young scholar, has been taught since his boyhood that "one's moral performance during his lifetime will be responsible not only for his own well-being but also his offspring's."[62] It is exactly the same moral message as in many of the ledgers of merits and demerits and the short tales about examination scholars' sexual ethics discussed earlier in this chapter. The assiduous preaching and close surveillance by his father and tutor result in Lü's behavioral pattern of misogyny, as he is afraid that any personal contact with a young woman can make him succumb to the temptation, which will in turn ruin his chance in the examinations. After his parents' deaths, however, Lü Zaisheng, now a licentiate at the Imperial Academy in Nanjing, becomes the local courtesans' favorite. As the most handsome scholar in town, he virtually becomes a "prostitute" for the prostitutes, as the women scramble to pay in order to sleep with him. As his service is in such great demand, a courtesan's access to him becomes a barometer of her status: those who are fortunate enough to have been "appraised and appreciated" (*jianshang*) by Lü become known as top courtesans and have their market value enhanced, and those who have not become regarded as low-class hookers and see their business diminish. As "his personal choice becomes the criterion in classifying good courtesans from bad ones," the young scholar who once tended to shun all women in order to protect his chance in the examinations now plays the role of "examiner" of women.[63] When a beautiful but jealous widow, Cao Wanshu, wishes to marry Lü, she sends a matchmaker for the scholar; upon his arrival, the "examiner" once again conducts a meticulous "examination":

> He saw Cao Wanshu dressed plainly and wearing light makeup, with thousands of charms but not the slightest affectation. The matchmaker had encouraged her to exhibit all her feminine tenderness. The woman accordingly let him scrutinize every part of her body. She even allowed him to lift her three-inch golden lotuses in his hands and hold her waist in his arm to check on its exquisite slenderness. After that, she took out a writing brush, an ink stone, and paper, and asked him to set a topic and give her a test in poetic composition. Lü Zaisheng therefore chanted a poem and then told her to compose another one on the same rhyming scheme.[64]

The result of this "examination" is quite satisfactory to both the "examiner" and the "examinee," leading to a blissful wedding soon afterward.

## THE CARNAL PRAYER MAT:
## AN EROTIC GAME OF EXAMINATION AND SELECTION

In Li Yu's twenty-chapter novel *The Carnal Prayer Mat* (Rou putuan), one finds the most fully developed figure of erotic scholar-lover and most sophisticated narrative operation based on the metaphoric bond between official selection and sexual selection.[65] Much of the narrated eroticism in *The Carnal Prayer Mat* is driven by an intriguing dynamic between the opposite positions in visual experience, the positions of the examiner and the examinee. The sexual escapades of the libertine scholar Weiyang Sheng, whose name Patrick Hanan has felicitously rendered Vesperus, usually starts with his sneaky peeping at a woman in order to appraise her beauty. If she is truly beautiful in his judgment, he appears before her in person, trying to attract her attention to his handsome features. Other characters in the narrative participate in similar visual games. The one who initially sets his or her eyes on the sexual prey thus shifts into a position of being preyed upon by the eyes of the person of the opposite sex. The economy of the narrative hinges on this constant alternation between looking and being seen, between the active and the passive, and between the masterful and the mastered. Since the polarity of looking and being seen between the lovers suggests a relationship of assessment and appraisal, it becomes associated with the dichotomy of the examiner and the examinee. While *The Carnal Prayer Mat* is remarkably exuberant in figurative imagery and the use of multiple metaphors, the examination metaphor is the only one that is consistently evoked throughout the entire work.

As do many other works of fictional eroticism, the novel establishes the symmetry between success in academic pursuit and success in sexual conquest early in the narrative. In chapter 2, when Vesperus visits the reclusive monk Lone Peak (Gufeng Zhanglao), it becomes clear from their conversation that the scholar's top two wishes are "to be the most brilliant poet in the world" and "to marry the most beautiful girl in the world."[66] To justify that symmetry, Vesperus cites what he considers the perfect compatibility between a beautiful girl (*jiaren*) and a brilliant poet (*caizi*): "The two terms *beautiful girl* and *brilliant poet* have always been inseparable. For every brilliant poet there has to be a beautiful girl somewhere to form a pair, and vice versa."[67]

However, Li Yu is obviously much more interested in the same set of positions that is involved in both the examination experience and the erotic experience—the positions of examiner and examinee—and the power relations suggested therein. The heightened narrative interest in those positions renders the narrated erotic experience remarkably comparable to the experience in the examinations. Much of the narrative therefore revolves around the metaphoric bond between selection of scholars and selection of women. One example is Vesperus's use of the Daoist temple as his vantage point for assessing female beauty. Here the narrator states that "it was Vesperus's idea to treat the temple as an examination hall," and then he goes on to liken the young man's peeping at the worshipping women to the state examiner's evaluation of the candidates. One realizes that the analogy is indeed driven home in light of Miyazaki Ichisada's description of the Baohe Palace, the site of the palace examinations during the Qing period, and the ceremony of the examination therein:

> Early in the morning of the twenty-first day of the fourth month the candidates passed through the main palace gate, the Wumen, or Meridian Gate, and assembled in front of the Taihe Gate, which rose straight ahead.... At the top of the ramp, under the curving eaves of the palace, an incense table had been set up. When the candidates had finished lining up on the terrace below, the senior academician of the grand secretariat appeared beneath the eaves at the east, bearing a packet containing the printed examination papers.... The master of ceremonies led the examination officials, from readers on down, to the table, where he lined them up to perform the full kowtow in unison at his command. Next it was the candidates' turn to do the same, again at the command of the master of ceremonies.... Deep in the interior of the Baohe Palace was the emperor's throne. During the examination he was supposed to show himself and review the candidates.[68]

The resemblance between the temple in *The Carnal Prayer Mat* and the Baohe Palace is quite clear. Just like the ceremony in the palace examination, the religious worship in the Daoist temple involves kowtowing and incense burning. Even the purposes of praying are not very different: while the women in the temple pray for a divine bestowal of fertility, the scholars in the palace sought the imperial grant of a *jinshi* degree so that their many years spent studying the classics would not end up being fruitless.

However, the analogy is not so much between the two venues per se as between Vesperus's visual testing of the women and the examiner's screening of the candidates. Indeed, as a record of his visual examination of each woman, Vesperus enters a note for her in his notebook, with her personal information as well as his comment on and grade for her beauty.

In doing so, according to the narrator, he works in the same manner as an examiner "lenient about admitting people to the examination, but... extremely strict in his grading."[69] Even the symbols that he uses in ranking a woman, a certain number of circles in red ink by her name, are precisely those that a state examiner would use in grading an examination candidate: "Beside her name, Vesperus drew in red ink to indicate her ranking: three circles for *summa cum laude* [*tedeng*]; two for *magna cum laude* [*shangdeng*], and one for *cum laude* [*zhongdeng*]. After each name he added comments in parallel-prose style like those written on local examination papers, to describe the woman's good points."[70]

Having observed and examined many women, Vesperus comes to realize that his wife, beautiful as she is, is by no means "the most beautiful girl in the world" as he used to think. Like a state examiner, Vesperus refuses to settle for a *bangyan* or a *tanhua,* and is determined to find a *zhuangyuan,* the most beautiful.[71] He is equally enthusiastic about two young women whom he calls Pale Rose Maid and Lotus Pink Beauty in his notes and draws three circles beside each of their names. Indeed, as the two women look equally beautiful to him, he has to admit that mere visual testing is not sufficient for ranking and that "only the Oral Examination will determine the top candidate."[72] Later in the novel, when Vesperus meets the two beauties again through the good offices of Cloud, he has to add one more circle to the original two for Cloud, "raising her from a *magna* to a *summa,*" in order to avoid a possible storm of jealousy among the three women. He does not completely succeed, however. When these young women find in Vesperus's notebook that Flora (Huachen), an older woman, has received the same ranking as they have, they quickly become resentful of his grading methods and criteria. The narrative here carefully maintains the examination metaphor, referring to the women as "pupils" (*mensheng*) and Vesperus as "the chief examiner" (*zhusi*): "Vesperus wanted to make a clean breast of everything and persuaded them that one person's luck rubs off on everyone present, but his three pupils were raising such a commotion that the examiner could not get a word in edgewise."[73]

What is closely "examined" in *The Carnal Prayer Mat* is very often not only a woman's physical looks but also her sexual skills, and the intensity of the testing in this regard is also likened to that in the civil service examinations. Speaking of his preference of experienced women to virgins, Vesperus compares the skills of lovemaking to those of writing the eight-legged essay. Again, he puts himself in the position of the examiner, evaluating and judging the performance of his sexual partner: "For real enjoyment you need a woman in her twenties who will know something about opening, development, reversal, and closure. Because sex is really like an essay, in which each section has its mode of organization and each stage its type of parallelism. This is well beyond the capacity of a child just learning how to write."[74]

In this vein, the women who have convincingly proved themselves to Vesperus as good sexual partners are likened to candidates who have successfully passed the examinations. As Cloud's affair with Vesperus becomes known to her two cousins who had once attracted Vesperus's eyes but have not yet begun their liaisons with him, they "resembled nothing so much as two failed candidates for the provincial examinations meeting a newly successful one—a mixture of humiliation and envy."[75] They ask Cloud all kinds of questions about Vesperus, obviously hoping to get ready for their own turns. The analogy to the examinations continues, for the two girls are said to be "like candidates for an examination buttonholding a friend outside the hall and asking them about the paper."[76]

Such erotic examination and selection has a most hilarious moment in chapter 17, where Flora and her three younger rivals have a contest to settle the order for wine and sex. The four women play "prima guess-fingers" (*zhuangyuan quan*), a drinking game similar to the one called Name the Candidate played by many late Ming courtesans as described by some modern scholars.[77] Again, the titles decided by the game are exactly the same as those by a palace examination. All three winners of the finger-guessing game—*zhuangyuan, bangyan,* and *tanhua* as they are called respectively—are all privileged to have sex with Vesperus, the examiner and selector, while the loser, who is called disparagingly Old Scholar (*laoru*) or a "perennial failure in the examinations," is only allowed to stand by watching the orgy.

The testing and examining of a sexual partner can go both ways between the male and female lovers. Sometimes it is the woman who is compared to the examiner, judging not only the looks but also the virility and stamina of the man, who is likened to a scholar under the examiner's stringent scrutiny. When Vesperus, on realizing the limits of his sexual prowess, plans to resort to aphrodisiacs, his friend the Knave ridicules him by comparing him to a desperate and untalented examination candidate who counts vainly on the help of ginseng. He says sardonically that there is no way for an "empty-headed" candidate to impress the examiner "even if he swallowed pounds of the tonic."[78] Before Vesperus embarks on his adventure with Fragrance, the Knave again admonishes the young scholar to try his very best to pass the woman's test: "You'll have to do your damnedest not to let her flunk you. Otherwise you'll be admitted to a first examination but not to a second or a third." The narrator does not lose the opportunity to create suspense at the end of the chapter: "The time would come for Vesperus's examination. But we do not yet know what method the examiner will adopt and will have to wait until the questions are handed out."[79] When the time arrives for the questions to be delivered, they are indeed tough ones. Fragrance makes an unusual arrangement, letting her ugly neighbor serve as her substitute to test the young man's capacity, while she herself monitors the examination in the darkness. Vesperus's performance during the examination turns out to be very impressive. At the end, when the ugly woman, with her true identity revealed, declares to the man that he has "passed the test," Fragrance comes to the foreground and takes the man into the second round of the "examination."[80] In such situations, the woman briefly plays the role of the examiner only before she allows herself to be further examined by the man. As Vesperus is always the epicenter of the sexual game, ultimately it is up to the scholar to test and select his sexual partners.

The inextricable intertwinement of the examination experience and the erotic experience punctuates Vesperus's transformation from a scholar into a lover. As Vesperus relinquishes his aspirations in the examinations and sets out to "look for the most beautiful girl in the world," he refuses to be examined and assumes instead the role of an examiner: to look, to appraise, and to select. Instead of striving to become a top candidate in the examinations, Vesperus makes himself the judge to determine the selection of the top women candidates. Unlike the thousands of scholars who competed with each other through the examinations hoping to be "netted" into civil bureaucracy, Vesperus now becomes the one who casts the net, catching the most beautiful girls in the empire. In this light, *The Carnal Prayer Mat* is a story about an examinee's desire to become an examiner in a changed power game.

## THE OPERATION OF THE EXAMINATION METAPHOR

The motif of examination is omnipresent in many works of the seventeenth-century fictional eroticism centered on the scholar-lover. While the examination experience is incorporated in the narrative in different ways, most often it serves as the central metaphor for the erotic experience. Its relationship to the scholar's sexual quest is both disjunctive and conjunctive, both digressive and congruous. As a rhetorical device, a metaphor is the locale for the meeting of two concepts that are assigned the roles of "tenor" and "vehicle" respectively. While they are comparable because of certain shared attributes, the tenor is the subject to which the attributes are ascribed and the vehicle is the object whose attributes are borrowed in order to heighten those of the subject. Obviously, the tenor is the real topic of the discussion or thinking, while the vehicle, just as the term itself suggests, facilitates the discussion or thinking. Thus the tenor is primary and essential whereas the vehicle secondary and subsidiary. However, this hierarchical order can become destabilized or even reversed when the vehicle becomes more active than usual in correlation with the tenor.[81]

If the erotic scholar-lover's sexual adventures function as "a mere excuse" for the introduction of the metaphor of the examinations, the work would cease to be an erotic narrative but become an allegory instead. That, however, is obviously not the case in the works discussed here, where the scholar-lover's escapades are narrated in such exuberant details that they defy any consistently allegorical reading. Nevertheless, the motif of examination is so extensive throughout these narratives that it is clearly not merely subservient to local rhetorical or stylistic purposes. In fact, since the examination appears to be such a master trope, it becomes a hallmark of the fictional eroticism surrounding the scholar-lover.

Based on the erotic scholar-lover's personal experience in the two worlds, the one of an aspiring office-seeker and the one of a cynical womanizer, the narrative generates two different sets of signifiers, substituting each other by turns. One can see how this has changed the relationship between the tenor and the vehicle: each set of signifiers becomes both the tenor and the vehicle because the movement of signification leads both to it and away from it. Indeed, if the juxtaposition of academic experience and sexual experience results in the eroticization of the examinations, arguably the most venerated social institution in premodern China, one can perhaps say equally well that it somehow academicizes the erotic experience. The examination metaphor, in this light, becomes a "metaphor for metaphor," creating a mirror effect of metaphorizing. Such a reading turns the meaning of the erotic scholar-lover problematic, transforming him from a Don Juan-like rake into a more complex figure loaded with intriguing ambiguities.

Metaphor, in Paul Ricoeur's words, "is the trope of resemblance *par excellence*," resemblance between two things that are otherwise apparently incongruous.[82] It hinges on the affinity in one signifier as seen from the vantage point of another. When what happens in official selection is presented as analogous to what happens in sexual selection, the former is clearly seen from the viewpoint of the lover. Similarly, when sexual adventures are portrayed as comparable to the pursuit of a civil service degree, sexual love is seen from the perspective of the examination scholar. Between the scholar part and the lover part of the protagonist is a mutual gaze, so to speak, with each seeing in the other some resemblance to the self and then letting its own resemblance to the other be seen. There is a similar dynamic between the two different sets of signifiers, the signifiers for official selection and for sexual selection. When one set of the signifiers is activated in the narrative, the other set is temporarily repressed, but never completely out of the scene. The activated or exhibited signifiers of the erotic scholar-lover's sexual selection are constantly gauged, in terms of the metaphoric connection, by the latent voyeuristic eye of the signifiers for scholarly selection, which in turn become activated into the foreground, but only to be surveyed by the temporarily repressed signifiers for sexual selection again.

The operation of the scholar-lover's desire is thus like a game of juggling: at each moment there is only one ball—sexual selection or scholarly selection—in the juggler's hand, but at each moment the ball in the hand tends to be displaced by the one in the air. The game is therefore driven by the desire to catch the "other" ball, the one that is not in the hand. As in Cai Qizun's poetic line quoted earlier in this chapter, a scholar was, at least theoretically, unable to "have it at both ends." A failed examination candidate like Li Yu could have made the same lamentation as the *zhuangyuan* Cai Qizun, although from the opposite end. Just as in Cai's poem, the scholar-lover's desire always directs toward something that is lacking at the moment. The open chain of signifiers in the metaphoric operation incessantly creates new gaps for desire to traverse and thus cuts desire from ultimate fulfillment. The result is an almost interminable production of substitutes, which constitute the narrative text. Very often, to end this chain of substitutions the narrative has to resort to a deus ex machina. Thus at the end of *Romance of the Embroidered Screen* the scholar-lover Zhao Yunke, following the advice of an itinerant Daoist master, retreats with his five wives to an islet in the middle of a lake. In a similar vein, Wei Yuqing and his six wives all become immortals at the end of *Shadows of the Peach Blossoms*. The erotic narrative is able to end only when the scholar-lover is no more interested in further sexual adventures or new bureaucratic positions. In *The Carnal Prayer Mat* the narrative ends in a more drastic manner—namely, castration. After the repentant Vesperus joins the Buddhist order, he continues to find himself pestered by "the root of evil" and has to cut off the organ that was once augmented with dog's flesh. Yet the penis does not merely represent the scholar-lover's sexual desire in a biological sense, for it is a symbol of all desires, both *in* the narrative and *of* the narrative. With the castration, Vesperus's desire ceases, and so does the desire of the narrative. The metaphoric interplay between the sexual experience and the examination experience now comes to an end, and for that reason the alternation and mutual substitution between these two sets of signifiers are terminated as well.

## THE SUBVERSIVE POWER OF THE EXAMINATION METAPHOR

As demonstrated in the affinity between the selection of scholars for civil bureaucracy and the selection of women for the imperial harem, the metaphorical bond between the examination experience and the sexual experience in the works of fictional eroticism is rooted in a familiar analogy. This metaphor is remarkably productive, opening up new territories not only for fiction making but also for fiction interpretation. As the sexual act is consistently presented in the language of the examinations, fictional eroticism centered on a scholar's selection of women becomes a powerful parody of the institution of official selection.

It may be no exaggeration to say that the examination system, as the primary channel for selection of officials, had been the lifeline of the imperial state ever since its inception. Precisely because of its crucial importance, it was always under the direct control and surveillance of the imperial court. During the late dynasties, the court not only determined the quota for all provincial examinations across the empire but also appointed their chief and associate examiners, many of whom were courtiers. The selection of *jinshi*, holders of the highest degree from the examination system, had regularly involved the emperor in person since the Tang period. Emperor Taizong, for instance, was the mastermind for the formal development of the *jinshi* examination in the early Tang from its fledgling precursor in the preceding Sui dynasty.[83] The tradition of "testing the candidates in the palace" (*dianqian shiren*) started in 689, when Empress Wu Zetian tested metropolitan examination graduates on policy questions (*cewen*) for consecutive days.[84] Yet the palace examination did not become fully institutionalized until the Song. In 973, a scholar named Xu Shilian, who had been eliminated from the metropolitan examination that year, accused the chief examiner Li Fang of being unfair in the selection. Emperor Taizu intervened by holding a reexamination in the palace, which he himself presided over as the chief examiner.[85] Since then, palace examination had always functioned as the final and ultimate stage in the process of official selection. In 1397, Zhu Yuanzhang, suspecting a political conspiracy, annulled the results of the metropolitan examination. Afterwards he graded the papers from a reexamination himself and then selected the new *jinshi* from the ensuing palace examination. What he did set the tone for his successors, as the subsequent Ming rulers dutifully followed the practice of "the Son of Heaven in person testing on policy questions at court" (*tianzi qin ce yu ting*).[86] The questions for the palace examination were usually drafted by Hanlin academicians but always finalized by the emperor himself. Qing rulers largely followed the Ming regulations on the palace examination. For some years in the early Qing, Emperor Kangxi even conducted a reexamination to verify the result of the regular metropolitan examination as a prelude to the palace examination.[87]

Apparently, much of the prestige of the examination system, especially on its highest levels, was derived from its close association with the imperial court. In particular, the emperor's personal involvement in the palace examination bestowed a luster of imperial majesty and augustness on the institution of official selection. With the emperor serving as the examiner, all graduates from the metropolitan and palace examinations became automatically "disciples of the Son of Heaven" (*tianzi mensheng*). Thus, Senior Licentiate Yan in *The Scholars* (Rulin waishi), who is otherwise a brazen and incorrigible liar, is actually telling a stark truth when he brags: "Our examinations are a great affair of the imperial court" (*chaoting dadian*).[88] Compounded with the pronounced Confucian commitment to government service, the proximity to the center of state power created a sense of grandeur and magnitude about the examinations in public perception.

In contrast, traditional Chinese culture consistently consigned sexual love to a low level in the hierarchy of values. One important reason was the androcentric prejudice against women, as suggested in this Confucian line: "Of all people, women and servants are the most difficult to behave to. If you are familiar with them, they lose their humility. If you maintain a reserve toward them, they are discontented."[89] While the Confucian sages never attempted to deny sexual desire as part of human nature, they considered sexual passion a potential menace to one's moral and political obligations. Thus, feeling the malaise of his contemporary society, Confucius found good reason to complain: "I have not seen one who loves virtues as he loves beauty" (*Wu weijian haode ru haose zhe ye*).[90] As the master saw it, love of virtue (*haode*) and love of female beauty (*haose*) were mutually exclusive and repulsive. Based on this conviction, a scholar's erotic experience would compromise the moral worth and political correctness of his participation in the examinations, the "great affair of the imperial court." That is precisely the message in many ledgers of merits and demerits and anecdotal narratives about sexual ethics discussed earlier in this chapter.

Thus, while selection of officials and selection of women were comparable in some ways that enable them to function respectively as the tenor and vehicle in the examination metaphor, they actually belonged to two vastly different levels in the moral and political scales of social life. The obscene and bawdy sexual selection as the subject matter in fictional eroticism is apparently incongruous with the elevated and stately "examination language" used to present it, and this incongruity is a major source of the comic effect of the erotic scholar-lover. As the selection of women parodies the selection of officials, the discourse of eroticism intertwines with the discourse of the examinations. As a result of the inter-illumination and inter-contamination between these two discourses, the examination system is relegated from a lofty height where it is constantly valorized by state power to a low level where it becomes comparable to and compatible with the indecency and debauchery in sexual escapades.

Obviously, the fictional eroticism discussed here does not parody the different levels of examinations equally. Instead, it targets the palace examination in particular, where the imperial ruler determined the selection of top scholars in person. Given the parallel between the imperial selection of palace women and the civil service examinations, this focus on the examiner and selector on the highest level makes the subversive power of the examination metaphor in fictional eroticism all the more formidable. By using this metaphor, of course, the author could have been simply "playing with his ink and writing brush" (*youxi bimo*) in order to win a laugh from his reader. Yet, as M. M. Bakhtin puts it, it is precisely laughter that "in general destroys any hierarchical (distancing and valorized) distance."[91] Amused by the comic juxtaposition of official selection with sexual selection, the reader's laughter mitigates the fear and awe for the imperial authority and diminishes the piety and reverence toward the examinations.

The metaphorical bond between selection of scholars and selection of women originated in late imperial Chinese society itself. In a sense, the multiple power relations in the sociopolitical structure were like a mutable host of metaphors and metonymies. The fictional erotic scholar-lover emerged precisely from that understanding. By metaphorizing the examinations, fictional eroticism places its scholar protagonist in the tension and interaction between competing perspectives. Yet the examination metaphor is more than a mere literary game. "Metaphorical meaning," as Paul Ricoeur proposes, "is not the enigma itself, the semantic clash pure and simple, but the solution of the enigma, the inauguration of the new semantic pertinence."[92] Using the Confucian canon and commentaries as the yardstick for official selection, the examination system became in the late dynastic periods the most important mechanism for the state to appropriate the *daotong* and manipulate the value system of society. By eroticizing and vulgarizing the institution of official selection, the examination metaphor amounts to an almost prankish reaction to the scrutinizing gaze from the imperial state, the ultimate examiner and selector.

CHAPTER 4

# *The Scholars*

## *Trudging Out of a Textual Swamp*

The eighteenth-century novel *The Scholars* (Rulin waishi) has posed a hermeneutic challenge to generations of scholars and critics. Despite their admiration for its stylistic and narrative innovations, the readers often feel perplexed by its seeming lack of thematic consistency. Traditionally the work was considered a satirical attack on social institutions, particularly the civil service examinations.[1] Yet, while the examination system is a main topic in the first half of the work, it seems to fade into the background in the later chapters. Even in that early part, the narrative involves many other things apart from the examinations.[2] Furthermore, the attitude toward the examinations reflected in the novel is nuanced, as some of the high-minded characters suffer no qualms about participating in the examinations.[3] While it is fair to say that the novel presents a voice of dissent with regard to the examination system, the examinations are not the overarching issue throughout the entirety of the novel.[4]

As some Qing commentators suggested, the assemblage of the scholars in a ceremony in honor of the ancient sage Tai Bo, the main episode in chapter 37, represents the climax of the novel.[5] Taking that view as the point of departure, Shuen-fu Lin argues in a seminal article that the novelist Wu Jingzi (1701–54) "has effectively used the element of *li* (ritual) as the central integrative principle in his novel," central "not only to the structure of the novel but also to the moral vision of the author as well."[6]

More recently, Stephen J. Roddy and Shang Wei have treated Confucian ritualism as the focal point in their respective studies of *The Scholars*.[7] Given the eighteenth-century intellectual setting that led to a surge of Confucian ritualism and Wu Jingzi's ties to the Yan Yuan–Li Gong school, the thematic and structural significance of ritualism in *The Scholars* is indisputable, yet the treatment of ritual performance in the novel is by no means consistent. If the Tai Bo ceremony represents the culmination of the effort to revive the ritualized Confucian way of living, that effort, as made clear in the later chapters, ends only in futility. "Why," as Stephen Roddy wrestles with the question, "does the novel articulate a vision of literati self-renewal through ritual, only to document its failure in subsequent events?"[8] Roddy's own answer to that question is a broadened notion of *li* that encompasses both ritual and ritual propriety: while the idealist scholars claim to be heirs to the tradition of ritualism, they themselves fail the test of ritual propriety, which contributes to the general decline of literati mores.[9] To Shang Wei, that contradiction in the novel reflects one in the novelist himself: while he recommends ritualized life as a remedy for the social ills that he diagnoses, he is fully aware of the limitations and inadequacies of that remedy. The novel, as a result, "demonstrates a dynamic process of critical inquiry and self-questioning that resists any definite conclusion."[10] These are powerful arguments; yet, if ritual is the central issue in *The Scholars*, it is not immediately clear how it coexists with some of the other major issues in the novel, including examination essay writing and literary inquisition, in a coherent narrative structure.

This chapter considers the examinations and poetic writing, although two seemingly separate topics in *The Scholars,* as related components of a continuous textual culture, which the imperial state manipulates with the lure of fame and rank on one hand and the terror of literary inquisition on the other. In this light, the performance of the Tai Bo ceremony and the reorientation in the later chapters to the practice of *li yue bing nong* (ritual, music, military training, and farming) represent the literati's endeavors to break out of the capsule of a textual culture into the world of praxis and to switch from serving *tianzi* (the ruler) to serving *tianxia* (society and civilization). While the novel envisions a rugged and tortuous path for that quest, it concludes on an optimistic note with the four "extraordinary figures" (*qiren*), harbingers of a new generation of intellectuals who are able to make vocational decisions independently, out of the textual culture. With a tapestry of stories about different types of scholars, *The Scholars* presents a reflection on the identity and social roles of the literati that is more meaningful than one can find in any earlier works of vernacular fiction.

## THE LITERATI AND THE YONGZHENG REIGN

As Wu Jingzi started writing the novel soon after his relocation from Quanjiao to Nanjing in 1733, a couple of years before the end of the Yongzheng reign, what happened during the Yongzheng years is most relevant to our discussion. During Emperor Kangxi's long and successful reign (1662–1722), the Qing government solidified state power by putting down all the political and military resistances and rebellions. In the meantime, the Manchu conquerors anointed themselves the new standard-bearers of the Cheng-Zhu school of learning. In Kangxi's lifetime, as mentioned earlier, some of the top Confucian scholars already venerated him as Zhu Xi's spiritual heir. With its firm commitment to the neo-Confucian doctrines, the Qing government successfully diluted much of the anti-Manchu nationalist sentiments among the Han literati. However, the state's usurpation of the leadership role in the *daotong* tradition caused considerable dismay and anxiety among the intellectual elite.

In 1722, Yongzheng inherited from his father his dual status, serving as both the head of the secular state and the spiritual leader of the Cheng-Zhu school of learning. The new emperor wasted no time in exercising his authority. In 1725, a scholar-official named Qian Mingshi (1660–1730) was accused of fawning on the disgraced general Nian Gengyao (d. 1726) with panegyric poems.[11] The punishment that Yongzheng meted out for Qian, bizarre as it might appear, was profoundly meaningful. Having removed Qian from office, Yongzheng humiliated him with a tablet that carried the imperial inscription "Criminal against Confucianism" (*mingjiao zuiren*), which the emperor made Qian hang at the main entrance of his residence. Furthermore, Yongzheng ordered each of the officials in the capital with an examination degree to compose a poem to castigate Qian. He decreed that everybody submit the poems to him for censorship before he had the selected poems delivered to Qian, who in turn was to sponsor the publication of the collection financially.[12] Most interesting was Yongzheng's explanation of this penalty: "Since Qian Mingshi offended Confucianism by fawning on a villain with his writing, we on our part will also use writing in lieu of the law of the state" (*yi wenci wei guofa*).¹³ In another edict, the emperor proclaimed that "we wanted all officials to know that, for a sinner against Confucianism, it would be more painful to live in shame than to die by execution."¹⁴ Apparently, by calling Qian a "criminal against Confucianism," Yongzheng meted out the punishment not in the name of the imperial court but in his self-assumed capacity as the supreme arbiter within Confucianism itself.

Even more demonstrative of the political situation in the early eighteenth century was Yongzheng's handling of the Zeng Jing case. Inspired by the ideas of the Ming loyalist Lü Liuliang (1629–83), Zeng Jing, a licentiate from Hunan, denounced what he called Yongzheng's several crimes, including usurpation of the throne, and attempted to instigate Yue Zhongqi, governor-general of Sichuan and Shaanxi, to rebel against the Manchu court. After Zeng was arrested and forced to write his statement of repentance, Yongzheng had the statement, along with his edicts on the case and the record of the interrogations, published in a volume titled *Record of Being Awakened from Befuddlement by the Cardinal Principles* (Dayi juemi lu). The emperor then distributed copies of the book to all scholars empire-wide for mandatory reading, and used Zeng, whose life he decided to spare (until Zeng was executed by Yongzheng's son and successor, Emperor Qianlong), as a living example of scholarly revolt subjugated. Apart from the anti-Manchu ethnic sentiment that Zeng Jing had inherited from Lü Liuliang, this case reflects the clash between the throne and literati who were disgruntled with the imperial appropriation of the moral primacy of the *daotong*. In his seditious tract titled *Record of Learning the New* (Zhixin lu), Zeng defiantly challenged the legitimacy of imperial rulers, who, according to him, lacked moral credentials for sitting on the throne:

> The imperial throne should belong to masters in our Confucian tradition, not to heroes in the mundane world [*shilu shang yingxiong*]. Most of those on the throne knew nothing of scholarly learning, and were simply heroes in the mundane world. Some of them were even wily and crafty fellows, like those who were commonly called scoundrels [*guanggun*]. Speaking of legitimacy, the throne of the Spring and Autumn period should have gone to Confucius, and that of the Warring States period to Mencius. After the

Qin, those like the Cheng brothers and Master Zhu should have become emperors, and Master Lü should have been emperor in the late Ming. However, the throne was always seized by despots [*haoqiang*]. Masters in our Confucian tradition are best qualified to be emperors. What did those heroes in the mundane world know about being emperors?[15]

To this, Emperor Yongzheng responded angrily:

The reason Confucius and Mencius became great sages was that they elucidated the ethical relations, rectified people's minds, and illuminated the great principles for thousands of generations. How could Confucius or Mencius have wanted to become an emperor? Confucius said, "One should fully observe the rules of propriety in serving one's prince" [*shijun jinli*], and "Ministers should serve their prince with faithfulness" [*chen shijun yi zhong*].[16] He also said, "The prince is prince, and the minister is minister; the father is father, and the son is son" [*jun jun, chen chen, fu fu, zi zi*].[17] In the chapter "Xiangdang" [of *Lunyu*] you see Confucius being extremely reverent and cautious in front of the prince and ancestors.[18] Mencius said, "I hope to be a minister and fulfill a minister's obligations" [*yu wei chen, jin chen dao*]; and he also said, "No man from the Qi respects the King as much as I do" [*Qi ren mo ru wo jing wang zhe*].[19] That Confucius and Mencius were in positions to practice the *dao* was precisely because they dutifully observed the rules for subjects. How could they, as virtuous but untitled scholars [*weibu rusheng*], have wanted to become emperors?[20]

This exchange illustrates the rivalry and contention between the *daotong* and the state power throughout much of China's imperial history. As the ones to carry on the tradition of the *daotong*, the Confucians had considered themselves holders of the moral primacy overriding even the political authority of the secular rulers, as expressed in the dictum *dao zun yu shi* (*dao* is a higher authority than political power). That was the reason that Zi Si rebuffed the summons from Duke Miao of the Lu (Lu Miao Gong).[21] Similarly, Marquis Wen of the Wei (Wei Wen Hou) (r. 445–396 BCE) willingly conceded the moral superiority of the scholar Duan Ganmu when he said: "Duan Ganmu is glorious for his virtue and I am for my power; Duan Ganmu is rich in righteousness and I am in wealth. Power is not as revered as virtue, and wealth not as exalted as righteousness."[22]

In Qing China, however, the literati were in no position to expect similar respect, as the *dao* learning had become largely a vehicle for consolidating the state power. Zeng Jing was thus not simply an individual rebel but an audacious spokesman for the mostly muted educated gentry longing to regain the lost status of the *daotong*. By saying that Confucian masters were best qualified to be emperors, Zeng advocated the convertibility of moral authority into political authority. In reality, however, the conversion always went in the opposite direction. Under Yongzheng's intimidation, Zeng quickly gave in. In his statement of repentance, he maintained that the ancient sage-kings, Yao, Shun, Yu, Tang, Wen, and Wu, became rulers because they were exemplary men of virtue and learning. Then he hastened to add that "His Majesty on the throne today . . . is a sage who is also thoroughly conversant in scholarly learning" and that "the virtues of the emperors of the current dynasty were not different from those of Yao, Shun, Yu, and Tang."[23] In the end, the exponent of the primacy of *daotong* was brought to his knees by the throne that was not only the supreme representative of political sovereignty but had become the ultimate moral and intellectual arbiter as well.

## THE SIGNIFICANCE OF THE WANG MIAN STORY

Viewed against the political setting of Wu Jingzi's time, especially the balance of power between the *daotong* and the *zhengtong*, the significance of the Wang Mian story in the opening chapter of *The Scholars* becomes considerably clearer. The chapter starts with a piece of *ci*, which the commentator of the Qixingtang edition (1874) calls the "essential point of the whole book" (*quanshu zhunao*).[24] In the middle of the *ci* there are these lines:

> Rank and fame, riches and privileges
> May vanish without a trace.
> Then aspire not for these,
> Wasting your days.[25]

The Chinese original for "Rank and fame, riches and privileges" is *gongming fugui*, which the commentator in an early version of the work, the Woxian Caotang edition (1803), considers the "general rubric" (*da zhu-*

*nao*) of the novel that the author "wrote about in myriads of ways."[26] Yet the novel obviously does not treat *gongming* (rank and fame) and *fugui* (riches and privilege) equally. It is *gongming* that many of the scholars in the novel seek, for they know only too well that once they attain "rank and fame," "riches and privileges" will follow as a matter of course. In the case of those few lofty-minded scholars, it is their imperviousness to *gongming*, which Timothy Wong terms Confucian eremitism, that separates them from the others.[27] The ultimate distributer of *gongming* was of course the imperial power. Apart from a limited number of cases where *gongming* was decided by hereditary statuses such as those of bondservants and Manchu nobilities, the Qing imperial state allocated rank and fame primarily through the examinations as a way to win the support and cooperation from the literati.

Wang Mian's indifference toward rank and fame sets the tone for the entire novel, or "points to the moral of the book" (*gaikuo quanwen*) as the heading of the chapter states (*RLWS* 1; *Scholars* 3). As modern scholars have repeatedly made clear, the novel's account of Wang Mian's life and career is significantly different from a number of widely known biographies of the late Yuan scholar-artist.[28] This idealized eremite in the novel is, therefore, Wu Jingzi's invention. The Qing commentator Zhang Wenhu calls Wang Mian "the forefather of all the *mingshi* [scholars with no official appointments] in the whole book"; this is not because of his "vast erudition," but because of his unswerving refusal to serve in officialdom.[29] When the county magistrate sends for Wang Mian on behalf of the bigwig Wei Su, who has taken a liking to Wang's paintings, the brief dialogue between Wang and the bailiff succinctly sums up the dynamic between the literati and political power. When the bailiff insists that an invitation from the magistrate is just as compulsory and binding as a summons, Wang replies: "If I receive a summons from the magistrate, how dare I refuse? But you have brought an invitation, which means I am under no compulsion. I don't want to go. His honor must excuse me" (*RLWS* 7; *Scholars* 9). This brief episode is strongly reminiscent of a passage in *Mencius*. When Wan Zhang asks Mencius why a commoner who is "well-informed" and "good and wise" should refuse to answer the summons by a feudal lord, the master answers: "If it is for the reason that he is well-informed, even the Emperor does not summon his teacher, let alone a feudal lord. If it is for the reason that he is a good and wise man, then I have never heard of summoning such a man when one wishes to see him."³⁰ By rejecting the invitation from the imperious official, as Wang Mian intimates later to his neighbor Old Qin, he is emulating the ancient sages of Duan Ganmu and Xie Liu, who resorted to extreme measures to avoid unwanted visitation from feudal lords.³¹

Years later, Zhu Yuanzhang, the prince of Wu and future founding emperor of the Ming dynasty, comes to Wang Mian's door. He appears to show some sincere appreciation of Wang Mian's learning and talent, as he claims to "have come specially to pay [his] respects" instead of issuing a summons. When the ruler solicits Wang Mian's counsel on the strategies for pacifying Zhejiang, Wang's native province, the scholar advises him to "use goodness and justice to win the people" (*yi renyi fu ren*), a typical Confucian line on governance that meets the prince's approving reception (*RLWS* 14; *Scholars* 15). The episode may appear to be another variation of the recurrent scene in vernacular Chinese fiction of a ruler's enlistment for the service of a man of talent. Yet, the ostensible depiction of Zhu Yuanzhang as a respectful and appreciative recruiter of talents may well be ironical in light of Zhu's historical maltreatment of his civil officials, which must have been common knowledge in Wu Jingzi's time. In particular, the reader could easily associate Wang Mian with his two contemporary fellow Zhejiang natives, Liu Ji (1311–75) and Song Lian (1310–81), both leading scholars of the early Ming whose careers as Zhu Yuanzhang's top advisers ended unhappily.³² Thus, after his rather good-natured interview with the ruler, Wang Mian's eventual rejection of the official appointment from Zhu Yuanzhang, now Emperor Hongwu, by no means comes as a surprise to the reader. By the time the imperial envoy arrives at his village with much fanfare, Wang Mian has already left home to hide at Kuaiji Mountain. Whether or not this incident is true of the historical Wang Mian is debatable, as the narrator coyly suggests at the end of the chapter, but it is certainly consistent with the idealized eremite that the novel creates.³³

Yet, if the Wang Mian story "points to the moral of the book" as proclaimed in the chapter heading, in what ways is it pertinent to the portrayal of all kinds of scholars in the rest of the novel? The answer lies in the beliefs and values that the scholar-artist stands for. While he does not completely shun government affairs—after all, he does offer counseling to Prince Wu from a Confucian perspective—he scorns those who are haughty and arrogant in the positions of power and despises those who are covetous for status and fame. For him, the Confucian ideal of *rushi*, or participation in social affairs, does not necessitate office holding. In his case, because of his mother's deathbed exhortation that he should not become an official, his practice of eremitism, despite its apparent tint of Daoism, becomes his way to fulfill the utmost Confucian principle of filial piety. When Wang Mian learns from the official bulletin about the rules of the civil service examinations, he reacts by expressing his concern that the system may put the educated elite in a moral jeopardy: "Once future candidates know there is such a path to fame and glory, they will disdain genuine scholarship and correct behavior" (*RLWS* 15; *Scholars* 16–17). As Wang Mian sees it, the official recruitment by the imperial state, if associated with fame and prestige, has an erosive effect on the moral integrity of the intellectual elite.

Wang Mian loves to read and has attained remarkable erudition, but he is portrayed in the novel primarily as an artist, much more devoted to painting than textual learning. He is deeply concerned that the examinations are based exclusively on texts and textual production. For him, indulgence in textual knowledge and compositional virtuosity may be detrimental to "genuine scholarship and correct behavior." And that is the reason for his outcry: "These rules are not good" (*RLWS* 15; *Scholars* 16). In his own case, having an artistic pursuit and a professional commitment away from the world of texts enables him to earn a living without relying on the emolument of office. His vocational choice guarantees an economic autonomy for him, which in turn strengthens his moral stance in resisting the temptations of rank and fame that accompany an official appointment.

Related to Wang Mian's aversion for officialdom is his view of his position as a literatus in the social structure. Unlike earlier reclusive scholars such as the third-century "Seven Worthies of the Bamboo Grove" (*zhulin qixian*), especially Ruan Ji (210–263) and Ji Kang (224–263), who were forced out of the center of power, Wang Mian voluntary stays away from office and is content with his eremitic life. He is, as a modern scholar has suggested, more like Yan Ziling of the early Eastern Han (25–220), who declined an offer of official position from his former schoolmate Liu Xiu, now Emperor Guangwu (r. 25–56).[34] Yet Wang Mian, even more so than Yan Ziling, finds life in the lower social stratum perfectly congenial. While he snubs the dignitary Wei Su and the country magistrate, he thoroughly enjoys the friendship with his neighbor Old Qin, an elderly farmer whose buffalos he attends during his youth. Indeed, one may take the buffalos as a symbol for Wang Mian's rustic but idyllic village life that is disturbed by the intrusion of Prince Wu's horses, which are associated with hegemonic political power.[35] Near the end of the chapter, Wang Mian and Old Qin set a small table on the threshing ground and sit down to drink amid the serenity of the early evening. It is obviously a scene of simple and crude life; Wang Mian, however, feels himself fortunate to be in a position where he can take pity on the educated elite of the future: "Scholars of the later generations will have hard times ahead" (*RLWS* 16; *Scholars* 17, translation modified).

The Wang Mian story thus raises a number of important questions for the literati: If rank and fame become the goal for passing the examinations, what are the moral repercussions? While Confucianism upholds the principle of social participation, would not the examination system, supposedly the apparatus for selecting public servants, actually estrange the scholars from public life by burying them under stacks of texts? Does servitude to the imperial power mean the same thing as serving the nation and society? In other words, should office-holding, in the context of spread literacy and the evolving relationship between the literati and political authorities, still be considered the ultimate vocational goal for the educated elite? These were crucial and burning questions particularly pertinent in Wu Jingzi's time, when the intellectual climate was under the influence of the early Qing reinvigoration of Confucianism spearheaded by Gu Yanwu, Huang Zongxi, and Wang Fuzhi (1619–92) as well as the so-called Learning of Substance represented by Yan Yuan and Li Gong. The Wang Mian story thus serves as a point of departure for the novelistic approach to these questions in the main body of the novel.

### THE MORAL EROSION OF *GONGMING*

When Wang Mian cries out, "scholars of the later generation will have hard times ahead," he expresses his concern not only for those who fail to reach *gongming* but also those who succeed in attaining it. What his mother says—"I'm afraid becoming an official is not something that would bring glory to your forefathers. The officials I have seen have all come to a bad end"—turns out to be not only an allusion to the past but also a prophecy for the future (*RLWS* 12; *Scholars* 14, translation modified). Starting with Zhou Jin and Fan Jin, the novel presents a series of moral casualties of *gongming*. After repeated failures Zhou Jin eventually has a successful run in the examinations, but not before he makes an ugly scene at the examination hall that draws for him a financial sponsorship from a group of merchants, whom the old village school teacher obsequiously addresses as "my foster-parents" (*RLWS* 33; *Scholars* 34). In the more amplified story of Fan Jin, the report of his long-awaited *juren* degree immediately turns the perennial examination failure mad, and the newfound wealth that follows his success costs his mother first her wit and then her life. In each case, the culprit seems to be a fit of emotions, or an "attack by some pestilent elements" (*zhong'e*) (*RLWS* 32; *Scholars* 32, translation modified). That may be true, but the source of those "pestilent elements" is precisely their many years' obsession with *gongming*, as the Qing critic Zhang Wenhu suggested.[36]

In the young scholar Kuang Chaoren, one sees even more clearly a downward moral spiral. After making his debut in the novel as an innocent lad of exemplary filial piety, Kuang enters a gradual but continual process of moral degeneration once he begins his pursuit of *gongming*. His father's deathbed admonition—"Fame and fortune are external things after all; it's goodness [*dexing*] that really counts"—clearly echoes that of Wang Mian's mother, but Kuang, unlike Wang, turns a deaf ear to the parental instruction, which completely vitiates his seemingly dutiful mourning over his father's death afterward (*RLWS* 210; *Scholars* 221).[37] As Kuang embraces rank and fame wholeheartedly and turns his back on virtue and integrity—the complete opposite of his father's exhortation—the advice from his friend Ma Chunshang that *gongming* is the surest way to "reflect credit on your family" and show "the greatest piety" is rendered scathingly ironical.

Behind the vanity and ambitions of Kuang Chaoren and many other characters in *The Scholars* is a sense of servitorship to the imperial power, the ultimate dispenser of rank and fame. For them, the path for pursuing *gongming* is also a pilgrimage to the imperial court and the emperor himself, in both literal and figurative senses. For that reason, they swagger about in plumes borrowed from the state power and regularly use the assumed affiliation with the political authorities to cover their moral deficiencies. Kuang Chaoren, after being selected to enter the Imperial

Academy and then passing the qualifying examination for tutors, returns to his native province to get the testimonial from the local authorities. The young man at the threshold of officialdom now brags about his propinquity to the imperial house: "Scholars like myself who reach officialdom through proper channels are imperial tutors whose pupils are the sons of nobles" (RLWS 244; Scholars 259). Refusing to visit a former friend and benefactor in prison, the tutor, who has just committed the crime of bigamy, attempts to cloak his ingratitude and heartlessness with the bravura rhetoric of serving the throne and the state: "It's a pity he is in this fix! I would have gone to the gaol to see him, but my position has changed. As a servant of the throne I have to abide by the law; and to call on him in such a place would show no respect for the law" (RLWS 245; Scholars 260).

The same is true of Senior Licentiate Yan (Yan Gongsheng). After his younger brother's death, Yan comes home from the provincial examinations with a plan to seize his brother's property. To justify his failure to bid farewell to his departing brother, the older Yan calls his participation in the examinations his attendance to state business: "As the proverb says, 'Public business comes before private affairs. The state comes before the family.' Our examinations are a great affair of state, and since we were busy on state business [*wei chaoting banshi*], even if we had to neglect our own relatives we need feel no compunction" (RLWS 77; Scholars 77). Saying so, Yan gilds his personal ambitions and greed with the luster of moral and political correctness. Thus, even before he can secure an official appointment, his participation in the examinations has already won him significant moral and political capital. That in turn feeds the local bully's arrogance and self-importance when he denounces his commoner neighbors who have brought up a lawsuit against him: "How dare these common people take such liberties with gentlemen?" (RLWS 78; Scholars 78).

## MA CHUNSHANG: MORAL SUSTENANCE FROM THE IMPERIAL POWER

Many of the *mingshi* in the novel, scholars who are ostensibly indifferent to officialdom, are equally under the spell of political power. Just like those who are obsessed with an examination degree, they know all too well that lasting fame and prestige can be founded only on an alliance with political authorities. The amateur poet Zhao Xuezhai is hailed as a celebrity because his poems attract high-ranking officials, whose visits to his residence augment his personal fame. The ruffian Niu Pulang wants to learn how to compose poems, because he knows that "a man who can write poems doesn't have to pass the examinations in order to make friends with great officials" (*RLWS* 253; *Scholars* 268). He steals the identity of the poet Niu Buyi, and when Dong Ying, a metropolitan examination candidate, pays him a visit, he uses the arrival of the "high official" at his door to impress his in-laws with whom he lives. In contrast to Wang Mian's genuine disinterest in office holding, the pretended detachment from political power is merely another means to angle fame and prestige. As a Western scholar has put it, "the more loudly the *mingshi* insist on their detachment, the more they reveal their resemblance to bureaucrats."[38] This line from Du Shenqing, himself a *mingshi*, summarizes their affectations most succinctly: "It is such a vulgar way of showing refinement" (*ya de zheme su*) (*RLWS* 346; *Scholars* 370). Indeed, the schizophrenia in Du's attitude toward women—he marries a seventeen-year-old concubine while vowing his misogyny by citing Emperor Hongwu: "If not for the fact that I was born of a woman, I would kill all the women in the world"—characterizes equally well the attitude of the *mingshi* toward state power and officialdom (*RLWS* 352–53; *Scholars* 377).

For these scholars, the imperial power is the supreme authority not only politically but also morally, indeed with its political and moral sides reinforcing and fortifying each other. That is the reason that they all scramble, in one way or another, to forge some kind of connection to the imperial court. An interesting but slightly different case is Ma Chunshang, a pedantic but honest compiler of pamphlets of sample eight-legged essays. Sauntering along the bank of the West Lake (Xihu) in Hangzhou and dazzled by both the natural beauty and the tempting sights of the market, Ma comes to a pavilion, where he unexpectedly sees on the wall an inscription by Emperor Renzong (r. 1023–63) of the Song dynasty: "Ma Chunshang gave a start when he saw this, and hastily straightened his cap, adjusted his sapphire-blue gown, and took from his boot a fan, which he carried as the tablet courtiers hold in the presence of the emperor. Then, very reverently he faced the wall, advanced in the manner prescribed by court etiquette, and bowed five times" (*RLWS* 180; *Scholars* 188).

As a professional compiler of anthologies of exemplary examination essays, Ma Chunshang may be obsessed with the authority of the throne, the ultimate judge on the quality of all examination writings. But the meaning of this encounter goes beyond that. When the scholar feels his moral frailty in front of the varicolored temptations, the sight of the imperial inscription becomes for him a timely warning, or, in a modern Chinese scholar's words, "a head-on blow and a shout" (*dangtou banghe*) that remind him of the importance of his "intellectual responsibility" and "moral decency."[39] The scholar, after a moment of mental drifting, finds a moral anchor in the tablet. Leaving the pavilion, Ma returns to the market, jostling his way through women dressed seductively in silk and brocade. This time, however, "the women paid no attention to him, nor he to them" (*RLWS* 181; *Scholars* 189). All of a sudden, he becomes immune from all the temptations "as if he were thickly armored."[40] Obviously Ma Chunshang is a different type of scholar from Kuang Chaoren, Senior Licentiate Yan, or Niu Pulang. Instead of deceptively parading a connection to the political authorities for ulterior purposes as the others do, Ma may be sincere in showing his reverence for the inscription, an icon of imperial augustness. Yet he shares with the others the same belief in their complete moral as well as political dependence on the imperial authority. Particularly interesting is Ma's meticulous imitation of the court etiquette in bowing to the tablet in all seriousness, and the use of the fan from his boot as a substitute for *huban*—a small tablet an official held before his breast when received in audience by the emperor—generates a comical effect.[41] It serves as a lampoon of Ma's undying ambition for a bureaucratic career and his almost intuitive submission to imperial power. Yet, as Ma Chunshang is actually several hundred years removed from Emperor Renzong's time, the temporal distance bestows a transcendent nature on this episode. The novel depicts Ma Chunshang as a figure of somewhat middling moral and social standing, and to that extent he may be seen as an average and representative scholar. One may therefore argue that Ma's encounter with Renzong's inscription is a reification of the state-literati relationship, when the imperial state had secured its position as the master in the *daotong* tradition.

## SERVING *TIANZI* OR SERVING *TIANXIA*?

The *dao* in Chinese culture, as Yu Yingshi has reminded us, originated in the ancient practice of ritual and music. "It was fundamentally a cultural tradition of managing the social order.... From the very beginning, Chinese intellectuals took it upon themselves to attend to Caesar's affairs."[42] That explains their intense sense of social responsibility, which was best expressed in Fan Zhongyan's (989–1052) celebrated motto: "Be the first one under heaven to feel concerned and the last one under heaven to enjoy happiness" (*Xian tianxia zhi you er you, hou tianxia zhi le er le*).[43] While the intellectuals were expected to be active in participating in social affairs, particularly in administrative roles, their sense of responsibility based on the Confucian ideal was supposed to go to "all people under heaven," or *tianxia*, rather than the sovereign himself, who was also known as *tianzi*, or the Son of Heaven. Idealistically, a literatus's service in officialdom was merely a means for reaching the ultimate goal of *ping tianxia*, bringing peace and prosperity to all under heaven.

Mencius made clear the difference between serving the ruler and serving the empire: "There are men whose purpose is to serve a prince. They will try to please whatever prince they are serving. There are men whose aim is to bring peace to the country and the people [*sheji*]. They attain gratification through bringing this about."[44] Confronting their contemporary reality of the lopsided balance of power between the *zhengtong* and the *daotong*, many scholars in the late imperial times reaffirmed that Mencian ideal. According to Lü Kun (1536–1618), what a scholar-official was supposed to serve ultimately was not the imperial power (*shi*) but the moral principle (*li*): "Between heaven and earth *li* and *shi* are the highest authorities. However, *li* is the authority over all other authorities [*zun zhi zun*]. If *li* is upheld in the court, the empire will not be completely dominated by *shi*. Even if it is, *li* will still extend to many generations to come. What is called *shi* is the power of the throne, and *li* is the power of the sages. Without *li* the power of the throne can sometimes go astray."[45]

During the early Qing, when the topic of political sovereignty became extremely sensitive under Manchu rule, Gu Yanwu's attempt to differentiate *guo*, the state, from *tianxia*, society or civilization, became particularly significant:

> What is the difference between loss of the state [*wang guo*] and loss of civilization [*wang tianxia*]? Here is the answer: Having the name of the dynasty changed is called loss of the state, and having beasts prey on humans and having people eat each other is called loss of civilization....

Therefore, one should know how to defend the civilization before knowing how to defend the state. Defending the state is what the sovereign, the ministers, and the noblemen have on their minds, while defending the civilization is the obligation of the common people.[46]

Gu's differentiation between *guo* and *tianxia* is akin to Huang Zongxi's distinction between *si* and *gong*. In his *Ming yi dai fang lu,* Huang questioned the legitimacy of the political sovereignty that made the ruler's "private and personal interest" (*da si*) appear as the "common interest of all people under heaven" (*tianxia zhi gong*). The ruler, as Huang argued, was supposed to be the one to spend his lifetime managing the business for all the people. Therefore, "*Tianxia* should be considered principal and the ruler only subsidiary" (*tianxia wei zhu jun wei ke*), as had been the case in the ancient time of the sage-kings. In Huang's own time, however, it turned the other way around as "the ruler came to be considered principal and *tianxia* only subsidiary" (*yi jun wei zhu tianxia wei ke*).[47] The different perceptions of the relationship between *tianzi* and *tianxia* led to different views of the nature of bureaucratic service. Because *tianxia* was so large and could not be ruled by the emperor alone, as Huang Zongxi proceeded to argue, the governance had to be a collective effort joined by many men of talent and wisdom. To enter officialdom, therefore, "was for the sake of *tianxia* rather than the sovereign, for the sake of myriads of people rather than one family." Unfortunately, as Huang lamented, many of his contemporaries mistakenly thought that official positions were instituted by the emperor and for the emperor: "The sovereign allocated me part of his *tianxia* to govern, and the sovereign gave me some of his people to rule. All the people under heaven were thus seen as private property in the sovereign's pocket."[48]

As we know, the relationship between *tianzi* and *tianxia* in imperial China was never black-and-white but always subtle and complex. However, at a time when the imperial power was usurping the moral supremacy from the *daotong,* making this distinction became many scholars' strategy in challenging the moral standing of the sovereign. Even though there is little evidence for direct influence on Wu Jingzi from either Gu Yanwu or Huang Zongxi, the legacy of Gu and Yan certainly had an enormous impact on the general intellectual climate of Wu's time.[49] The literati's stupefaction in confusing *tianzi* with *tianxia,* which was spiritedly attacked by Gu and Huang, is caustically satirized in *The Scholars*. Almost everyone that attempts to gain moral capital by approaching the imperial power eventually suffers moral bankruptcy. In contrast, the high-minded scholars in the novel are well aware of the distinction between servitude to the imperial state and dedication to society. Following Wang Mian, Du Shaoqing refuses the invitation to participate in the special examinations, even going to the extreme of feigning illness, as he knows he will not be allowed to achieve anything as an official (*RLWS* 393; *Scholars* 425). Compared to the somewhat unconventional and unbridled Du, Zhuang Shaoguang is obviously a more orthodox Confucian. When the emperor summons him to the capital for an audience, he feels obligated to go as a subject, but his attitude toward an official appointment is quite similar to Du's. When he realizes that "it does not seem as if our Confucian ways will avail in this age" (*wo dao bu xing*) he requests to be allowed to return home immediately (*RLWS* 411; *Scholars* 445).

For both Du and Zhuang, a political relationship to the sovereign becomes completely meaningless if it does not facilitate the Confucian moral agenda. In Zhuang's case, what seems to prevent him from a more thoroughgoing conversation with the emperor on the issues of ritual and music is "a stab of pain on the top of his head" that is caused, as he finds out later outside the palace, by a scorpion in his cap (*RLWS* 411–12; *Scholars* 445). Yet the sting of the scorpion is not exactly the unexpected mishap that it appears to be, for Zhuang already made up his mind to decline any offer of official appointment even before his departure from home, when he promised his wife that he would "come straight back" (*RLWS* 403; *Scholars* 436). The scorpion therefore serves as a painful reminder of the predicament he is in—"It does not seem as if our Confucian ways will avail in this age"—rather than the cause of it.

Yu Yude, "the number one person in the work" (*shuzhong diyi ren*) as the commentator in the Woxian Caotang edition calls him, is not completely averse to bureaucratic service, but totally indifferent to rank and fame.[50] He receives the *jinshi* degree at the age of fifty. While appointing other candidates in their fifties or sixties as Hanlin academicians, the emperor consigns Yu, the only old candidate who reports his true age, to be a professor at the Imperial Academy in Nanjing. Yu, on his part, is actually happy for being pushed away from the center of political power in Beijing. He lives contentedly with his family in Nanjing on his modest salary and heartedly enjoys making friends and practicing virtue. Du Shaoqing compares him to the ancient sages of Bo Yi and Liuxia Hui as well as the fifth-century hermitic poet Tao Yuanming (*RLWS* 425; *Scholars* 461). Among the three, as a modern Chinese scholar suggests, the closest parallel for Yu should be Liuxia Hui (fl. 634 BCE), to whom Mencius gave this commendation: "Liuxia Hui was not ashamed of a prince with a tarnished reputation; neither did he disdain a modest post. When in office, he did not conceal his talent, and always acted in accordance with the Way. When he was passed over he harbored no grudge, nor was he distressed even in straitened circumstances."[51] That is the reason Mencius gave him the honorific title "the sage who was easy-going" (*sheng zhi he zhe*).[52] Like Liuxia Hui, Yu Yude maintains an eremitical mentality while serving on an official post, and thus becomes a "hermit within officialdom" (*liyin*).[53] Impervious to the temptations of rank and fame, Yu is unaffected by any change to his status and remains unperturbed by any material losses or gains. Compared to Du Shaoqing's resolute boycott of the state's recruitment, Yu's "hermitage within officialdom" represents a more sophisticated form of detachment from the imperial power. It allows office holding to be considered a way of living without compromising one's moral integrity and intellectual independence.

## BEIJING AND NANJING: A TALE OF TWO CITIES

One can thus consider Yu Yude's departure from Beijing for Nanjing after his reception of the *jinshi* degree more than just a geographical relocation. "Nanjing is a fine place," he exclaims with joy, and considers his teaching job in Nanjing much better than that of a Hanlin academician in the "northern capital" (*RLWS* 422; *Scholars* 458). That enthusiasm for Nanjing is, significantly, shared by his friends. To answer his wife's question why he has declined the court's invitation to become an official, Du Shaoqing calls it "absurd" (*dai*) to leave Nanjing for Beijing. While he and his wife can go out "in the spring and autumn to look at the flowers and drink wine" in Nanjing, Beijing, according to him, "is a cold place," and "one gust of wind there would freeze [one] to death" (*RLWS* 395; *Scholars* 427–28). In a similar vein, Zhuang Shaoguang, on his way back home from Beijing, cries out in delight as his boat approaches Nanjing: "Today I shall see the beauties of the Yangtze again" (*RLWS* 414; *Scholars* 449).

Wu Jingzi of course lived in Nanjing for many years and was very fond of the city. In his *Yijia fu* he offers a description of his leisured and uninhibited life there: "Outside the house were brilliant flowers, and above the curtain was a shining sun. The gentle breeze brushed the bamboos in the yard, and [in winter] the fallen snow stopped at the window screen. I was often skillfully and casually catching lice on my body, or looking above following the soaring geese with my eyes."⁵⁴ What most significantly enriched his life in Nanjing, however, was the spiritual companionship of the literati who had lived in the city in the past, especially Ji Kang, Ruan Ji, and others of the Six Dynasties period who were known for their unbridled expressions of political dissent. That was the reason that Wu Jingzi would, again in his own words, "think of those outstanding figures of the Six Dynasties, and suddenly become sad and shed tears" (*Diao Liudai zhi yingcai, hu chuangyan er yunti*).⁵⁵ The same sentiment is expressed in such lines in *Wenmu shanfang ji*:

> Incidentally I purchased a residence on the Qinhuai River,
> So much better I liked it than I did my native village.
>
> . . . . . . . . . . . . . . . . . . . .
>
> As I was to live in seclusion,
> I invited Ruan Ji and Ji Kang;
> Coats draping on our shoulders and our legs extended,
> We drank till we were all blue.⁵⁶

Nanjing, the cultural center of Jiangnan, was traditionally where literati assembled, and Wu Jingzi identified particularly with those historical figures in Nanjing who were banished from the center of political power. Like the novelist, the high-minded scholars in *The Scholars* clearly share an enthusiasm for Nanjing, which becomes even stronger in contrast to their indifference toward Beijing. The novel almost presents Nanjing as the capital for the literati, in counterpoise to Beijing as the political center of the empire.⁵⁷

As mentioned earlier, it is a scholarly consensus that the ritual in honor of Tai Bo in chapter 37 marks the climax of the novel. Tai Bo, as the legend goes, was the oldest son of King Tai of Western Zhou (Xi Zhou) and heir apparent to the throne. As he found out that his father favored his nephew Ji Chang, he ran away to the Jiangnan area of Wu so that King Tai could pass on the throne to his third son Ji Li and through Ji Li to Ji Chang, who was to become King Wen (Wen Wang). Meanwhile, Tai Bo became the founder of the Wu civilization. In the Confucian tradition, Tai Bo was venerated as the one who embodied "supreme virtue" (*zhide*) by his persistent yielding (*rang*) of the throne.[58] As he relinquished political power and worked instead to promote the well-being of the people in a less culturally developed area, he also exemplified the Confucian ideal of *rushi* that, as Gu Yanwu and Huang Zongxi understood it, upheld service for *tianxia* above service for *guo* or *tianzi*.

Chi Hengshan, the initiator of the project of the Tai Bao temple, praises Tai Bo as "the worthiest man our Nanjing has produced, past or present" (*RLWS* 393; *Scholars* 425). By identifying Tai Bo with Nanjing, Chi also identifies himself and his friends in Nanjing with the ancient sage who moved here from the political center in the north. The ritual in the temple is therefore not only a tribute to Tai Bo himself, but also a celebration of the spirit of "yielding" that the scholars have inherited from their ancient precursor. In that sense the high-minded literati's migrations to Nanjing, especially Yu Yude's, can be considered lesser replicas of the classical paradigm set by Tai Bo. While the scholars in pursuit of fame and status yearn for the center of imperial power in Beijing, Nanjing becomes the destination for those who have higher goals in life than a bureaucratic position.

Interestingly, the narrative of the Tai Bo ceremony is preceded almost immediately by the account of another ceremony in chapter 35, the ceremony at the imperial palace right before Zhuang Shaoguang's reception in audience with the emperor. Part of the account goes as follows: "In the glare of a hundred torches the prime minister arrived, Wu Men, the main gate, was opened, and the officials entered through side gates. They proceeded through Fengtian Gate to Fengtian Palace, where heavenly music was being played and they could barely hear the herald bid them take their places. A whip cracked three times, eunuchs trooped out from the inner palace bearing golden censers of ambergris, and palace maids with long-handled fans escorted the emperor to his throne. Then the officials hailed the Son of Heaven and prostrated themselves in obeisance" (*RLWS* 409; *Scholars* 443).

It is apparently a ceremony that heightens the awe-inspiring imperial authority and dramatizes the submission of the officials to the throne. Right before the ritual, it is announced in an imperial edict: "We have heard that a good sovereign reveres his ministers as teachers. Indeed, this has been proved true since ancient times" (*RLWS* 409; *Scholars* 443). The ruler-ministers relationship demonstrated in this ceremony renders those words from the emperor a caustic mockery of the once-revered tradition of the *daotong*. Thus the juxtaposition of these two ceremonies, one at the imperial court in Beijing and the other at the Tai Bo temple in Nanjing, becomes profoundly meaningful. While the former celebrates the imperium's appropriation of the *daotong*, the latter is a symbolic gesture to evoke the intellectuals' autonomy and independence of the state power. A modern Chinese critic has compared the congregation of the scholars at the Tai Bo ceremony to the assemblage of the Liangshan bandit heroes in *Water Margin*.[59] Indeed, the analogy does not stop with the similar structural function of the gathering of the characters. The ritual performed by the literati in the Tai Bo temple, though not as blatant a revolt as the Liangshan rebellion, is presented clearly as a political gesture as it serves as a counterweight to the ceremony at the imperial court.

## SNARED IN A TEXTUAL CULTURE: THE OBSESSION WITH SAMPLE EXAMINATION ESSAYS

In chapter 34, having declined the invitation to participate in the special examinations, Du Shaoqing exclaims to himself joyfully, "Good! This is the end of my career as a licentiate. I shall not sit for the provincial examination or the yearly tests again, but take life easy and attend to my own affairs" (*RLWS* 396; *Scholars* 428). This outcry of relief posits an opposition between the examinations and a literatus's "own affairs." However, how does the state power intervene and manipulate the literati's intellectual agenda and prevent them from "attending to [their] own affairs?"

*The Scholars* provides a panoramic exposition of the dynamics between the state and the literati in different sectors of textual culture. The most prominent sector is no doubt that of examination learning, especially the writing of the eight-legged essay (*bagu wen*). It should be noted that, while the examination system was attacked by numerous literary figures, the eight-legged essay as a form of prose was not without its merit.[60] Even Huang Zongxi, one of the fiercest early Qing critics of the examination system, gave this form of prose writing its due as he included seventy-eight prefaces to a variety of *bagu* collections in *Ming wenhai*.[61] Even when the eight-legged essay was under attack, in many cases people treated it as a synecdoche for the examination system, rather than as a form of essay writing per se. What was more controversial, however, was the content of the writing, or what was actually carried by the vehicle of the essay. Liang Zhangju (1775–1849) summarized two conflicting attitudes toward the content of the *bagu* essays among Qing scholars: "Those who respect it say that the essay establishes words on behalf of the sages and worthies [*dai shengren liyan*] and that the writing leads to the *dao* [*yin wen jian dao*].... Those who look down on it say that the essay carries nothing but empty words and therefore has no practical use at all."[62] Neither side, as Liang insisted, had the whole truth, but it was a fact that by the eighteenth century scholars had become much less interested in, if not completely disillusioned with, the alleged moral function of the eight-legged essay as the appropriate vehicle for expounding the Confucian teachings. That change was reflected in the scholarly discussions of the eight-legged essay, which shifted their focus from the content of the writing to the essay format and style.[63] "In the evolution of prose theory," as Stephen Roddy rightly states, "we can detect a definite trend toward the weakening of an ethical linkage between the essay form and the teachings of the classics and Four Books."[64]

There were multiple reasons for this exaltation of form over content. Apparently, an immediate reason was the proliferation of anthologies of successful examination essays. Gu Yanwu complained about the easy availability of such sample writings and deplored their foul influence: "People in the empire know these are things that can enable you to succeed in the examinations and to enjoy fame and prestige. They call these books scholarship, and read no other books at all." Gu therefore saw a reason to be concerned that the formalistic imitation of the sample essays would lead to a neglect of the moral teachings in the classics: "Alas! The eight-legged essay is flourishing while the Six Classics are declining. The eighteen-hall writings are rising while the Twenty-One Histories are abandoned" (*Bagu sheng er liujing wei, shibafang xing er nianyishi fei*).[65] Qing government certainly understood the importance of establishing textual models as a manner of ideological control and as part of the process of preparing the examination candidates. In the early Qing, the state and private publishers actually competed with each other in producing collections of sample *bagu* essays. Particularly popular were collections compiled by Lü

Liuliang, a Ming loyalist and recognized scholar in classic learning who had failed to pass the provincial examination.[66] However, the government soon banned publication and circulation of model examination essays by private booksellers, and virtually monopolized the business itself. In 1723, Emperor Yongzheng put the Board of Rites (Libu) and the Hanlin Academy in charge of selecting model eight-legged essays to be collected in anthologies. Soon after his ascension in 1735, Emperor Qianlong authorized Fang Bao (1668–1749) to compile an official collection of examination essays, which came out in 1740 under the title *Imperially Authorized Edition of Essays on the Four Books* (Qinding Sishuwen).[67] Following its publication, the court repeatedly demanded that the criteria set forth in the imperial anthology, which became the official reference for examiners, be strictly observed in the local and metropolitan examinations.[68]

By setting these officially endorsed textual models for all examination candidates, the Manchu state attempted to curb all examination writings within the frame of neo-Confucian orthodoxy. In the meantime, as the government enforced the standard of the model essays, they became the key to success in the examinations and opened up a shortcut to *gongming*. For many pursuers of fame and status, these selected essays superseded the Confucian canon itself as the most essential readings. They became more concerned with the formal features of the model essays than with the moral and ethical content of the classics. The situation became even worse than that in the seventeenth century as described by Gu Yanwu, simply because the new anthologies of eight-legged essays had the backing of the political authorities.

Wu Jingzi's composition of *The Scholars* coincided with the prevalence of the official editions of eight-legged essays, especially the *Imperially Authorized Edition of Essays on the Four Books*. The rage of the model eight-legged essays that Wu may have witnessed is well documented in his novel. In chapter 15, Ma Chunshang urges Kuang Chaoren to start preparing for the examinations. After citing the cliché—"In study one finds golden mansions, one finds bushels of rice, and one finds beautiful women"—the compiler of *bagu* anthologies acclaims the value of the model examination essays with this rhetorical question: "What is study today if not our anthologies of selected *bagu* compositions?" (*RLWS* 193; *Scholars* 203, translation modified). Wei Tishan, another compiler of *bagu* anthologies, is equally boastful: "Only those essays selected and annotated by us are assured of immortality" (*RLWS* 223; *Scholars* 237). As the novel is set in the Ming period, Ma, Wei, and others in the trade are all private editors, but they frequently suggest that the criteria for *bagu* composition is ultimately determined by the state, and that they are the ones who can demonstrate and explicate the relationship between the imperial power and the stylistic changes in the examination writing. In a conversation with Qu Xianfu in chapter 13, Ma Chunshang observes that "during the reigns of Hongwu and Yongle we find one style, and during the reigns of Chenghua and Hongzhi another" (*RLWS* 166; *Scholars* 172). Wei Tishan echoes this almost verbatim in chapter 15. When Kuang Chaoren expresses his perplexity about the rules on *bagu* composition, Wei delivers this admonition to the younger scholar: "Essays express the teachings of the sages, and they must be written according to definite rules, unlike other frivolous forms of literature which you may write as you please. Thus from an essay you should be able to see not only the writer's rank and fortune, but also whether the empire is passing through a period of prosperity or decline. The Hongwu and Yongle periods had one set of rules; the Chenghua and Hongzhi periods had another. Each reign has its particular rules which have been handed down from one group of scholars to another, forming an orthodox tradition" (*RLWS* 223; *Scholars* 236–37).

Interestingly, what Ma and Wei describe here is precisely the way the *Imperially Authorized Edition of Essays on the Four Books* was organized, which consisted of five collections (*ji*) with each of the first four devoted to the reign periods of two Ming emperors and the fifth to the Qing. Thus, the first collection included essays from the Chenghua (1465–88) and Hongzhi (1488–1506) periods, the second from the Zhengde (1506–22) and Jiajing (1522–67) periods, and so forth.[69] Whether by Ma's and Wei's words the novelist alludes to the *Imperially Authorized Edition of Essays on the Four Books* remains unclear, but it is evident that the novel, using Ma and Wei as mouthpieces, associates the evolution of the *bagu* writing to manipulation from the political authorities.

Thus the imperial state, as the novel suggests, is to blame for vitiating most of the ethical content of the examinations and turning it largely into a play of form. While the examination writing was supposed to "establish words on behalf of the sages and worthies," the candidates' reiteration of the Confucian moral philosophy always had to be constricted into a stylistic form dictated by the state, for political purposes that could change from one period to the next. That is exactly what Ma Chunshang implies in this observation:

> By the Tang dynasty, scholars were chosen for their ability to write poetry. Even if a man could talk like Confucius or Mencius, it would not get him a post; so all the Tang scholars learned to write poems. That was the civil service of the Tang dynasty. By the Song dynasty, it was even better: all the officials had to be philosophers. That was why the Cheng brothers and Zhu Xi propagated neo-Confucianism. That was the civil service of the Song dynasty. Nowadays, however, we use essays to select scholars, and this is the best criterion of all. Even Confucius, if he were alive today, would be studying essays and preparing for the examinations instead of saying, "Make few false statements and do little you may regret." Why? Because that kind of talk would get him nowhere: nobody would give him an official position. No, the old sage would find it impossible to realize his ideal. (*RLWS* 168; *Scholars* 174)

The message here is clear: what can possibly lead to an official position is not so much faithful adherence to the moral teachings of the ancient sages as perfect conformity to the form of writing endorsed by the imperial state.

## THE TEXTUAL CRISIS OF NEO-CONFUCIANISM

Another factor that contributed to the estrangement of form from content in examination writing was the imperial state's stance on what can be called a textual crisis of neo-Confucianism itself. With the movement of evidential scholarship on the rise, the early decades of the eighteenth century witnessed a growing distrust of the Cheng-Zhu exegetical tradition. Back in the early Qing, Chen Que (1604–77) had forcefully and daringly challenged the authenticity of the *Great Learning* (Daxue), a text that was long believed to have been authored by Confucius's disciple Zeng Shen (505–436 BCE) and regarded as a cornerstone of the Cheng-Zhu school of learning.[70] Chen's contemporary Pan Pingge (1610–77) also attacked both the Cheng-Zhu and the Lu-Wang schools as being adulterations with either Buddhism or Daoism. Decades later, the meticulous textual study by Yan Ruoqu (1636–1704) confirmed definitively a long-standing doubt that the Old Text portion of the *Book of Documents* (Shangshu), a perennial component of the examination curriculum, was not written by the ancient sage-kings as had long been assumed but a forgery of much later dating. Another scholar, Hu Wei (1633–1714), was able to reveal that the so-called *Diagram of the Great Ultimate* (Taiji tu), which served as the foundation for the cosmology of the neo-Confucian pioneer Zhou Dunyi (1017–73), actually was of a Daoist origin. Such scholarly findings severely damaged the textual integrity of the neo-Confucian orthodoxy, which, consequently, lost much of its halo among the literati during the early half of the eighteenth century.

In the meantime, the Manchu state was concerned that the results of such philological studies might lead to ideological disturbances and impair their political control over the educated elite. Supported by some conservative Confucian scholar-officials, the imperial government repeatedly refused to make adjustments to the examination curriculum to accommodate the new scholarly developments. In the 1690s and the 1740s, for instance, scholars submitted memorials to the throne calling for elimination of the Old Text portion of the *Book of Documents* from the official text used in the examinations, but each time the request was ignored.[71] In the metropolitan examinations of 1730 and 1737, the Old Text continued to be cited in the questions "with no indication of the philological controversy surrounding its authenticity."[72] Even as many results of evidential studies gained general acceptance, "those who aspired to enter the civil service were still better off studying in the Zhu Xi tradition."[73] It was not until the late eighteenth and early nineteenth centuries that evidential scholarship finally managed to find its way to the metropolitan examinations. Even then, the change was largely confined to the policy questions of Session Three, while the much more important Sessions One and Two "remained, for the most part, unchanged in content and governed by orthodox Cheng-Zhu interpretations."[74]

There was thus an evident incongruity between the diminished authority of the neo-Confucian texts in the larger scholarly world and the continued dominance of the Cheng-Zhu orthodoxy within the examination regime itself. The damaged textual integrity weakened the credibility of the moral teachings in the neo-Confucian canon. In *The Scholars*, Du Shaoqing is one of those who are perceptive enough to see this not as a problem of the Song neo-Confucians themselves but of the forces behind the ideological manipulation. His complaint in chapter 34 is thus highly pertinent: When Zhu Xi put forward his opinions, he perhaps expected posterity to compare them with others'. It was only because of "the narrow-mindedness of later generations" that Zhu's words became unfairly lifted to the height of infallible and untouchable authority (*RLWS* 400; *Scholars* 433). If the Cheng-Zhu school were treated as one voice amid many others, the flaws in its textual corpus would have been condoned without causing much uproar. However, since it was now the core of the examination curriculum and thus the passport to officialdom, scholars were compelled to follow certain texts of questionable status. In other words, they had to read and write what they did not truly believe. Consequently, the examinations became largely a business of texts and writings, and the ethical messages became something on paper only and largely extraneous to the real world.

Much of the degeneration of the literati mores in *The Scholars* can be attributed to the divorce of form from content and of textual discourse from real-world practice. Fan Jin, right after his success in the provincial examinations, totally disregards the ritual propriety taught in the Confucian classics. He feels no qualms devouring "large shrimp balls" during the mourning period for his mother, while hypocritically insisting on using bamboo chopsticks instead of silver or ivory ones (*RLWS* 58; *Scholars* 58). In the case of Kuang Chaoren, his moral deterioration coincides with his diligent study of the classics in preparation for the examinations. Beyond their textual existence, the teachings in the classics have no efficacy for him other than serving as a stepping-stone to fame and rank. Elsewhere, Mr. Gao, a reader in the Hanlin Academy, calls Du Shaoqing's father, the late Prefect Du, a "fool" (*daizi*) because the older Du is said to have taken the moral messages on paper too seriously: "While in office he showed no respect for his superiors but simply tried to please the people, talking nonsense about 'fostering filial piety and brotherly love, and encouraging agriculture.' Such phrases are mere figures of speech to be used in compositions, yet he took them seriously, with the result that his superiors disliked him and removed him from his post" (*RLWS* 398; *Scholars* 431).

It should be noted here that the imperial state was by no means unaware of the moral detriment caused by this disconnection between text and praxis. Emperor Kangxi, in particular, took a strong personal dislike to those scholar-officials who paid only lip service to the moral teachings in the Confucian canon.[75] As early as 1663, the emperor approved the memorial from the Board of Rites to discontinue the eight-legged essay in both provincial and metropolitan examinations, but had to reverse that decision only five years later.[76] In Wu Jingzi's time, Shu-ho-te (1711–77), a Manchu official well versed in the classics, stated in a 1744 memorial to Emperor Qianlong: "Today's contemporary-style essays [*shiwen*, i.e., eight-legged essays] are nothing but empty words and cannot be applied to any use. This is the foremost reason why the civil examinations are inadequate for selecting men."[77] What he said was obviously true, even to the Manchu rulers themselves. Then why did the imperial state keep the form of the examination writing in place while knowing its defects? An answer was provided by the Manchu official O-erh-tai (1680–1745), a staunch apologist for the examination system: "It is not that I don't know that the eight-legged essay is useless. But for the purpose of captivating scholars of aspirations [*laolong zhishi*] and commanding men of talent [*quce rencai*], there is no better means."[78] The eight-legged essay, after all, was more than merely empty words; for the imperial power, the form itself became a most effective strategy of political control and ideological manipulation.

## POETIC TEXTS AND THE LITERARY INQUISITION

Following the practice of the Ming, the Manchu state prioritized the examination essay over belletristic writing in its prescribed agenda for the literati. In chapter 3 of *The Scholars*, Zhou Jin, the education commissioner, reprimands a young candidate who has showed some liking for poetic composition: "Since the emperor attaches importance to essays, why should you bring up the poems of the Han and Tang dynasties?" He denigrates the poetic composition as "heterodox studies" (*zalan*) while upholding the practice of the examination essay as the "real work" (*zhengwu*) (*RLWS* 36–37; *Scholars* 36). To indicate the extent to which that agenda was embraced by the educated gentry, the novel presents a *bagu* fanatic: Qu Xianfu's wife, Miss Lu (Lu Xiaojie). She faithfully follows her father's exhortation that mastery of the skills in the eight-legged essay writing is a prerequisite for any other genres of literary composition, even though as a woman she clearly will win no official appointment with her assiduous practice of the essay.[79] When Qu Xianfu is asked to demonstrate his skills with the eight-legged essay, he disappoints both his wife and father-in-law with two compositions that bear more resemblance to poetry than examination writing (*RLWS* 140–41; *Scholars* 142–44). For Ma Chunshang, the eight-legged essay is a pure form of writing that should not be adulterated with any "poetical sensibility" (*cifu qi*), which "is likely to have a bad influence on later scholars" (*RLWS* 166; *Scholars* 172). To be sure, much of this is based on genre considerations, but clearly the reverence for the eight-legged essay depicted in the novel demonstrates the impact of the state policy on the literary taste of the day: the political value of the form was translated into an aesthetic value.

Yet the imperial state's focus on the examination essay does not mean it treated other sectors of textual culture with a laissez-faire attitude. In *The Scholars*, poetic composition, while not quite as prominent and privileged as examination writing, is another important cultural activity for the literati, particularly those who ostensibly have given up their aspirations for a bureaucratic career. It is thus another contact zone between the literati and the state. The amateur poets in the novel, Jing Lanjiang, Zhao Xuezhai, and others, are depicted as a bunch of shams who "do not have rank or wealth and therefore envy others who do," as the commentator of the Woxian Caotang edition put it.[80] In chapter 18, Zhi Jianfeng, a merchant and self-proclaimed poet, almost gets arrested by the patrolling police for gesticulating on the street and wearing a scholar's hat in his drunkenness. Apart from that brief episode, the state power seems to leave these poets alone in their self-deluded dream for fame and prestige. That, however, is not true, for looming largely in the background is the turbulence surrounding the manuscript copy of a collection of poems by Gao Qi (1336–74), an early Ming scholar-official who was executed by Emperor Hongwu allegedly for his seditious writings.

Several characters in the novel are involved in the turmoil centered on Gao Qi's writings. The manuscript is initially in the possession of Wang Hui, a treasonous official who is on the run as a fugitive after the rebellion he has been implicated in is put down. From the perspective of the imperial state, that the texts originally belonged to a rebel may have augmented their subversive power. Indeed, they may appear to be an even more dangerous and enduring menace than the rebellion itself, for the court continues to hunt them down long after its military triumph over the revolt. When Qu Xianfu receives the manuscript in a casket from Wang Hui, he puts it in print, setting his own name on it as editor. After winning some fame for him initially, Qu's ownership of the manuscript quickly becomes a liability. His mutinous servant blackmails him by threatening to use the casket for the manuscript as evidence for Qu's tie to Wang Hui. Qu is in real trouble until Ma Chunshang comes to his rescue by redeeming the casket with the royalties on his anthologies of model eight-legged essays. That, however, does not end the case, which resurfaces in chapter 35. On his way to Beijing for an audience with the emperor, Zhuang Shaoguang meets Lu Xinhou, a young scholar who has managed to collect works of all famous writers of the Ming dynasty, including those by Gao Qi. To his new friend Zhuang offers this cautionary advice: "Your interest in old books shows your respect for learning, sir. But it is better to have nothing to do with forbidden books. Although there is nothing treasonable in the writings of Gao Qingqiu [i.e. Gao Qi], since Emperor Hongwu took a dislike to him and his works are now banned, I would advise you not to read them" (*RLWS* 408; *Scholars* 442). Zhuang Shaoguang is obviously seasoned enough to know that the state power is too formidable for a scholar to mess with. Sure enough, Lu Xinhou is arrested while paying a visit to Zhuang in Nanjing, and Zhuang has to use his newly gained influence with some dignitaries in Beijing to get his friend released.

What happens in the novel surrounding Gao Qi's writings, according to a Qing critic, may allude to the case of Dai Mingshi, who was executed by Emperor Kangxi in 1713.[81] A closer parallel, however, may be the traumatic experience of Wu Jingzi's friend Liu Zhu. In 1733, Liu, while visiting Cheng Tingzuo, was wrongly accused of carrying a forbidden book and consequently tortured and imprisoned for seven years.[82] Yet, as the Gao Qi case in the novel involves multiple characters and different locales, it makes more sense to consider it not so much as an allusion to any specific case but rather as an epitome of the rampant literary inquisition during the early half of the eighteenth century in general. That conjecture is reasonable, because literary inquisition, following the Dai Mingshi case in the late Kangxi reign, became even more intensified during the Yongzheng period.[83]

The case of Gao Qi's poetic manuscript, therefore, reflects the political climate of Wu Jingzi's time. For those amateur poets in the novel, it represents a potential disaster lurking in the background, and renders their fantasies about fame and prestige all the more ludicrous. The thematic thread of poetic writing may appear extraneous to the topic of the examinations, which is obviously a major concern in much of the narrative. Yet, if one reads *The Scholars* as a fictional approach to the power relations between the literati and the imperial state, one may argue that the juxtaposition of examination writing and poetic writing in the novel is actually part of a masterful structural design, which encompasses writings in and out of the examination system as two major sectors of textual culture that are separate but related. Combined, they form a panoramic picture of the literati indulgence in a textual culture largely insulated from other aspects of social reality. In both sectors, "textual composition is taken as the stepping-stone for fame and rank" (*yi weizi wei gongming zhi jie*) as the commentator in the Qixingtang edition put it.[84]

## THE ENDEAVORS TO BREAK OUT OF THE TEXTUAL CULTURE

In contrast to most of their fellow scholars, the few "true Confucians" (*zhen ru*) are on a quest for a spiritual renewal of the literati. Du Shaoqing's proclamation to "attend to my own affairs" while turning down the invitation to take the examinations can be considered, in an enlarged context, a common manifesto of these high-minded scholars to seek a certain degree of autonomy. Among their *own* affairs, one of the most important is the ceremony in the Tai Bo temple. The selection of Tai Bo from among the many ancient sages is in itself significant, as there is no way to better express their determination to detach themselves from the imperial power than paying tribute to "the forefather to all eremites throughout the ages."[85] As a gesture to reject the bait of rank and fame from the state, the ceremony itself reverberates with the ancient sage's escape from court politics.

It is no longer a new topic in modern scholarship that Wu Jingzi may have received influence, especially via his friend Cheng Tingzuo, from Yan Yuan and Li Gong.[86] At the kernel of Yan-Li thought was a critical skepticism of the epistemological function of textual discourse without the proof and support from praxis. For Yan Yuan, the most crucial phase in the process of knowledge acquisition, as suggested by the name of his study Xizhai (Studio of Practice), was to "use the hands to actually do the thing" (*fanshou shizuo qi shi*).[87] Li Gong, while in his later years showing more interest in textual studies than Yan, agreed with his master that "the ancients comprehended the principle by the means of facts and actions [*shishi*] rather than empty words [*kongwen*]."⁸⁸ "Without seeing in your own eyes and trying it in person," he asked rhetorically, "how can you tell what truth is?"⁸⁹ Yan and Li thus pointed to a new direction for intellectual and moral cultivation, superseding textual scholarship with "substantial learning" (*shixue*), which included, in particular, the practice of ritual, music, martial training, and farming (*li yue bing nong*).⁹⁰ One may therefore consider the ritual in the Tai Bo temple a major attempt by the "true Confucians" to extricate themselves from the "empty words" on paper and start "actually doing the thing." It is in that spirit that Chi Hengshan, upon proposing the Tai Bo project to Du Shaoqing, complains about many of their contemporaries' indulgence in the *bagu* composition and poetic writing while neglecting the practice of ritual and music. Chi continues to justify his proposal to build the Tai Bo temple by saying: "There is not a single temple [in Nanjing] dedicated to him, though you find temples to the God of Literature (Wenchang Miao) and God Guan (Guandi Miao) everywhere" (*RLWS* 393; *Scholars* 425, translation modified). Clearly, Chi opposes Tai Bo to the two deities that are popularly believed to be guardians of literature and writing.

The Tai Bo ceremony thus signifies the effort of the "true Confucians" to detach themselves from the imperial power on two different but related levels. By honoring Tai Bo, they openly identify with the ancient sage who walked away from the court to promote the welfare of the people in the culturally backward south, demonstrating more loyalty to *tianxia* than the state. In the meantime, the practice of the ritual marks their tentative endeavor to break out of a textual culture that the imperial power manipulates with the lure of examination degrees on one hand and the threat of literary inquisition on the other. Finally, Du Shaoqing and his friends are able to fulfill their wish to "attend to their own affairs." Indeed, starting with chapter 31, where scholars begin the congregation in Nanjing that eventually leads to the Tai Bo ceremony, the narrative seems to shift its focus away from textual culture, which is clearly in the spotlight in the early portions of the novel.⁹¹ Right after the Tai Bo ritual in chapter 37 a narrative stretch about a series of *actions* begins. In chapter 38, Guo Tieshan embarks on an arduous trek in search of his long-missing father, punctuated by Guo's hazardous encounters with monsters and bandits. The journey is depicted clearly as a ritualized expression of filial devotion. Chapter 39 tells about Xiao Yunxian's martial feat and Marshal

Ping's (Ping Shaobao) successful campaign against the mutinous tribesmen. In chapter 40, Xiao Yunxian, as both a local administrator and a garrison commander, leads the efforts in constructing farmland and irrigation systems and building new schools. The chapter also features a ceremony to worship the God of Agriculture (Xiannong). The narrative interest in actions continues in chapter 43, which is about General Tang's (Tang Zongzhen) suppression of the Miao tribesmen's rebellion. Clearly, this portion of the novel is devoted to the practice of ritual, music, martial training, and farming.

The story of Shen Qiongzhi, in chapters 40 and 41, may appear to be a digression. A young woman running away from an arranged marriage to a salt merchant, Shen commands much admiration from the reader for her courage and defiance. In the meantime, however, some of her behaviors—such as stealing the gold and silver utensils from the merchant's house in a manner reminiscent of the bandit hero Lu Zhishen in *Water Margin* and selling poems openly on the streets of Nanjing—may reveal, in Stephen Roddy's words, "a willingness to flaunt standards of female propriety."[92] In that regard her story may seem to undercut the theme of reviving the practice of ritual. Yet, upon a closer examination, the story of the woman escaping her imposed status as a concubine parallels the scholars' endeavor to break away from servitude to the imperial power. Both Shen Qiongzhi and the scholars have to get out of their confinement—a boudoir for the woman and closed studios for the scholars—to seek liberation in the larger world. Even the story of the dissipated Tang brothers in chapter 42 may not be completely irrelevant to the other chapters in this stretch. As the Tangs are dandies who speak of their experience in the examinations while visiting prostitutes, they in a way signify the tarnished and almost morbid examination culture that contrasts sharply with the dynamic and robust world of actions presented elsewhere in this part of the novel.

## IS TEXTUAL CULTURE AN IMPENETRABLE PRISON HOUSE?

To be sure, the major characters involved in the later portion of the novel—Guo Tieshan, Xiao Yunxian, Marshal Ping, and General Tang—are most likely educated men but not necessarily scholars by profession. Yet they seem to sustain the effort that the scholars themselves have initiated at the Tai Bo ceremony: to renounce the world of texts that has become corrupted by rank and fame and to revive true Confucian ethics in praxis. However, the result, as it becomes known before long, is highly paradoxical. The Tai Bo ceremony is obviously a big success and goes a long way in restoring the forgotten tradition of ritual practice, as evidenced by the reaction of the old Nanjing natives among the audience who are enthralled by the event, which they have never before witnessed (*RLWS* 437; *Scholars* 473). Yet the narration of the ritual in chapter 37, which has long been considered as the climax of the novel, may appear instead "singularly anticlimactic," as a Western scholar has put it.[93] It is unbearably tedious and monotonous, in contrast to the enthusiastic reception of the ceremony itself by the audience. Indeed, what one reads in chapter 37, "a bald summary of the proceedings," may well be the same thing as the program of the ceremony (*yizhudan*) and order of the processions (*zhishidan*) that Wang Yuhui reads in chapter 48 on the dust-covered wall, when he visits the ruined Tai Bo temple years later (*RLWS* 558; *Scholars* 607).[94] As Shang Wei has pointed out with much insight, the account of the Tai Bo ceremony, which may be based on some Confucian ritual manual, ends up becoming another copy of that manual.[95] It is a symbolic moment when the significance of the ritual practice becomes cancelled: if the ritual was an endeavor by the scholars to break out of the world of texts, they have instead come full circle and arrived in exactly the same place from where they departed. In this aspect, the novel again shows a strong affinity with *Water Margin*, where the rebels eventually capitulate to the imperial court and thus cause no change to the social order.[96] However, by dramatizing the futility of the literati's efforts to extricate themselves from the textual swamp, the novelist also bestows a certain amount of tragic heroism on such efforts.

One character that embodies this retrogression to texts is Xiao Yunxian, who ironically also exemplifies the ideal of *li yue bing nong* more fully than anyone else. The district under Xiao's governance enjoys harmony and prosperity on a scale that contrasts sharply with the poverty and chaos that Zhuang Shaoguang witnesses elsewhere on his way to the capital. Ironically, however, in the schools that Xiao has established, children are not taught how to practice *li yue bing nong*, but how to write well formulated *bagu* essays. Just like the other men of success and abilities such as Marshal Ping and General Tang, Xiao Yunxian is deprived by the imperial state of the rewards he fully deserves. When Xiao meets Wu Shu in chapter 40, he expresses his admiration for Wu's poems, and then requests that the scholar honor his achievements in writing so that they "will not be forgotten." In response, Wu promises to "confer immortality" on Xiao's adventures and "rescue them from oblivion" (*RLWS* 469; *Scholars* 507–8). In the end, Xiao Yunxian, the disillusioned man of action, has to seek shelter in written words.

In Wang Yuhui the inertia of textual culture finds a most profound expression. As an old licentiate, Wang obviously has given up any hope for an official appointment. Taking everything in the Cheng-Zhu doctrine as *literally* true, he is another "pedantic scholar" (*shudaizi*), not unlike the other aged licentiate Ni Shuangfeng in chapter 25, whose decades of study of the "lifeless dogma" (*sishu*) leads him to destitution. However, unlike Ni who turns to mending musical instruments for a livelihood, Wang remains steadfast in his pursuit of the textual truth. Devoting his time to compiling three books, "one on ceremony, one on etymology, and one on country etiquette" (*RLWS* 551; *Scholars* 599), he is, as some modern critics call him, the most "religious" believer of ritual propriety in *The Scholars*.[97] Wang's third daughter is apparently his most faithful disciple. As the young widow kills herself in order to join her husband in the grave, Wang, while saddened, hails her suicide as a glorious deed that will enable her name "to be recorded in history" (*RLWS* 553; *Scholars* 601). Reprimanding his grief-stricken wife for being a "silly old woman," Wang insists that their daughter has died a most proper death for a good *timu*. The Chinese word *timu*, in its rich polysemy, can mean "cause" as well as "topic" or "subject matter" for a textual composition. That semantic ambiguity is most meaningful here, as the daughter dies for a "good cause" which in turn becomes a "good topic" for books such as her father's that preach ritual propriety. Wang Yuhui's ethical conviction, in Shang Wei's words, is "based on a simple maxim: Select a rubric for yourself so that others can write you into the sacred texts of history."[98] It is not coincidental that his books are completed about the same time as his daughter dies. It can be said that they are written in both the old licentiate's ink and the young woman's blood. The simultaneous death of a human life and birth of the new writings mark an astounding moment of the old scholar's return to the world of texts.

The young widow's death eventually wins recognition from the government. On an official decree, a shrine is made and a sacrificial ceremony conducted in her honor. Again, with the ritual properly practiced, Wang Yuhui's thought turns to his writings, as he leaves home trying to find a printing firm for his manuscripts. On his way to visit a friend, Wang takes a tour of Suzhou, and, most interestingly, the narrative of his tour is remarkably similar to Ma Chunshang's tour of West Lake in chapter 14. Like Ma, Wang's sense of moral propriety is shaken while out sightseeing. While Ma Chunshang receives a moral "recharge" by kowtowing to the inscription of a past emperor, Wang Yuhui pays a visit to the Tai Bo temple to seek spiritual sustenance after his arrival in Nanjing. In the dust-covered text of the ritual program posted on the dilapidated wall, Wang Yuhui perhaps sees the future of his own ritual manuals before they are even in print: the moral contents of the writings will be subjected to oblivion and the texts will be reduced to mere empty words.

Again, the parallel between Wang Yuhui and Ma Chunshang, compilers of ritual manuals and *bagu* anthologies respectively, is part of a larger design to demonstrate the quandary for the literati. For all their endeavors to lift themselves out of a textual culture that is manipulated by political power and sullied by the avarice for rank and fame, they end up being ensnared even more deeply. Wang Yuhui may be a devoted advocate of ritual propriety, but in the final analysis, he is just another Ma Chunshang, offering new additions to an already congested realm of texts that is sealed off from the world of praxis. Not surprisingly, the participants of the Tai Bo ceremony disperse in different directions soon after the event. Several of them leave for official positions in Beijing, even Chi Hengshan, the principal organizer of the event. As ritual now retreats from real-life practice back to the form of textual dogma, it loses much of its moral efficacy.

## A NEW GENERATION OF EDUCATED MEN

The experiment with *li yue bing nong* thus ends in failure. In their quest for an identity independent of the imperial state, the literati do not appear to be any more effective than Sun Wukong's attempt to somersault out of the Buddha's palm. The opening paragraph of chapter 55, for good reason, expresses a somber sense of futility and helplessness:

> By the twenty-third year of the Wanli period, all the well-known scholars had disappeared from Nanjing. Of Dr. Yu's generation, some were old, some had died, some had gone far away, and some had closed their doors and paid no attention to affairs outside. Pleasure haunts and taverns were no longer frequented by men of talent, and honest men no longer occupied themselves with ceremony or letters. As far as scholarship was concerned, all who passed the examinations were considered brilliant and all who failed fools. And as for liberality, the rich indulged on ostentatious gestures while the poor were forced to seem shabby. You might have the genius of Li Bai or Du Fu and the moral worth of Yan Hui or Zeng Shen, but no one would ask your advice. So at coming of age ceremonies, marriages, funerals or sacrifices in big families and in the halls of the local gentry, nothing was discussed but promotions, transfers and recalls in the official world. And all impecunious scholars did was to try by various tricks to find favor with the examiners. (*RLWS* 820; *Scholars* 676)

The struggle of Yu Yude, Du Shaoqing, and their friends has caused little change, as the values in the literati culture continue to be dictated by the imperial state with its ways of distributing rank and fame. Yet the quest for liberation from imperial servitude does not end. The four "extraordinary figures" (*qiren*) who make their debut at the very end of the novel herald a new phase in the evolution of the relationship between the state and the educated elite.

Each of these four men excels in one of the four accomplishments traditionally associated with literati cultural cultivation: zither (*qin*), chess (*qi*), calligraphy (*shu*), and painting (*hua*). Apparently, they are well educated and culturally cultivated, but they all refuse to "use written words as stepping-stones to fame and rank." Instead, by taking up mundane occupations, they become true owners of their knowledge and skills and are able to live a simple but dignified life without having to curry to the whims of political authorities. From the very end of the novel they resonate with Wang Mian, with whom the novel begins. Indeed, they are the spiritual heirs of Wang Mian—who is portrayed in the novel more as a painter than a man of textual learning—and they are also successors to the failed cause of scholars of the older generation in Nanjing. Jing Yuan, a vocal tailor and skilled zitherist, may be taken as the spokesman of the quartet, and what he says in justifying his vocational commitment is strongly reminiscent of Du Shaoqing's pronounced wish to "attend to my own affairs": "I am not disgracing my studies by tailoring. Those college scholars don't look at things the way we do. They would never be friends with us. As it is, I make six or seven silver cents a day; and when I've eaten my fill, if I want to strum my zither or do some writing, there's nobody to stop me. I don't want to be rich or noble, or to make up to any man. Isn't it pleasant to be one's own master like this?" (*RLWS* 628; *Scholars* 684). That these four men correspond neatly to the four arts in literati culture is obviously intended to be symbolic. Rather than taking them as individual hermits, it makes more sense to consider them representatives of a new generation of intellectuals that the novel invokes. With literacy overflowing the examinations into other cultural spheres, the social disparity between the educated elite and the common "townsfolk" (*shijing ximin*) was narrowing. For these newcomers, government office, the ultimate goal of a traditional scholar's prolonged toil in textual studies, is no longer the only acceptable vocational choice. By steering away from textual learning, the traditional avenue to fame and prestige, they are less susceptible to political manipulation and at least one step closer to becoming their own masters, to echo Jing Yuan's words. Meanwhile, as suggested by their proficiency in *qin, qi, shu,* and *hua,* which is clearly a synecdoche for their cultural competence, they make meaningful contributions to social growth and cultural enrichment. Thus these four "extraordinary figures" are truly the ones that "link the past with the future" (*shuwang silai*), as the opening couplet of the chapter has it.

CHAPTER 5

# The Stone in *Dream of the Red Chamber*

## *Unfit to Repair the Azure Sky*

Among premodern Chinese fiction writers, perhaps nobody had more traumatic memories of the erratic power of the imperial state than Cao Xueqin (ca. 1715–64), author of *Dream of the Red Chamber* (Honglou meng). The splendid edifice of the Cao family, which once had enjoyed untouchable prestige and prosperity under the blessing of Emperor Kangxi, was leveled to debris under the wrath of Emperor Yongzheng. Cao Xueqing, who lived for most of his adult life under the Qianlong reign, was so poverty-stricken that he eventually had to rely on financial help from friends.[1] However, in *Dream of the Red Chamber,* especially in the depiction of the protagonist Jia Baoyu, there is a concern that goes far beyond any personal level. Indeed, further enriching the novel's remarkable polysemy is a careful rethinking of the historical role of the literati that had long been dictated in the teachings of the *daotong*.

### DREAM OF THE RED CHAMBER AND THE QIANLONG REIGN

When Emperor Qianlong ascended the throne in 1735, he took over a prosperous empire, and the Han intellectual gentry had largely been tamed by his shrewd imperial grandfather and father. Elated with the prospect of achieving even greater heights during his reign, Qianlong did not conceal his aspiration to have his name ranked with the ancient Three Generations (*san dai*) of sage kings, Yao, Shun, and Yu. Two months after his inauguration, he proclaimed complacently: "The order of the Three Generations will definitely be restored, and the *dao* of Yao and Shun will definitely be practiced."[2] Following that, top civil officials vied with each other acclaiming the advent of the new "sage king." In 1745, for instance, Grand Councilor O-erh-tai sang the praise of the young emperor in a memorial to the throne: "Your Majesty concentrates on the constancy and adheres to the golden mean [*jing yi zhi zhong*], and venerated the orthodox learning. He has unified the minds of all people under heaven [*yi tianxia zhi renxin*]. . . . Both the heavenly virtue and the kingly way are fully embodied here."[3] A few months later, Zhang Tingyu (1672–1755), another Grand Councilor, joined O-erh-tai in presenting this eulogy: "Your Majesty emulates Yao and Shun and has far surpassed Emperor Taizong of the Tang."[4]

Indeed, following an extended period of prosperity in the empire, Qianlong was apparently in a better position than his predecessors to speak of a successful return to the glory of the Three Generations, which was characterized by a seamless harmony between the *dao* and political power. However, what happened in 1768 ruthlessly proved Qianlong's ambition completely unviable. As rumors about mysterious soulstealers sinisterly hovered across several provinces, the emperor found himself at constant odds with his civil bureaucracy on local levels. He first coerced doubtful local officials into taking hard-line actions on the sorcery cases, and then, after the cases turned out to be overblown, cast all the blame on his provincial officials. Qianlong took advantage of the crisis and quickly turned it into an opportunity to terrorize the potentially intractable intellectual elite. To borrow Philip Kuhn's succinct words about the emperor's vermilion rescripts on officials' missives, "The *context* . . . was the prosecution of sorcerers, but the *content* was the control of bureaucrats."[5]

Although this sorcery crisis took place a few years after Cao Xueqin's death, it was symptomatic of a long-term disease that had started much earlier, a disease in the relationship between what Kuhn calls the ruler's "arbitrary power" and the bureaucracy's "routine power." Concluding his book on the sorcery scare, Kuhn wonders on the possibility for Qianlong's civil officials to curb the ruler's arbitrary power "by invoking a superior code under which all human governments might be judged": "To do so required that they regard themselves as something more than servants of a particular regime. Such self-confidence could persist only among men who believed themselves to be certified carriers of a cultural tradition. In late imperial politics, such gumption was scarce enough, even at the highest levels of ministerial power."⁶ In the context of imperial China, that "cultural tradition" whose "superior code" could possibly be invoked to restrain imperial power was precisely the *daotong*. However, the *daotong* had, by Qianlong's time, lost its last carriers to intimidation from state power. Indeed, to indicate the intensity of the intimidation, there were more cases of literary inquisition during the Qianlong reign than those of the Kangxi and Yongzheng periods put together. Thus, when Qianlong spoke of a return to the Three Generations, he did not think of any harmonious coalescence of the *zhengtong* and *daotong* but simply muffling the voice of the latter. The damage to the *daotong* was severe: if the spirit to curb state power had been the soul of the *daotong*, it had now nearly lost its soul and started to wilt.⁷

Against this sociopolitical backdrop, Jia Baoyu's famous aversion to bureaucratic service in the novel is no surprise at all. Nor is his pungent sarcasm on "scholars dying demonstrating with the emperor and generals dying fighting for the empire" (*wen si jian wu si zhan*) difficult to understand.⁸ Indeed, to support this contextual reading of fiction, one finds this indifference toward government service not unique to Jia Baoyu but shared by main characters in other major novels of the Qianlong period. Tan Shaowen in Li Lüyuan's (1707–90) *Warning Light for the Wrong Path* (Qi lu deng), for instance, is a profligate son from a literati family, who obstinately disregards his father's admonitions to study for the examinations. After his father's death, he indulges in sensual pleasures to the complete negligence of his obligation for the state and family, until he finally reforms. Likewise, Wen Ruyu, son of a governor-general in Li Baichuan's (ca. 1720–71) *Trace of the Immortals on a Green Land* (Lüye xianzong), is a good-for-nothing dandy who dissipates the family's wealth in the pleasure quarters, ignoring his father's constant urges to prepare for officialdom. After a dream in which he is made a high-ranking official and the emperor's son-in-law, he becomes totally disillusioned with official service and converts to Daoism.

In real life, however, most literati of the Qianlong period who had lost interest in government service did not just idle away their time as the fictional characters Tan Shaowen and Wen Ruyu. Indeed, a scholar's decision to enter a profession outside civil officialdom was often difficult and painful. As the ultimate distributor of social capital and material benefits, the imperial state was able to make the pursuit of an examination degree the *normal* mode of behavior for the literati. Valorized by the political power, the practices within the institution of official selection were regularized and routinized. When a scholar removed himself from that institution and took on a new profession, he became, in the contemporary Chinese scholar Wang Xuetai's vocabulary, a *tuoxuren,* or a breakaway from the established social order.[9] By doing so, he was stepping out of a familiar territory and onto an uncharted path strewn with perils and hardships. Yet, the unprecedented level of economic development and commercialization in the Qianlong period made it relatively easy for scholars to find other means of livelihood in different cultural fields. If in previous times most scholars had been forced to find other ways to make a living after their examination failures, now many of them voluntarily turned away from government service to embrace other professions.[10] "There was an expanded definition of what a respectable career was," as Susan Naquin and Evelyn Rawski observe on the situation for eighteenth-century literati. "High degrees and government office, becoming so difficult to obtain, were no longer seen as the only acceptable form of achievement."[11] As the *daotong* declined, it was no longer the cohesive agent it had been to bind the fate of the intellectual gentry to that of the state. Yet, if the literati's replacement in society was in a way their reaction to the much weakened status of the *daotong,* it was also made possible by the changed economic conditions.

What happens at the closure of *The Scholars* reflects this phenomenon of the High Qing period: the four "extraordinary figures," all well educated, make adequate living in their mundane professions far removed from government service. Xu Ke's (1869–1928) *Classified Anecdotes of the Qing Dynasty* (Qing bai lei chao) contains numerous accounts of Qing scholars, including many of the Qianlong period, who migrated to different cultural realms and became physicians, bibliophiles, painters, calligraphers, musicians, merchants, and even fortune-tellers.[12] Another important profession was legal counseling, as some of the scholars became law specialists or private advisers to officials.[13] One special cultural role that some scholars would adopt outside officialdom was fiction writing. Just like elsewhere in literati culture, fiction writing was an area dominated by "breakaways" from the mainstream political life regulated by the imperial power. Different from his counterparts in other cultural realms, however, a fiction writer could recapture, in fictional language, a scholar's experience of cultural marginalization and adjustment of vocational choices. Since his own chosen profession is fiction writing, fiction can therefore become intensely reflexive in presenting the making of a fiction writer.

In *Dream of the Red Chamber,* a mythic stone is deemed as "talentless" and dismissed from a goddess's project of heaven reconstruction. After that it takes a human incarnation, and finally resumes its form as a supernatural stone with a narrative of its human experience inscribed on its surface. This narrative frame of the novel may be interpreted as an account of the transition from failed "official-making" to successful "fiction-making." In this reading, Jia Baoyu is remarkably akin to the four "extraordinary figures" in *The Scholars*. Going one step further, however, *Dream of the Red Chamber* dramatizes all the emotions and commotions involved in the process of a young literatus's repudiation of the examinations and officialdom. Through Baoyu's vocational decision, the novel calls into question one of the time-honored precepts in the *daotong* tradition, namely, the political commitment to government service, which is symbolized in the novel with the master trope of "mending heaven" (*butian*).

## SIGNIFICANCE OF THE "FANLI" STATEMENT

The *jiaxu* (1754) manuscript copy of *Honglou meng,* the earliest-known version of the novel, carries a prefatory piece titled "Fanli" (Statement of general principles), possibly written by one of the novel's earliest commentators.[14] The statement contains a long passage, allegedly by the novelist Cao Xueqin himself:

> Having made an utter failure of my life, I found myself one day, in the midst of my poverty and wretchedness, thinking about the female companions of my youth. As I went over them one by one, examining and comparing them in my mind's eye, it suddenly came over me that those slips of girls—which is all they were then—were in every way, both morally and intellectually, superior to the "grave and mustachioed signior"

I am now supposed to have become. The realization brought with it an overpowering sense of shame and remorse, and for a while I was plunged in the deepest despair. There and then I resolved to make a record of all the recollections of those days I could muster—those golden days when I dressed in silk and ate delicately, when we still nestled in the protecting shadow of the Ancestors and Heaven still smiled on us. I resolved to tell the world how, in defiance of all my family's attempts to bring me up properly and all the warnings and advice of my friends, I had brought myself to this present wretched state, in which, having frittered away half a lifetime, I find myself without a single skill with which I could earn a decent living. I resolved that, however unsightly my own shortcomings might be, I must not, for the sake of keeping them hid, allow those wonderful girls to pass into oblivion without a memorial. . . . I might lack learning and literary aptitude, but what was to prevent me from turning it all into a story and writing it in the vernacular? In this way the memorial to my beloved girls could at one and the same time serve as a source of harmless entertainment and as a warning to those who were in the same predicament as myself but who were still in need of awakening. (*HLM* 1:1; *SS* 1:20)

In the subsequent versions of the novel, starting with the slightly later *gengchen* (1760) manuscript copy, part of the "Fanli," including the passage here, is incorporated into the novel proper and becomes the beginning paragraph of the opening chapter.[15] As the statement has since become such a crucial part of the work, one would think that Cao Xueqin himself "should have penned just one such preface," as Wai-yee Li has suggested.[16]

Most significantly, this long passage, with its first-person self-reference, presents a penitent and apologetic novelist whose sense of shame over his dissipated past motivated him to write about his female companions. That image, in turn, is reinforced elsewhere. In the *jiaxu* text, the "Fanli" is followed by a heptasyllabic poem that ends with these lines:

Each word looks like blood,
Ten years' toil was extraordinary.
(*Zizi kanlai jieshi xue, shinian xinku bu xunchang.*)[17]

Consistent with it, there is another short poem in the opening chapter, a pentasyllabic one, which was retained in all subsequent versions of the novel:

> Pages full of idle words
> Penned with hot and bitter tears:
> All men call the author fool
> None his secret message hears.
> (*HLM* 1:4; *SS* 1:51)

This portrayal of a poignant novelist is also corroborated by the words of the novel's earliest commentators, especially Red Inkstone (Zhiyanzhai). In a marginal note, Red Inkstone emotionally laments Cao Xueqin's premature death: "Only the one who knew [the secret message] could shed his bitter tears with which to write this book [*ku cheng ci shu*]. On the New Year's Eve of the year of *renwu*, Xueqin departed this world after having exhausted his tears, leaving his book unfinished. I wept so much for Xueqin that my tears became nearly exhausted as well."[18] Obviously, such textual reverberations in the opening chapter add to the significance of the long passage in the "Fanli." Of course one should not be so credulous as to follow some of the 20th-century Chinese Redologists in equating the novelist constructed in the "Fanli" with Cao Xueqin, regardless of whether the long quote was indeed penned by Cao himself.[19] Yet one has to agree that this fictionalized novelist at the beginning of the narrative imposes an additional layer of signification on the fictional text. If the "Fanli" offers a sketch of a novelist's life and delineates the process of his conversion to fiction writing, in what ways does it bear on the meanings of the narrative action and the portrayal of the characters in the novel, especially Jia Baoyu?

## "UNFIT TO REPAIR THE AZURE SKY": BAOYU, THE STONE, AND THE FICTIONALIZED NOVELIST

In chapter 34, after Jia Baoyu is severely thrashed by his father Jia Zheng, the girls in the Great Prospect Garden (Daguanyuan) come to show their deep concern and shed their tears. Their expressions of affection not only alleviate Baoyu's pains but also set him to fantasizing about their even deeper grief at the time of his death. In an almost ecstatic inner monologue,

Baoyu calls that imagined moment a great accolade for which "the loss of a life's ambitions would be a small price to pay" (*HLM* 2:402; *SS* 2:156). It is a moment similar to the one in chapter 36, when Baoyu again fantasizes the end of his life, with his dead body floating on a river formed by the tears of his beloved girls (*HLM* 2:436; *SS* 2:206). To him, to die as a martyr of love would be much more glorious than to die as a martyr of the imperial state, and he scornfully calls those who die remonstrating with the emperor or fighting on the battlefield "whiskered idiots" (*xumei zhuowu*).

Now, as Xue Baochai, Baoyu's female cousin and future wife, inquires about the cause of the beating, the answer of Baoyu's maid Aroma (Hua Xiren) may implicate Baochai's uncouth brother Xue Pan. To dissolve the embarrassment for Baochai, Baoyu quickly interrupts Aroma's words and dismisses that suggestion as groundless. Already badly shaken at the sight of Baoyu's injuries, Baochai is now deeply touched by the boy's gentle care and thoughtfulness: "'What delicacy of feeling!' she thought, '—after so terrible a beating and in spite of all the pain, to be still able to worry about the possibility of someone else's being offended! If only you could apply some of that thoughtfulness to the more important things of life, my friend, you would make my Uncle so happy; and then perhaps these awful things would never happen . . .'" (*HLM* 2:402; *SS* 2:156–57). Obviously, what Baoyu calls "a life's ambitions" (*yisheng shiye*) is perfectly synonymous with what Baochai terms "the more important things of life." The Chinese phrase Baochai uses here, *waitou dashi*, literally means "the big things outside," which of course refers to the preparation for an official career and participation in political affairs as opposed to matters in domestic life.

The celebrated dictum *qi jia, zhi guo, ping tianxia* underscores the Confucian family-society analogy, regarding the regulation of the family (*qi jia*) as the initial stage in a scholar's progression toward his ultimate goal, *ping tianxia*. The latter phrase, which literally means "to smooth the world under heaven," comes close to suggesting an act of cosmic refurbishment: the surface of the world was rough and therefore needed to be smoothed out. Little wonder that, for the Confucian ideal of government service, the myth of Nüwa's cosmic re-creation lent itself as an apt metaphor. An official's meritorious service to the imperial state was thus often likened to the goddess's exploit of *butian*, patching the breakage of heaven.[20] By the same token, the state's recruitment of talented scholars into officialdom, arguably the most crucial institutional measure to buttress the imperial rule, was also seen as analogous to the mythic act of cosmic reconstruction. That analogy is registered, for instance, in these lines by the eleventh-century poet Huang Tingjian (1045–1106):

> The imperial court nowadays recruits only Confucian scholars
> Who are made into hands mending the heaven with five[-colored] stones.[21]

In the outer frame in *Dream of the Red Chamber,* or the "over-narrative" as Henry Y. H. Zhao calls it, Nüwa uses thirty-six thousand and five hundred blocks of stone in her project of rebuilding the sky.[22] She rejects an extra stone block as unworthy, abandoning it at the foot of the mountain called Qinggeng Feng. The Stone "became filled with shame and resentment and passed its days in sorrow and lamentation" (*HLM* 1:2; *SS* 1:47). One does not have to be a meticulous reader to notice the parallel between the abandoned Stone and the fictionalized novelist in the "Fanli": both feel shame and humiliation for having failed to achieve something important. What is more, both turn to something ostensibly less significant as an alternative, namely, fiction making: while the novelist in the "Fanli" takes to "turning [his experience] into a story and writing it in the vernacular," the Stone travels to the mundane world and comes back with a narrative about its human experience inscribed on its surface. In light of this parallel, the tale of the mythic Stone can be considered a dramatization of the experience of the fictionalized novelist, his conversion to fiction writing after "a life's ambitions" are stymied and thwarted. As stated in the "Fanli," the fictionalized novelist "uses what the Stone remembers/recollects/records [*shitou suo ji zhi shi*] as an analogy [*pi*] for himself."[23] The word *pi,* which denotes the compatibility and comparability between humans and things, is found at the heart of traditional Chinese moral philosophy and philosophy of language.[24] Used in the "Fanli," it sums up the nature of the relationship between the Stone, Baoyu, and the fictionalized novelist, a set of relationships built on metaphorical affinity.

The main body of *Dream of the Red Chamber* is of course a story about Jia Baoyu, the Stone's anthropomorphosis, and his female companions. Yet, as it is embedded in the narrative frame about the mythic Stone, it becomes not only the end product of the Stone's trip to the human world but also an account of that trip itself. Indeed that meaningful ambiguity is well reflected in one of the alternative titles for the novel, *Story of the Stone* (Shitou ji), which can mean both "what is remembered/recollected/recorded *about* the Stone" and "what is remembered/recollected/recorded *by* the Stone," suggesting the Stone's dual status as the protagonist as well as the author.[25] The rich polysemy of the word *ji* felicitously reveals the stone fiction as being a "record" of the past experience based on recollections—a historian style of fiction making—as well as a "record" of the process of recording/recollecting itself. In that light, the "Story of the Stone" can be considered both the "memoir" that the novelist in the "Fanli" declares he will write and an account of the process in which that "memoir" comes to be written.

That the "Story of the Stone" is based on the activities of *ji* is also manifested in the quatrain that the Daoist priest Vanitas (Kongkong Daoren) spots on the back of the stone block after he has finished reading the inscribed narrative:

> Found unfit to repair the azure sky
> Long years a foolish mortal man was I.
> My life in both worlds on this stone is writ:
> Pray who will copy out and publish it?
> (*HLM* 1:2; *SS* 1:49)

That the inscribed narrative is about the Stone's "life in both worlds" (*shenqian shenhou shi*) reflects a Buddhist understanding of memory that serves as a crucial link in transmigration. Referring to the Stone's life in the mythic realm as well as his human incarnation as Baoyu, the phrase strongly suggests an act of reminiscing as the basis of fiction writing. Yet, in light of the parallel between the Stone and the fictionalized novelist, it may also be a hint of the two "incarnations" of the novelist himself, his "half a lifetime" that was "frittered away" (*bansheng liaodao*) and his later "ten years of toil" (*shinian xinku*) as a novelist. Thus it can be said that *Dream of the Red Chamber* is about his prenovelistic experience—"the female companions of my youth," "those golden days when I dressed in silk and ate delicately," and so on—as well as his novelistic experience of recollecting the past and then turning the remembrances into a fictional text.

What is most interesting about the quatrain, however, is the way it summarizes the Stone's trajectory of becoming a creator of fiction. Even after the completion of its fiction, the Stone still remembers (*ji*) that its mission of fiction making started with its humiliating rejection from the project of cosmic creation. The narrative text inscribed on its surface now testifies to its potency in a different type of creation—and indeed it is the record of that creation itself. The first line of the poem—"Found unfit to repair the azure sky"—can be considered a succinct expression of—in Red Inkstone's words—"the gist of the book" (*shu zhi benzhi*).[26] Throughout the novel, one sees a constant conflict between two different demands for talent (*cai*), from the imperial state on one side and the individual and aesthetic pursuits on the other. Since the Stone's fiction creation involves its "life in both worlds," that disgruntlement about being excluded from the project of mending the azure sky is inherited by Jia Baoyu, the Stone's human form.[27] In Baoyu, it is turned into a persistent antipathy toward bureaucratic service, of which *butian* is often evoked as a morally and politically charged metaphor. With either the Stone or Baoyu, it is against the hegemonic discourse of mending heaven that an interest in fiction making engenders and develops. As dramatized by the experiences of both the Stone and Baoyu—"my life in both worlds"—fiction creation as a cultural activity can be in itself not only an alternative but also an audacious challenge to what is considered to be the ethical and political norm for the literati.

Toward the end of the opening chapter and right before the Stone takes its debut in the human world, an interesting character, Jia Yucun, steps into the narrative spotlight. A poor student who has to lodge at a temple with no money for traveling to the capital for the examinations, Jia Yucun eventually manages to acquire a *jinshi* degree and find his way into officialdom. It is important to note that he is from "a family of scholars and bureaucrats" that "has fallen on bad times." Indeed, what he shares with Jia Baoyu is more than just their surname, as Baoyu is also born at "the time of twilight" (*moshi*) of his once influential and wealthy clan, even though he, unlike Yucun, does not have to live in poverty. What Yucun does—to "search for fame and success and restore the family's fortune"—is precisely what Baoyu is expected to do (*HLM* 1:7; *SS* 1:56, translation modified). Since all the other male members of the Jia clan "get more degenerate from one generation to the next," as the merchant Leng Zixing reports, Baoyu becomes the only hope to reinvigorate the family's stock, if he can—just as Yucun has done before him—succeed in the examinations (*HLM* 1:18; *SS* 1:74). The early debut of Jia Yucun in the novel is therefore meaningful: he is presented as a contrast to Baoyu even before the latter's advent, suggesting a career model Baoyu is expected to follow but instead relentlessly rejects.

What Baoyu refuses to be is another block of stone to be used in a project of family rebuilding. In chapter 5, when the spirits of Baoyu's ancestors, the Duke of Ningguo (Ningguo Gong) and the Duke of Rongguo (Rongguo Gong), meet Goddess Disenchantment (Jinghuan Xianzi), they reminisce about the past glory of their clan in serving the throne and express their wish that Baoyu become the one to prevent their family's further decline and degeneration:

> In the hundred years since the foundation of the present dynasty, several generations of our houses have distinguished themselves by their services to the Throne and have covered themselves with riches and honors; but now its stock of good fortunes has run out, and nothing can be done to replenish it. And though our descendants are many, not one of them is worthy to carry on the line. The only possible exception, our great-grandson Baoyu, has inherited a perverse, intractable nature and is eccentric and emotionally unstable. . . . Could you perhaps initiate him in the pleasures of the flesh and all that sort of thing in such a way as to shock the silliness out of him? In that way he might stand a chance of escaping some of the traps that people fall into and be able to devote himself single-mindedly to the serious things of life (*ruyu zhenglu*). (HLM 1:59; SS 137)

Thus Baoyu is expected to focus on the "serious things" (*zhenglu*), to enter service for the imperial state, which is seen as the only way to preserve the family's prestige and prosperity. Yet, as suggested by his behavior at his one-year birthday party—where the baby plays with "some women's things" (HLM 1:19; SS 1:76)—Baoyu seems to have an innate distaste for the "serious things," which may indeed have been carried over from his previous incarnation as the Stone that is dismissed from a business most "serious" of all.

That imperviousness to the "serious things" now prognosticates Baoyu's failure to carry on the family line "properly." In chapter 110, almost as an echo to what happened at that early birthday party, the dying Grandmother Jia gives her last admonition to Baoyu, her coddled grandson: "My boy, you must promise to do your very best for the family" (*ni yao zhengqi cai hao*) (*HLM* 4:1389; *SS* 5:192). Her last outcry summarizes her frustrated expectations as a grandmother as well as the unyielding obduracy of her grandson, now a married man, in resisting the call to familial duties. The Chinese term *zhengqi,* which means to win credit or earn respect for one's parents and ancestors, was often used in a close association with filial piety (*xiao*). Thus a son who failed to bring dignity and esteem to his parents by having a successful career would be stigmatized as *bu zhengqi,* which was almost synonymous with *bu xiao,* or not filial. Furthermore, with the Confucian tradition of regarding the family as an epitome of the nation and filial piety in a close affinity to political loyalty (*zhong*), the failure to fulfill one's duty to the family (*jia*) would be easily translated into negligence of service to the state (*guo*). As early as chapter 3, when Baoyu meets Daiyu for the first time, the novel offers a poem that contains these lines about the boy:

> Regrettably so many precious hours he wastes,
> For the family and the empire he will be of no use.
> (*HLM* 1:36; *SS* 1:102, translation modified)

That verdict remains just as pertinent toward the end of the novel, as clearly indicated by the grandmother's deathbed exhortation.

Thus one sees a triplex parallel between the fictionalized novelist in the "Fanli," the Stone in the mythic frame, and Jia Baoyu in the main body of the novel. While the fictionalized novelist in the "Fanli" has made an "utter failure" of the first half of his life, the Stone is found unqualified for heaven rebuilding, and Baoyu is considered to be of no use "for the family and the empire." There is therefore an intriguing resonance, not only between the mythic and human forms of the Stone but also between the Stone's "life in both worlds" and the fictionalized novelist. In each case, the "failure"—which is clearly in a moral and political sense—turns out to be the prelude to a success in fiction making.

## AESTHETIC WRITINGS VERSUS EXAMINATION LEARNING

Even more than Grandmother Jia, Baoyu's father Jia Zheng feels great anxiety over his son, who appears to be such a "doltish mule, to study disinclined" (*yuwan pa du wenzhang*) (*HLM* 1:36; *SS* 1:102). The austere father makes persistent efforts to pressure Baoyu into earnest preparations for the examinations, which, however, only further strains the father-son relationship. "No reader of *Hongloumeng* will dispute the contention," as Anthony Yu points out, "that one constant source of conflict between Bao-yu and his father lies in the boy's ostensible lack of self-discipline in his studies."[28] Indeed there should be no question about Baoyu's intelligence. While often depicted in the novel by such pejorative epithets as *chun* (stupid), *dai* (moronic), *sha* (silly), and *chi* (imbecile), Baoyu is, as the inscription on his talisman—"Precious Jade of Luminous Intelligence" (*tongling baoyu*)—suggests, a young man of remarkable acumen.[29] He of course fully understands the moral, political, and financial remunerations that success in the examinations will bring for himself and his family. His obstinate reluctance to study for the examinations therefore merits close scrutiny.

In addition to his instinctive aversion for the bureaucratic recruitment and the "career worms" like Jia Yucun, Baoyu has a particular dislike for the format of the examination writing, the eight-legged essay (*bagu wen*), which he considers "nothing more than a shoddy way of worming into a job" (*HLM* 3:1059; *SS* 4:52). Despite his father's dictatorial insistence that he should "thoroughly understand and learn by heart the whole Four Books" before anything else (*HLM* 1:107; *SS* 1:204), Baoyu demonstrates no impressive knowledge of the Confucian canon that formed the kernel of the examination curriculum. His vivacious and almost wayward disposition obviously is not conducive to the memorization-based learning essential for a success in the examinations. In chapter 73, hastily preparing for his father's possible checkup of his examination studies, Baoyu realizes in consternation that he can remember little of the classics:

> He found that there was little more than *The Great Learning*, *The Doctrine of the Mean* and the two halves of the *Analects* that he could be absolutely sure of. The first half of *Mencius* he knew reasonably well, but certainly not well enough to be able to carry on from any sentence given him at random. The second half was virtually *terra incognita*. Of the Five Classics he was fairly familiar with the *Poetry Classic* because he was frequently having to read bits of it in connection with his own versifying. Though far from word-perfect, he probably knew it well enough to scrape through a test. He could not remember any of the other classics at all; but fortunately his

father had so far never asked him to study them, so probably it would not matter. When it came to Old Style Prose, the case was rather different... he had not done any serious work on them. There was certainly no question of his being able to remember them. There was even less likelihood of his being able to pass muster on the Examination Essay. He had always detested this style of writing in any case. (*HLM* 3:935–36; *SS* 3:436–37)

On another occasion, when Baoyu makes himself work on the Four Books, he immediately experiences a "familiar sinking feeling," as all the textual details seem to "slip from his grasp." Helplessly, he says to himself: "Poems are easy, but I can't make head or tail of this stuff" (*HLM* 3:1060; *SS* 4:53–54). Despite his eventual acquisition of a *juren* degree following a spurt of intensive study urged by everyone around him, Baoyu is clearly aware that what he is endowed with is a different type of talent. The anthropomorphosis of the Stone, just like his former mythic incarnation, remains "unfit to repair the azure sky."

Baoyu's feeling about the relative easiness of poetry is bolstered by his experience of versification. "Although the boy showed no aptitude for serious study," so is Jia Zheng informed by Baoyu's tutor Jia Dairu, "he nevertheless possessed a certain meretricious talent for versification, not undeserving of commendation" (*HLM* 1:186; *SS* 1:326). Indeed, one of the routine activities for Baoyu and the girls in the Great Prospect Garden is composing poems. Although he usually defers the laurels of the poetry club to Lin Daiyu or Xue Baochai, he is able to handle different topics with admirable facility. The most impressive exhibitions of Baoyu's poetic aptitude are, quite ironically, in Jia Zheng's presence. In chapter 17, after the construction of the Great Prospect Garden is completed, Jia Zheng demands poetic lines from Baoyu to be inscribed at different sites in the garden. In chapter 78, in another of his attempts to test Baoyu's talent, Jia Zheng orders his son to compose an elegy on Fourth Sister Lin (Lin Siniang), a legendary woman warrior. In both situations Baoyu demonstrates his facile imagination and remarkable dexterity in poetic composition. On the latter occasion, his "archaic-style" (*guti*) ballad honoring Fourth Sister Lin gives him the inspiration for a piece of rhapsody (*fu*) with the title "Hibiscus Dirge" (*Furong lei*), which he composes in mourning over his beautiful and innocent maid Skybright (Qingwen) who has lost her young life to calumny and slander.

Thus the young man who dreads the civil service examinations actually excels in a different type of examination, one on literary composition. Significantly, during both tests by his father, Baoyu's performance wins admiration from Jia Zheng's guests, mostly his fellow officials. What these former civil service examination graduates say—"Our young friend with his natural talent and youthful imagination succeeds immediately where we old pedants fail"—may be more than just a routine compliment (*HLM* 1:187; *SS* 1:328). Jia Zheng's attitude, however, is quite ambivalent. While not totally unpleased by his son's literary feats, he ultimately decides on both occasions to dampen Baoyu's enthusiasm on poetic writing with his typical paternal severity. He is concerned that Baoyu's enthusiasm with belletristic composition may be the very reason for his lack of interest in the examination essays, and that concern is once again expressed in his conversation with Baoyu's tutor Jia Dairu, when he takes his son back to school:

> Today I've myself brought him [Baoyu] here, because I felt the need to entrust him to you personally. He is no longer a child, and if he is to shoulder his responsibilities and earn a place in the world, it is high time he applied himself conscientiously to preparing for his exams. At home, unfortunately, he spends all his time idling about in the company of other children. He may be able to compose a few poems, but they are for the most part gibberish and nonsensical. Even the better ones are about nothing more than the wind and the cloud, the moon and the dew—frivolities that have nothing to do with the proper business of his life [*yisheng de zhengshi*]. (*HLM* 3:1056; *SS* 4:47, translation modified)

The tutor immediately chimes in: "Not that one should entirely neglect poetic composition. But there is surely time enough for that later on in one's career" (*HLM* 3:1056; *SS* 4:47).[30] This exchange between the father and the tutor reflects the prevalent view in late imperial China, which privileged government service over any other professions and the examination essay over any other forms of writing.[31] Within the novel itself, the tutor's words here echo his earlier report on Baoyu's "meretricious talent for versification" (*HLM* 1:186; *SS* 1:326). The Chinese original for "meretricious talent" is *waicai*, a derogatory term that means, literally, a devious and crooked gift or an aptitude that goes awry. Meanwhile, studies for the examinations are constantly referred to, as in Jia Zheng's words quoted earlier, as *zhengshi,* literally, a "straight" or "upright" matter. The antithesis between these two terms, *waicai* and *zhengshi,* clearly indicates the moral valorization for government service in the prevalent value system and vividly illustrates the perceived incompatibility between the talent for literary creation and the learning for the civil service examinations.

During the Ming and Qing periods, the examination curriculum was almost exclusively based on the Confucian canon and Song scholastic commentaries.[32] With the exceptions of the special *buoxue hongci* examinations, belletristic writings were almost completely eradicated from the examinations until 1757, when Emperor Qianlong decreed that the provincial examinations include the composition of a pentasyllabic poem.[33] The tension between literary creation and canonic learning had a strong impact on many literati's vocational decisions. According to the late-Ming poet and artist Dong Qichang (1555–1636), Wang Shizhen (1526–90), one of the famous "Latter Seven Scholars" (*houqizi*), "exhorted his disciples not to work on poetry" because of his concern that poetic composition might become "a professional impediment for examination candidates" (*juzi yebing*).[34] This relegation of the belletristic tradition in favor of examination scholarship quickly found expressions in fiction. In the early Qing story "Pretense Became Reality in the Seven-Pine Garden" (Qisongyuan nongjia chengzhen) collected in *The World-Illuminating Cup* (Zhaoshi bei), the young scholar Ruan Jianglan decides to give up poetry composition altogether and concentrate on preparations for the examinations in order to win back his beloved girl Wanniang. The narrator comments on his decision approvingly: "How much talent can one be endowed with? The more talent is spent on poetry, the less of it will be left for the examinations."[35] A still better-known example is in chapter 3 of *The Scholars,* mentioned earlier in chapter 5 of this book: when an examination candidate brags about his skills in versification and knowledge in poetry, the chief examiner Zhou Jin reprimands him sternly: "Since the emperor attaches importance to essays, why should you bring up the poems of the Han and Tang Dynasties?"[36]

This abrasive censure resonates with Jia Zheng's scolding of Baoyu. Ironically, in chapter 37 Jia Zheng is appointed commissioner for education in one of the provinces, a position similar to the one Zhou Jin holds in *The Scholars.* His departure for office leaves Baoyu free to "play in the Garden to his heart's content without the least fear of restraint or reprisal"

(*HLM* 2:440; *SS* 2:213). Almost immediately, he joins his sister Tanchun and other girls forming a poetry society, the Crab Flower Club (Haitang She).[37] So, while the father, just like Zhou Jin, is away "at the imperial command to examine essays," the son at home indulges himself in "heterodox studies" and "miscellaneous literary forms" to the total negligence of "real work."

Baoyu's penchant for poetry is thus perfectly consistent with his antipathy for the examinations and government service. Yet, having "life in both worlds," the Stone/jade/Baoyu has a mission that transcends the daily dabbling in poetry, a mission to turn his mundane experience into a narrative text. Indeed, that is precisely the mission that the fictionalized novelist proclaims for himself in the "Fanli" and then entrusts to his trifurcated novelistic agent, the Stone/jade/Baoyu. Baoyu's poems, along with those by other characters, are materials for making the "Story of the Stone." Macrocosmically, therefore, his primary literary engagement is not poetic composition but the creation of a fictional text. In comparison with poetry, fiction was further downgraded in the hierarchy of intellectual prioritization. As a Qing scholar put it, "Moral and ethical doctrines, classics and histories—these are the important ones among all writings [*yan zhi da zhe ye*]. Poems and songs, miscellaneous notes and fictions—these are the trifling ones [*yan zhi xiao zhe ye*]. Among all writings, fiction is the most trifling of the trifling ones [*yan zhi you xiao zhe*]."[38] In comparison with his practice of poetic composition, Baoyu's fiction making amounts to an even more drastic and more resolute repudiation of a bureaucratic career, or the service of "mending heaven" for both the imperial state and the family.

## DREAMS AND ILLUSIONS (*MENGHUAN*): INSPIRATIONS FOR FICTION MAKING

That the ultimate product of the Stone's experience in the human world is to be a text of fiction is suggested early in the *jiaxu* manuscript copy of the novel. In the opening chapter, Zhen Shiyin sees in his dream the Buddhist monk and Daoist priest carry the jade to Goddess Disenchantment. Along the way, the two immortals converse about the Stone's metamorphosis into Divine Luminescent Page (Shengying Shizhe), who is in turn destined to descend to the human world along with the celestial plant Crimson Pearl (Jiangzhu Xiancao). In a passage that somehow became obliterated in the later typographical editions, these clergymen make it quite clear that the Stone's imminent journey to the mundane world will become a story (*gushi*): "It seems this story is going to be more detailed [*suosui*] and more exquisite [*xini*] than all the wind-and-moon stories [*fengyue gushi*] that have ever existed."³⁹

The Stone's—also Baoyu's or the *baoyu*'s—authorship of the inscribed "Story of the Stone" is further emphasized, still in the opening chapter, in the dialogue between the Stone and the itinerant Daoist, Vanitas. As the priest expresses his doubt about the moral value of the narrative, the Stone's eloquent observations on its entertaining efficacy eventually convert the distrustful reader into a willing transmitter of the text. The authorship of the narrative is clearly claimed by the Stone and acknowledged by the priest: while Vanitas refers to it as "this story of yours," the Stone calls it "my story of the stone" (*HLM* 1:2–3; *SS* 1:49). In light of this, the poem at the end of the inscribed narrative becomes intriguingly ambiguous. The line that David Hawkes has aptly translated as "My life in both worlds on this stone is writ" (*ci xi shenqian shenhou shi*) can also mean, in consistence with the emphasis on the Stone's authorship, "My life in both worlds I've writ on this stone" (*HLM* 1:2; *SS* 1:49). ⁴⁰

Two words, "dreams" (*meng*) and "illusions" (*huan*), frequently occur in the text in relation to fiction creation and therefore particularly merit our attention. In the "Fanli," dreams and illusions are associated with the conception and inception of the fiction with the fictionalized novelist: "The author stated that he had experienced a series of dreams and illusions. He therefore concealed the real events and, by means of the Precious Jade of Luminous Intelligence, related this story of the stone. Hence the name Zhen Shiyin" (*HLM* 1:1). At the end of the long passage, the reader is reminded of the unusual significance of "dreams" and "illusions" in the main body of the novel, which are said to be "the very essence of this book" (*ci shu benzhi*) (*HLM* 1:1). The pairing of dreams and illusions, along with the Nüwa myth and the metamorphosis of the magic Stone itself, constitutes a chimerical textual ambience in a striking contrast to the realistic fabric of daily-life details in the main body of the novel. *Dream of the Red Chamber* is intensely interested in the dichotomy between what is real and what is false and its ramifications for fictional imagination.⁴¹ The tension between these two seemingly opposite orientations in signification—both toward and away from reality—is precisely what characterizes fictional literature. Chinese *xiaoshuo*, just like the Western novel, had to circumscribe its territory between reality and truth on one side and illusion and falsehood on the other. In that sense, *Dream of the Red Chamber* is more directly concerned with the nature of fiction and more intensely reflexive on the art of fiction-making than any Chinese fictional work prior to it. While the words "dreams" and "illusions" certainly carry a Buddhist tinge, what is presented here is not so much religious wisdom as the wisdom for literary creation. By employing these terms, "the author has succeeded in turning the concept of world and life as dream into a subtle but powerful theory of fiction that he uses constantly to confound his reader's sense of reality," to borrow Anthony Yu's astute words.[42]

According to the fictionalized novelist in the "Fanli," the writing of his fiction is both subsequent to and contingent upon "a series of dreams and illusions."[43] To be sure, the "dreams and illusions" mentioned here are quite ambiguous. They can signify on a literal level, but metaphorically they can also refer to the fictionalized novelist's memory of his life experience that feels dreamlike when viewed retrospectively. The latter possibility seems more likely, as it is more consistent with the rest of the paragraph where the fictionalized novelist offers a brief account of his own life. In either case, however, dreams and illusions do not refer to his experience per se but a mental transformation of it, a process that must necessarily involve "concealment of real events" (*zhenshi yin*). Yet the dreams and illusions, as made quite clear here, are the source of the inspirations for the creation of fiction: the mental transformation leads to an aesthetic one.

Since the "Fanli" anticipates the dreams and illusions in the main body of the novel and calls them "the essence of this book," one may wonder in what ways they are related to the "series of dreams and illusions" of the fictionalized novelist in the "Fanli" itself, especially since it was those dreams and illusions that have initiated his transformation into a fiction writer. If the "Story of the Stone" is considered here not only as a textual outcome of that transformation but also a theatrical recuperation of that transformation itself, can some of Baoyu's dreams and illusions be interpreted in a similar light, in terms of their function in the progress toward the completion of the stone narrative? In other words, if the fictionalized novelist's fiction writing is initiated by a "series of dreams and illusions," does Baoyu, the surrogate of the fictionalized novelist in the main body of the novel, have similar inspirational experiences?

Baoyu's most important dream is, of course, the one in chapter 5, in which he visits Taixu Huanjing, the Illusory Land of Great Void, or the Land of Illusion as David Hawkes renders it. The term *taixu*, or Great Void, was deeply entrenched in classical Chinese thinking. In the chapter "Knowledge Wonders North" (Zhi bei you) of *Zhuangzi*, *taixu* seems to refer to a metaphysical space of vacuity that provides an access to ultimate truth because of its transcendence over all the mutations of matters and affairs.[44] With Confucian scholars in later periods, however, the concept of *taixu* came to be drastically reshaped. For the seventh-century Confucian exegete Kong Yingda (574–648), *taixu* was a grand realm where the transmutations and transformations of all substances took place: "How can the myriads of things be put in motion [by an outer force]? With no exceptions they all take their shapes from the Great Void on their own [*mo bu du hua yu taixu*] and create themselves instantly."[45] Zhang Zai (1020–77), one of the Northern Song pioneers of neo-Confucianism, took over the idea of *taixu* and further developed it. For Zhang, *taixu* was not a space of nothingness as perceived by the Daoists, for nothingness, as Zhang argued, simply took no space. Rather, it was filled with what he termed *qi*, or the ether, which, although invisible to the human eye, was in a constant movement to form and then reform all types of existences: "The Great Void is formless and is filled with *qi*. Its condensation and dispersion are nothing but the changes of the transitory forms of existence" (*qi ju qi san, bianhua zhi kexing er*). "The Great Void cannot be without *qi*. The *qi* cannot but conglomerate into myriads of things, and myriads of things cannot but disperse to constitute the Great Void."[46] Zhang Zai's theory on *taixu* and *qi* influenced Cheng Yi (1033–1107) and Zhu Xi,[47] and, through them, had an impact on some of the major thinkers of the Ming and Qing periods, especially Wang Fuzhi (1619–92).[48]

If *taixu* was traditionally conceived as the space where all forms of existence were to be created and then re-created, it is indeed quite befitting that it becomes transformed in *Dream of the Red Chamber* into a symbolic space of fiction making. Before its journey to the mundane world, the Stone travels to the Illusory Land of Great Void. The nature of this celestial realm is well summarized by the couplet inscribed on either side of the arch:

> Truth becomes fiction when the fiction's true;
> Real becomes not real where the unreal's real.
> (*HLM* 1:6; *SS* 1:55)

That the couplet deliberately blurs the line between the real and the unreal and between facts and fabrications has been so well explicated that it does not bear another repetition here, but the background of *taixu* in Chinese philosophical thinking may provide a new perspective for us. What the couplet suggests, the metamorphosis between the real (*zhen*) and the unreal (*jia*) and between existence (*you*) and nonexistence (*wu*), is quite comparable to what happens in the realm of *taixu* as Zhang Zai characterized it. If the metaphysical *taixu* is where things are formed and reformed amid the continuous movement of the ether, it may be said that the Illusory Land of Great Void performs a similar function in the world of *Dream of the Red Chamber*. It is in Disenchantment's Sunset Glow Palace that the Divine Luminescent Page, transformed from the magic Stone, irrigates the celestial plant of Crimson Pearl. When the plant sheds off her vegetable shape and becomes a fairy girl, she decides to repay the Page's favor with her tears in the human world, where they are destined to be reborn respectively as Jia Baoyu and Lin Daiyu, the male and female protagonists of the novel. This series of successive rebirths here is quite similar to the constant reshaping of material forces in Zhang Zai's *taixu*. It is significant that *Dream of the Red Chamber* starts with such successive metamorphoses of its main characters. The "Story of the Stone," just to reiterate, can be read as a fictional elaboration of the life experience of the fictionalized novelist conjured up in the "Fanli." Yet to fictionalize that experience, what is "real" has to be concealed, or rather, reprocessed, and the successive metamorphoses of the Stone and Crimson Pearl Plant signify that process of transforming the "real" into the fictional. Taixu Huanjing, seen in this light, becomes a symbolic realm of the creative power of fictional imagination.

The first five chapters of the novel have often been considered an elaborate prologue, unfolding the mythic frame of the fiction and then setting the stage for the drama in the Jia household. It is by no means accidental that in chapter 5, right before the story of the Stone's human experience starts to evolve, Baoyu visits the realm of the Goddess of Disenchantment in his dream. His other dream trip there takes place in chapter 116, where the Illusory Land of Great Void is given a different name, the Paradise of Truth (Zhenru Fudi). These two visits are at two points perfectly symmetrical in the 120-chapter version of the novel, respectively near the beginning and the end. The meaning of this arrangement becomes apparent in light of the symbolic-allegorical function of Disenchantment's realm and Baoyu's role as the destined fiction maker, as these two visits mark, respectively, the initiation and completion of Baoyu's mission of fiction-making.

The first dream trip, which is certainly "one of the longest and most celebrated, complex, and well-wrought literary dreams in the history of Chinese literature," particularly deserves a careful scrutiny.[49] That day, while attending a party in the Ningguo mansion, Baoyu feels tired and sleepy. Grandmother Jia lets Qin Shi, her favorite great-granddaughter-in-law, put Baoyu to an afternoon nap. The young lady conducts Baoyu into a room, where he sees on the wall a painting featuring the Han scholar Liu Xiang assiduously reading a book that is dutifully illuminated for him by an immortal holding a flaming torch. On either side of the painting is this couplet in calligraphy:

> True learning implies a clear insight into human activities,
> Genuine culture involves the skillful manipulation
>    of human relationships.
> (*HLM* 1:52; *SS* 1:126)

As Baoyu bluntly expresses his dislike for the place, Qin Shi takes him to her own chamber, where he is greeted by a delicious fragrance and a sumptuous but elegant décor:

> The fragrance of wine overwhelmed one with its flower-like scents. On a table stood an antique mirror that had once graced the tiring-room of Empress Wu Zetian. Beside it stood the golden platter on which Flying Swallow once danced for her emperor's delight. And on the platter was that very quince which An Lushan once threw at Lady Yang, bruising her breast. At the far end of the room stood the priceless bed on which Princess Shouchang was sleeping under the eaves of the Hanzhang Palace. Over it hung a canopy commissioned by Princess Tongchang entirely fashioned out of ropes of pearls. (*HLM* 1:52–53; *SS* 1:127, translation modified)

Baoyu is delighted with everything he sees and decides to take his nap here. Qin Shi, the proud owner of the room, then makes the bed for Baoyu: "She unfolded a quilted coverlet, whose silk has been laundered by the fabulous Xi Shi, and arranged the double head-rest that Hong-niang once carried for her amorous mistress" (*HLM* 1:53; *SS* 1:127).

Baoyu's repugnance for the first room is not surprising, as the exaltation of pedantic learning and the glorification of a bureaucratic career presented in the painting and the couplet certainly will not win the renegade's heart. Yet the reason behind his love for the second room is not immediately clear. One may say that the pubescent boy is attracted to the décor suggestive of sexual love. Yet, none of the objects in the room—the mirror, the platter, the quince, the bed, or the canopy—suggests anything at all until they become associated with the name of a woman celebrated in fictional literature.[50] In that sense, they constitute an iconography of fictional sensuality and point to a prominent sector of Chinese fictional literature.[51] Even the objects themselves may be just "fictional," as their "authenticity" exclusively hinges on that of the stories they are associated with, stories that have evolved a long way into fictional literature from whatever factual or historical origins they might have once had. "If you take them for what they are called, you will be once again tricked by the author," as Red Inkstone cautions the reader in his interlinear comment.[52] So, if the décor in Qin Shi's room is indeed arousing to Baoyu, it perhaps does not arouse the adolescent boy's sexual desire as much as the budding fiction maker's imagination for literary creation.

Amid this aura in Qin Shi's room, Baoyu has his dream trip to Disenchantment's celestial realm. To explain her reason for the invitation, Disenchantment observes that "a full exposure to the illusions of feasting, drinking, music and dancing may succeed in bringing about an awakening" in Baoyu (*HLM* 1:59; *SS* 1:137). She accordingly lets Baoyu have a glimpse of the files of women around him, become intoxicated with her celestial tea and fairy wine, watch a sumptuous song-and-dance suite, and, ultimately, sleep with her younger sister Jianmei. Baoyu's dream experience, as Shuen-fu Lin has pointed out, presents "a program for the rest of the book."[53] The main and supplementary registers of the "Twelve Beauties from Jingling" (*Jinling shi'er chai*) foretell the destinies of dozens of women characters in enigmatic verses and pictures, and the prophecies about the twelve ladies in the "main register" (*zhengce*) are reiterated in the song-and-dance suite called "Dream of the Red Chamber" (*Honglou meng*). It is by no means a coincidence that the titles for the registers and the music suite are identical with two of the alternative titles for the "Story of the Stone" given in the opening chapter of the novel. Obviously, the novelist makes a conscious effort to suggest that Baoyu is here given a preview of the outline of the stone narrative. Guiding Baoyu through the dreamland by hand and offering the fiction maker a prognostic glimpse into his own fiction, the goddess is to Baoyu what the Muses were to the Greek bards. Indeed Red Inkstone demonstrates his remarkable perceptivity when he calls Baoyu and Disenchantment "the two persons that are the key to the entire work" (*tongbu dagang*).[54] On the level of signification where *Dream of the Red Chamber* is read as a fiction about the making of a fiction writer, the goddess should be considered the primary source of inspiration.

That Baoyu's experience in the dreamland does leave its imprint on his mind is made clear in chapter 17. When he follows his father on a tour of the newly completed Great Prospect Garden, all of a sudden he is overcome by an unaccountable feeling that "he must have known a building somewhat like this before—though where or when he could not for the life of him remember" (*HLM* 1:195; *SS* 1:343).[55] The boy lives his mundane life—or, rather, advances his "Story of the Stone"—by following the "program" revealed to him in the dream. Actually, the novel wastes no time in suggesting the inspirational nature of Baoyu's dream. Right after the account of the dream in chapter 5, the narrative suddenly assumes a different tone in this passage near the beginning of chapter 6:

> The inhabitants of the Rong mansion, if we include all of them from the highest to the humblest to our total, numbered more than three hundred souls, who produced between them a dozen or more incidents in a single day. Faced with so exuberant an abundance of material, what principle should your chronicler adopt to guide him in his selection of incidents to record? As we pondered the problem *where to begin,* it was suddenly solved for us by the appearance as it were out of nowhere of someone from a very humble, very insignificant household who, on the strength of a very tenuous, very remote family connection with the Jias, turned up at the Rong mansion on the very day of which we are about to write. (*HLM* 1:68; *SS* 1:150)

This Shandean-style apology, suggesting the diffidence and coyness of a novice narrator, marks the inauguration of this stone-turned-fiction writer. The novelist, as one scholar puts it, intends at this point "to hand over the authorship to the Stone."[56] What appears to be an account of

Baoyu's mundane experience, as the passage indicates, is coeval with his experience of fiction creation. Indeed, the "series of dreams and illusions" that initiated the fiction writing of the fictionalized novelist in the "Fanli" becomes thus dramatically reenacted in Baoyu's dream visit to Disenchantment and her realm.

In chapter 116, Baoyu has his second dream trip to the celestial realm, now called the Paradise of Truth (Zhenru Fudi). This time he sees on either side of the arch a couplet somewhat different from the one he saw during his first trip:

> When Fiction departs and Truth appears, Truth prevails;
> Though Not-real was once Real, the Real is never unreal.
> (*HLM* 4:1457; *SS* 5:285)

Like the one he saw before, this couplet also heightens the dialectic between the real and the unreal. Yet, if the original one introduces Baoyu to the land of fictional imagination by accentuating the illusory nature of what appears to be real, this one, near the completion of the "Story of the Stone," asserts the truthfulness in the product of the fictional imagination. Significantly, Baoyu does not see Disenchantment and her celestial cohorts this time. As he has fulfilled the mission of fiction making, creative inspirations are no longer needed. Instead, Baoyu finds himself in a place that dimly reminds him of the Great Prospect Garden and encounters the spirits of several women who have shared his mundane life. If Baoyu during his first dream trip is given a fleeting preview of the fiction he is to make, now he is having a retrospective summary of the fiction he has completed. As Baoyu feels dazed by what he sees, he asks the Buddhist monk, who has escorted him to the celestial land, whether he is in a dream or in the real world. The answer by the monk, once again, echoes the statement in the "Fanli" that the fictionalized novelist "uses what the Stone remembers/recollects/records as an analogy for himself." Although deliberately obscure and evasive, the monk's words carry a strong suggestion that what Baoyu sees is precisely his own recollection (*ji*): "As long as you have dutifully remembered/recollected/recorded all the details of what you experienced [*ba jingli guo de shiqing xixi ji zhe*], I shall explain it to you further when we meet again" (*HLM* 4:1462; *SS* 5:293, translation modified). Their next meeting, of course, takes place in the final chapter of the novel, where Baoyu, following the Buddhist monk and the Daoist priest, leaves Red Dust for good. The author of the "Story of the Stone"—just like Vanitas, its first reader—experiences passion before finally advancing from the phenomenal world to the ultimate truth of void. Yet, by ending his adventures in the mundane world, he also ends the fiction he has been "remembering/recollecting/recording."

## PERSONAL AND PRIVATE FEELINGS AS MATERIAL FOR FICTION MAKING

Baoyu's dream in chapter 5 ends on a sensual note. After watching the performance of the song-and-dance suite, Disenchantment takes Baoyu to a sumptuously furnished room, where he sees a beautiful fairy girl. Then the goddess delivers an extended lecture on the connection between love and sex and the difference between lust of the flesh and lust of the mind (*yiyin*) before she offers her younger sister, the fairy girl in the room, to be his bride:

> In principle, of course, all lust is the same. But the word has many different meanings. For example, the typically lustful man in the common sense of the word is a man who likes a pretty face, who is fond of singing and dancing, who is inordinately given to flirtation; one who makes love in season and out of season, and who, if he could, would like to have every pretty girl in the world at his disposal, to gratify his desires whenever he felt like it. Such a person is a mere brute. His is a shallow, promiscuous kind of lust. But your kind of lust is different. That blind, defenseless love with which nature has filled your being is what we call here "lust of the mind." "Lust of the mind" cannot be explained in words, nor, if it could, would you be able to grasp their meaning. Either you know what it means or you don't. Because of this "lust of the mind" women will find you a kind and understanding friend; but in the eyes of the world I am afraid it is going to make you seem unpractical and eccentric. It is going to earn you the jeers of many and the angry looks of many more.... And now I am going to give you my little sister Two-in-One—"Keqing" to her friends—to be your bride. The time is propitious. You may consummate the marriage this very night. My motive in arranging this is to help you grasp the fact that, since even in these immortal precincts love is an illusion, the love of your dust-

stained, mortal world must be doubly an illusion. It is my earnest hope that, knowing this, you will henceforth be able to shake yourself free of its entanglements and change your previous way of thinking, devoting your mind seriously to the teachings of Confucius and Mencius and your person wholeheartedly to the betterment of society. (*HLM* 1:64; *SS* 1:146)

This lengthy admonition is truly intriguing. If Baoyu's dream visit to the Illusory Land of Great Void is a trip for fictional inspirations, why does the goddess want Baoyu's initiation as a fiction maker to coincide with his sexual initiation? Her pronounced purpose of thrusting Baoyu into the illusion of sensual pleasures in order to disillusion him may well be ironic, as it is immediately vitiated by Baoyu's sexual experiment with his maid Aroma when he is back in the "dust-stained, mortal world" after the dream. Equally ironic is her exhortation to Baoyu on the importance of Confucian learning. The goddess is, in her own words, "a person in the know" (*gezhong ren*), who is completely aware of the "origin" (*laili*) of the stone-turned-boy and his destined mission in Red Dust.[57] As one recalls, Disenchantment is the one who has sent both Divine Luminescent Page and Crimson Pearl Plant, along with other "amorous souls" (*qinggui*), down to the mundane world. She of course knows that the Stone and the Plant, formerly two inhabitants of her own realm, are in Red Dust to redeem their "debts of passions" (*qingzhai*). And of course she also knows that Baoyu is, as goes the opening line in the prelude of the song-and-dance suite performed in her palace, the most devoted lover (*qingzhong*) ever since "first the world from chaos rose" (*kaipi hongmeng*).[58] Quite obviously, the goddess's "earnest" hope to see Baoyu turn away from love and devote his mind to "the teachings of Confucius and Mencius" does not sound genuinely earnest at all.

In a way Disenchantment's younger sister Jianmei is a truly illusory figure in the goddess's land of illusion. Unlike the voluble goddess herself and the other clamorous fairies—who complain loudly about their "pure, maidenly precincts" being contaminated by the intrusion of a "disgusting" male—Jianmei is completely voiceless and motionless even when Disenchantment brings Baoyu into her chamber and declares her his bride. All that is known about her is that she appears to Baoyu as resembling both his female cousins, Daiyu and Baochai. While that may indeed justify Hawkes's translation of the name as Two-in-One, Jianmei literally means simply "combined beauty." Even though she reminds Baoyu of the two girls he is most intimate with, the name itself suggests a sense of generality rather than specificity. Her other name, Keqing, happens to be the same as that of Baoyu's niece-in-law Qin Shi, who is to die very soon.[59] The pairing of these two names thus forms a paradox about their owner as being both omnipresent and nonexistent, pertaining both to women in general and to a particular one who is soon to be no more. One therefore has reason to believe that the shadowy fairy is meant to represent not any specific woman or women but the abstract notion of womanhood. If that is the case, Baoyu's sexual intercourse with her becomes a highly symbolic act, through which the boy's naive and innocent preference for girls—"Girls are made of water and boys are made of mud"—now evolves into *qing*, the most intricate and complex feeling of a sexually awakened young man (*HLM* 1:19; *SS* 1:76). What may appear to be a self-contradiction on Disenchantment's part—it seems that she distinguishes Baoyu's "lust of the mind" (*yiyin*) from others' "lust of the flesh" and then ostensibly feels the need to disillusion him of the corporeal pleasures—may not be a self-contradiction after all, if Baoyu's wedding with Jianmei is seen as a ritual to mark both his puberty and his entry into the domain of the most complex feelings in personal and private life.

It is clear from the beginning of Baoyu's dream visit that Taixu Huanjing, as a land of inspirations for fictional imagination, is enveloped in an aura of personal desire and passion. At the entrance of the land, after seeing the famous couplet celebrating the paradox of fiction, Baoyu is immediately greeted by this line inscribed above the lintel: "Sea of emotions and skies of passions" (*niehai qingtian*). That line is accompanied by another couplet inscribed vertically on either side:

Ancient earth and sky
    Marvel that love's passion should outlast all time.
Star-crossed men and maids
    Groan that love's debts should be so hard to pay.
(*HLM* 1:55; *SS* 1:130)

Once within Disenchantment's realm, Baoyu sees an array of buildings each with a board above it indicating the name of the department housed in it. Those names virtually form a nomenclatural kaleidoscope of personal emotions: Department of Fond Infatuation (Chiqing Si), Department of Cruel Rejection (Jieyuan Si), Department of Early Morning Weeping (Zhaoti Si), Department of Late Night Sobbing (Muku Si), Department of Spring Fever (Chungan Si), Department of Autumn Grief (Qiubei Si), among many others (*HLM* 1:55; *SS* 1:131). Through all these names, along with the files auguring the fates of Baoyu's female companions, Disenchantment reveals to Baoyu all possible scenarios in the drama of love and desire. At the same time, however, the goddess ostensibly assumes the role of an agent of Baoyu's illustrious ancestors in urging him to shake himself free of the entanglement in passion and make himself ready for government service. By doing so the goddess prophesies a tension in Baoyu's emotional and intellectual growth, the tension between *qing*, his personal and private feelings, and the public and bureaucratic role expected of him, of which *li* (principle), the central concept in the Cheng-Zhu orthodoxy and potentially the passport to officialdom, may serve as an emblem.[60] While *Dream of the Red Chamber* does not spurn *li* altogether, *qing* is clearly the main source for the fiction-making material. However, the novel is not about *qing* per se; rather, it contextualizes private desire and passion in a constant conflict with the discourse of the examinations and government service.

In the mythic frame of the novel, the Stone, after being rejected from Nüwa's heaven rebuilding, lies at the foot of the mountain called Qinggeng Feng (Green Ridge Peak). Part of that name, *qinggeng*, as Red Inkstone pointed out, puns meaningfully on the word *qinggen*, or the root of passions.[61] In light of the affinity between the Stone and the fictionalized novelist in the "Fanli," the allegorical signification becomes fulfilled here: just as the ostensible futility of the fictionalized novelist's days with his female companions turns out to be seminal for his fictional creation, the Stone, during what seems to be its idle abandonment, is nourished by the vitality of "the roots of passions" before it becomes a fiction maker. While the Stone was previously "melted" and "molded" (*duanlian*) by the goddess for her *heavenly* project, it now undergoes a different preparation for its impending mission to the *earthly* world. The effect of that preparation is soon evident. Transformed into Divine Luminescent Page in Disenchantment's realm, the Stone conceives such a fancy for the beautiful Crimson Pearl Plant that it takes to "watering her everyday with sweet dew, therefore conferring on her the gift of life" (*HLM* 1:5; *SS* 1:53). Even before it embarks on the journey to the human world, the Stone not only has its first experience of love but also witnesses for the first time the wonder of the creative power of personal passion: "Thanks to the vitalizing effect of the sweet dew, she was able to shed her vegetable shape and assume the form of a girl" (*HLM* 1:5; *SS* 1:53).

It may be said that the Stone, in order to become a fiction maker, is first made a *qingzhong,* a destined lover. Yet the Stone's anthropomorphosis, as son of an aristocratic and bureaucratic family, is not immune from the conflict between *qing* and *li*. Apart from the bitter father-son feud on the priority between aesthetic writing and examination learning, Baoyu's development as a fiction writer is also punctuated by the clash between two different attitudes toward personal and private feelings. A figure in point is Qin Zhong. As handsome and affectionate as Baoyu, Qin Zhong may be considered Baoyu's double, or another *qingzhong* as his name may suggest. Also like Baoyu, Qin Zhong finds scholastic learning totally insufferable, and when they are fellow students at Jia Dairu's school the duo are a major reason for much of the tumult there. Yet, in the *jiaxu* manuscript copy of the novel, one hears Qin Zhong express his deep repentance to Baoyu in the last moment of his curtailed life: "Finally I've realized that we spoiled ourselves. I still hope you will become determined to pursue *gongming* and earn fame and prestige."[62] One can only imagine these words' shocking effect on Baoyu, especially because they are from a dying friend who has during his lifetime totally immersed himself in love and passion.

To a greater extent, however, the opposition between *qing* and *li* is dramatized by the dynamic between Jia Baoyu and his namesake, Zhen Baoyu. While the Zhen family in Nanjing is for the most part kept in the background of the narrative, the first reference to the Zhens takes place as early as chapter 2. The Zhens and the Jias are almost mirror images of each other: both families are wealthy and prestigious, "though rich yet given to courtesy" (*fu er hao li*) (*HLM* 1:21; *SS* 1:80). As the narrative proceeds, both families turn out to share the same fate of falling out of imperial favor before regaining, perhaps only partially, lost glory. Red Inkstone notices in an interlinear comment in chapter 2 that the family of Zhen 甄, which puns on *zhen* 真 (real), is presented here as a double for the family of Jia 賈 / *jia* 假 (false) in a ploy to problematize the true-false opposition: "Another 'real' family [*zhenzheng zhi jia*] that confronts the 'false' family [*jia jia*]. Thus, from what is written about the 'false' one can learn about the 'real'" (*xie jia ze zhi zhen*).⁶³ This mutual complementariness between the two families is corroborated in chapter 16, where the Zhens are said to be the only family to have "received the Emperor *four times*" (*HLM* 1:180; *SS* 1:314), clearly an allusion to the fact that Cao Xueqin's grandfather Cao Yin (1658–1712), as the textile commissioner in Nanjing, acted as the host for Emperor Kangxi on his four imperial tours to the south.⁶⁴ If the depiction of the Jia household is to some extent based on the history of the Cao family, the creation of the Zhens shares the same prototype. Certainly Red Inkstone has a point in this interlinear comment in chapter 16: "This Zhen family is the key to all important things, and should not be taken as idle chatter."⁶⁵

Yet the most extraordinary about these two families is the similitude of the two boys, Jia Baoyu and Zhen Baoyu. Their physical likeness amazes everyone that has seen them both, and equally striking is the similarity of their personalities. Exactly like Jia Baoyu, Zhen Baoyu loathes going to school with boys and prefers to spend his time with girls. It seems that this Zhen boy, like his Jia counterpart, would be fully devoted to personal feelings and private sensibility and apathetic to the prescribed educational course for government service. In chapter 93, however, it is reported that Zhen Baoyu, after a dream visit to Disenchantment's realm, becomes thoroughly transformed: "None of his old game appealed to him any more. Now it was all books and studying. And nobody could distract him" (*HLM* 4:1199; *SS* 4:270). While Jia Baoyu's dream trip to Taixu Huanjing is inspirational for making fiction with personal and private sentiments, Zhen Baoyu's trip becomes an effective reaffirmation of the political commitment to the imperial state.

The relationship between the two Baoyus, however, may not be so clear-cut. In chapter 56 Jia Baoyu has a dream in which he visits the garden of the other Baoyu, whose maidservants all mistake him for their master. He then drifts into a courtyard that looks just like his own. Once inside the building he sees the other Baoyu lying in bed, relating to the maids around him about *his* dream visit to the garden of his Jia counterpart. So Jia Baoyu dreams of Zhen Baoyu who is in turn dreaming of Jia Baoyu himself. The two Baoyus all of a sudden become like the ever-receding images in a hall of mirrors. Whether there is ontologically another boy named Zhen Baoyu is irrelevant, because for Jia Baoyu, at least for that moment, the other Baoyu is just his own mental projection, as the account of the dream strongly suggests.

This encounter of the two dream-souls foreshadows the only meeting of the two young men in chapter 115, when Zhen Baoyu pays a visit to the Jia household. Jia Baoyu, who has expected to find in the other Baoyu a true friend, is soon disappointed, as Zhen Baoyu starts to prattle about glory of the family name and service to the state. Yet the parting of the two Baoyus is actually preordained. Despite all their physical likeness, Zhen Baoyu was not born with a piece of jade in his mouth. He is called Baoyu only because he is his grandmother's "treasure" with "such a milky-white complexion" (*HLM* 2:713; *SS* 3:81). In other words, the Zhen boy, exactly as his family name Zhen (real, true) suggests, is not a destined maker of fiction (*jia*). Yet, because of his complementariness to Jia Baoyu that is sustained throughout much of the novel, he may be said to represent a tendency in Jia Baoyu himself. In his course of becoming a fiction writer, Jia Baoyu cannot fail to feel the coercing demand from his family and the imperial state as well as the temptations of all the remunerations of a bureaucratic career. By rejecting Zhen Baoyu as another "career worm," Jia Baoyu ultimately repudiates one latent part of his own ego, or a potential possibility to succumb to the hegemonic discourse of government service. Zhen Baoyu may proceed to win an official appointment and prove to be a "real precious jade" (*zhen baoyu*) for both his family and the state; in contrast, Jia Baoyu, because of his decision to turn away from government service in order to "attend to [his] own affairs"—to borrow the words of Du Shaoqing in *The Scholars*—becomes a breakaway from what is valorized as the *norm* for a member of the educated gentry. Consequently, he will "seem unpractical and eccentric" in the eyes of the world just as Disenchantment has predicted (*HLM* 1:65; *SS* 1:146). With all his good looks and intelligence, he will be seen as a "spurious precious jade" (*jia baoyu*), which is to be cherished not in the "real" (*zhen*) world but only in the "false" realm of fiction (*jia*).

Yet Jia Baoyu proves that he is a different jade but by no means inferior. Toward the end of the novel, he takes the provincial examinations and wins a *juren* degree before he leaves the mundane world for good. As he wins the degree only after he has completed the "Story of the Stone," he successfully reverses the intellectual and vocational prioritization rigorously prescribed by his father and tutor—and indeed by the imperial state and society at large. The Chinese word for joining the Buddhist order is *chujia*, which means to renounce one's familial ties, but in Baoyu's case the timing makes his *chujia* all the more meaningful: as he departs after the examinations without awaiting the official appointment, he does not only relinquish his familial duties but disclaims all political obligations to the imperial state as well.

Eventually the Stone resumes its original form in the supernatural world, with the narrative of its mundane experience inscribed on its surface. The fiction "of the Stone" and "by the Stone" is now "published by the Stone," in the most enduring form of publication, stone carving. The Stone's fiction-making mission is now completed, in the fullest manner possible. More interestingly, it "publishes" its fiction at precisely the same site where it was once declared by Nüwa as "unfit to repair the azure sky." That ruling was correct: the Stone has indeed remained "unfit to repair the azure sky" in both its lives, as its anthropomorphosis Jia Baoyu would willingly agree. For over two millennia, Chinese intellectuals, by participating in government service, offered themselves as blocks of stone to mend the heaven for the imperial state. As the *zhengtong-daotong* partnership was approaching its date of expiration, more and more intellectuals found themselves "unfit to repair the azure sky." However, they should be able to find uses for themselves other than mending heaven, as demonstrated by the Stone in *Dream of the Red Chamber*.

# Coda

*Out of the Imperial Shadow*

Near the closure of *Dream of the Red Chamber,* when Jia Baoyu has completed his earthly journey and is leaving the mundane world, he meets his father Jia Zheng for the last time on a cold and snowy day. Jia Zheng's boat is moored in the canal and his servants are all ashore, leaving him alone on board:

> There, up on deck . . . was the figure of a man with shaven head and bare feet, wrapped in a large cape made of crimson felt. The figure knelt down and bowed to Jia Zheng, who did not recognize the features and hurried out on deck, intending to raise him up and ask him his name. The man bowed four times, and now stood upright, pressing his palms together in monkish greeting. Jia Zheng was about to reciprocate with a respectful bow of the head when he looked into the man's eyes and with a sudden shock recognized him as Bao-yu. (HLM 4:1510; SS 5:359)

This is a moment full of pathos and symbolic meanings. Jia Baoyu's life has been of course marred by a long-standing feud with Jia Zheng. As a staunch exponent of one's political commitment to the state and obligation for the family, Jia Zheng is a typical literatus who belongs to the world that Baoyu is now leaving behind. Yet the departing son finds himself unable to cleanly sever his emotional ties to his once tyrannical father.

While Baoyu is moving forward into the future, he actually shows, by his deep and silent bows to his father, a lingering attachment to the past.

In a sense, this sentimental moment bridging the past with the future catches much of the essence of late imperial Chinese vernacular fiction. As it came into existence on the eve of the expiration of the ancient social covenant between the *daotong* and the *zhengtong*, vernacular fiction questions the soon-to-be-outdated *daotong* teaching on the literati's political duty of government service, but not without some ambivalence and nostalgia for the past glory of the *daotong-zhengtong* collaboration. Different from some of the more radical and audacious thinkers of their time, vernacular fiction writers rarely had head-on confrontations with the imperial state. Instead of complaining about the political system itself, they presented a challenge, unmistakable even though often subtle and nuanced, to the ideological system that was sustained by the political power. So, with one foot still planted on the soil of the past, Chinese vernacular fiction was steadily stretching its other foot into the future. Again, in this regard Jia Baoyu's finale in *Dream of the Red Chamber* becomes almost allegorical. Before the father and son can have a conversation, the two immortals accompanying Baoyu remind him sternly: "Come, your earthly karma is complete. Tarry no longer." With that, the three of them "strode off into the snow," and Baoyu never looks back (*HLM* 4:1510; *SS* 5:359).

In a way, the works of Chinese vernacular fiction discussed in this book punctuate a lingering yet eventually resolute departure of Chinese intellectuals from the age of government service. *Romance of the Three Kingdoms*, as we have seen, loudly protests against the imperial state's suffocating control over the literati, but it still wishes for a new type of political sovereignty and improved ruler-subject relationship. Zhuge Liang, the sagacious and astute statesman and strategist in the novel, mercilessly ridicules the pedantry of the "textually bound" scholars, a thinly veiled innuendo about the examination system in late imperial times. However, the novel does not completely lose hope in the imperial power, as we can tell from the idealistic portrayal of Liu Bei as a ruler with sincerity and humility in treating men of talent. In some of the seventeenth-century fictional works, the experience of the erotic scholar-lover can be read as a parody or travesty of the civil service examinations. In particular, by adopting the examination as a master trope for sexual act, these erotic narratives desanctify the institution of official selection that was valorized and perpetuated by the political power. At the same time, however, the bitter satire in these works is often tempered with good-natured humor and playfulness. In *The Scholars*, Wu Jingzi exposes much of the malaise in the literati mores and calls for emancipation of the literati from the textual capsule that the imperial state had entrapped them in. Here one finds a much deeper concern about the crisis in the *shi* (士)–*shi* (勢) relationship and a much more serious contemplation of the literati's historical mission, conglomerated in the wish that is repeatedly expressed by the literati figures in the novel to "attend to [their] own affairs." Finally, Cao Xueqing's *Dream of the Red Chamber* presents an adolescent Jia Baoyu and his relentless resistance against the call from his family and society to prepare for a bureaucratic career, as well as his persistent pursuit of his individual interests and a profession of his own choice. Indeed, in Baoyu's departure from his father at the end of his mundane karma one can almost read a growing awareness among the literati of late imperial times that their "karma" for government service was approaching its completion.

Obviously, these works are selected to be illustrative rather than exhaustive. While divergent in their storylines and ways of characterization, collectively they document the final stage of the convoluted evolution of the bond between Chinese intellectual elite and the imperial state. Indeed, what happened between the *daotong* and the *zhengtong* was perhaps the biggest paradox in the history of imperial China. It was under the blessing of the state power that Confucianism had become the official ideology of the Chinese empire, but the close alliance of Confucianism with the imperial power in turn facilitated the state's appropriation of the *daotong* and accelerated the latter's decline. More specifically, the Confucian teaching on the political obligation of intellectuals to go into government service had been the cohesive agent that bound the fate of the *shi* (literati) to that of the *shi* (political state), but as the state took over that doctrine from the *daotong* and privileged government service in its official discourse, the literati contingent, ironically, became a force preponderantly outside civil officialdom.

The ultimate Confucian goal in collaborating with the state, as Qian Mu saw it, was not to promote and fortify but to curb and restrain the imperial power.[1] Yet, while the Confucian intellectuals' dream of *dejun xingdao*—getting the rulers to practice the *dao*—became ruthlessly shattered during the late dynasties, the imperial power seized what had originally been Confucian ideas, especially the ones on government service, and privileged them as the cornerstone of the value system of the culture, or the symbolic order. In the meantime, by using the examinations as a vehicle for its influence and control, the state successfully made itself the center of the nation's intellectual life. Rewarding examination success with fame and prestige, the state placed itself in a position where it could manipulate the symbolic order, align it with its own interest, and impose it upon the entire society as legitimization of the institutional structure. Thus, buttressed by the state power, both the symbolic system and political institutions of the empire were largely in a relationship of reciprocation, reinforcing and perpetuating each other.

The imperial state's appropriation of the *daotong* and shaping and molding of cultural values in late imperial China can perhaps be best summarized by the phrase that O-erh-tai used in his eulogy of Emperor Qianlong quoted earlier in this book: "unifying the minds of all people under heaven." This endeavor on the part of the political authority to unify people's thinking was akin to what Pierre Bourdieu has termed "symbolic violence," by which he refers to the "capacity to impose the means for comprehending and adapting to the social world by representing economic and political power in disguised, taken-for-granted forms."[2] Different from the traditional Marxist emphasis on the economic structure of society, the concept of symbolic violence helps uncover the operation of the symbolic dimension of power relations. In late imperial China, the imperial power, equipped with state apparatus, could recruit men of talent into government service by sheer coercion, as we have seen with Zhu Yuanzhang's penal code against "the literati who refuse to be employed by the sovereign." More often, however, it did so by resorting to a symbolic order through the complicity of the populace, who would tend to forget that the society's ideological system was largely the result of the adroit manipulation by the state's unseen hand as illustrated by a Song emperor's doggerel of "Exhortation to Studies" quoted earlier in chapter 1. Omnipresent and permeating not only in government propaganda but also in proverbs, sayings, moral maxims, and many other forms of "popular wisdom," the symbolic system fulfilled a political function by trying to lull the public into a docile acquiescence in the social order and the domination of the state power.

Under this symbolic order carefully maintained by state power, it became almost a public consensus that a well-educated man could seek his fullest personal fulfillment only by winning an official appointment with an examination success. In this view, educational capital could be convertible in most favorable terms to social and symbolic capital only in the field of government service. Thus Du Shaoqing in *The Scholars*, who rebuffs invitations to the examinations, is seen as an eccentric; and in *Dream of the Red Chamber*, Jia Baoyu's obstinate rejection of a bureaucratic career earns him the "jeers of many and angry looks of many more" (*HLM* 1:64; *SS* 1:146). As government service was placed at the very top of the hierarchy of symbolic values, those who were barred from it were not only degraded politically but also marginalized culturally, with their social and symbolic capital severely diminished.

The imperial state's appropriation of the Confucian doctrine, of which government service was a key component, prompted the gradual decline of the *daotong* in late imperial times. In the meantime, bolstered by both the government apparatus and the usurped moral primacy from the *daotong*, the state ideology became the dominant and authoritative discourse, sustaining the symbolic order of the society and potentially suffocating all other discourses. However, like the Western novel, Chinese vernacular fiction is a realistic representation of human experience, and it requires that each character bring his or her unique and individual discourse into the fictional world. A hegemonic and forcefully unifying discourse, endorsed by a spiritual or a secular authority, tends to be prohibitive of other discourses. It is therefore resistant to being dialogized or double-voiced, and does not belong to the world of the novel where different discourses intersect and interlock each other.[3] In a sense, the world in Chinese vernacular fiction is characterized by a "centrifugal" force, which tends to displace an authoritative and homogenous voice with individual and heterogeneous ones.[4]

This notion that fictional literature rises and grows while contesting and counteracting a dominant and hegemonic discourse was not actually foreign to traditional Chinese scholars and critics. In his preface to *Stories Old and New* (Gujin xiaoshuo), Feng Menglong makes this famous statement: "*Xiaoshuo* began to rise when the tradition of historiography started to decline" (*Shitong san er xiaoshuo xing*).[5] Apparently, Feng uses the term *xiaoshuo* here to refer to a literary genre that had started with some of the pre-Qin works in prose narrative, works that can be called fiction only in a broad sense. Yet, to our purpose here, the definition of the term *xiaoshuo* as Feng Menglong uses it is not as pertinent as Feng's view on what happened between the early *xiaoshuo* and the tradition of historiography. As history writing was a political institution under the direct control of the state in ancient China, historiography had been the dominant and authoritative narrative genre for a long time. Consequently, *xiaoshuo*, as an unofficial and unorthodox narrative form, could only negotiate with historiography for a certain amount of legitimacy.

The situation for vernacular fiction in late imperial times was in a way comparable to that for the earliest works of *xiaoshuo* as Feng Menglong saw it. The emergence of vernacular fiction as a major narrative genre was conditioned by the literati's continued haggling with the authoritative discourse of government service. There was, however, a major difference. What happened between vernacular fiction and the discourse on government service was not a collision or conciliation between two different narrative genres, one old and one new, as had been the case between historiography and the early *xiaoshuo* as Feng Menglong described. Instead, the discourse on government service had an influence that went far beyond narrative literature. Indeed, it permeated all aspects of social life and fed into the symbolic order at large. In the meantime, however, the discrepancy between what was taught in the discourse on government service and the social reality was becoming increasingly obvious. "In the most densely populated and prosperous regions," as Susan Naquin and Evelyn Rawski have observed, "a sharpening of examination competition turned many intellectuals away from orthodox careers to activities in the cultural realm."[6] There was thus an exodus of literate and intellectual forces that was unprecedented in Chinese history in scale. Since the literati's educational capital did not convert to symbolic capital in the field of civil bureaucracy, they reinvested it elsewhere, mostly in cultural fields. As the seventeenth-century scholar Gui Zhuang (1613–73) put it, once a literatus was "unfortunately rejected in the examinations," he had, "for the rest of his life, to repose on poetry and wine and the use of other artistry" (*jiyu shijiu, tuoyu jiyi*).[7] The literati culture that flourished in late imperial times was largely created by those who were outside government service. Their personal misfortunes in office seeking, paradoxically, became a blessing for the growth of many cultural fields. In that sense, the examination system functioned as a great "culture-booster": intended to serve as the main avenue for recruiting talent for the imperial state, it in fact constantly redirected educational and intellectual capital away from government service and pumped it instead into various cultural sectors.

This broadening gap between the symbolic order and social reality was a major reason for much of the frustration and bewilderment of the literati in different cultural fields, including vernacular fiction writing. Li Yu grumbled in a private letter that he was ill-fated with his "hundred skills" in writing, which only made him "hundred times poorer."[8] Cheng Jinfang (1718–84), writing a poem in mourning of Wu Jingzi, had good reason to express the regret that his late friend, with all his outstanding talent, "should have been remembered *merely* for his fiction" (*jing yi baizhuan chuan*).[9] In the meantime, critics and commentators such as Li Zhi, Jin Shengtan, Mao Zonggang, and many others were nearly obsessed with the word "genius" (*caizi*) in their references to writers of vernacular literature.[10] Yet, they were so emphatic in using that word, precisely because they knew that those writers were *not* generally recognized as geniuses. Much of the anxiety and bitterness of the fiction writers, expressed so frequently in the motif of unjustly neglected talent, should therefore be considered a reaction to the growing incongruity between the symbolic order of the society and the prevalent trend of massive transfer of literacy and intelligence away from government service into cultural realms. Vernacular fiction writers spearheaded that flow of educational capital; by exposing the bigotry in the symbolic order sustained by the state ideology, they also attempted to remove a major impediment to that flow.

The rise of vernacular fiction in late imperial China was a complicated cultural phenomenon that is not to be explained by any single reason. Among all the factors in the social setting, including the changed relationship between the educated gentry and the imperial state, none was solely responsible for the advent of vernacular fiction. While the literati's disenchantment with the examinations and government service did not inevitably lead to fiction writing by itself, it was organically interwoven with other factors in the general social and cultural climate that proved conducive to the new narrative genre. The commercial market, for instance, played an enormous role in shaping the tastes and habits of the public and in the production and consumption of fictional works. Yet the growth of the commercial market was inextricably related to the accelerated flow of educational capital. Since more and more intellectual elites no longer considered government service their ultimate professional destination, many of them became merchants. As the status distinction between literati and merchants tended to be blurred, it became possible for them to develop common interests.[11] Typically, merchants who were actively involved with the production and consumption of vernacular fiction were those who emulated the scholarly style and way of life, since scholars had now become much more approachable.[12] Thus the coalescence of commerce and culture, which was an indispensible premise for the full flourish of vernacular fiction, did not take place in isolation but was enhanced by the reshuffle of cultural and intellectual forces in the wake of the examinations.

The massive relocation of literate and intellectual forces also facilitated the preparation of writers of vernacular fiction. By turning away from the examinations and government service, these former examination candidates no longer had to bury themselves in volumes of the classics and exegetic commentaries and came to be in closer contact with commoners, not only their fellow scholars but also merchants, craftsmen, and peasants. Indeed, what Ian Watt has remarked of the Western novel to a large extent goes for Chinese vernacular fiction as well: "the novel is a full and authentic report of human experience, and is therefore under an obligation to satisfy its reader with such details of the story as the individualities of the actors concerned, the particulars of the times and places of their actions."[13] Living in the midst of ordinary people, fiction writers now could have a circumstantial view of human life. The result is what Robert Hegel has aptly termed "quotidian realism" that characterizes so many works of Chinese vernacular fiction.[14]

This redistribution of men of letters was also a prerequisite for the rise of the written vernacular as a new literary language for fictional literature. In contrast to classical poetry, where writing and reading typically took place within the largely homogeneous circles of the literati themselves, vernacular fiction had audiences covering all social strata, from scholar-officials to shop assistants and from learned schoolmasters to functionally literate housewives.[15] Particularly enhancing its appeal to readers from all walks of life was the use of either a mixture of vernacular with simplified classical Chinese, as in *Romance of the Three Kingdoms*, or full-fledged written vernacular, as in *Water Margin* and many other works. As the men of letters now found themselves in proximity to the plebeians, they were in a position to familiarize themselves with different social dialects. The written vernacular, by emulating the whole spectrum of social dialects, proved a much more capable vehicle for "linguistic mimesis," presenting a fictional simulacrum of the polyphonic social life.[16]

Yet the impact of the advent of the written vernacular went well beyond fiction itself. Language is always a form of power. Different people and different cultural institutions, to promote their respective interests, always privilege and elevate certain speech forms while demoting and disparaging others. As classical Chinese was the written language for classical studies and the examinations, it was a language valorized by the imperial state and, as such, bestowed with lofty symbolic values. In this context, the adoption of the written vernacular as the literary language in fiction carried considerable political ramifications, as it claimed a marked linguistic distinction outside the established symbolic order. Pu Songling, despite the fact that his *Strange Tales from Liaozhai* (Liaozhai zhiyi) was written in classical Chinese, was clearly aware of the power of language forms. In one of his stories, Wang Zi'an, a frustrated scholar, pledges bitterly that, if anyone dares to present him with written phrases such as *qiefu* and *changwei*, typical *wenyan* formulations frequently used in the examination essays, "I will definitely chase him out with a spear in hand" (*dingdang caoge zhu zhi*).[17] In the meantime, language forms, like other cultural symbols, embody and advance the interests of certain social groups. As reflected in Feng Menglong's famous maxim that "there are few refined minds but many crude ears under heaven," language forms are informed by, even though not reducible to, social structural forms.[18] By embracing the language of the masses, vernacular fiction writers carved a large linguistic market for themselves and formed a broad alliance in combating the established symbolic order. Thus, like other linguistic and literary conventions, the predominant use of the written vernacular in late imperial Chinese fiction "can be appreciated only as a product of, and a means for reproducing, specific historical and political relations."[19]

Late imperial China witnessed a quiet and gradual process of the intellectual elite's refocusing of their interest and expectations from political power to common people and from the ruler (*tianzi*) to society and civilization (*tianxia*), a process that can be traced back to Wang Yangming, if not earlier.[20] Admittedly, on an individual level a literatus's exit from the examinations was often involuntary, but the massive transfer of educational and intellectual capital from political domains into cultural realms was consistent with the sustained endeavor of the literati to redefine their relationships with the state and society, respectively. Thus, the rise and boom of vernacular fiction, perhaps more so than many other branches of the literati culture in late imperial China, was closely related to the exodus of legions of highly educated men away from government service, an institution so strictly controlled by and so closely associated with the state power that one may wish to call it an "imperial shadow." Vernacular fiction was one of the products of that exodus from the imperial shadow, as the redistribution of intellectual forces helped make the new narrative genre possible culturally and linguistically. Yet vernacular fiction is also an *image* of that exodus itself, as we can see in works such as *The Scholars* and *Dream of the Red Chamber*, where literati figures turn away from government service and start to "attend to their own affairs."

In its contemplation of the literati's historical destiny, late imperial Chinese vernacular fiction portends a future moment when Chinese intelligentsia finally parted ways with government service, at least in a formal sense. For that moment, history would have to wait till the abolishment of the civil service examinations in 1905, or even the May 4th Movement over a decade later. Yet it seems that our fiction writers discussed in this study already discerned a historical momentum toward that end, as the two-millennium-long partnership of Chinese intellectuals and imperial state became increasingly rugged in the late dynasties. Chinese *shi*, as mentioned earlier, emerged as a self-conscious social group during the Spring and Autumn period in a historic "breakthrough," a moment when "rituals corrupted and music crumpled" (*lihuai yuebeng*). If ritual and music serve as a metaphor for the system of Confucian moral and intellectual convictions in general, the times our vernacular fiction writers lived in can perhaps be called another moment of *lihuai yuebeng*, a moment that witnessed the decline of the *daotong* and the fossilization of the *dao* learning in the hand of the imperial state. Once again, this became a moment for the intellectuals to start regrouping themselves and redefining their historical missions. As if history advances in a cyclical movement, this déjà vu eventually would result in another breakthrough, of which late imperial Chinese vernacular fiction may be considered a harbinger. If the earlier breakthrough catalyzed an age-long partnership between Chinese intellectuals and the state power, this later breakthrough would see the intellectuals marching out of the obsolete symbolic system in anticipation of the advent of modernity. Indeed, it would be a future of many uncertainties for them, but, just like Jia Baoyu in his departure from the mundane world, they would never turn back.

# Notes

## INTRODUCTION

1   For a case in point, compare C. T. Hsia's *A History of Modern Chinese Fiction* and his *The Classic Chinese Novel: A Critical Introduction*. It is apparent that the approach in the former is much more political than in the latter.
2   Chen Xizhong et al., eds., *Shuihu zhuan huipingben*, 1:28.
3   Yang Minglang, "*Yingxiong pu* juanshou," reprinted in Zhu Yixuan and Liu Yuchen, eds., *Shuihu zhuan ziliao huibian*, 231.
4   Tianhuazang Zhuren, *Ping Shan Leng Yan*, 10–15.
5   Shuhui Yang, *Appropriation and Representation*, 126.
6   Lukacs, *Theory of the Novel*, 45.
7   Aristotle, *The Poetics*, 17.
8   See, for example, Hayden White, "Getting Out of History."
9   Hans Georg Gadamer, for instance, maintains in *Truth and Method* (New York: Continuum, 2004) that hermeneutic consciousness is in motion because it constantly merges the horizon of the past with that of the present.
10  Gallagher and Greenblatt, *Practicing New Historicism*, 7.
11  Ibid., 15.
12  For a discussion of *shi* and its evolution from a military term for "strategic advantage" to the concept of a ruler's "political purchase," see Ames, *The Art of Rulership*, 65–107.
13  For more thorough discussions of the origins of the terms *shi* and *shidafu*, see

Yan Buke, *Shidafu zhengzhi yansheng shigao,* 29–72, and Ge Quan, *Quanli zaige lixing,* 4–19.
14. *Cihai* (Shanghai: Shanghai cishu, 1979), 515.
15. Bol, "On the Problem of Contextualizing Ideas," 73.
16. Naquin and Rawski have noted that a "source of unresolved tension" for the Qing government during the eighteenth century "was the discrepancy between the state's desire to reach outside the bureaucracy and control localities and its inability to do so without the cooperation of local elites." See Naquin and Rawski, *Chinese Society in the Eighteen Century,* 11.
17. Fei Xiaotong has argued that the separation of the *daotong* from the *zhengtong*, or lineage of political power, started with the reverence for the legendary Duke of Zhou (Zhou Gong), the regent for King Wu of the Zhou (Zhou Wu Wang) (r. 1115?–1079? BCE), and was completed with the advent of Confucius himself. See Fei Xiaotong, "Lun shiru," 26. Mencius dwelled on the succession of "virtue" (*de*) among the ancient sages. He was very close to proposing a lineage of the *daotong*, even though he did not use the term.

    Among Confucian scholars of the subsequent ages, Han Yu (768–824) was the one who first attempted a formal lineage of the *daotong*, which, according to him, came from the ancient sage kings (Yao, Shun, Yu, Tang, Wen, and Wu) down to Duke of the Zhou, and then to Confucius and Mencius. Han Yu expressed his anxiety, which was perhaps shared by many other Confucian scholars of the time, that "nobody has taken over the legacy since the death of Meng Ke." Yet that anxiety itself, paradoxically, evidences a continuous consciousness among leading Confucian scholars of the lineage of the *dao* learning. See *Han Yu xuanji,* 267.

    According to Yu Yingshi, it was Zhu Xi's (1130–1200) student and son-in-law Huang Gan (1152–1221) who extended the lineage of the *daotong* to reach the Northern Song Confucians Zhou Dunyi, the Cheng brothers, and Zhang Zai, and finally Zhu Xi himself. See Yu Yingshi, *Zhu Xi de lishi shijie,* 1:16. On the specific names in the *daotong*, there was never a true consensus among Confucian scholars, especially in the late imperial periods. For instance, there was a debate whether Zeng Shen (505–436 BCE) or Yan Yuan (521–490 BCE) should be regarded as the link between Confucius and Mencius. For the purpose in this book, however, such details are not very important, because *daotong* here refers more to the Confucian tradition at large than a list of sages' names.
18. Tu Wei-ming, "The Sung Confucian Idea of Education," 147.
19. Gramsci, *An Antonio Gramsci Reader,* 235.
20. Foucault, *Power,* 329.

21  Ibid., 340.
22  Wang Dingbao, *Tang zhiyan*, 1:3.
23  It is generally believed that the examination system had its inception in the Sui period (589–618), but it was during the Tang, especially under the reign of Emperor Taizong, that the system took significant steps of development. It is stated in Wang Dingbao's *Tang zhiyan* (1:3): "The *jinshi* examinations originated in the middle of the Daye period of the Sui and flourished in the late Zhenguan and early Yonghui periods of the Tang. Even high-ranking officials would not feel good about themselves without a *jinshi* degree." Also see Chen Maotong, *Zhongguo lidai xuanguan zhidu*, 110–68; Wang Daocheng, *Keju shihua*, 2–9. However, it was not until the Song that "the most important positions in government were occupied by *jinshi*," as the function of the examination system shifted from restricting the power of the aristocracy during the Tang into establishing a civil bureaucracy. See Ichisada Miyazaki, *China's Examination Hell*, 115–16
24  Elman, "Changes in Confucian Civil Service Examinations," 111.
25  Elman, *A Cultural History*, xvii.
26  Foucault, *Power*, 333. Expounding the nature of pastoral power, Foucault writes: "This form of power is salvation-oriented (as opposed to political power). It is oblative (as opposed to the principle of sovereignty); it is individualizing (as opposed to legal power); it is coextensive and continuous with life; it is linked with a production with truth—the truth of the individual himself" (333).
27  Yu Yingshi, *Shi yu Zhongguo wenhua*, 100.
28  Foucault, *Power*, 332.
29  Ibid., 332.
30  Clare O'Farrell, *Michel Foucault*, 46.
31  Ge Zhaoguang, *Zhongguo sixiang shi*, 477.
32  Hayden White, "Getting Out of History," 147.
33  Fredric Jameson, *The Political Unconscious*, 70.

## CHAPTER 1. A RUGGED PARTNERSHIP

1  Equally popular among schoolboys was a poem by the Song scholar Wang Zhu (11th cent.), which includes these lines: "The Son of Heaven values heroes, / And wants you to study the writings. / All occupations are inferior, / Exalted is only book-learning."
2  Legge, *Confucian Analects*, 302–3; translation modified.
3  Yang Bojun, *Mengzi yizhu*, 2:321.

4   Yang Bojun, *Mengzi yizhu*, 2:303; D. C. Lau, trans., *Mencius*, 183.
5   Wan Sida, "*Ming ru yanxinglu* xu," in Shen Jia, *Ming ru yanxinglu*, 1:1/a-b.
6   Yu Yingshi, *Shi yu Zhongguo wenhua*, 92.
7   Fei Xiaotong, "Lun shiru," 24.
8   Legge, *Confucian Analects*, 210–11; translation modified.
9   Ibid., 212; translation modified.
10  It may be ironic that the expression first appears in the chapter "Tianxia" in *Zhuangzi*. That, however, did not prevent the Confucians from adopting it as a most succinct dictum for their mutually complementary intents of moral cultivation and political participation.
11  Legge, *Confucian Analects*, 357–59.
12  Yang Bojun, *Mengzi yizhu*, 2:304; D. C. Lau, *Mencius*, 183.
13  Tu Wei-ming, "The Sung Confucian Idea of Education," 145.
14  Ban Gu, *Qian Han shu*, 24.2/b.
15  Liu Baonan, *Lunyu zhengyi*, 405.
16  Yang Bojun, *Mengzi yizhu*, 1:142; D. C. Lau, *Mencius*, 108.
17  Wang Xianqian, *Xunzi jijie*, 104.
18  Anonymous, *Guoyu*, 6.3/b-4/a.
19  Following elaborate performances of the ritual and music at court, a delighted Liu Bang uttered the outcry: "I finally got to know the majesty of being the emperor today." See Sima Qian, *Shi ji, juan* 99, 8:2723.
20  When Liu Bang bragged about having won the empire by fighting on horseback, Lu Jia, a scholar-official and exponent of education and cultural cultivation, retorted with the question: "You have won it on horseback, but how can you rule it on horseback as well?" See Sima Qian, *Shi ji, juan* 97, 8:2699.
21  Ban Gu, *Qian Han shu*, 1B.20/b.
22  Fan Wenlan, *Zhongguo tongshi jianbian*, 2:50–51.
23  Dongfang Shuo, "Da ke nan," 45.3/b-4/a.
24  Wu Han, *Zhu Yuanzhang zhuan*, 160–61; also Wu Han, "Lun shenquan," in Wu Han, Fei Xiaotong et al., *Huangquan yu shenquan*, 51.
25  See, for example, Yu Yingshi, *Song Ming lixue yu zhengzhi wenhua*.
26  Li Tao, *Xu Zizhi tongjian changbian*, 221.5/b.
27  According to Yu Yingshi, the pledge of "No killings of courtiers and remonstrators," allegedly made by the founding emperor Taizu (r. 960–75), was not to be found in firsthand historical sources; however, it did become a tenet for subsequent Song rulers in general. See Yu Yingshi, *Song Ming lixue yu zhengzhi wenhua*, 15. Gu Yanwu (1613–82) considered the relatively benign treatment of the intellectuals one of the four major reasons for the longevity of the Song dynasty, which lasted over three hundred years. See *Ri zhi lu jishi*, 15:1224–25.

28  See Yu Yingshi, *Zhu Xi de lishi shijie*.
29  Shen Defu, *Wanli yehuobian*, 2: 454–83. About the early Ming officials terrified by Zhu Yuanzhang's tyranny, Zhao Yi (1727–1814) gave this account: "Every morning when the officials in the capital went to the court, they would always bid farewell to their wives and children. If they came back home safe and sound in the evening, they would always celebrate with their families for having lived another day." See Zhao Yi, *Nianershi zhaji*, 9:680–81.
30  Liu Zongzhou, *Liuzi yishu*, 2.15/b.
31  For an analysis of the demise of the Ming, see, e.g., Shinian Kanchai, *Wan Ming qishi nian*, 275–301.
32  The work is said to "discuss moral integrity (*dexing*), self-cultivation (*xiushen*), caution with words (*shenyan*), caution with action (*jinxing*), diligence (*qinli*), vigilance (*jingjie*), thrift (*jiejian*), charity (*jishan*), following the sages' teaching (*chong shengxun*), admiring the worthies (*jing xianfan*), waiting upon the parents (*shi fumu*), serving the ruler (*shi jun*), waiting upon the parents-in-law (*shi jiugu*), ancestry worship (*feng jisi*), motherhood (*muyi*), familial harmony (*muqin*), love for children (*ciyou*), support for the subordinates (*daixia*), and proper treatment for marriage relatives (*dai waiqi*)." See Cao Renhu and Ji Huang, *Qingding xu wenxian tongkao*, 173.-15/b.
33  In 1473 an official reported to Emperor Chenghua (r. 1465–87) that errors had been found in the texts collected in *Wujing sishu daquan*, but the emperor rejected the proposal. In 1484, a Confucian scholar from Wuxi submitted his revised version of Zhu Xi's *Sishu jizhu* (Commentaries and annotations on the Four Books), but Emperor Chenghua would not tolerate any tampering with Zhu Xi's words and had the scholar imprisoned.
34  Liang Qichao, *Zhongguo jin sanbainian xueshushi*, 3.
35  Ethnical sentiments, however, should not be considered the sole reason for all the boycotts of the Manchu regime. Lynn A. Struve has pointed out that this ambivalence regarding office-holding "should be viewed integrally with long-standing misgivings toward the civil service examinations (whether under Ming or Qing auspices), and toward public service itself." See Struve, "Ambivalence and Action: Some Frustrated Scholars of the K'ang-hsi Period," 327.
36  About the economic and cultural prominence of the Lower Yangzi region for much of the Qing dynasty, see Susan Naquin and Evelyn S. Rawski, *Chinese Society in the Eighteenth Century*, 147–58.
37  In addition to a series of banquets, Kangxi made a gesture of respect toward the candidates by announcing that the examination would have been unnecessary if not for the purpose of providing an opportunity for them to demonstrate their erudition. The emperor's conciliatory overture was also reflected

by the topic line for the poetic composition as part of the examination: "All people under heaven are one family" (*Tianxia wei yijia*). See Xu Ke, *Qing bai leichao*, 2:706–7. Furthermore, the emperor was exceptionally generous in passing and grading the candidates. See Chen Maotong, *Zhongguo lidai xuanguan zhidu*, 428–29.

38 Jiang Liangqi, *Donghua lu*, 122.
39 Xu Ke, *Qing bai leichao*, 1:241.
40 See, for example, Luther Carrington Goodrich, *The Literary Inquisition of Ch'ien-lung*; Ding Yuanji, *Qingdai Kang Yong Qian sanchao jinshu yuanyin zhi yanjiu*.
41 Chen Dongyuan, *Zhongguo jiaoyu shi*, 416–17.
42 Elman, *A Cultural History*, 135.
43 Li Guangdi, *Rongcun quanji*, 10.3/b–10.4/a.
44 Aixinjueluo Xuanye, *Qing Shengzu Ren Huangdi yuzhi wenji*, 19.4/b.
45 Inspired by the ideals of the Ming loyalist Lü Liuliang (1629–83), Zeng Jing, a licentiate from Hunan, denounced what he called Yongzheng's several crimes, including usurpation of the throne, and attempted to instigate Yue Zhongqi (1686–1754), the governor-general of Sichuan and Shaanxi, to rebel against the Manchu court. After Zeng was arrested and forced to write his statement of repentance, Yongzheng had Zeng's statement, along with his edicts on the case and the record of the interrogation, publicized in a volume titled *Dayi juemi lu* (Record of being awakened from befuddlement by the cardinal principles). Yongzheng then distributed copies of the book to all scholars empire-wide for mandatory reading, and used Zeng, whose life he decided to spare (until he was executed by Yongzheng's son and successor, Emperor Qianlong), as a living example of a scholarly revolt subjugated.
46 Zeng Jing, "Gui ren shuo," 180.
47 This is clear from the transcripts of the interrogations of Zeng Jing that are included in *Dayi juemi tan*. Besides the issue of ethnicity of the Manchu rulers, which Zeng Jing had exploited in his seditious instigation, the interrogations actually touched upon many other topics ranging from the civil service examinations to disaster relief and even mintage of copper money. The topic that was debated most extensively was, not surprisingly, that of the ruler-subject relationship.
48 Pei Songzhi has this comment on Zhuge Liang: "He served as prime minister and was heartily respected by all the courtiers. That was because of the full trust from Liu Bei as well as his own outstanding abilities. He acted as regent over all state affairs, had all the powers but remain prudent, and made decisions on behalf of the sovereign yet did not incur suspicions. That was why

he was beloved by the ruler, the officials, and the common people." See Chen Shou, *Sanguo zhi*, 5:934.

49 Despite all the differences between Wang Anshi's *xinxue* (New School) and Zhu Xi's *lixue* (School of Principle), Zhu Xi and other Southern Song neo-Confucians actually followed Wang's model of *dejun xingdao*, when they tried, although unsuccessfully, to win the support from emperors Xiaozong (r. 1163–89) and Guangzong (r. 1190–94). See Yu Yingshi, *Zhu Xi de lishi shijie*, 2: 850–53.
50 Li Tao, *Xu Zizhi tongjian changbian*, 233.22/b.
51 Zhang Tingyu et al., *Ming shi*, 19:5652.
52 Yu Yingashi, *Song Ming lixue yu zhengzhi wenhua*, 38.
53 Zhang Tingyu et al., *Ming shi*, 8:2284 and 8:2318. Also see Zhao Yi, *Nianershi zhaji*, 9:677.
54 Wang Yangming, *Wang Wencheng quanshu*, 4.26/a.
55 Fei Xiaotong, "Lun shenshi," 7.
56 Wm. Theodore de Bary, ed., *Self and Society in Late Ming Thought*, 6.
57 See de Bary, "Individualism and Humanitarianism in Late Ming Thought," 145–247.
58 Lü Kun, *Shenyin yu*, 79.
59 Gu Yanwu, *Ri zhi lu jishi*, 3:1014.
60 Huang Zongxi, *Ming yi dai fang lu*, 1–2.
61 Tang Zhen, *Qian shu*, 196.
62 For an account of Fang Yizhi's reinterpretation of *gewu*, see William J. Peterson, "Fang I-chih: Western Learning and the 'Investigation of Things.'"
63 Yan Yuan, *Cun xue bian*, 2.
64 Li Gong, *Shugu hou ji*, 1:39.
65 Yan Yuan, *Xizhai jiyu*, 1:3.
66 Hu Shi has observed that the success of the evidential scholars derived from four characteristics of their research: their historical vision, their use of philology as a tool, their inductive methodology, and their emphasis on evidence. See Hu Shi, "Dai Dongyuan de zhexue," 31.
67 Liang Qichao, *Zhongguo jin sanbainian xueshushi*, 27.
68 Guo Kangsong, *Qingdai kaojuxue yanjiu*, 66.
69 Qian Mu, *Guoxue gailun*, 276.

CHAPTER 2. ROMANCE OF THE THREE KINGDOMS

1 Zhang Xuecheng, *Zhang shi yishu waibian*, juan 1. Excerpted in Zhu Yixuan and Liu Yuchen, eds., *Sanguo yanyi ziliao huibian*, 692.

2   In his *Sanguo yanyi kaoping,* Zhou Zhaoxin notes the difference between the ways of selecting narrative material in the novel and Chen Shou's (233–97) *Sanguo zhi.* While Chen Shou attempts to provide a panoramic view of that historical period, the novelist "only selects what would serve his own purpose and plan" (74). Similarly, Wu Zuxiang observes that the writer of *Three Kingdoms* "utilizes the Three Kingdoms stories to express his political views on the reality of his time and projects in them his own ideals and wishes." See *Shuo bai ji,* 20.

3   Peter R. Moody, "*The Romance of the Three Kingdoms* and Popular Chinese Political Thought," 178.

4   Shelley Hsueh-lun Chang, *History and Legend,* 134.

5   This is what Robert E. Hegel suggests in his discussion of the late imperial Chinese writers of historical fiction: "By presenting their fiction as popularized history, thus as a recognized way of transmitting proper moral values to posterity, novelists could nominally identify with Confucian historiography even if facetiously. Official histories seldom provided sufficient details to make a good story; hence a novelist was free to make up what he needed, ostensibly secure in the belief, although perhaps less than totally seriously, that he was performing a somewhat meritorious act of writing." See Hegel, *Reading Illustrated Fiction,* 29.

6   See, for example, Zhang Peiheng, "Guanyu Luo Guanzhong de shengzu nian," 107–11.

7   See Zhang Guoguang, "*Sanguozhi tongsu yanyi* chengshu yu Ming zhongye bian," 270–71.

8   For instance, Shanzhou, one of those Yuan place-names that appear in the interlinear notes, was officially renamed Yilingzhou during the Ming. But in an epigraph for the fifteenth-century official Yang Wenke (d. 1465) collected in *Ming wenhai* (*Siku quanshu* ed., 442.12/b-13/a), it is said that one of Yang's sons was appointed to an official position in Shanzhou (*ling Shanzhou panguan*). Also mentioned in the notes is Jiankang, a Yuan name for the Nanjing area. According to *Ming yitong zhi* (*Siku quanshu* ed., 6.5/b-6/a), the jurisdiction of Jiankang Lu (Jiankang Prefecture) was established in the early Yuan, but it was renamed Jiqing Lu (Jiqing Prefecture) in 1329. Zhu Yuanzhang in 1356 adopted the name Yingtian Fu (Yingtian Prefecture) for the area, and after the founding of the Ming in 1368 it started to be referred to officially as Nanjing, or the Southern Capital. Yet the name Jiankang may have continued to be used during the Ming. In *juan* 71 of *Ming shi* (6:1711), it is said that Zhu Yuanzhang summoned a group of Confucian scholars "to Jiankang." In another epigraph collected in *Ming wenhai* (434.6/b), the Southern Capital

is referred to as "the imperial capital Jiankang." In the Wanjuanlou edition of *Sanguo yanyi*, the interlinear notes on place-names often refer to *Ming yitong zhi*, a geographic work published in 1461, yet some of the notes still contain place-names such as Yidu Lu, which is obviously a Yuan term. It may seem that people in the Ming were either remarkably liberal or irredeemably sloppy in their use of place-names. Whatever the case, the use of place-names from the previous Yuan period did not seem to be a politically sensitive issue.

9   See Zhang Peiheng, "Guanyu Jiajing ben *Sanguozhi tongsu yanyi* xiaozhu de zuozhe"; Yuan Shishuo, "Ming Jiajing ben *Sanguozhi tongsu yanyi* nai Yuanren Luo Guanzhong yuanzuo"; Ouyang Jian, "Shilun *Sanguozhi tongsu yanyi* de chengshu niandai."

10  For a debate on the significance of the Ming place-names in the interlinear notes, see Ouyang Jian, "Shilun *Sanguozhi tongsu yanyi* de chengshu niandai"; Zhang Guoguang, "*Sanguozhi tongsu yanyi* chengshu yu Ming zhongye bian"; and Zhang Peiheng, "Zaitan *Sanguozhi tongsu yanyi* de xiezuo niandai wenti."

11  The twentieth-century Chinese scholar Zheng Zhenduo (1898–1958) observed: "There remains skepticism about the authorship of *Water Margin*. As for *Three Kingdoms*, however, there is little doubt that it was written by Luo Guanzhong." See Zheng Zhenduo, "*Sanguozhi yanyi* de yanhua," 192. Indeed, little has changed since Zheng Zhenduo made that assertion in 1930s.

12  In the second entry following that for Luo Guanzhong, for example, the biographic note for the early Ming playwright Gu Zijing mentions Gu's expertise on *Zhou Yi*, his knowledge in medicine, his oratory eloquence, and his exquisite *yuefu* poems. See Jia Zhongming, *Luguibu xubian*, 281–82.

13  *Luguibu xubian*, 281. The date for *Luguibu xubian* cannot be earlier than 1424, because the compiler states that more than sixty years had passed since he had met Luo Guanzhong for the last time in 1364.

14  *Sanguozhi tongsu yanyi*, 1:5.

15  Of those Yuan place-names in the interlinear notes throughout the 1522 edition, two stand out as the most significant because they contain the term *lu*, the Yuan equivalent to the Ming term *fu* (prefecture). Indeed, one of those two, Yizhou Lu, occurs in *juan* 2. That could suggest that it was before or shortly after the demise of the Yuan when the novelist was at that early point of the composition. The lone other instance of *lu* is in the name Guiyang Lu. It takes place in *juan* 11, but its status is more ambiguous because it is not unequivocally referred to as a "contemporary place-name."

16 Zheng Zhenduo asserted that all extant versions of the novel were derived from the 1522 edition, with minimal and negligible textual variations ("*Sanguozhi yanyi* de yanhua," 213). Anne E. McLaren has challenged that view by pointing out that the opening chapters in one of the pictorial editions contain considerably fewer written characters but cover more narrative details than their counterparts in the 1522 edition. See McLaren, "Popularizing *The Romance of the Three Kingdoms*," 173.

17 See Liu Cunren [Ts'un-yan Liu], "Luo Guanzhong jiangshi xiaoshuo zhi zhenwei xingzhi," 82–83. Yu Chaogui has noted that the 1522 edition does not feature the character Hua Guan Suo, the Shu general Guan Yu's third son, as the *zhizhuan* editions do. From there Yu speculates that the earliest Three Kingdoms text might contain a Hua Guan Suo ingredient, which could have been dropped out in *Tongsu yanyi* but kept intact in the *zhizhuan* tradition. See Yu Chaogui, "*Sanguo yanyi* banben er ti," 204–5. Gail King has also informed us of a textual discrepancy between the Hua Guan Suo episode in the Württemberg fragment dated 1592 and its counterpart in the 1605 Lianhuitang edition. King suggests that, as that discrepancy was most likely caused by a scribal error in the 1592 text, the inclusion of Hua Guan Suo in the novel "dates from before 1592." See King, "A Few Textual Notes Regarding Guan Suo and the *Sanguo yanyi*," 91.

18 Andrew Plaks, *The Four Masterworks of the Ming Novel*, 365.

19 One of the embedded poems in the 1522 edition has been identified as a composition by a fifteenth-century writer, Yin Zhi (1427–1511). See Wang Liqi, "Luo Guanzhong yu *Sanguozhi tongsu yanyi*," 254. Wang asserts that that poem, along with several others in the 1522 edition, could have been inserted by Zhang Shangde, the author of one of the prefaces and possibly the editor of the edition. Additionally, there are interlinear notes in the 1522 edition that may suggest revisions over an earlier version, and that process of revision could have been a multi-tiered one if those notes themselves were inherited from a textual antecedent, rather than written by the editor of the 1522 edition himself. Yu Chaogui has called our attention to some of such notes ("*Sanguo yanyi* banben er ti," 55).

20 Yuan Shishuo considers it "most likely" that the 1522 edition retains all the features from the Luo Guanzhong text, and he regards the citation of a fifteenth-century poem in *juan* 21 an isolated interpolation by the editor(s). See Yuan's "Ming Jiajing kanben *Sanguozhi tongsu yanyi* nai Yuanren Luo Guanzhong yuanzuo."

21 Yang Bojun, *Mengzi yizhu*, 1:186; D. C. Lau, *Mencius*, 128.

22 What happened in the court between Zhu Yuanzhang and his top civil offi-

cials concerning the *Mencius* was particularly revealing of the confrontation between the imperial authority and the intellectual elite. The emperor threatened to have any protestors executed. Risking his life, Qian Tang remonstrated defiantly: "If I die for Meng Ke [Mencius] it will be a glorious death." Miraculously, Zhu Yuanzhang was moved by Qian's audacity and sincerity, and left Mencius's status in the official pantheon intact. See *Ming shi*, 13:3982. According to Chen Jian's *Huang Ming tongji jiyao*, however, Zhu Yuanzhang ordered the archers to shoot at Qian Tang, but afterward sent him to the imperial hospital to have his wounds treated (4:465).

23  See Zhu Ronggui, "Cong Liu Sanwu *Mengzi jiewen* lun junquan de xianzhi yu zhishifenzi zhi zizhuxing"; Yin Xuanbo, *Zhongguo Mingdai jiaoyu shi*, 28.

24  Zhu Yizun, *Jingyi kao*, 235.17/b.

25  Song Lian's biography in *Ming shi* states that Song died in Kuizhou on his way to exile to Sichuan, but curiously mentions no cause of his death. See *Ming shi*, 12:3788. According to Gu Yingtai's *Mingshi jishi benmo*, Song died of illness (2:58–59). Based on some unofficial sources, however, one modern scholar has suggested that Song could have committed suicide out of despair. See Zhan Changhao, "Shilun Ming chu daru Song Lian zhi si."

26  *Ming shi*, 6:1697.

27  During the Hongwu reign the academy had two campuses, located respectively in the capital Nanjing and Zhu Yuanzhang's hometown Fengyang of Anhui. The Fengyang campus was much smaller and became defunct in 1393, and the instructors and students moved to the Nanjing campus. In 1402, Emperor Yongle set up a new campus in Beijing. The two campuses coexisted for the remainder of the Ming dynasty, though the Nanjing campus remained the larger one for many years even after Beijing replaced Nanjing as the primary capital in 1421. As an indicator of the size of the Imperial Academy in the early Ming, the numbers of the students for some years during the Hongwu reign are recorded in *Nanyong zhi*: 2728 in 1371; 577 in 1382; 766 in 1383; 980 in 1384; 969 in 1390; 1532 in 1391; 1309 in 1392; 8124 in 1393; and 1829 in 1397. See Chen Maotong, *Zhongguo lidai xuanguan zhidu*, 270.

28  Chen Maotong, *Zhongguo lidai xuanguan zhidu*, 277; Yin Xuanpo, *Zhongguo Mingdai jiaoyu shi*, 54.

29  *Ming shi*, 13:3952.

30  *Nanyong zhi*, juan 10, quoted in Chen Maotong, *Zhongguo lidai xuanguan zhidu*, 278–79.

31  *Ming shi*, 13:4019; also Gu Yingtai, *Ming shi jishi benmo*, 3:48–49.

32  For some of the so-called Jianwen martyrs—Qi Tai, Huang Zicheng, Fang

Xiaoru, Lian Zining, Zhou Xuan, Zhuo Jing, Chen Di, and others—see *Ming shi*, 13:4013–30; *Ming shi jishi benmo*, 3:48–61. Benjamin A. Elman has offered a vivid English retelling of the Fang Xiaoru story in his "'Where is King Ch'eng?' Civil Examinations and Confucian Ideology during the Early Ming, 1368–1415."

33 It is stated in *Lunyu*: "The Master said, 'Extreme is my decay. For a long time, I have not dreamed, as I was wont to do, that I saw the Duke of Zhou." See Legge, *Confucian Analects*, 196. Zhu Xi has made this comment on those words from Confucius: "In his prime years Confucius had aspired to follow the *dao* of Duke Zhou, and that was why he sometimes met him in his dreams." See *Lunyu jizhu* (*Siku quanzhu* ed.), 4.2/a.

34 Zhu Yizun, *Jingyi kao*, 235.17/a-b.

35 Elman, *A Cultural History*, 118.

36 Ibid., 79.

37 For the sake of convenience, I refer to the author of the *Mencius* simply as Mencius, but this does not amount to an unquestioning acceptance of the master's authorship of the work.

38 Yang Bojun, *Mengzi yizhu*, 1:219; D. C. Lau, *Mencius*, 144.

39 Yang Bojun, *Mengzi yizhu*, 1:171; D. C. Lau, *Mencius*, 121–22.

40 Yang Bojun, *Mengzi yizhu*, 2:328; D. C. Lau, *Mencius*, 196.

41 *Yupi tongjian gangmu, juanshou shang*, 18/b.

42 Mao Zonggang, "Du *Sanguo zhi* fa," in *Sanguo yanyi ziliao huibian*, 293–94; David T. Roy, trans., "How to Read *The Romance of the Three Kingdoms*," in David L. Rolston, ed., *How to Read the Chinese Novel*, 152.

43 Cheng Yizhong argues that *Three Kingdoms* is much more critical of the late Han emperors and the corrupt court politics than *Sanguozhi pinghua* and that the novel's attitude toward most members of the imperial clan, such as Liu Biao and Liu Zhang, is largely derogatory: "Luo Guanzhong truly is not partial for anyone only because he is a Liu." See Cheng, "Chongti jiu'an shuo Cao Cao," 173. Another scholar, Liu Xiaoyan, considers "orthodox rule" (*zhengtong*) an issue related to but separate from the pro–Liu Bei stance in *Three Kingdoms*, with the former inherited from the histories and the latter from the popular *Sanguo* cycles. See his "Zhengtongguan yu *Sanguo yanyi*," 84. Zhou Zhaoxin also argues against the view that the characterization of Liu Bei may have been influenced by the notion of "orthodox rule": "Even those who believed in orthodox rule would not necessarily venerate Liu Bei as the orthodox ruler or to denigrate Cao Cao. The idea of orthodox rule should not be mixed up with the pro-Liu and anti-Cao tendency [in the novel]." See Zhou Zhaoxin, *Sanguo yanyi kaoping*, 98. Zhou Jialu makes

a similar argument in his "Shilun *Sanguozhi tongsu yanyi* dui chuantong sixiang wenhua de fansi," 63–64.

44  See, for instance, Luo Guanzhong, *Sanguozhi tongsu yanyi* (hereafter *SGZT-SYY*), 1:245; 3:1401; 3:1909; 4:2557. On another occasion (4:1624), it is Zhuge Liang who voices that argument on behalf of Liu Bei himself, for the purpose of retaining Jingzhou and thwarting Zhou Yu's demand of handing it over to the Wu. My English translations of the excerpts from the novel are all based on the 1522 edition of *Sanguozhi tongsu yanyi*. Compare with corresponding passages in Moss Robert's excellent translation *Three Kingdoms: A Historical Novel*, which is based on the Mao Zonggang version.

45  Chen Shou, *Sanguo zhi*, 4:877. The same passage, in slight verbal variation, is also found in Zhu Xi's *Yupi Tongjian gangmu*, 13.83/b.

46  *Sanguozhi pinghua*, 813.

47  Mao Zonggang, "Du *Sanguo zhi* fa," 295; David T. Roy, "How to Read *The Romance of the Three Kingdoms*," 156, translation slightly modified.

48  In the 1522 edition, Cao Cao blames Xu Chu and holds an elaborate funeral for Xu You. Following that passage there is an interlinear comment: "This is an example of Cao Cao's unscrupulousness. He wishes to have Xu You killed but doesn't want to stir up a controversy. So he pretends to say something like that" (*SGZTSYY*, 2:1069). Mao Zonggang observes in his chapter commentary: "The one that kills Xu You is Cao Cao, not Xu Chu. Xu You affronted Cao several times and Cao had wanted to get rid of him for a long time. If he killed Xu You he would have been criticized for having slain a friend and meritorious adviser. So he uses Xu Chu's hand to do it." See *Sanguo yanyi ziliao huibian*, 351. Another commentator, Li Yu, holds a similar view on the incident. See *Li Liweng piyue Sanguo zhi*, 365.

49  From the password "chicken ribs" that Cao Cao has issued, Yang Xiu sees Cao's undeclared intent and tells his men to get ready for a retreat: the battle is like a chicken rib, with little meat on it but some remaining flavor. Cao has Yang executed on the charge of ruining the morale of the soldiers, which may be merely an excuse. The narrator of the *yanyi* offers the comment: "Although Cao could employ men of abilities, he was jealous of them all his life and didn't want to see anyone's talent superior to his own" (*SGZTSYY*, 4:2318).

50  Hua Tuo's proposal to cleave open Cao Cao's skull is not found in *Sanguo zhi* or *Hou Hanshu* (History of the Later Han). In both sources, the physician is said to stall Cao Cao's summons with a fabricated excuse of his wife's illness. When Cao finally found out the truth, he put Hua in prison and soon had him executed. See Chen Shou, *Sanguo zhi*, 3:802–3; Fan Ye, *Hou Hanshu*,

112B.11/b. In both works, Cao Cao did not die shortly after the execution of Hua Tuo as the novel has it, although in *Sanguo zhi* Hua's death is said to be followed by the death of Cao Cao's son Cangshu.

51  *Sanguozhi pinghua*, 806.
52  *Zizhi tongjian* (*Siku quanshu* ed.), 61.5/b.
53  Yang Bojun, *Mengzi yizhu*, 1:83; D.C. Lau, *Mencius*, 84.
54  In his commentary on chapter 36, Mao Zonggang notes the structural relationship between the Xu Shu story and the debut of Zhuge Liang: "Before Zhuge Liang's numerous clever strategies and shrewd tactics later in the work, Shan Fu's casual display of his talents serves as an introduction." See *Sanguo yanyi ziliao huibian*, 357.
55  In his memorial to Liu Bei's son and successor, Liu Shan, the historical Zhuge Liang put down these lines: "Despite my lowly status, the Previous Emperor deigned to visit me three times in my thatched cottage and consulted me on the current matters of the empire." The whole text of the memorial is included in "Zhuge Liang zhuan" (Biography of Zhuge Liang) in Chen Shou, *Sanguo zhi* (4:920).
56  Chen Shou, *Sanguo zhi*, 4:912.
57  According to Pei Songzhi, it was stated in some earlier sources that Zhuge Liang went to see Liu Bei in Fancheng. Liu treated the young visitor as just another ordinary scholar before he became impressed by Zhuge's incisive analysis of the military situation. Pei Songzhi refutes that account by citing Zhuge Liang's *Chushi biao*. See *Sanguo zhi* 4:913–14. Pei's dismissal of those earlier sources is not compelling, as the two accounts are not mutually exclusive—to say Liu Bei went to visit Zhuge Liang three times does not preclude the possibility that Zhuge had visited Liu before.
58  Andrew Plaks has noted that many sequences of action in *Sanguo* plays and fiction are based on the pattern of "triple occurrence," relying upon "trebling effect" as typical of folklore and popular literature (*Four Masterworks*, 383–84). Elsewhere I consider the frequent use of the number of three in *Shuihu zhuan* a residue from the novel's oral antecedents, where it could have been used as a mnemonic device by the storytellers (*Out of the Margins*, 84).
59  Cao Xuewei argues that Zhuge Liang should be considered primarily a Confucian figure who nevertheless demonstrates Daoist elements in his thinking and actions, but he maintains a difference between Daoism in the regular sense and the Daoist tendency in Zhuge Liang, which he calls "Daoism at a more sophisticated level." See Cao Xuewei, "Daojiao yu Zhuge Liang de xingxiang suzao."
60  *Sanguo zhi pinghua*, 807–9.

61 Zheng Qian, ed., *Jiaoding Yuan kan zaju sanshizhong*, 397.
62 Apart from *Bowang shaotun*, I have perused these *Sanguo zaju* plays that feature Zhuge Liang as a major character: *Liu Xuande zui zou Huanghelou* (The intoxicated Liu Xuande goes to Yellow Crane Tower), *Zou Fengchu Pang lue si jun* (Pang Tong, the fledgling phoenix, takes four districts), *Cao Cao ye zou Chencang lu* (Cao Cao moves to Chencang at night), *Yangpingguan wu ma po Cao* (Five warriors defeat Cao Cao at Yangping Pass), and *Shoutinghou nu zhan Guan Ping* (Marquis of Shouting kills Guan Ping in fury). Another *zaju*, *Shiyangjin Zhuge lun gong* (Zhuge Liang dwells on meritorious service), should not be considered a *Sanguo zaju* because it features Zhuge Liang as a ghost, but even the ghost follows the same format of Daoist self-introduction. Except for *Bowang shaotun*, all these plays, even though some of them might be of Yuan origins, are extant only in Ming texts, and are all collected in Wang Jilie, ed., *Guben Yuan Ming zaju* and Zang Jinshu, ed., *Yuanqu xuan*.
63 Yi Yin was a legendary counselor to King Tang, founder of the ancient Shang dynasty (ca. 16th cent.—ca. 11th cent. BCE). Jiang Ziya, also known as Jiang Shang or Lü Shang, was the chief adviser to King Wen, founder of the Zhou dynasty (ca. 11th cent.—256 BCE), who later helped King Wu, King Wen's son and successor, in overthrowing the tyrannical Zhou, the last ruler of the Shang. Both Zhang Liang and Chen Ping were counselors and strategists for Liu Bang, founding emperor of the Han dynasty. Geng Yan and Deng Yu were both aides to Liu Xiu (r. 25–56), who defeated the usurper Wang Mang and founded the Eastern Han (23–220).
64 *Li Liweng piyue Sanguo zhi*, 476.
65 One of the measures the Han state took to maintain the dominance of Confucianism over other schools of thinking was to establish positions of academic officials (*xueguan*) each specializing in one of the Confucian classics. The title for those officials was *boshi*. There were *boshi* for such canonized texts as *Classic of Poetry*, *Analects*, *Spring and Autumn Annals*, *Classic of Filiality*, *Mencius*, and *Erya*. Each *boshi* was entitled to take fifty students, or *boshi dizi*, who were qualified for official appointments. See Chen Dongyuan, *Zhongguo jiaoyu shi*, 24 and 44.
66 There were two different channels of recommendation in the *chaju* system: *xianliang fangzheng* (virtuousness and righteousness) and *xiaolian* (filiality and honesty). As the terms may suggest, both forms of recommendation were supposedly more heavily dependent on a moral evaluation than textual scholarship. While *xianliang fangzheng* was operational in the early Han, *xiaolian* became the regular form of recommendation throughout the rest

of the dynasty. Even though the recommended candidates were usually not tested on the classics, starting with Emperor Wen (r. 179–157 BCE) they had to pass a test of "policy questions" (*cewen*) before they became qualified for official appointments. See Chen Maotong, *Zhongguo lidai xuanguan zhidu*, 58–62; Xie Qing and Tang Deyong, eds., *Zhongguo kaoshi zhidu shi*, 34–36.

67 See Chen Dongyuan, *Zhongguo jiaoyu shi*, 249. It is stated in *Ming shi*: "[The examination writing] basically imitated that of the Song *jingyi*, but in the tone of the ancients. It was in the format of parallelism, and was called *bagu*" (6:1693). According to Gu Yanwu, Wang Anshi, in his late years, came to regret instituting the *jingyi shi* as the standard format for the examination writing: "I intended it to turn pedants into scholars, and did not expect it to turn scholars into pedants!" See Gu Yanwu, *Rizhilu jishi*, juan 18.2:1410.

68 Liu Bei refers here to chapter 10.7 of the *Mencius*. See Yang Bojun, *Mengzi yizhu*, 2:248; D. C. Lau, *Mencius*, 157–58. Confucius highly commended the gamekeeper's refusal to answer Duke Jing's summons.

69 The text of the 1522 edition contains an interlinear note that retells the story of Duke Huan. Slightly different versions of the same story can be found in Chen Houyao's *Chunqiu Zhanguo yici* (*Siku quanshu* ed.) 17. 8/a, and Xue Yuji's *Chunqiu biedian* (*Siku quanshu* ed.) 2.3/b-4/a.

70 *Ming shi*, 8:2318.

71 Yang Bojun, *Mengzi yizhu*, 1:89; D. C. Lau, *Mencius*, 87.

72 Yang Bojun, *Mengzi yizhu*, 1:248; D. C. Lau, *Mencius*, 157.

73 Yang Bojun, *Mengzi yizhu*, 2:297–98; D. C. Lau, *Mencius*, 180–81.

74 Zhou Zhaoxin has noted that historically, these two battles were won by Liu Bei before his recruitment of Zhuge Liang. See Zhou, *Sanguo yanyi kaoping*, 111–12. Obviously, the novelist attributes these victories to Zhuge Liang to make Zhuge's debut as a strategist more dramatic and impressive. Zhou Wuchun has noted a similar effort in the novel to bolster Zhuge Liang's image as a resourceful military adviser. The elaborate event of Zhuge Liang "borrowing" arrows from Cao Cao with boats full of straw bundles may have been based on the similar but much sketchier episodes in *Sanguo zhi* and *pinghua* where the feat is attributed, respectively, to Sun Quan and Zhou Yu. See Zhou Wuchun, "Cong *Sanguo yanyi* Chibi zhi zhan tan lishi he xiaoshuo de guanxi," 34–35.

75 See Andrew Plaks, *The Four Masterworks*, 436.

76 In his commentary on chapter 85, Mao Zonggang observes: "You may want to ask whether the Previous Emperor's proposal of Kongming taking over the imperial authority is genuine or phony. The answer is: It is genuine if you take it as genuine, and it is phony if you take it as phony. It is impossible

to make Kongming do what Cao Pi has done, because out of his personal honor he will neither dare nor bear to do such a thing. Because he knows Kongming will neither dare nor bear to do it, [the Previous Emperor] lets him hear these words, so that he will support the heir apparent all the more wholeheartedly." See Zhu Yixuan and Liu Yuchen, *Sanguo yanyi ziliao huibian*, 439.

77 Here is one example of the use of the term *shouzu* in describing the way Liu Bei treats his sworn brothers: When Guan Yu is surrounded by the Wu forces and the Wu official Zhuge Jin tries to persuade Guan Yu to surrender, Guan says this in reply: "I was but a warrior from Jieliang. By his favor my lord has treated me like his hands and feet [*yi shouzu dai zhi*]. How can I betray my honor and surrender to the enemy?" (chap. 76, 4:2454). Xiong Du considers the sworn brotherhood in *Three Kingdoms* and *Water Margin* a trope for the idealized ruler-minister relationship. See Xiong Du, "Zhongguo fengjian junchen guanxi de bianqe yanbian."

78 According to *Ming shi jishi benmo* (3:48), Zhu Di, in response to Fang Xiaoru's denouncement, ordered soldiers to cut Fang's mouth, and "the cut was so deep as to reach both ears." Fang was forced to watch the executions of his relatives and friends before he was put to death by dismembering.

79 Xu Qianxue, *Zizhi tongjian houbian* (*Siku quanshu* ed.) 4.5/b. In 966, Emperor Taizu accidentally found from the back of a copper mirror that his current reign title Qiande had been used in an earlier period. He was disappointed and blamed it on the ignorance of his civil officials, especially the prime minister Zhao Pu, who was not a scholar and therefore not very knowledgeable of history.

80 Huang Zongxi, *Ming yi dai fang lu*, 5.

81 See the comment (*zan*) at the end of the biographies of Li Shanchang and Wang Guangyang. *Ming shi*, 12:3775.

82 *Ming shi*, 26:7907.

83 Ibid., 12:3781 and 27:7906.

84 Su Tongbing has proposed this hypothesis in his "Mingdai xiangquan yanjiu," 1–9.

85 Huang Zongxi, *Ming yi dai fang lu*, 5.

86 Those works include the Judge Bao *cihua* collected in *Ming Chenghua shuochang cihua congkan* (Collection of chantefables from the Chenghua reign of the Ming dynasty) and works of fiction such as *Bao Longtu pan baijia gong'an* (Bao Longtu judges a hundred cases), *Longtu gong'an* (Bao Longtu cases), *Longtu erlu* (Recorded Bao Longtu stories), *Sanxia wuyi* (Magistrate Bao and his valiant lieutenants), and others.

## CHAPTER 3. THE SCHOLAR-LOVER IN EROTIC FICTION

1 Elman, *A Cultural History*, xxiv.
2 I conceive a continuous spectrum of eroticism covering some of the late Ming and early Qing fictional works that feature a young scholar as lover. For my purpose here, I consider the difference in the degrees of eroticism among these works less significant than what they share in common, namely, the dynamic interplay between the man's sexual quest and his experience in the examinations. In that sense, a work such as *The Carnal Prayer Mat* may be regarded as more akin to *Ping Shan Leng Yan*, a typical work of the scholar-beauty genre with few explicitly sexual scenes, than it is to a work that is equally pornographic but features no scholar-lover, such as *Xiuta yeshi* (Unofficial history of the embroidered couch). This approach here partially overlaps with that of Keith McMahon in his *Misers, Shrews, and Polygamists*, where he makes a useful distinction between the "chaste 'beauty-scholar' romance" and the "erotic 'scholar-beauty' romance" (103, 127).
3 *Zhao Feiyan waizhuan*, putatively written by Ling Xuan of the Han period, tells the story of Zhao Feiyan, the empress of Emperor Cheng of the Han (r. 33–7 BCE), and her enchantment of the emperor. *Daye shiyiji*, also known as *Sui yilu* (Previously unrecorded accounts of the Sui) and *Nanbu yanhua lu* (Record of the courtesans of the south), was traditionally attributed to Yan Shigu of the Tang. It narrates the sexual escapades of Emperor Yang of the Sui (r. 604–18) during his trip to the southern city of Yangzhou. *Yang Taizhen waizhuan*, allegedly authored by Yue Shi of the Song, describes Tang Xuanzong's (r. 712–56) life in the palace chamber with his favorite concubine Yang Yuhuan.
4 According to Li Shiren, the earliest publication of *Ruyijun zhuan* could be roughly dated to the reign periods of Chenghua (1465–87) and Hongzhi (1488–1505). See Ouyang Jian and Xiao Xiangkai, *Zhongguo tongsu xiaoshuo zongmu tiyao*, 48. For modern scholarship and an annotated English translation of *Ruyijun zhuan*, see Charles R. Stone, *The Fountainhead of Chinese Erotica*.
5 Li Zhi, *Fen shu, yuan* 1. *Fen shu Xu Fen shu*, 40.
6 Yuan Hongdao, "Letter to Mr. Gong Weichang," *Yuan Hongdao jijian jiao*, 1:205.
7 Zhang Dai, *Langhuan wenji*, 199.
8 Patrick Hanan, *The Chinese Vernacular Story*, 80. Hanan states that at one extreme of the spectrum of Feng Menglong's personae is "the wit, the ribald humorist, the bohemian, the drinker, the romantic lover." Also see Zhao Yi, *Nian'ershi zhaji*, 9:718.

9   For a discussion of Zhu Xi's stance on sexual desire and sexual love, see Ping-cheung Lo, "Zhu Xi and Confucian Sexual Ethics."
10  Kai-wing Chow argues that Confucianism in the Ming was eroded by a movement of syncretism within itself, a tendency to tolerate and compromise with both Buddhism and Daoism. See Chow, *The Rise of Confucian Ritualism in Late Imperial China*, 22–33.
11  For a study of these moral handbooks, see Cynthia J. Brokaw, *The Ledgers of Merit and Demerit*.
12  Both texts of these ledgers of merits and demerits, along with many others, are collected in *Daozang jiyao* (Collectanea of selected Daoist texts).
13  R. H. van Gulik, *Sexual Life in Ancient China*, 246–50.
14  These sources include, but obviously are not limited to: Lü Xiangxie's *Kechang yiwenlu*, which includes *Guochao kechang yiwenlu*, *Qian Ming kechang yiwenlu*, *Zhisheng kechang yiwenlu*, and *Xiaoshi kechang yiwenlu*; Qian Yong's *Lüyuan conghua*; Li Diaoyuan's *Danmo lu* and *Zhiyike suoji*; Huang Zuo's *Hanlin ji*, Liang Gongchen's *Chishang caotang biji*, and the anonymous *Dengke lu* and *Dengke lu zhuan*.
15  Lü Xiangxie, *Qian Ming kechang yiwenlu*, 1.3/b. The phrase *bu ke* is a pun here. It usually means "should not" or "be prohibited from," but it was also used among examination candidates to refer to the almost unattainable status of *zhuangyuan*, the top graduate from the palace examinations. Apparently, the Cao Nai story was well known among the examination candidates of later times. In Yu Jin's *Xichao xinyu* (337), Chen Zhihua, the *zhuangyuan* of 1724, rejects the advances of a beautiful young woman from a neighboring household while he was preparing for the examinations. Following Cao Nai's example, he writes the four characters *Cao Nai bu ke* on a slip of paper and pastes it to the right of his seat.
16  Wang Jian. *Qiudeng conghua*, 1:23–24.
17  Lü Xiangxie, *Guochao kechang yiwenlu*, 1.6/a.
18  Guan Yu, the famous general of the Three Kingdoms period, came to be worshiped as a deity during the Tang period. In the numerous imperial decrees of the Tang and Song times, Guan Yu was referred to by his lifetime title of nobility, Han Shoutinghou. During the Yuan, he was often referred to as Guan Wang (Prince Guan)—as in Guan Hanqing's (fl. 1279) *zaju* play *Guan Dawang dufu dandaohui* (Prince Guan attends the meeting all by himself with a single broadsword)—or Wu'an Wang (Prince of Wu'an). In the middle of the Ming, Guan Yu was even given an imperial status and referred to as Guan Di (Emperor Guan), a practice continued by the Manchu rulers of the Qing. On the evolution of the worship of Guan Yu, see Luo

Kanglie, "Wenxue he lishi zhong de Guan Yu"; Li Huiming, "Chuanshen wenbi xie Guan Yu: Guan Yu yishu xingxiang shenshenghua zhi lishi bianqian." Kam Louie's *Theorizing Chinese Masculinity* contains a chapter that discusses Guan Yu as the representative of what Louie calls *wu* masculinity (22–41). However, it is interesting to note that in numerous anecdotes from Qing sources Guan Yu, a warrior in his lifetime, was made a deity that decided on the reward or punishment for a scholar in the examinations. To that extent, his function overlapped with that of Wenchang Dijun, the deified icon of Confucius who was generally regarded as the god in charge of scholars' fame and success.

19  Wang Shizhen, *Chibei outan*, 2:526–27.
20  Lü Xiangxie, *Guochao kechang yiwenlu*, 1.10/a. According to Shen Defu's *Wanli yehuobian* (2:413), body searches at the examination sites were very rigorous during the Jiajing reign period (1522–65), when two imperial counselors (*yushi*) were put "particularly in charge of the searches and inspections" at the entrances. Offenders were to be pilloried in front of the Ministry of Rites for a month, before sentenced to imprisonment. Later, the searches became increasingly stringent, and the candidates had to "unbutton their garments and take off their hats to be searched thoroughly."
21  Lü Xiangxie, *Guochao kechang yiwenlu*, 3.3/a.
22  Yu Jin, *Xichao xinyu*, 61.
23  Li Wa is the heroine in Bai Xingjian's (776–826) *wenyan* tale "Li Wa zhuan" (Story of Li Wa). As a courtesan, Li Wa nurtures her distressed scholar lover Young Master of Yingyang (Yingyang Gongzi) and encourages him to return to the examinations, which leads to his success.
24  Ji Yun, "Ming Yi'an huanghou waizhuan," 2–3.
25  *Qinding Daqing huidian zeli* (*Siku quanshu* ed.), 172.24/b-25/a. Also see Rawski, *The Last Emperors*, 170.
26  *Qinding Daqing huidian zeli*, 172.27/b.
27  Spence, *Emperor of China*, 123.
28  Xu Ke, *Qing bai lei chao*, 2:485.
29  Empress Dowager Cixi (1835–1908) may be a case in point. She was selected by Emperor Xianfeng (r. 1851–61) in 1852 as a concubine of the sixth rank, but she rapidly reached the zenith of political power in about a decade.
30  There were fourteen ranks for palace women during the Han dynasty. For the Tang period, palace women were organized in six "bureaus" (*ju*) and twenty-four "departments" (*si*). In the early Ming, Zhu Yuanzhang followed the Tang model but simplified the system to six "bureaus" and one additional "department," with the position of bureau leader in the sixth rank (*liupin*).

See Zhang Tingyu et al., *Ming shi*, 12:3503–4. The ranks of imperial concubines were of course higher. During the Tang, imperial concubines with titles of *guifei, shufei, defei*, and *xianfei* were all in the first rank, the so-called nine ladies (*jiu pin*) in the second rank, and the nine with the title *jieyu* in the third rank. The other members of the imperial harem were in the range from the fourth to the eighth rank. Later Ming and Qing rulers inherited this institution of stratified imperial harem. During the Qing, the imperial consorts were also differentiated in eight ranks, with the empress at the top, followed in descending order by the status groups of *huangguifei, guifei, fei, pin, guiren, changzai*, and *daying*. See Rawski, *The Last Emperors*, 132.

31  About the corruption in the examination system, especially bribery and favoritism, see Benjamin A. Elman's *A Cultural History of Civil Examinations in Late Imperial China*, 195–207, 224–28.

32  In Ban Gu's *Qian Han shu*, Wang Zhaojun (i.e. Wang Qiang, fl. 33 BCE), a palace woman under Emperor Yuan (Yuan Di) (r. 49–33 BCE), is said to have volunteered to be married to the king of the Xiongnu in a noble act of self-sacrifice for peace after the Xiongnu proposed an alliance by marriage (*Siku quanshu* ed., 94.12/b-13/a). In *Xijing zaji* (Miscellaneous records of the western capital), however, the cause of Wang's exile is said to be Mao Yanshou's misrepresentation of her beauty (*Siku quanshu* ed., 2. 1/a-b). The Wang Zhaojun story also appears in Liu Yiqing's *Shishuo xinyu*, where Mao Yanshou is referred to as a "palace painter" but not by name (142).

33  The Tang poets Li Bai (701–62) and Bai Juyi (772–846), each composing numerous poems on Wang Zhaojun, could be considered representatives of the sustained poetic fascination with the legendary palace beauty. Wang Anshi (1021–86) of the Song also left us with two famous poems on Zhaojun, titled "Mingfei qu" (Tunes on Mingfei). The earliest known prose story in the Zhaojun tradition is perhaps "Zhaojun bianwen" (Transformation story on Zhaojun). During the Yuan, a number of *zaju* plays were based on the Zhaojun story, including Guan Hanqing's *Han Yuandi ku Zhaojun* (Emperor Yuan of the Han laments on Zhaojun), Ma Zhiyuan's (1251?–1321?) *Han gong qiu* (Autumn in Han palace), and Zhang Shiqi's (13th cent.) *Zhaojun chusai* (Zhaojun travels to the northern frontiers). See Zhong Sicheng, *Luguibu* (Registry of ghosts), 105, 108, and 112.

Among these Zhaojun plays of the Yuan, only *Han gong qiu* is extant. The Ming and Qing periods witnessed a proliferation of Zhaojun plays, including the anonymous *He rong ji* (A story of pacifying the frontier) and *Zhaojun zhuan* (Story of Zhaojun), Xue Dan's (fl. 1644) *Zhaojun meng* (Dream of Zhaojun), Chen Yuxiao's (16th cent.) *Zhaojun chusai*, Chen Zongding's

(Ming dynasty) *Ning hu ji* (A story of placating the barbarians), You Tong's (1618–1704) *Diao pipa* (Lamenting over the *pipa*), and Zhou Leqing's (1785–1855) *Pipa yu* (Words from the *pipa*), to mention only a few extant ones. For an account of the evolution of the Wang Zhaojun tradition in premodern Chinese literature, see Zhang Wende, Wang *Zhaojun gushi de chuancheng yu shanbian*.

34  In his long poem *Li sao* (Encountering sorrow), Qu Yuan uses the images of fragrant plants and beautiful women to refer allegorically to his own lofty personality under the siege of political calumnies. For a discussion of Qu Yuan's description of the ruler-minister relationship by using language and images pertaining to sexual union, see Paul Rakita Goldin, *The Culture of Sex in Ancient China*, 34–37. Qu Yuan's practice marks the beginning of a literary convention. As Hellmut Wilhelm has pointed out, some works of *fu* during the Han period evoke the image of a neglected wife that is often an expression of an official out of the favor with the ruler. See Wilhelm, "The Scholar's Frustration: Notes on a Type of Fu." For a discussion of the gender implications in *Li sao*, see Song Geng, *The Fragile Scholar*, 43–60.

35  Zou Yang wrote a letter in prison to the prince Liu Wu, which contained these lines: "Beautiful or ugly, a woman would be a target of jealousy once admitted to the palace. Worthy or unworthy, a *shi* would suffer from calumny once he is at the court." See Sima Qian, *Shi ji*, juan 83.

36  *Ming Taizu wenji* (*Siku quanshu* ed.), 13.16/b.

37  Shen Defu, *Wanli yehuobian*, 2:621.

38  See Martin Huang, *Negotiating Masculinities in Late Imperial China*, 72–86.

39  Zhao Yuan, *Ming Qing zhi ji shidafu yanjiu*, 317.

40  See Yong Zheng, *Dayi juemi tan*, 159.

41  Huang Zongxi, *Mingyi daifang lu*, 2.

42  No name, real or pseudonymous, is ascribed to this twelve-chapter novel, although it is said to have been compiled by a certain Qishan Zuochen and commentated by Li'an Jushi. The work is also known under the title *Huqiu hua'an yishi* (Story of the flower adjudication in Huqiu). In his foreword to the modern facsimile edition of the novel in the *Guben xiaoshuo jicheng*, Wang Xiaohai calls attention to the novelist's mention of a carnival known as *saishen yinghui*, which was popular in the Jiangnan area during the late Ming and the early Qing before the local authorities cracked down on it in 1685. The novelist describes the festival as being "all the rage twenty years ago." Wang Xiaohai also informs us that the artist for the illustrations in the novel was Huang Shunji, who was also responsible for the illustrations in the 1660 edition of *Xu* Jin Ping Mei (A sequel to *Jin Ping Mei*). Based on

such evidence, Wang tentatively dates *Nükaike zhuan* to the early years of the Kangxi reign (1662–1722).

The general plotline of the novel seems to conform well to the scholar-beauty fiction, but the fact the leading women characters here are courtesans, instead of maidens from elite families, puts the novel in a smaller company with such nineteenth-century works as *Pinhua baojian* (Treasured mirror for ranking flowers), *Hua yue hen* (Traces of flowers and the moon), and *Qinglou meng* (Dream of the courtesans). However, none of these later novels contains an examination for female scholars in the plot. *Nükaike zhuan*, therefore, is unique as a precursor of both the "courtesan novels" and the novels like *Lü mudan* (The green peony) and *Jinghua yuan* (Flowers in the mirror) that feature an examination for women. The earliest work in either group is *Lü mudan*, which was first published in 1800. It is remarkable that *Nükaike zhuan* predates both groups of works by at least a century.

43 *Nükaike zhuan*, 15.

44 Ibid., 128.

45 The scholar-courtesan romance in *Nükaike zhuan* reflects a fascinating seventeenth-century phenomenon in the major cities of Jiangnan—what may be called an interfusion of literati culture and courtesan culture. Several prominent literati figures enjoyed romantic relationships with leading courtesans with remarkable literary and/or artistic accomplishments. The most celebrated couples included Qian Qianyi (1582–1664) and Liu Rushi (1618–64); Wu Weiye (1609–72) and Bian Yujing (1623–65); Mao Xiang (1611–93) and Chen Yuanyuan (1624–81) and, later, Dong Xiaowan (1623–51); and Hou Fangyu (1618–55) and Li Xiangjun (1624–?). The last couple of course becomes immortalized in Kong Shangren's (1648–1718) *chuanqi* play *Taohua shan* (The peach blossom fan).

For recent studies of famous late Ming and early Qing courtesans and their liaisons with literati figures, see the articles collected in Ellen Widmer and Kang-I Sun Chang, eds., *Writing Women in Late Imperial China*, including Apul S. Ropp: "Ambiguous Images of Courtesan Culture in Late Imperial China," 17–45; Wai-yee Li: "The Late Ming Courtesan: Invention of a Cultural Ideal," 46–73; and Dorothy Ko: "The Written Word and the Bound Feet: A History of the Courtesan's Aura," 74–100. Also see Allan H. Barr, "The Wanli Context of the 'Courtesan's Jewel Box' Story," *Harvard Journal of Asiatic Studies* 57, no. 1 (June 1997): 107–41.

46 Timothy Brook observes that, for many late imperial Chinese scholars, "taking a courtesan became an act of allegory. Highly cultured males could fictionalize their dilemma as tragic men by buying women trained in certain

culturally admired ways and taking on the courtesan's persona of the suffering female to express their sense of victimization." See Brook, *The Confusions of Pleasures*, 231.

47  *Nükaike zhuan*, 30.

48  For all titles of Qing examination officers, including *zhukao* (chief examiner), *tongkao* (associate examiner), and *jianlin* (superintendent), see Liu Zhaobin, *Qingdai keju*, 29–34.

49  This description reflects a close simulation of the postexamination celebrations during the Qing. For an account of the celebratory activities of the successful candidates following the palace examinations during the Qing, see Chen Dongyuan, *Zhongguo jiaoyu shi*, 399–400.

50  Dorothy Ko, "The Written Word and the Bound Feet," 83. According to Ko, the most popular drinking game among courtesans in the late Ming was called "Name the Candidate," during which the women were ranked and named with the titles for top examination graduates. That drinking game soon led to a flourish of the practice of ranking the courtesans with the titles of the degree-holders, commonly known as *hua'an* (flower adjudication) or *huabang* (flower roster). Li Yu's play *Shen luan jiao* (The cautious lovers) offers a good illustration of the mutual mirroring between sexual selection and the civil service examinations. In the play, a group of young scholars plan for a *hua'an* for the courtesans. They begin the game by selecting the female *zhuangyuan, bangyan,* and *tanhua*, ranked with the same titles as the top graduates from the palace examinations, and then let those top courtesans select their clients from among the scholars, who are in turn called the male *zhuangyuan, bangyan,* and *tanhua*. See *Li Yu quanji*, 2:431–32.

In chapter 30 of *Rulin waishi*, two scholars sponsor a similar competition for theatric female impersonators. See Wu Jingzi, *Rulin waishi*, 358–61; *The Scholars*, 383–86. Xu Ke's *Qing bai lei chao* contains several accounts of such "flower adjudications" and "flower rosters" for actresses and courtesans in Beijing and Jiangnan during the early Qing (11:5096; 11:5149–50). Xu is insightful on the cause of the rage of this practice: "Literati scholars were obsessed with the examinations wherever they were, and they unwittingly let that obsession find a way to express itself when they used the terms in the examinations such as *zhuangyan, bangyan,* and *tanhua* in ranking the women" (11:5096).

51  The work is attributed to the pseudonymous Su'an Zhuren, or "Master of the Taoist temple in Suzhou." A preface by the pseudonymous writer Nongxiang Zhuren (Master of handling the incenses) is dated 1670, which suggests that the novel may have appeared in print in that year or slightly later.

52  Su'an zhuren, *Xiu ping yuan*, 8.
53  A modern edition of the novel was published in 1994 by Taiwan daying baike gufen youxian gongsi. There are no explicit indications of the date of the work in the text or its prefatory materials. However, the pseudonymous author, Zuili Yanshui Sanren (Wanderer in the mist and water of Zuili), is the same as that of *Nücaizi shu* (Story of talented women), *Yuanyang mei* (Matching of the destined lovers), and a number of other fictional works. As the earliest known edition of *Nücaizi shu* is dated to the Shunzhi reign (1644–61), and *Yuanyang mei* is said to be emendated by Tianhuazang Zhuren, to whom several seventeenth-century fictional works are attributed, the author of *Taohua ying* may have lived in the early Qing, most likely contemporaneous with Tianhuazang Zhuren.
54  Keith McMahon considers such a potent polygamist as Wei Yuqing "the sexual boss who sits at the top of society." See McMahon, *Misers, Shrews, and Polygamists*, 10.
55  In another erotic novel, *Xinghua tian* (Days of apricot blossoms), attributed to Gutang Tianfang Daoren, the parallel of the polygamist's womenfolk to an imperial harem is even more obvious. The principal wife, when formerly inaugurating her position, has all ten concubines seated on her sides in the order of their ranks. She then issues her decree on the management of the house, designating each of the concubines for specific duties. See *Xinghua tian*, 259.
56  Li Yu, *Shi'er lou*, 24.
57  Ibid., 22. The expression "snapping off a cassia twig" (*zhe gui*) is frequently used in traditional Chinese literature, especially poetry, as a metaphor for a success in the civil service examinations. It originated in the biography of Que Shen in *Jin shu* (History of the Jin). When Emperor Wu of the Jin (i.e., Sima Yan, r. 280–289) asked Que Shen for his self-evaluation, the latter replied: "When I took the policy examination for the recommended *xianliang*, I won the first place among the candidates from across the land. It was like [snapping off] the first twig from the cassia grove." See *Jin shu* (*Siku quanshu* ed.), 52.6/b-7/a. The Tang poet Wen Tingyun (812?–866) wrote the lines in a poem congratulating a friend of his on passing the metropolitan examinations: "Delighted to know my old friend snapped the cassia twig recently / I pity myself as still wandering lonely and adrift." See *Quan Tang shi* (*Siku quanshu* ed.), 578.14/a-b. Subsequently, the expression "snapping off a cassia twig" set off what may be considered a chain of metonymic associations. "As people believe there is a cassia tree in the moon, the 'cassia twig' comes to refer to the 'cassia in the moon' [*yuegui*]. Again, as there is said

to be a toad [*chan*] in the palace of the moon, 'cassia' in the expression is sometimes substituted by 'toad,' and 'receiving the degree' [*dengke*] is sometimes referred to as 'reaching the toad' [*dengchan*]." See Pan Yongyin, *Song bai lei chao*, 5.19/b-20/a. Obviously, Li Yu's usage of the expression in the story, where he associates a success in the examinations with the beautiful moon goddess Chang'e, represents a further extension of the metonymic signification.

58  Li Yu, *Shi'er lou*, 92.
59  Ibid., 93.
60  In the title of the story, Mengmu, or Mother Meng, refers to Mencius's mother. It is said that the woman moved her residence three times before finally settling down near a school in order to give her son a wholesome upbringing. For the story, see Liu Xiang, *Gu lienü zhuan* (Stories of ancient women) (*Siku quanshu* ed.), 1.15/a. For centuries, this story remained a model for parental teaching and moral edification. One therefore feels the thrust of parody to see that allusion become part of the title for a story about male homoerotic love, which was, even though by no means uncommon in seventeenth-century China, considered by many to be a form of perversion.
61  Li Yu, *Wusheng xi*, 111–14.
62  Li Yu, *Liancheng bi*, 371.
63  Ibid., 376.
64  Ibid., 382.
65  The novel, also known as *Jue hou chan* (The Chan Buddhist converted after his awakening), is ascribed on its first page of the text to a Qingchi Fanzheng Daoren (Daoist transformed from his former self as a crazy lover). It was first explicitly attributed to Li Yu by the seventeenth-century scholar Liu Tingji in his *Zaiyuan zazhi* (Miscellaneous notes of Zaiyuan). Liu, however, did not document any source for that attribution, which leaves room for the debate on Li Yu's authorship among modern scholars. Chun-shu Chang and Shelley H. Chang, for instance, assert in their *Crisis and Transformation in Seventeenth-Century China* that Li Yu's authorship "has not been proved by logically acceptable evidence." Their conclusion is based on three arguments: There were no contemporary records associating the work with Li Yu; if Li Yu was indeed the author, he should have no reason not to claim the authorship, since he was already known as notoriously unconventional; and if Li Yu did write the work, there is no explanation as to why he did not try to make a profit out of it when he was in financial difficulties (234–35). In contrast, modern Chinese scholars on vernacular fiction such as Lu Xun and Sun Kaidi either accepted or acquiesced in Li Yu's authorship of *The Carnal Prayer Mat*.

Most Western scholars of Chinese fiction support the attribution as well. In their *Li Yü*, Nathan Mao and Liu Ts'un-yan endorse the attribution by making a detailed study of the similarities between *The Carnal Prayer Mat* and Li Yu's other writings (91–95). Patrick Hanan, in his *The Invention of Li Yu*, observes: "So distinctive is his brand of fiction that although the novel has never actually been proved to be by Li Yu, one has only to read it alongside his stories to feel the truth of the attribution" (76). Robert Hegel proclaims in his *The Novel in Seventeenth-Century China* that the attribution is "at least . . . as justifiable as the identification of most earlier novelists" (183). Recent studies by Chinese scholars on the authorship of *The Carnal Prayer Mat* include Huang Qiang's "*Rou putuan* wei Li Yu suo zuo neizheng," which enumerates a large number of verbal parallels between the novel and Li Yu's other works. Based on the overwhelming thematic and stylistic affinities between *The Carnal Prayer Mat* and those works indisputably by Li Yu, I believe the attribution of the novel to Li Yu is well grounded. Obviously, however, the issue of authorship is not essential to my discussion of the novel here.

66 Li Yu, *Rou putuan*, 154; Hanan, *The Carnal Prayer Mat*, 24.
67 Li Yu, *Rou putuan*, 155; Hanan, *The Carnal Prayer Mat*, 25.
68 Miyazaki Ichisada, *China's Examination Hell*, 76–79.
69 Li Yu, *Rou putuan*, 216; Hanan, *The Carnal Prayer Mat*, 79.
70 Li Yu, *Rou putuan*, 215–16; Hanan, *The Carnal Prayer Mat*, 78–79. During the Qing period, the metropolitan and palace examination papers were usually graded by a group of imperially appointed examiners, fourteen in the early Qing and eight after the Qianlong reign. According to Shang Yanliu, five different symbols were used in the grading: circle, triangle, slant line, vertical line, and cross. Those papers that were graded the top rank were usually marked with circles from all the examiners, and those with one or two triangles would be slightly inferior, so on and so forth. So the number of circles from the examiners was an indicator of the grades of the candidates. See Shang Yanliu, *Qingdai keju kaoshi shulu*, 114–15. Zhu Pengshou, who served as an examiner for the last palace examination of the Qing, reports a slightly different grading system consisting of only four symbols: circle, triangle, dot, and vertical line. See Chen Maotong, *Zhongguo lidai xuanguan zhidu*, 401.
71 Li Yu, *Rou putuan*, 216–17; Hanan, *The Carnal Prayer Mat*, 79–80.
72 Li Yu, *Rou putuan*, 221; Hanan, *The Carnal Prayer Mat*, 84.
73 Those candidates who had passed the examinations would consider themselves disciples of the examiner who granted them the success and would call themselves *mensheng* (pupils) in front of their mentor. According to Wang Shizhen, this mentor-protégé relationship was very significant in the Ming

period, especially during the Wanli reign (1573–1620): "Once the mentor-disciple relationship was established, it became a lifetime bond." Starting in 1658, the Qing government tried to reverse the trend, banning the appellations of "mentor" and "pupil" on public occasions between the officials who had been examiners and those they had passed in the examinations. See Wang Shizhen, *Chibei outan*, 1:18. Li Yu, *Rou putuan*, 417; Hanan, *The Carnal Prayer Mat*, 243.

74  Li Yu, *Rou putuan*, 259; Hanan, *The Carnal Prayer Mat*, 115.
75  Li Yu, *Rou putuan*, 391; Hanan, *The Carnal Prayer Mat*, 222.
76  Li Yu, *Rou putuan*, 395–96; Hanan, *The Carnal Prayer Mat*, 225.
77  See, for example, Dorothy Ko, "The Written Word," 83–84.
78  Li Yu, *Rou putuan*, 237; Hanan, *The Carnal Prayer Mat*, 96.
79  Li Yu, *Rou putuan*, 277; Hanan, *The Carnal Prayer Mat*, 131.
80  Li Yu, *Rou putuan*, 299; Hanan, *The Carnal Prayer Mat*, 148.
81  I. A. Richards has observed: "At one extreme the vehicle may become almost a mere decoration or coloring of the tenor, at the other extreme, the tenor may become a mere excuse for the introduction of the vehicle, and so no longer be 'the principle subject.'" See Richards, *The Philosophy of Rhetoric*, 100.
82  Paul Ricoeur, *The Rule of Metaphor*, 173. Original italics.
83  The ninth-century scholar Zhao Gu, referring to the examination system during the Tang, left us with these lines: "Emperor Taizong came up with a really farsighted strategy / which made all men of talent work hard till their heads turned gray" (*Taizong Huangdi zhen chang ce / Zhuande yingxiong jin baitou*). See Wang Dingbao, *Tang zhiyan*, 1:1.
84  Ma Duanlin, *Wenxian tongkao*, 29.6/a.
85  Tuo Tuo et al., *Song Shi*, juan 440.
86  Zhang Tingyu et al., *Ming shi*, 6:1693. One conspicuous exception among the Ming rulers was Emperor Wanli. Because of his long-term stalemate with his top civil officials over the designation of an heir to the throne, the reclusive sovereign developed an inveterate apathy toward state affairs, and often failed to show up in person at the palace examinations.
87  Chen Maotong, *Zhongguo lidai xuanguan zhidu*, 392.
88  Wu Jingzi, *Rulin waishi*, 77; Yang and Yang, trans., *The Scholars*, 77; translation slightly modified.
89  Legge, *Confucian Analects*, 330, translation slightly revised.
90  Ibid., 222.
91  M. M. Bakhtin, *The Dialogic Imagination*, 23.
92  Paul Ricoeur, *The Rule of Metaphor*, 214.

CHAPTER 4. THE SCHOLARS

1   See, e.g., Hu Shi, "Wu Jingzi zhuan"; Qian Xuantong, "*Rulin waishi* xin xu."
2   C. T. Hsia observes that "the objects of ridicule comprise many other types besides scholars and pseudo scholars obsessed with examinations." See Tsia, *The Classic Chinese Novel*, 225.
3   See Timothy C. Wong, *Wu Ching-Tzu*, 62. Wong also refutes other critical approaches that consider *The Scholars* as "nationalistic, or democratic, or pro women's rights," but those views have been much less influential.
4   See Paul S. Ropp, *Dissent in Early Modern China*, 89–119.
5   The commentator in the Wuxian Caotang edition calls chapter 37 "the first culmination of the book" (*diyige da jieshu*). See *Rulin waishi huijiao huiping ben*, 2:461 and 2:515.
6   Shuen-fu Lin, "Ritual and Narrative structure in *Ju-lin wai-shi*," 249 and 256.
7   Stephen J. Roddy, *Literati Identity*; Shang Wei, *Rulin waishi and Cultural Transformation*.
8   Stephen J. Roddy, *Literati Identity*, 131.
9   Ibid., 130–46.
10  Shang Wei, *Rulin waishi and Cultural Transformation*, 26.
11  Nian Gengyao, one of Yongzheng's confidants and ablest aides before his succession, quickly fell out of favor with the new emperor despite his meritorious service in the positions of governor-general of Sichuan and governor-general of Shaanxi and Gansu. After demoting and then imprisoning him, Yongzheng finally ordered Nian to commit suicide. Qian Mingshi was implicated in the Nian case because he praised Nian in his poems, even though they were written before Nian fell out of imperial favor.
12  Jiang Liangqi, *Donghua lu*, 452.
13  Shanghai shudian chubanshe, ed., *Mingjiao zuiren tan*, 5.
14  Ibid., 49.
15  *Dayi juemi lu*, in Yong Zheng, *Dayi juemi tan*, 174.
16  Both quotations are from the chapter "Ba you" in *Lunyu*. The first line is taken from the sentence that reads: "The Master said, 'The full observance of the rules of propriety in serving one's prince is accounted by people to be flattery" (*Shijun jinli ren yi wei chan ye*). The second quotation is from the sentence, "Confucius replied, 'A prince should employ his ministers according to the rules of propriety; ministers should serve their prince with faithfulness" (*Jun shi chen yi li, chen shi jun yi zhong*). See Liu Baonan, *Lunyu zhengyi*, 62; Legge, *Confucian Analects*, 161.

17  *Lunyu*, "Yan Yuan." See Liu Baonan, *Lunyu zhengyi*, 271; Legge, *Confucian Analects*, 256.

18  Yongzheng here refers to the sentence that reads: "When [Confucius] was in the ancestral temple or in the court, he spoke minutely on every point, but cautiously." See Liu Baonan, *Lunyu zhengyi*, 196; Legge, *Confucian Analects*, 227, translation slightly modified.

19  Yang Bojun, *Mengzi yizhu*, 1:89; D. C. Lau, trans., *Mencius*, 86. When Gongsun Chou accuses Mencius of not showing enough respect for the King of Qi, the master argues that he was actually more respectful by trying to discuss with the King "the way of Yao and Shun" (*Yao Shun zhi dao*) while many other scholars in the Qi did not even consider the King a worthy interlocutor on benevolence and righteousness (*he zu yu yan ren yi ye*). In other words, Mencius showed his respect for the ruler by trying to enlighten him.

20  *Dayi juemi lu*, 174–75.

21  Yang Bojun, *Mengzi yizhu*, 1:248; D. C. Lau, *Mencius*, 157.

22  Gao You, annotated, *Huainanzi*, 334.

23  *Dayi juemi lu*, 176–177.

24  Wu Jingzi, *Rulin waishi huijiao huiping ben*, 1:1.

25  *Rulin waishi*, hereafter *RLWS*, 1; *The Scholars*; hereafter *Scholars*, 3, translation modified.

26  *Rulin waishi huijiao huiping ben*, 1:32.

27  See Timothy C. Wong, *Wu Ching-tzu*, 70ff.

28  See, e.g., C. T. Tsia, *The Classic Chinese Novel*, 210–11; Stephen J. Roddy, *Literati Identity*, 113–14; Zhang Guofeng, *Rulin waishi shilun*, 27–28; Shang Wei, *Rulin waishi and Cultural Transformation*, 125–26.

29  *Rulin waishi huijiao huiping ben*, 1:5.

30  Yang Bojun, *Mengzi yizhu*, 1:247–48; D. C. Lau, *Mencius*, 157.

31  Duan Ganmu climbed over a wall to avoid meeting with an official, and Xie Liu bolted his door to refuse admittance to a visiting official. Both anecdotes are mentioned in *Mencius* (Yang Bojun, *Mengzi yizhu*, 1:152; D. C. Lau, *Mencius*, 112).

32  For the ends of Liu Ji and Song Lian, see Zhang Tingyu et al., *Ming shi*, 12:3781; 12:3789–90; Gu Yingtai, *Ming shi jishi benmo*, 2:58–59.

33  At the end of the opening chapter, the narrator challenges those "writers and scholars" for referring to Wang Mian as commissioner of records (*canjun*) and insists that Wang "never served as an official for a single day" (*RLWS* 17; *Scholars* 18). In *Ming shi*, Wang Mian is said to have been recruited by Zhu Yuanzhang and was made a commissioner of records (*ziyi canjun*) when Zhu captured the district of Wuzhou (*Ming shi*, 24:7311). The narrator of *RLWS*,

as Stephen J. Roddy informs us, may be echoing Zhu Yizun's (1629–1709) version of Wang Mian's biography, where Zhu in a similar manner questions the credibility of Wang Mian's acceptance of the official position. See Roddy, *Literati Identity*, 114–15. It may be irrelevant to verify which theory is more reliable, as the fictional version of Wang Mian is obviously not obligated to be consistent with its historical counterpart. At any rate, however, the novelistic Wang Mian's avoidance of officialdom seems consistent with a prevalent practice of intellectuals in the early Ming, when many of them turned down offers of administrative positions. See, e.g., Zhao Yi, *Nianershi zhaji*, 9:677–78.

34. C. T. Hsia, *The Classic Chinese Novel*, 212.
35. Following the line in the novel that Prince Wu's attendants "tethered their horses beneath the willows by the lake," Zhang Wenhu comments in an interlinear note: "These were the trees that the buffalos used to be tethered to, and all of a sudden they were used to tether the horses! The buffalos would probably say, 'Your Majesty has unexpectedly encroached upon our domain.'" See *Rulin waishi huijiao huiping ben*, 1:13.
36. See *Rulin waishi huijiao huiping ben*, 1:32.
37. The novelist may be deliberate in contrasting Kuang Chaoren with Wang Mian. Apart from the similar deathbed scenes, the episode that Kuang Chaoren reads at night in a temple and draws the attention from the country magistrate who happens to be passing by (*RLWS* 204; *Scholar* 214) mirrors part of the Wang Mian biography in *Ming shi* (24:7311).
38. Marston Anderson, "The Scorpion in the Scholar's Cap," 265.
39. Yue Hengjun, "Ma Chunshang zai Xihu," 142.
40. Ibid.
41. That comical effect is noted by Zhang Wenhu. See *Rulin waishi huijiao huiping ben*, 1:204. *Huban* was a tablet that an official would hold in hand when received in audience by the emperor.
42. Yu Yingshi, *Shi yu Zhongguo wenhua*, 107.
43. Fan Zhongyan, *Fan Wenzheng ji*, 7.5/b.
44. Yang Bojun, *Mengzi yizhu*, 2:308; D. C. Lau, *Mencius*, 185, translation slightly modified.
45. Lü Kun, *Shenyin yu*, 54.
46. Gu Yanwu, *Ri zhi lu jishi*, 13:1014.
47. Huang Zongxi, *Ming yi dai fang lu*, 2.
48. Ibid., 3.
49. Paul Ropp sees a similarity between Wu Jingzi and Gu and Huang in their critical attitude toward the examination system, but he maintains that simi-

larity "suggests not so much their intellectual influence on him as the persistence of serious problems in the system itself" (*Dissent in Early Modern China*, 100–101). Zhang Guofeng, in contrast, believes in a more substantial intellectual link between Wu and the two early Qing thinkers. Wu's close friend Cheng Tingzuo (1691–1767) was not only associated with Yan Yuan and Li Gong but also a tremendous admirer of Gu Yanwu and Huang Zongxi. Cheng Jinfang (b. 1718), another close friend of Wu's, was a devout follower of Gu and Huang while keeping a distance from the more iconoclastic stance of Yan and Li. See Zhang Guofeng, *Rulin waishi shilun*, 12–17.

50  *Rulin waishi huijiao huiping ben*, 2:501.
51  Li Hanqiu, *Rulin waishi yanjiu*, 95.
52  Yang Bojun, *Mengzi yizhu*, 1:232–33; D. C. Lau, *Mencius*, 150.
53  The notion of *liyin* may have an origin that can be traced to the Western Han dynasty (206–24 BCE). Dongfang Shuo, a palace humorist, observed: "One can escape from the world and keep one's self intact by living in the palaces. Why should he have to hide in the deep mountains and in a thatched cottage?" Inspired by Dongfang Shuo, the Tang poet Li Bai (701–762) expressed disillusionment of his official career in these lines: "People in the world know no Dongfang Shuo, / A great hermit within the Golden Gate is the Banished Immortal" (*zhexian*, i.e., Li Bai himself). The fourth-century writer Wang Kangju has left us the celebrated couplet: "Petty hermits hide in hills and marshes, / Great hermits hide in the court and marketplaces" (*Xiaoyin yin lingsou, dayin yin chaoshi*). Traditionally the practitioners of *liyin* were considered "middling hermits," or *zhongyin*, between great hermits (*dayin*) and petty hermits (*xiaoyin*). Examples of *liyin* include the Tang poet and bureaucrat Wang Wei (701–61) and the Song scholar-officials Wang Anshi and Ouyang Xiu (1007–72) in their late years. See Wang Debao, *Shi yu yin*, 80–85. For another typical example of *liyin* in the Tang poet Bai Juyi (772–846), see Xiaoshan Yang, *Metamorphosis of the Private Sphere*, 11–50.
54  Wu Jingzi, *Yijia fu bing xu*. In Zhu Yixuan, ed., *Ming Qing xiaoshuo ziliao xuanbian*, 2:886–87. Li Hanqiu suggests that the two lines that contain "catching lice" and "following the soaring geese with my eyes" allude to Ji Kang. See Li Hanqiu, *Rulin waishi yanjiu*, 218.
55  Wu Jingzi, *Yijia fu bing xu*. In Zhu Yixuan, ed., *Ming Qing xiaoshuo ziliao xuanbian*, 2:887.
56  Wu Jingzi, *Wenmu shanfang ji, juan* 4. Excerpted in Zhu Yixuan, ed., *Ming Qing xiaoshuo ziliao xuanbian*, 2:891.
57  This point is made even more piquant by the historical fact that, during the Ming, in which *RLWS* is set, Nanjing was indeed one of the two capitals

for the empire. It was made the capital of the empire after the founding of the dynasty in 1368. In 1421 Emperor Yongle moved his imperial court from Nanjing to Beijing, which became the principal capital for the rest of the dynasty, but Nanjing retained both its name and status as the "southern capital." See *Ming shi*, 1:99. In 1645, the second year after his inauguration in Beijing, Emperor Shunzhi of the Qing decreed to demote the status of Nanjing and made it the capital of the province of Jiangnan. See Jiang Liangqi, *Donghua lu*, 80. Among modern scholars, Shang Wei argues that the novel gives Nanjing "its role as the center for the revival of the Confucian ritual by setting it in a binary contrast with Beijing, the political center of the empire," and he also suggests that the literati taste and sensibility in Nanjing contrasts with the "philistines, hypocrites, and shams" in the other Jiangnan city of Hangzhou (*Rulin waishi and Cultural Transformation*, 291).

58  *Lunyu*, "Taipo." In Liu Baonan, annotated, *Lunyu zhengyi*, *Zhuzi jicheng*, 1:154.

59  Li Hanqiu, *Rulin waishi yanjiu*, 81.

60  See, e.g., Huang Zongxi, *Mingyi daifang lu*, 7–14; Gu Yanwu, *Ri zhi lu jishi*, *juan* 16 and *juan* 17; Gu Yanwu, "Shengyuan lun" (three essays), in Li Guojun, ed., *Qingdai qianqi jiaoyu lunzhu xuan*, 1:233–237; Cheng Tingzuo, *Qingxi wenji*, especially *juan* 9; Ruan Kuisheng, *Chayu kehua*, especially *juan* 16.

61  See Liang Zhangju, *Zhiyi conghua*, 26.

62  Ibid., 4.

63  See the numerous comments on the *bagu* writing collected in Liang Zhangju's *Zhiyi conghua*, especially those by Li Guangdi, Zhang Boxing (1652–1725), Fang Bao (1668–1749), and Yu Zhengxie (1775–1840). It should be noted that the style of the *bagu* essay was more than a purely formal issue. As it was also referred to as *shiwen* (modern or contemporary prose), it might, on the one hand, be regarded as a relatively new form of writing and thus carry some appeal as such. On the other hand, the *bagu* essay, with rigid structural rules of its own, had ties to several other prose forms of past ages. As suggested by the prevailing slogan "use the ancient style in the modern prose" (*yi guwen wei shiwen*), the *bagu* essay had certain stylistic affinities to the classics in pristine Confucianism, the parallel prose (*pianti wen*) of the Han period, and the forceful but largely unadorned writings of Tang-Song essayists, especially Han Yu (768–824), Liu Zongyuan (773–819), Ouyang Xiu (1007–72) and Wang Anshi. It may therefore be argued that the form of the *bagu* essay was ideologically rooted in a long tradition of prose literature.

64  Stephen J. Roddy, *Literati Identity*, 54.

65  Gu Yanwu, *Ri zhi lu jishi*, 16:1247. The so-called *shiba fang* (eighteen halls)

refers to the eighteen associate examiners in assistance to the two principal examiners during the Ming period, each of whom was supposed to read the examination answers on a certain topic in a separate room. A published anthology of sample *bagu* essays written by such examiners, who were believed to be particularly familiar and skilled with the essay form, was often called *shiba fang ke* (eighteen-hall printings).

66 Benjamin Elman has noted that the *bagu* collections compiled by Lü Liuliang, Dai Mingshi (1653–1713), and other early Qing editors "turned the official ranking of eight-legged essays by the examiners inside-out. In effect, there were now two public tribunals for the genre. One derived from the official rankings of candidates. The other represented the views of literati outside the official compounds" (*A Cultural History*, 409). I suspect that this "unofficial" attitude toward the selected essays may have been an important reason for the popularity of such privately compiled collections.

67 For detailed information and discussions of this particular anthology, see R. Kent Guy, "Fang Pao and the *Ch'in-ting Ssu-shu-wen*," 160–72; Kai-wing Chow, "Discourse, Examination, and Local Elite," 192–95.

68 Kai-wing Chow, "Discourse, Examination, and Local Elite," 194.

69 See Liang Zhangju, *Zhiyi conghua*, 12–13; R. Kent Guy, "Fang Pao and the *Ch'inting Ssu-shu-wen*," 164.

70 In his "*Daxue* bian" (A Scrutiny of the *Great Learning*), Chen made the assertion: "The language [in the *Great Learning*] is ostensibly from the sages but the meanings are actually taken from Buddhism. The words are drifting and rootless, deceptive but ultimately going nowhere." Quoted in Zhao Jihui et al., eds., *Zhongguo ruxueshi*, 777.

71 See Elman, *A Cultural History*, 505.

72 Ibid., 506.

73 Naquin and Rawski, *Chinese Society in the Eighteenth Century*, 66.

74 Elman, *A Cultural History*, 518–19.

75 For examples of Emperor Kangxi's remarks against the pseudo moralists, see Jiang Liangqi, *Donghua lu*, 203 and 315.

76 Jiang Liangqi, *Donghua lu*, 140 and 149.

77 Quoted in Elman, *A Cultural History*, 538.

78 Quoted in Zhang Guofeng, *Rulin waishi shilun*, 96–97.

79 That view may have been shared by many Qing scholars and writers. Wang Shizhen (1634–1711) once met a commoner who was known to be a good poet. When Wang read some of his poems, he found them to be rather awkward. Wang afterward mentioned it to one of his friends, who responded by saying: "That was exactly because the man had never practiced the contemporary

essay!" The anecdote was cited approvingly by Liang Zhangju, who observed: "While the contemporary essay is different from poems and archaic writings, one will not be able to present his ideas systematically in those forms without first becoming at home with the *bagu* essay" (*Zhiyi conghua*, 35).

80  *Rulin waishi huijiao huiping ben*, 1:247.
81  Jin He, "*Rulin waishi* ba," in Zhu Yixuan, ed., *Ming Qing xiaoshuo ziliao xuanbian*, 2:919.
82  Hu Shi was the one who first suggested the parallel. See his "Yan-Li xuepai de Cheng Tingzuo," 132–33.
83  Major cases of literary inquisition during the Yongzheng reign included the Wang Jingqi case in 1726, the Xie Jishi case and the Zha Siting case in 1727, the Zeng Jing case in 1729, the Lu Shengnan case in 1730, the Qu Dajun case and the Fan Shijie case in 1731, and the Shen Lun case and the Wu Maoyu case in 1735, among others. The Qianlong period is also known for its harsh literary inquisition, but most cases were dated later than 1750, after *Rulin waishi* was completed.
84  *Rulin waishi huijiao huiping ben*, 1:234.
85  According to Jin He's "*Rulin waishi* ba," Wu Jingzi, soon after moving to Nanjing, led a project joined by other scholars to build a temple called *xianxian ci* (Sanctuary for the ancient worthies) in the southern outskirts of the city, in honor of Tai Bo and over two hundred and thirty other sages. See "*Rulin waishi* ba," in Zhu Yixuan, ed., *Ming Qing xiaoshuo ziliao xuanbian*, 2:918.
86  See, e.g., Hu Shi, "Yan-Li xuepai de Cheng Tingzuo"; Chen Meilin, "Yan-Li xueshuo dui Wu Jingzi de yingxiang," in his *Wu Jingzi yanjiu*, 1–14; Paul Ropp, *Dissent in Early Modern China*, 76 and 105; Stephen Roddy, *Literati Identity*, 63–73; Shang Wei, *Rulin waishi and Cultural Transformation*, 36–52; Li Hanqiu, *Rulin waishi yanjiu*, 78–80; Zhang Guofeng, *Rulin waishi shilun*, 9–18. Zhang, however, warns against attaching too much importance to Wu Jingzi's tie to the Yan-Li school. He suggests that Gu Yanwu and Huang Zongxi's influence on Wu was perhaps just as significant.
87  Zhong Ling, *Yan Xizhai xiansheng yanxing lu*, 20.
88  Qian Mu has observed that while Yan Yuan was staunch in rejecting textual studies, his disciple Li Gong "was not completely able to follow the master's path." See Qian Mu, *Guoxue gailun*, 267. Engaged in annotating the classics such as *Lunyu*, *Zhongyong*, *Shou yi*, and *Shi jing*, Li Gong demonstrated an interest in textual scholarship that placed him in a kinship with scholars of the Qian-Jia Han Learning.
89  Li Gong, *Lun xue*, *juan* 2, quoted in Zhao Jihui et al., eds., *Zhongguo ruxue shi*, 781.

90 It is interesting to note that the word *shixue*, or in the same sense, *shi*, is used a couple of times in *The Scholars*, quite ironically, to refer to a mastery of the *bagu* skills. In chapter 3, Fan Jin rebukes the examination candidate Wei Haogu for wasting his time on "miscellaneous studies" (*zaxue*) while "neglecting the real business" (*buwushi*) (RLWS 36–37). In chapter 10, Compiler Lu (Lu Bianxiu) speaks of Yang Zhizhong in front of the visiting Lou brothers: "Among people like him, many appear to be brilliant but few have genuine learning [*shixue*]. If he is truly a good scholar, why did he fail to pass the examinations?" (RLWS 127).

91 This is basically consistent with C. T. Hsia's division of the novel into three parts "flanked by a prologue and an epilogue." According to Hsia, part 1 (chaps. 2–30) is about those "in search of rank, fame, and wealth." Part 2 (chaps. 31–37) is about "the good scholars" who "gather to perform the ritual of worship at the Tai Bo Temple." Part 3 (chaps. 37–54) "comprises a miscellaneous group of stories without apparent design" (*The Classic Chinese Novel*, 224). The verdict that the final part is "without apparent design," however, may well be debatable, as my discussion shows.

92 Stephen Roddy, *Literati Identity*, 137.

93 Marston Anderson, "The Scorpion in the Scholar's Cap," 268.

94 C. T. Hsia, *The Classic Chinese Novel*, 237

95 Shang Wei, Rulin waishi *and Cultural Transformation*, 90.

96 Robert Hegel has made this comment on the conclusion of *Water Margin*: "The novel thus ends where it began, with little accomplished and no new era of reinvigorated rule to replace the corruption of the past." See Hegel, *Reading Illustrated Fiction*, 31.

97 Hu Yiming and Zhou Yueliang, *Rulin waishi yu Zhongguo shi wenhua*, 33.

98 Shang Wei, Rulin waishi *and Cultural Transformation*, 87.

## CHAPTER 5. THE STONE IN *DREAM OF THE RED CHAMBER*

1 While information of Cao Xueqin's life remains inadequate, several poems by Cao's friends Dunmin and Duncheng, marginalized members of the Manchu imperial clan, offer us a glimpse into the novelist's wretched situation in Beijing. For Cao's relationship to Dunmin and Duncheng, see Wu Enyu, "Dunmin, Duncheng he Cao Xueqin"; for selected poems by the two Manchu poets, see Yi Su, ed., *Honglou meng juan*, 1–7.

2 *Qing Gaozong shilu*, *juan* 3, 9:195–96.

3 Ibid., *juan* 211, 11:709.

4 Ibid., *juan* 227, 11:933.

5 Philip Kuhn, *Soulstealers*, 221, original italics.
6 Ibid., 232.
7 According to the late Qing scholar Li Yuerui (1862–1927), some of the leading scholars of the Qianlong period sank to an unprecedented depth in their efforts to curry favor with the throne. Li claimed that the volumes of *Twenty-Four Histories* (Ershisi shi), a compendium that was compiled under Emperor Qianlong's auspices, were filled with errors. Instead of results of negligence on the part of the compilers, these errors, as Li Yuerui believed, were deliberately created in order to be corrected by Qianlong, the ultimate proofreader. The emperor and scholars colluded with each other to create an illusion of the ruler's academic superiority over the scholars. Ironically, Qianlong took delight in the flattery but not the toil of proofreading itself, leaving many of the errors permanent on the pages. See Wang Xuetai, "Kang Yong Qian san chao duiyu shiren de xunhua."
8 Cao Xueqin and Gao E, *Honglou meng*, henceforward *HLM*, 2:436; *The Story of the Stone*, trans. David Hawkes and John Minford, henceforward *SS*, 2:206.
9 Wang Xuetai, *Youmin wenhua yu Zhongguo shehui*, 69–70.
10 Contemporary Chinese scholar Liu Weiwei has noticed the change from the late Ming to the Qianlong period, using two scholar-artists, Xu Wei (1521–93) and Zheng Xie (i.e., Zheng Banqiao; 1693–1765), as examples. While Xu was dejected and eventually became deranged after he was compelled to give up his aspiration for a bureaucratic career and became a high-ranking official's staff member, Zheng calmly resigned from his office to become a professional painter. See Liu Weiwei, "Wan Ming yu Qing zhongye shanren xintai bijiao yanjiu."
11 Naquin and Rawski, *Chinese Society in the Eighteenth Century*, 124.
12 Most of such accounts are to be found in volume 5 and volume 9 of *Qing bai lei chao*. For failed examination scholars' professions, also see Ping-ti Ho, *The Ladder of Success*, 35–37 and 303; Rawski, *Education and Popular Literacy in Ch'ing China*; Naquin and Rawski, *Chinese Society in the Eighteenth Century*, 123–27; Robert Hegel, *Reading Illustrated Fiction in Late Imperial China*, 13–17.
13 Li Chen considers legal counseling a major profession for former examination candidate during the Qing. By Li's estimate, there could be "more than 3,000 legal advisors working in the local yamen in any given year" during the eighteenth century. See Li Chen, "Legal Specialists," 24.
14 In the *jiaxu* manuscript copy, there is a marginal note by Red Inkstone (Zhiyanzhai) that reads: "Xueqin used to have a book *Fengyue baojian* with a

preface by his younger brother Tangcun. Now Tangcun has passed away. When I saw the new [text] it reminds me of the old [text], and that was why I still followed it [*gu reng yin zhi*]." See *Zhiyanzhan chongping Shitouji: Jiaxu ben*, henceforward *Jiaxu ben*, 15. In the *Jiaxu ben*, the quote attributed to the novelist is included in the "Fanli," which precedes the opening chapter and is separated from the chapter head by a half-blank page. According to Wu Shichang, the "Fanli" was formerly Tangcun's preface to Cao Xueqin's *Fengyue baojian*, possibly an early version of his *Honglou meng*. Wu speculates that Red Inkstone followed the format in *Fengyue baojian* by retaining Tangcun's preface in the new text of *Honglou meng* in commemoration of Cao Xueqin's dead brother. See Wu Shichang, *Honglou tanyuan*, 107–8.

15  That practice in the *gengchen* text is then followed by all later recensions, including the earliest typographic editions (1791 and 1792) sponsored by Cheng Weiyuan and Gao E. In this study, I still refer to this opening statement of the novel as "Fanli," for the sake of convenience.

16  Wai-yee Li, *Enchantment and Disenchantment*, 164.

17  *Jiaxu ben*, 5.

18  *Jiaxu ben*, 16–17.

19  Yu Pingbo (1900–90), for example, believed the quote in the "Fanli" to be the most reliable channel for getting to know Cao Xueqin and his state of mind at the time of writing the novel: "If we do not even believe Mr. Cao's own words in the preface, what can be more reliable evidence?" See his "*Honglou meng* bian," 504.

20  For instance, the Southern Song (1127–1279) official Zhang Jun (1097–1164), one of the most staunch advocates of resistance against the invasion of the Jin (1115–1234), was praised as having achieved the "meritorious deeds of mending the heaven and bathing the sun" (*butian yuri zhi gong*). See Chen Bangzhan, *Song mo jishi benmo*, 16.9/a. In Cheng Shilong and Chen Si's *Liang Song mingxian xiaoji*, one sees these lines in Chen Si's elegy on Yue Fei (1103–42), the best known Southern Song anti-Jin general who was imprisoned and then executed by his political enemies: "Please collect those frail bones mottled with stains of moss, / And present them to our emperor as stones for mending the heaven" (356.1/b). Southern Song poet Xin Qiji (1140–1207) left us these lines expressing his tenacity to fight for the imperial state when the northern half of the empire was occupied by the Jin: "A man now has his heart hardened like steel, / In an effort to mend the fracture of the heaven." See *Jiaxuan ci*, 1.8/a-b.

21  Huang Tingjian, *Shangu ji waiji*, 2.11/a.

22  Y. H. Zhao, *The Uneasy Narrator*, 118.

23  *Jiaxu ben*, 1.
24  One of the most famous uses of the term is in the Confucian *Analects*, where Confucius dwells on the moral desirability of empathizing with others: "Now the man of perfect virtue, wishing to be established himself, seeks also to establish others; wishing to be distinguished himself, he seeks to distinguish others. To be able to judge *of others* by what is nigh *in ourselves* [*nengjin qupi*]—this may be called the art of virtue." See Legge, *Confucian Analects*, 194. Later, *qupi* became a key notion in Chinese understanding of the linguistic sign, suggesting the formation of many of the written characters as combinations of both mimetic and analogic elements in language. In *Shuowen jiezi*, Xu Shen (58?–147) considers *qupi* a crucial principle in forming the semantic-phonetic ideographs, or *xingshengzi*: "What are called *xingsheng* are those graphs that are named after the matter and supplemented by an analogic component [*yi shi wei ming, qupi xiangcheng*]. The graphs *jiang* and *he* are examples." See *Shuowen jiezi* (*Siku quanshu* ed.), 15.2/a.
25  As related in the opening chapter of the novel, the narrative inscribed on the surface of the mythic stone is brought into a long process of transmission, and five different titles are used at different stages of that process: "Shitou ji" (Story of the Stone), "Qingseng lu" (Record of Brother Amour), "Fengyue baojian" (Magic mirror for the romantic), "Honglou meng" (Dream of red mansions), and "Jinling shier chai" (Twelve Beauties of Jinling). While they could have been titles that Cao Xueqin tentatively used at different times for his work, they refer in chapter 1 to the inscription on the stone, rather than the novel itself. All known versions of the novel are titled either *Shitou ji*, as in the cases of the two earliest manuscript copies *Jiaxu ben* and *Gengchen ben*, or *Honglou meng*, as in the cases of *Qi xu ben* (a manuscript copy with a preface by Qi Liaosheng) and the Cheng-Gao typographic editions. In the "Fanli" at the beginning of the *Jiaxu ben*, three titles, *Honglou meng*, *Shitou ji*, and *Fengyue baojian*, are mentioned, but only *Honglou meng* is said to be the general title for the whole novel (*zong qi quanbu zhi ming*). See *Jiaxu ben*, 1.
26  *Jiaxu ben*, 11.
27  On the relationship between the Stone and Baoyu, there is an inconsistency in different versions of the novel. In the early manuscript copies like *Jiaxu ben* and *Gengchen ben*, the Stone is transformed into a jade of the size of a fan-pendant, either by the two wandering immortals or by its own magic power. When Divine Luminescent Page (Shenying Shizhe) is reincarnated as Baoyu to fulfill his predestined tragic love with Crimson Pearl Plant (Jiangzhu Xiancao), who is to be reborn as Lin Daiyu, the jade comes to the mun-

dane world with Baoyu, contained in the boy's mouth. In the Cheng-Gao editions, however, both the jade and Divine Luminescent Page who is to be reincarnated as Baoyu are said to be metamorphoses of the magic Stone. In the early manuscript copies, which seem to suggest a bifurcation of Baoyu and the *baoyu* (the precious jade transformed from the Stone), the latter is on several occasions granted the status of a detached observer or a scribe. Yet the narrative is by no means consistent in that regard, which may have necessitated the revision in the Cheng-Gao editions. Obviously this is not the occasion to discuss this issue fully. Suffice it to say, it may be well advised to consider Baoyu and the *baoyu* as two complementary components of the mythic Stone's sublunary existence. That seems to be corroborated by the fact in the novel that each time the jade is lost Baoyu becomes ill. Toward the closure of 120-chapter version of the novel, the novelist seems to have a good reason in making Zhen Shiyin say: "Baoyu is the Stone, the precious jade" (*Baoyu, ji baoyu ye*) (*HLM* 4:1518; *SS* 5:371).

28  Anthony Yu, *Rereading the Stone*, 179.

29  In chapter 5, when Goddess Disenchantment shows Baoyu the pictures and poems portending the fates of the girls around him, she begins to fear that she might be "in danger of becoming responsible for a leakage of celestial secrets," as she is aware how "intelligent and sharp-witted" Baoyu is (*HLM* 1:58; *SS* 1:135–36). In a marginal note, Red Inkstone observes: "Throughout the book all the words denigrate Baoyu and all the people ridicule Baoyu. All of a sudden these words come out of Disenchantment's mind. It is indeed a message that goes beyond all the other messages (*yiwai zhi yi*)!" See *Jiaxu ben*, 140.

30  What Jia Dairu says here carries a striking affinity to what Mr. Lu says to his daughter in chapter 11 of *Rulin waishi*, where he regards the skills in the examination composition as essential and prerequisite for all other forms of literary writings: "If you write *bagu* essays well, then whatever literary form you use—and this applies even to lyrics or descriptive poems—you will express yourself forcefully and exactly. If, however, you cannot write *bagu* essays well, then all your writing will be unorthodox and third-rate" (*Rulin waishi*, 139; *The Scholars*, 142).

31  Anthony Yu argues that Jia Baoyu's father and tutor express "a deeply entrenched view of what constitutes intellectual priority and ethical obligation for a young man of Bao-yu's social status and upbringing." See Anthony Yu, *Rereading the Stone*, 181.

32  In *Ming shi* there is this statement about the curriculum of the examinations during the Ming period: "The civil service examinations followed the past

models of the Tang and the Song, but the approach of evaluation was slightly modified: Questions for official selection were exclusively based on the Four Books and the Five Classics.... This was all decided by Emperor Taizu and Liu Ji" (*juan* 70, 6:1693). Despite the mention of the Tang and Song in that statement, however, Ming examination curriculum was closer to the Yuan model. One reason, according to Benjamin Elman, "was to get away from the purely literary criteria for the selection of imperial officials" that had been prevalent during part of the Tang and Song periods. Zhu Yuanzhang's personal distrust in literary talent may also have led to his political partiality for examination candidates from the culturally less developed north. See Elman, *A Cultural History*, 89–90.

33  Chen Maotong, *Zhongguo lidai xuanguan zhidu*, 369.
34  Dong Qichang, *Rongtai bieji, juan* 1; quoted in Qian Zhongshu, *Qian Zhongshu lunxue wenxuan*, 3:339.
35  Zhuoyuanting zhuren, *Zhao shi bei*, 62.
36  This rhetorical question, in two rhymed heptasyllabic lines in the Chinese original (*Dangjin tianzi zhong wenzhang, zuxia hexu jiang Han-Tang*), is most likely not the novelist's invention but may have been a common witticism among scholars of the seventeenth and eighteenth centuries. Chen Jitai, a late Ming scholar, had tried to borrow from his uncle a copy of *Can Tang* (The late Tang) before he eventually succeeded in the *jingshi* examinations in 1634. As the book was obviously irrelevant to the examination learning, the uncle replied in two lines that were only slightly different from Zhou Jin's in *Rulin waishi*: "*Dangjin tianzi zhong wenzhang, zuxia hexue song Han-Tang*" (Since the emperor attaches importance to the [eight-legged] essays, why should you read about the Han and Tang dynasties?). See Chen Dongyuan, *Zhongguo jiaoyu shi*, 344.
37  Maram Epstein considers Jia Zheng's departure an event that marks the shift toward "the aesthetic values associated with *qing*" in the garden: "From this point on, the cousins engage in poetry competitions, landscape painting, and musical composition." See Epstein, *Competing Discourses*, 158.
38  Wang Xilian, "*Xinping xiuxiang Honglou meng quanzhuan* juanshou." Excerpted in Zhu Yixuan, ed., *Ming Qing xiaoshuo ziliao xuanbian*, 2:680.
39  *Jiaxu ben*, 19.
40  If the magic Stone takes a biform sublunary existence in both Baoyu and the *baoyu* (jade), the former is indisputably its principal agent that is responsible for the making of the "Story of the Stone." Cao Xueqin from the outset may have attempted to create a fictional "author" of the stone fiction, but because of a dualistic approach to the jade and its human double, the authorship is

sometimes attributed solely to the jade. One example is in chapter 15. When Baoyu threatens to "settle accounts" in bed with his friend Qin Zhong, the jade cunningly refuses to go into details, citing its limited "point of view" caused by the fact that Wang Xifeng has put it under her pillow for the night (*HLM* 1:170; *SS* 1:300). Yet the jade's "point of view" obviously is not sustainable in the narrative, as it is not consistently in a position to witness all narrative events. Later editors of the novel may have been aware of that difficulty. In chapter 18 in the *gengchen* manuscript copy, when Yuanchun pays a visit to her family, the jade once again comes to the foreground of the narrative, marveling on the spectacular and extravagant scene and reminiscing about the misery and loneliness it once experienced as the abandoned stone block at the foot of the mountain. See *Zhiyanzhai chongping Shitou ji: Gengchen ben*, (henceforward *Gengchen ben*), 1: 377–78. That passage dramatizing the jade as a narrator separate from Baoyu came to be deleted in the Cheng-Gao typographic editions.

41  Wai-yee Li has observed that *Dream of the Red Chamber* is "probably more burdened with the implications of the reality-illusion, truth-falsehood (*zhen-jia*) dialectics, and the idea of emptiness (*kong*) than any other work in the Chinese *xiaoshuo* (narrative fiction) tradition." See Li's *Enchantment and Disenchantment*, 155–56.

42  Anthony C. Yu, *Rereading the Stone*, 141.

43  This is indicated by the word "therefore," or *gu* in the original: "He therefore concealed the real events and, by means of the Precious Jade of Luminous Intelligence, related this story of the stone." In her *Enchantment and Disenchantment,* Wai-yee Li has noticed this peculiar usage with insight: "The leap of logic in the word 'therefore' conceals a break between experience and the representation of experience. The causal connection asserted is fraught with ambiguity" (157). From the stance I am assuming here, that "break" can also be said to be between the dreams as mental/psychological illusions and a fiction as a textual illusion. In that sense what is concealed here is of course the entire process of fiction making. But that concealment may have been a deliberate one, as that missing gap is to be filled by the novel itself, which is, to reiterate, both a fiction and a fiction about the making of that fiction.

44  "Nonbeginning [Wushi] said: 'He who responds when asked about the Way does not know the Way. Thus, although one may ask about the Way, he doesn't learn anything about it. For the Way is not to be asked about, and questions about the Way are not to be answered. If one asks about what is not to be asked about, the question is futile. If one answers what is not to be answered, the answer is inane. In this fashion, those who counter futility

with inanity are unobservant of the universe without and unaware of the great origin within. Thus they cannot pass over Kunlun and wander in grand emptiness [*bu you hu taixu*]." See Victor H. Mair, trans., *Wandering on the Way*, 220.

45 Kong Yingda, *Zhouyi zhushu*, 11.19/b-20/a.

46 Zhang Zai et al., *Zhangzi zhengmeng*, 86–87. According to Fung Yu-lan, Zhang Zai's theory of *taixu* and *qi* takes as its premise certain ideas in the *Book of Changes* (Yi jing). See Fung Yu-lan, *A History of Chinese Philosophy*, 2:481. It is beyond any doubt that Cao Xueqin was familiar with the theory about *taixu* and *qi*. In chapter 31, Shi Xiangyun tries to enlighten one of the maidservants by saying: "The *yin* and the *yang* are from the ether. It is the ether that endows on things their distinctive forms" (*HLM* 2:378; *SS* 2:122, translation modified).

47 The concept of *qi* played a prominent role in the thought of Cheng Yi (1033–1107), who believed that the evolution and transformation (*hua*) of *qi* was responsible for the spontaneous generation of all forms of existence. Zhang Zai's influence was quite obvious, even though Cheng Yi did not acknowledge it explicitly. Assimilating Zhang Zai's proposition that *taixu* is filled with the material force of *qi*, Zhu Xi, as one modern scholar puts it, revised Zhang's philosophical system "by subordinating material force to principle, so that the principle became the ruler of material force." See Ren Jiyu, "Chu Hsi and Religion," in Wing-tsit Chan, ed., *Chu Hsi and Neo-Confucianism*, 363.

48 Among the Ming-Qing thinkers, Wang Fuzhi was probably the one most interested in the concepts of *taixu* and *qi*. In his annotation of *Zhangzi zhengmeng*, Wang makes this comment on the movement of *qi* in the space of *taixu*: "When [the ether] is dispersed into the Great Void, it resumes its original form of the mist [*yinyun*], but it does not become annihilated. When it condenses and gives births to all kinds of things, it is not a magic trick but caused by the constant nature of the mist. . . . The dispersion and condensation of the ether, the beginning and end of lives, the movements back and forth, in and out, are all spontaneous with an intrinsic tendency and cannot be stopped" (*Zhangzi zhengmeng*, 87). Modern Chinese scholar Hou Wailu considers the *yinyun* in Wang Fuzhi's thinking quite close to the philosophical—although not scientific—concept of "material." See Hou Wailu, *Zhongguo sixiang tongshi*, 5:57–58.

49 Shuen-fu Lin, "Chia Pao-yu's First Visit to the Land of Illusion," 78.

50 The Tang empress Wu Zetian is fictionalized in numerous works of premodern fiction, regularly as a beautiful but ruthless female ruler with an insatiable appetite for both power and sex. Lady Yang, whose name was Yang

Yuhuan (719–56), was the favorite concubine of Emperor Xuanzong (r. 712–56) of the Tang. The tragic love between them, celebrated in Bai Juyi's (772–846) famous poem "Changhen ge" (Song of everlasting regret), is repeatedly reenacted in works of fiction such as *Sui-Tang yanyi* (A popular history of the Sui and the Tang) and *Shuo Tang* (Telling of the Tang). Even in fictional works where she does not appear as a character, she is frequently referred to as a typical plump beauty. Flying Swallow, whose name was Zhao Feiyan (?–1 BCE), was the empress of Emperor Cheng (Cheng Di) (r. 32–7 BCE) of the Han. She is often celebrated in premodern Chinese fiction as the best representative of female slimness and gracefulness, especially in contrast with the buxom beauty of Lady Yang. Xi Shi, who lived in the fifth century BCE, was a native of the kingdom of Yue. Like Lady Yang, Xi Shi is frequently evoked in the *xiaoshuo* tradition as both a stunning beauty and a femme fatale. Hong-niang is a maidservant in the *chuanqi* story "Yingying zhuan" by the Tang poet Yuan Zhen (779–831). She serves as a facilitator of the love affair between her beautiful mistress Yingying and the young scholar Student Zhang (Zhang Sheng). The story later provided the subject matter for Wang Shifu's (fl. 1280) play *Xixiang ji* (Romance of the Western Wing), which happens to be one of the favorite books for both Baoyu and Daiyu in *Dream of the Red Chamber*.

51  The novel does not mention Baoyu's reading of any titles in fictional literature until chapter 23. When Baoyu feels bored, his servant Tealeaf buys him copies of fictional works from outside the Jia residence, including the ones about Flying Swallow, Empress Wu Zetian, and Lady Yang. Indeed these are exactly some of the figures that the decorative objects in Qin Shi's room are associated with, which corroborates the conjecture that the décor of Qin Shi's room does not suggest romantic love so much as fictional sensuality. That Baoyu is not shown reading any such books in earlier chapters does not mean he has his first contact with those books in chapter 23. Actually, when he receives those books from Tealeaf, he is obviously already well acquainted with their contents: he "took one look at this gift and was enraptured," even before he read a single line in any of those volumes (*HLM* 1:268; *SS* 1:462).

52  *Jiaxu ben*, 127.

53  Shuen-fu Lin, "Chia Pao-yü's First Visit," 101.

54  *Jiaxu ben*, 130.

55  Yu Yingshi has pointed out that the Great Prospect Garden is "an earthly projection of the Illusory Land of Great Void." Yu suggests that the description of the scenery in the garden in chapter 17 can be considered "an elabora-

56   tion and enlargement" (*jiaxiang he fangda*) of what Baoyu sees on his arrival at the celestial land. See Yu Yingshi, "*Honglou meng* de liangge shijie," 38.

56   Pan Zhonggui, *Honglou meng xinjie*, 92.

57   At the start of the song-and-dance suite of *Honglou meng*, Disenchantment cautions Baoyu that only those who are "in the know" (*gezhongren*) will be able to follow the meaning of the performance (*HLM* 1:60). In an interlinear note Red Inkstone asks: "Who are those that are in the know? Is Baoyu in the know? Is the Stone in the know? Is the author? Is the reader?" (*Jiaxu ben*, 144). Surprisingly, Red Inkstone does not include Disenchantment in his suggested list of possible "knowers," but obviously the goddess is more "in the know" than any other characters in the novel.

58   The line appears in the form of a question: "Since first the world from chaos rose, who is the most constant lover?" (*HLM* 1:60; *SS* 1:138, translation modified). Red Inkstone answers that question in his interlinear note: "Who else can that lover be if not the author? On second thought, I say anew: Not the author but the Stone" (*Jiaxu ben*, 145).

59   The name Qin Keqing, as has been suggested by numerous scholars and critics, can pun on different homophonic structures: *qing-ke-qin* (to be endeared for her passion), *qing-ke-qing* (to be toppled with passion), and *qing-ke-qing* (to be disdained for her passion). Toward the end of chapter 8, one is informed that Qin Shi has another name, Jianmei, which is identical to that of Disenchantment's younger sister. But throughout the novel nobody ever refers to Qin Shi by that name.

60   In chapter 111, the novel offers a gloss of *qing* in the words of Qin Keqing's spirit, where *qing* is called the "natural state" of love before the stirring of the passion within (*weifa zhi qing*): "Earthlings treat lust and love as one and the same thing. By this means they practice all manner of lechery and immorality, and pass it off as 'harmless romance.' They do not understand the true meaning of the word 'love' [*qing*]. Before the emotions of pleasure, anger, grief and joy stir within the human breast, there exists the 'natural state' of love; the stirring of these emotions causes passion. Our kind of love, yours and mine, is the former, natural state. It is like a bud. Once open, it ceases to be true love" (*HLM* 4:1402; *SS* 5:210).

61   In a marginal note, Red Inkstone exclaims: "Marvelous! It refers to itself as having fallen to the root of passions and therefore useless for the restoration of heaven." See *Jiaxu ben*, 7.

62   Ibid., 351.

63   Ibid., 58.

64   The four imperial visits to Cao Yin's residence took place in 1699, 1703, 1705,

and 1707. For an account of those visits, see Jonathan Spence, *Ts'ao Yin and the K'ang-hsi Emperor*, 138–51.

65  *Jiaxu ben*, 339.

## CODA

1  Yu Yingshi, "Qian Mu yu xin rujia," 51.
2  David Swartz, *Culture and Power*, 89.
3  Bakhtin has observed that an authoritative discourse is "located in a distanced zone, organically connected with a past that is felt to be hierarchically higher. It is, so to speak, the word of the fathers. Its authority was already *acknowledged* in the past. It is a *prior* discourse." See Bakhtin, *The Dialogic Imagination*, 342; original italics.
4  To some extent, this "centrifugal" force in Chinese vernacular fiction is comparable to that in the Western novel. Discussing the novelistic discourse, Bakhtin writes: "In the history of literary language, there is a struggle constantly being waged to overcome the official line with its tendency to distance itself from the zone of contact, a struggle against various kinds and degrees of authority." Ibid., 345.
5  Feng Menglong, *Yushi mingyan*, 1.
6  Naquin and Rawski, *Chinese Society in the Eighteenth Century*, 59.
7  *Gui Zhuang Ji, juan* 3. Quoted in Zhao Zifu, *Mingdai xuexiao yu keju zhidu yanjiu*, 304.
8  *Li Yu quanji*, 1:165.
9  *Mianxingtang shiji, juan* 2. Quoted in Zhu Yixuan, ed., *Ming Qing xiaoshuo ziliao xuanbian*, 2:899.
10  Jin Shengtan, in particular, was persistent in using *caizi* to refer to Shi Nai'an, whom he believed to be the writer of *Water Margin*, the novel that he called *The Fifth Book of Genius*.
11  In Wang Yangming's epitaph for a scholar-turned-merchant Fang Lin, Fang is said to have retorted his friend's question on his change of profession by saying: "How do you know that a scholar cannot become a merchant and a merchant cannot become a scholar?" Citing Wang Yangming's epitaph, Yu Yingshi considers Fang Lin a relatively early example of a scholar's conversion to commerce, an example to be followed by many more literati in the later Ming and Qing. See Yu Yingshi, *Shi yu Zhongguo wenhua*, 525–40.
12  One example is Yu Xiangdou (fl. 1596), a publisher and bookseller of vernacular fiction in Jianyang. Timothy Brook describes the ways in which the

merchant meticulously affected a scholar's style and demeanor in an idealized portrait of himself. See Brook, *The Confusions of Pleasure,* 213.
13  Ian Watt, *The Rise of the Novel,* 32.
14  Robert E. Hegel, *Reading Illustrated Fiction,* 59.
15  For a discussion of the broad and heterogeneous readership of vernacular fiction in late imperial China, see Hegel, *Reading Illustrated Fiction in Late Imperial China,* 63–65.
16  Using *Water Margin* as example, Liangyan Ge has presented a discussion of the significance and impact of written Chinese vernacular as a new literary language for fiction. See Ge, *Out of the Margins,* 186–97.
17  Pu Songling, *Liaozhai zhiyi,* 562.
18  Feng Menglong, *Yushi mingyan,* 1.
19  Edward LiPuma, "Culture and the Concept of Culture in a Theory of Practice," 19.
20  To be sure, early Qing scholars, including Gu Yanwu and Wang Fuzhi, denounced the influence of Wang Yangming and his disciples in the leftist Taizhou school, especially Li Zhi, as a reason for the collapse of the Ming rule. That, however, does not change the fact that their own ideas were largely developed on the basis of Wang's thinking. Liang Qichao, in his *Zhongguo jin sanbainian xueshushi,* put it this way: "They all had once been—perhaps they would be unwilling to acknowledge it—nurtured in the bosom of their 'mother,' the Wang Yangming school" (15).

# Glossary of Chinese Characters

Personal names and titles of publications presented in the Selected Bibliography are not listed here.

an 庵

ba jingli guo de shiqing xixi ji zhe 把經歷過的事情細細記著
Ba you 八侑
Bagu sheng er liujing wei, shibafang xing er nianyishi fei 八股盛而六經微，十八房興而廿一史廢
bagu wen 八股文
Bai Juyi 白居易
Bai Xindao 白信蹈
Bai Xingjian 白行簡
baihua 白話
baimian shusheng 白面書生
bansheng liaodao 半生潦倒
*Bao Longtu pan baijia gong'an* 包龍圖判百家公案
Bao Shuya 鮑叔牙
Bao Zheng 包拯
Baohe 寶和
Baoyu, ji baoyu ye 寶玉，即寶玉也
baqi lingmiguan 八旗領米官
Beijing 北京
benyi 本意
Bian Yujing 卞玉京
Bo Yi 伯夷
boshi dizi 博士弟子
boxue hongci 博學宏詞
bu ke 不可
bu wei buren buyi zhi shi 不為不仁不義之事
bu xiao 不孝
bu you hu taixu 不遊乎太虛
bu zhengqi 不爭氣
butian 補天
butian yuri zhi gong 補天浴日之功

buwushi 不務實

cai (talent) 才
cai (wealth) 財
Cai Qizun 蔡啟傳
caizi 才子
caizi jiaren 才子佳人
*Can Tang* 殘唐
Cangshu 倉舒
canjun 參軍
Cao Cao 曹操
*Cao Cao ye zou Chencang lu* 曹操夜走陳倉路
Cao Huan 曹奐
Cao Nai 曹鼐
Cao Nai bu ke 曹鼐不可
Cao Pi 曹丕
Cao Xueqin 曹雪芹
Cao Yin 曹寅
caotang 草堂
cewen 策問
chaju 察舉
chan 蟾
Chang'an 長安
*Changhen ge* 長恨歌
changming guan 唱名官
changwei 嘗謂
changzai 常在
chaoting dadian 朝廷大典
chen 臣
Chen Di 陳迪
Chen Houyao 陳厚耀
Chen Jitai 陳際泰
Chen Lin 陳琳
Chen Ping 陳平
Chen Que 陳確

chen shijun yi zhong 臣事君以忠
Chen Yuanyuan 陳圓圓
Chen Yuxiao 陳與效
Chen Zongding 陳宗鼎
Cheng 程
Cheng Di 成帝
Cheng Jinfang 程晉芳
Cheng Tingzuo 程廷祚
Cheng Wang 成王
Cheng Weiyuan 程偉元
Cheng Yi 程頤
Chenghua 成化
Cheng-Zhu 程朱
chi 痴
Chibi 赤壁
Chiqing Si 痴情司
chong shengxun 崇聖訓
chuanqi 傳奇
chujia 出家
chun 蠢
Chungan Si 春感司
chungui 春閨
*Chunqiu* 春秋
*Chunqiu biedian* 春秋別典
*Chunqiu chuanshuo huizuan* 春秋傳說匯纂
*Chunqiu Zhanguo yici* 春秋戰國異辭
*Chushi biao* 出師表
ci shu benzhi 此書本旨
ci xi shenqian shenhou shi 此系身前身後事
cifu qi 詞賦氣
*Cihai* 辭海
ciru 雌儒
Cixi 慈禧
ciyou 慈幼

# Glossary of Chinese Characters

cun tianli, mie renyu 存天理，滅人欲

da si 大私
da zhunao 大主腦
*Dagao* 大誥
Daguanyuan 大觀園
dai 呆
Dai Mingshi 戴名世
dai shengxian liyan 代聖賢立言
dai waiqi 待外戚
Dai Zhen 戴震
daixia 逮下
daizi 呆子
Dangjin tianzi zhong wenzhang, zuxia hexu jiang Han-Tang 當今天子重文章，足下何須講漢唐
Dangjin tianzi zhong wenzhang, zuxia hexu song Han-Tang 當今天子重文章，足下何須誦漢唐
dangtou banghe 當頭棒喝
dao 道
dao zun yu shi 道尊於勢
daohao 道號
daotong (Daoist novice) 道童
daotong (lineage of Confucian learning) 道統
Daotong zai shi, zhitong yi zai shi yi 道統在是，治統亦在是矣
daoxue 道學
Daoyan 道衍
*Daozang jiyao* 道藏輯要
*Daxue* 大學
*Daxue bian* 大學辨
Daxueshi 大學士
Daye 大業
*Daye shiyi ji* 大業拾遺記

*Dayi juemi lu* 大義覺迷錄
dayin 大隱
daying 答應
de 德
defei 德妃
dejun xingdao 得君行道
Deng Yu 鄧禹
dengchan 登蟾
dengke 登科
*Dengke lu* 登科錄
*Dengke lu zhuan* 登科錄傳
dexing (moral conduct) 德行
dexing (moral virtue) 德性
dianqian shiren 殿前試人
Diao Liudai zhi yingcai, hu chuangyan er yunti 吊六代之英才，忽愴焉而隕涕
*Diao pipa* 吊琵琶
dingdang caoge zhu zhi 定當操戈逐之
Dingyuan 定遠
*Diwu caizishu* 第五才子書
diyige da jieshu 第一個大結束
Dong Qichang 董其昌
Dong Xiaowan 董小宛
Dong Ying 董瑛
Dong Zhongshu 董仲舒
Dong Zhuo 董卓
Dongfang Shuo 東方朔
Du *Sanguo zhi* fa 讀三國志法
Du Shaoqing 杜少卿
Du Shenqing 杜慎卿
Duan Ganmu 段干木
Duan Yucai 段玉裁
duanlian 鍛煉
dufa 讀法
Duncheng 敦誠

Dunmin 敦敏
Duo jin lou 奪錦樓
duyou 督郵

*Ershisi shi* 二十四史
*Erya* 爾雅
eryan 邇言

fafen 發憤
Fan Jin 范進
Fan Shijie 范世傑
Fan Zhongyan 范仲淹
Fang Bao 方苞
Fang Lin 方麟
Fang Xiaoru 方孝孺
Fang Yizhi 方以智
Fanli 凡例
fanshou shizuo qi shi 犯手實做其事
fei 妃
feipin 妃嬪
feng jisi 奉祭祀
Feng Menglong 馮夢龍
*Fengshen yanyi* 封神演義
Fengyang 鳳陽
*Fengyue baojian* 風月寶鑒
fengyue gushi 風月故事
fenshu kengru 焚書坑儒
fu (prefecture) 府
fu (rhapsody) 賦
fu er hao li 富而好禮
Fu yun lou 拂雲樓
*Furong lei* 芙蓉誄

gaikuo quanwen 概括全文
Gao Qi 高啟
Gao Wenxiu 高文秀
Geng Yan 耿弇

gengchen 庚辰
gewu 格物
gezhong ren 個中人
gong 公
Gong Weichang 龔惟長
gongguoge 功過格
gongming fugui 功名富貴
gongnü 宮女
Gongsun Chou 公孫丑
*Gongyang* 公羊
gu 故
*Gu lienü zhuan* 古列女傳
gu reng yin zhi 故仍因之
Gu Zijing 古子敬
Guafu sheji zhui xinlang, zhongmei qixin duo caizi 寡婦設計贅新郎, 眾美齊心奪才子
*Guan Dawang dufu dandaohui* 關大王獨赴單刀會
Guan Di 關帝
Guan Hanqing 關漢卿
Guan Wang 關王
Guan Yu 關羽
Guan Zhong 管仲
Guandi Miao 關帝廟
Guandu 官渡
guanggun 光棍
Guangwu 光武
Guangzong 光宗
Gufeng Zhanglao 孤峰長老
Gui Youguang 歸有光
Gui Zhuang 歸莊
*Gui Zhuang Ji* 歸莊集
guifei 貴妃
guiren 貴人
Guiyang lu 桂陽路
*Gujin xiaoshuo* 古今小說

# Glossary of Chinese Characters

guo 國
Guo Kangsong 郭康松
Guo Tieshan 郭鐵山
*Guoyu* 國語
Guozijian 國子監
gushi (ancient times) 古時
gushi (story) 故事
Gutang Tianfang Daoren 古棠天放道人
guti 古體

Haitang She 海棠社
Han 漢
Han Fei 韓非
*Han gong qiu* 漢宮秋
Han Shoutinghou 漢壽亭侯
Han xue 漢學
Han Yu 韓愈
*Han Yuandi ku Zhaojun* 漢元帝哭昭君
Hangzhou 杭州
Hanlin 翰林
hao shan er wang shi 好善而忘勢
haode 好德
haohuo haose 好貨好色
haoqiang 豪強
haose 好色
he 河
he chang 鶴氅
He gui lou 鶴歸樓
*He rong ji* 和戎記
He Xinyin 何心隱
he zu yu yan ren yi ye 何足與言仁義也
Hong-niang 紅娘
Hongwu 洪武
hongyunhe daopao 紅雲鶴道袍
Hongzhi 弘治
Hou Fangyu 侯方域
houqizi 後七子

Hu Wei 胡渭
Hu Weiyong 胡惟庸
hua (to change, to melt) 化
hua (painting, to paint) 畫
Hua Guan Suo 花關索
Hua Tuo 華佗
Hua Xiren 花襲人
*Hua yue hen* 花月痕
hua'an 花案
huabang 花榜
Huachen 花晨
huan 幻
Huang Gan 黃幹
Huang Shunji 黃順吉
Huang Tingjian 黃庭堅
Huang Zicheng 黃子澄
huangguifei 皇貴妃
Huangshu 皇叔
Huanzhong shidafu buwei jun yong 寰中士大夫不為君用
huban 笏板
hubu 戶部
Hui Dong 惠棟
huishi 會試
Huizong 徽宗
*Huqiu hua'an yishi* 虎邱花案逸史

ji (remembrance, to remember) 記
ji (collection) 集
Ji Chang 姬昌
Ji Kang 嵇康
Ji Ping 吉平
jia (family, home) 家
jia (false) 假
jia baoyu 假寶玉
Jia Baoyu 賈寶玉
jia jia 假家

Jia Kui 賈逵
Jia Yucun 賈雨村
Jia Zheng 賈政
Jiajing 嘉靖
Jian'an 建安
jianben 簡本
jiang 江
Jiang Daqi 蔣大器
Jiang Gan 蔣幹
Jiang Shang 姜尚
Jiang Ziya 姜子牙
jianguo 僭國
Jiangzhu Xiancao 絳珠仙草
Jiankang 建康
Jiankang lu 建康路
jianlin 監臨
Jianmei 兼美
jianshang 鑑賞
Jianwen 建文
Jiao Hong 焦竑
Jiaqing 嘉慶
jiaren 佳人
jiaxiang he fangda 加詳和放大
jiaxu 甲戌
Jie 桀
jiejian 節儉
Jieting 街亭
jieyu 婕妤
Jieyuan Si 結怨司
jiming 記名
Jin 金
Jin He 金和
*Jin Ping Mei* 金瓶梅
*Jin shu* 晉書
Jin Wenzheng 金文徵
Jing Lanjiang 景蘭江

jing xianfan 景賢範
jing yi baishuo chuan 竟以稗說傳
jing yi zhi zhong 精一執中
Jing Yuan 荊元
*Jinghua yuan* 鏡花緣
Jinghuan Xianzi 警幻仙子
jingjie 警戒
*Jingshi gongguoge* 警世功過格
jingshi zhiyong 經世致用
jingyi shi 經義式
Jinling shi'er chai 金陵十二釵
jinnang miaoji 錦囊妙計
jinxing 謹性
Jiqing lu 集慶路
jishan 積善
jiu pin 九嬪
jiushi 舊時
jiyu shijiu, tuoyu jiyi 寄於詩酒, 托於技藝
ju 局
juanshou 卷首
juanshou shang 卷首上
juanyun guan 捲雲冠
*Jue hou chan* 覺後禪
juemin xingdao 覺民行道
jun 君
jun jun, chen chen, fu fu, zi zi 君君, 臣臣, 父父, 子子
Jun shi chen yi li, chen shi jun yi zhong 君使臣以禮, 臣事君以忠
junshi 軍師
junzi 君子
Junzi ai ren yi de 君子愛人以德
junzi zhi ru 君子之儒
juxian renneng, gejin qixin 舉賢任能, 各盡其心

# Glossary of Chinese Characters

juzi yebing 舉子業病

kaipi hongmeng 開闢鴻蒙
Kangxi 康熙
kaojuxue 考據學
Keqing 可卿
Kong Rong 孔融
Kong Shangren 孔尚任
Kong Yingda 孔穎達
Kongkong Daoren 空空道人
Kongming 孔明
kongwen 空文
ku cheng ci shu 哭成此書
Kuaiji 會稽
Kuang Chaoren 匡超人
Kuizhou 夔州

laili 來歷
Lao kefu yao 老客婦謠
laolong zhishi 牢籠志士
laoru 老儒
Leng Zixing 冷子興
li (principle) 理
li (ritual) 禮
Li Bai 李白
Li Baichuan 李百川
Li Fang 李昉
Li Gong 李塨
Li Lüyuan 李綠園
*Li sao* 離騷
Li Shanchang 李善長
Li Shiren 李時人
Li Shizhen 李時珍
Li Si 李斯
Li Wa 李娃
*Li Wa zhuan* 李娃傳

Li Xiangjun 李香君
Li Yiji 酈食其
li yue bing nong 禮樂兵農
Li Yuerui 李岳瑞
Li Zhi 李贄
Li'an Jushi 蠢庵居士
Lian Zining 練子寧
Liang 亮
liangzhi 良知
Lianhuitang 聯輝堂
Libu 禮部
lihuai yuebeng 禮壞樂崩
lijia 立枷
Lin Daiyu 林黛玉
Lin Siniang 林四娘
ling Shanzhou panguan 領陝州判官
Ling Xuan 伶玄
lingchi 凌遲
Liu Bang 劉邦
Liu Bei 劉備
Liu Biao 劉表
liu bu 六部
Liu Ji 劉基
Liu Jin 劉瑾
Liu Rushi 柳如是
Liu Sanwu 劉三吾
Liu Shan 劉禪
Liu Tingji 劉廷璣
Liu Wu 劉武
Liu Xiang 劉向
Liu Xie 劉協
Liu Xiu 劉秀
*Liu Xuande zui zou Huanghelou* 劉玄德醉走黃鶴樓
Liu Zhang 劉璋
Liu Zhu 劉著

Liu Zongyuan 柳宗元
liupin 六品
Liuxia Hui 柳下惠
lixue 理學
liyin 吏隱
*Longtu erlu* 龍圖耳錄
*Longtu gong'an* 龍圖公案
Longzhong 隆中
lu 路
Lu Bianxiu 魯編修
Lu Jia 陸賈
Lü Kun 呂坤
Lü Liuliang 呂留良
Lu Miao Gong 魯繆公
*Lü mudan* 綠牡丹
Lü Shang 呂尚
Lu Shengnan 陸生楠
Lu Su 魯肅
Lu Xiaojie 魯小姐
Lu Xinhou 盧信侯
Lu Xun 魯迅
luan tianxia zhe wei jun 亂天下者唯君
lun di 論地
*Lun xue* 論學
lunjin 綸巾
*Lunyu* 論語
*Lunyu jizhu* 論語集註
Luo Guanzhong 羅貫中
*Lüye xianzong* 綠野仙踪

Ma Chunshang 馬純上
Ma Rong 馬融
Ma Su 馬謖
Ma Zhiyuan 馬致遠
Mao Xiang 冒襄
Mao Yanshou 毛延壽
Mao Zonggang 毛宗岡

meitong kao'an 美童考案
meng 夢
Meng Ke 孟柯
Mengzi 孟子
*Mengzi jiewen* 孟子節文
mensheng 門生
*Mianxingtang shiji* 勉行堂詩集
Miao Gong 繆公
mifeng guan 彌封官
Min wei gui, sheji ci zhi, jun wei qing
    民為貴, 社稷次之, 君為輕
*Ming Chenghua shuochang cihua
    congkan* 明成化說唱詞話叢刊
*Ming Taizu wenji* 明太祖文集
*Ming wenhai* 明文海
*Ming yitong zhi* 明一統志
Mingfei qu 明妃曲
mingjiao zuiren 名教罪人
mingjun xianxiang 明君賢相
mingshi 名士
mingzhu 明主
mo bu du hua yu taixu 莫不獨化於太虛
moshi 末世
Muku Si 暮哭司
muqin 睦親
muyi 母儀

Nan Mengmu jiaohe sanqian 男孟母教
    合三遷
*Nanbu yanhua lu* 南部煙花錄
Nanjing 南京
*Nanyong zhi* 南雍志
nei sheng wai wang 內聖外王
neige 內閣
neiwufu dachen 內務府大臣
nengjin qupi 能近取譬
Ni Shuangfeng 倪霜峰

## Glossary of Chinese Characters

ni yao zhengqi cai hao 你要爭氣才好
Nian Gengyao 年羹堯
niehai qingtian 孽海情天
*Ning hu ji* 寧胡記
Ningguo Gong 寧國公
Niu Buyi 牛布衣
Niu Pulang 牛浦郎
nongchen 弄臣
Nongxiang Zhuren 弄香主人
*Nücaizi shu* 女才子書
Nüwa 女媧

Oboi 鰲拜
O-erh-tai 鄂爾泰
Ouyang Xiu 歐陽修

Pan Pingge 潘平格
Pang Tong 龐統
Pei Songzhi 裴松之
pi 譬
pianti wen 駢體文
pin 嬪
pindao 貧道
Ping Shaobao 平少保
ping tianxia 平天下
*Pinhua baojian* 品花寶鑒
*Pipa yu* 琵琶語

qi (chess) 棋
qi (air, ether) 氣
qi jia 齊家
qi jia, zhi guo, ping tianxia 齊家,治國,平天下
qi ju qi san, bianhua zhi kexing er 其聚其散,變化之客形耳
Qi Liaosheng 戚廖生
*Qi lu deng* 歧路燈

Qi ren mo ru wo jing wang zhe 齊人莫如我敬王者
Qi Tai 齊泰
*Qi xu ben* 戚序本
Qian Daxi 錢大昕
Qian Mingshi 錢名世
Qian Mu 錢穆
Qian Qianyi 錢謙益
Qian Tang 錢唐
Qiande 乾德
Qianlong 乾隆
qiefu 且夫
qifen shishi, sanfen xugou 七分事實,三分虛構
qin 琴
Qin Keqing 秦可卿
Qin Shi 秦氏
Qin Zhong 秦鐘
*Qinding Daqing huidian zeli* 欽定大清會典則例
*Qinding Sishuwen* 欽定四書文
qing 情
Qingchi Fanzheng Daoren 情癡反正道人
qinggen 情根
Qinggeng Feng 青埂峰
qinggui 情鬼
qing-ke-qin (to be endeared for her passion) 情可親
qing-ke-qing (to be toppled for her passion) 情可傾
qing-ke-qing (to be disdained for her passion) 情可輕
*Qinglou meng* 青樓夢
*Qingseng lu* 情僧錄
qingtan 清談
Qingwen 晴雯

qingzhai 情債
qingzhong 情種
qinli 勤勵
qiren (extraordinary person) 奇人
qiren (bannerman) 旗人
Qishan Zuochen 歧山左臣
Qisongyuan nongjia chengzhen 七松園
　　弄假成真
Qiubei Si 秋悲司
Qixingtang 齊省堂
Qu Dajun 屈大均
Qu Yuan 屈原
*Quan Tang shi* 全唐詩
*Quan xue wen* 勸學文
Quanjiao 全椒
quanshu zhunao 全書主腦
quce rencai 驅策人才
Que Shen 卻詵
Qufu 曲阜
qupi 取譬

rang 讓
renwu 壬午
renzheng 仁政
Renzong 仁宗
Rongguo Gong 榮國公
*Rongtai bieji* 容台別集
Rongyutang 容與堂
ru er jun zhe 儒而君者
ru shi zuoyoushou 如失左右手
Ruan Ji 阮籍
Ruan Jianglan 阮江蘭
*Rulin waishi* ba 儒林外史跋
rushi 入世
*Ruyijun zhuan* 如意君傳
ruyu zhenglu 入於正路

saishen yinghui 賽神迎會
san dai 三代
san jia 三甲
*San yan* 三言
*Sanguo yanyi* 三國演義
*Sanguo zaju* 三國雜劇
*Sanguo zhizhuan* 三國志傳
*Sanguo zhizhuan pinglin* 三國志傳評林
sanjuan guan 散卷官
*Sanxia wuyi* 三俠五義
sha 傻
Shan Fu 單福
Shang 商
shangdeng 上等
Shangshu 尚書
Shanzhou 陝州
sheji 社稷
Shen 莘
*Shen luan jiao* 慎鸞交
Shen Lun 沈倫
Shen Qiongzhi 沈瓊枝
sheng zhi he zhe 聖之和者
*Shengxue xinfa* 聖學心法
*Shengyu* 聖諭
*Shengyu guangxun* 聖諭廣訓
*Shengyu liuyan* 聖諭六言
*Shengyuan lun* 生員論
Shengzu 聖祖
shenqian shenhou shi 身前身後事
Shenwu 神武
shenxian 神仙
shenyan 慎言
*Shenying Shizhe* 神瑛侍者
Shenzong 神宗
shi (teacher, master) 師
shi (scholar, literatus) 士

# Glossary of Chinese Characters

shi (political power) 勢
shi fumu 事父母
*Shi jie gongguoge* 十誡功過格
shi jiugu 事舅姑
shi jun 事君
Shi Xiangyun 史湘雲
shiba fang 十八房
shiba fang ke 十八房刻
shiba qicai, buju weijian 視拔奇才，不拘微賤
shichen 師臣
shidafu 士大夫
shifu 師父
*Shijing chuanshuo huizuan* 詩經傳說匯纂
shijing ximin 市井細民
shijun jinli 事君盡禮
Shijun jinli ren yi wei chan ye 事君盡禮人以為諂也
shilu shang yingxiong 世路上英雄
shinian xinku 十年辛苦
shishi 實事
Shitong san er xiaoshuo xing 史統散而小說興
*Shitou ji* 石頭記
shitou suo ji zhi shi 石頭所記之事
shiwen 時文
shixue 實學
*Shiyangjin Zhuge lun gong* 十樣錦諸葛論功
shoujuan guan 收卷官
*Shoutinghou nu zhan Guan Ping* 壽亭侯怒斬關平
shouyu diwangjia 售予帝王家
shouzu zhi qing 手足之情
shu 書

Shu 蜀
shu zhi benzhi 書之本旨
shudaizi 書呆子
shufei 淑妃
Shu-ho-te 舒赫德
*Shuihu zhuan* 水滸傳
Shun 舜
Shunzhi 順治
*Shuo Tang* 說唐
*Shuowen jiezi* 說文解字
Shusun Tong 叔孫通
shuwang silai 述往思來
shuzhong diyi ren 書中第一人
si (department) 司
si (private) 私
*Siku quanshu* 四庫全書
Sima Yan 司馬炎
*Sishu* 四書
sishu 死書
*Sishu daquan* 四書大全
*Sishu jizhu* 四書集註
Song Lian 宋濂
Song Na 宋訥
*Song ru* 宋儒
Song Yingxing 宋應星
Su Qin 蘇秦
*Sui yilu* 隋遺錄
*Sui-Tang yanyi* 隋唐演義
Sun Ce 孫策
Sun Kaidi 孫楷第
Sun Quan 孫權
Sun Wukong 孫悟空
suosui 瑣事
suwang 素王

Tai Bo 泰伯

Tai 太王
Taihang 太行
*Taiji tu* 太極圖
taixu 太虛
Taixu Huanjing 太虛幻境
Taizhou 泰州
Taizong 太宗
Taizong Huangdi zhen chang ce /
　Zhuande yingxiong jin baitou 太宗
　皇帝真長策，賺得英雄盡白頭
Taizu 太祖
Tan Shaowen 譚紹聞
Tanchun 探春
Tang 湯
Tang furen you guo jin zhi ruzhe 唐婦人
　猶過今之儒者
Tang Ying 唐寅
Tang Zhen 唐甄
Tang Zongzhen 湯總鎮
Tangcun 棠村
Tao Yuanming 陶淵明
*Taohua shan* 桃花扇
tedeng 特等
Tian Feng 田豐
tianxia 天下
*Tianxia wei yijia* 天下為一家
tianxia wei zhu jun wei ke 天下為主
　君為客
tianxia zhi gong 天下之公
tianzi 天子
tianzi mensheng 天子門生
tianzi qin ce yu ting 天子親策於廷
tidiao guan 提調官
timu 題目
tingzhang 廷杖
tizhinei 體制內
tizhiwai 體制外

tongbu dagang 通部大綱
tongkao 同考
tongling baoyu 通靈寶玉
tongzi 童子
tuoxuren 脫序人
tupo 突破

wai 外
waicai 歪才
waitou dashi 外頭大事
Wan Zhang 萬章
Wang Anshi 王安石
Wang Fuzhi 王夫之
Wang Gen 王艮
Wang Guangyang 汪廣洋
wang guo 亡國
Wang Hui 王惠
Wang Jingqi 汪景祺
Wang Kangju 王康琚
Wang Mang 王莽
Wang Mian 王冕
Wang Niansun 王念孫
Wang Qiang 王嬙
Wang Shifu 王實甫
Wang Shizhen 王世貞
wang tianxia 亡天下
Wang Wei 王維
Wang Xiaohai 汪孝海
Wang Xilian 王希廉
*Wang xue* 王學
Wang Yangming 王陽明
Wang Yinzhi 王引之
Wang Yuhui 王玉輝
Wang Zhaojun 王昭君
Wang Zhu 汪洙
Wang Zi'an 王子安
wangnianjiao 忘年交

Wanjuanlou 萬卷樓
Wanli 萬曆
Wanniang 畹娘
Wei (river) 渭
Wei (kingdom) 魏
wei chaoting banshi 為朝廷辦事
Wei Tishan 衛體善
Wei Yuqing 魏玉卿
weibu rusheng 韋布儒生
weifa zhi qing 未發之情
Weiyang Sheng 未央生
Wen 文
Wen Chou 文丑
Wen Ruyu 溫如玉
wen si jian wu si zhan 文死諫武死戰
Wen Tingyun 溫庭筠
Wen Wang 文王
Wen Yanbo 文彥博
Wenchang Dijun 文昌帝君
Wenchang Miao 文昌廟
Wenmu shanfang ji 文木山房集
wenren 文人
wenwang tai mi 文網太密
wenyan 文言
wenziyu 文字獄
wo dao bu xing 我道不行
wobei 臥碑
Woxian Caotang 臥閒草堂
Wu (kingdom) 吳
Wu (King Wu of the Zhou) 武
wu (military, martial) 武
wu da kuaihuo 五大快活
Wu Maoyu 吳茂育
Wu Shu 武書
Wu weijian haode ru haose zhe ye 吾未見好德如好色者也
Wu Weiye 吳偉業

Wu Zetian 武則天
wu zhi Zifang 吾之子房
Wu'an Wang 武安王
wude rang youde 無德讓有德
Wujing Sishu daquan 五經四書大全
Wushi 無始
Wuwang fa Zhou shu 武王伐紂書
Wuxian 吳縣
Wuzhou 婺州
Wuzong 武宗

Xi Shi 西施
Xi Zhou 西周
Xia 夏
Xia yi lou 夏宜樓
Xian tianxia zhi you er you, hou tianxia zhi le er le 先天下之憂而憂，後天下之樂而樂
xianfei 賢妃
Xianfeng 咸豐
xiangcao meiren 香草美人
Xiangdang 鄉黨
xiangshi 鄉試
Xiangyang 襄陽
Xiangyang hui 襄陽會
xianliang 賢良
xianliang fangzheng 賢良方正
Xiannong 先農
xiansheng 先生
xianxian ci 先賢祠
xianzhu 先主
xiao 孝
Xiao Yunxian 蕭雲仙
xiaolian 孝廉
xiaoren zhi ru 小人之儒
xiaoshuo 小說
xiaoyin 小隱

Xiaoyin yin lingsou, dayin yin chaoshi 小隱隱陵藪, 大隱隱朝市
Xiaozong 孝宗
xie jia ze zhi zhen 寫假則知真
Xie Jishi 謝濟世
Xie Liu 泄柳
Xihu 西湖
*Xijing zaji* 西京雜記
Ximen Qing 西門慶
Xin Qiji 辛棄疾
xing 性
*Xinghua tian* 杏花天
*Xingli daquan* 性理大全
*Xingli jingyi* 性理精義
xingshengzi 形聲字
xini 細膩
*Xinping xiuxiang Honglou meng quanzhuan* 新評繡像紅樓夢全傳
*Xinping xiuxiang Honglou meng quanzhuan* juanshou 新評繡像紅樓夢全傳卷首
xinxue 新學
Xiongnu 匈奴
Xiuranzi 修髯子
xiushen 修身
*Xiuta yeshi* 繡榻野史
*Xixiang ji* 西廂記
*Xiyou ji* 西遊記
Xizhai 習齋
Xizong 熹宗
Xu Chu 許褚
Xu Da 徐達
Xu Guangqi 徐光啟
*Xu Jin Ping Mei* 續金瓶梅
Xu Qianxue 徐乾學
Xu Shen 許慎
Xu Shilian 徐士廉
Xu Shu 徐庶
Xu Wei 徐渭
Xu Xiake 徐霞客
Xu You 許攸
Xuande 玄德
xuanxiu 選秀
Xuanzong 玄宗
Xue Aocao 薛敖曹
Xue Baochai 薛寶釵
Xue Dan 薛旦
xue er you ze shi 學而優則仕
Xue Pan 薛蟠
xue yi ju wei yue shi 學以居位曰士
Xue Yuji 薛虞畿
xueguan 學官
xumei zhuowu 鬚眉濁物
Xun Shuang 荀爽
xunchuo guan 巡綽官
xunzhang zhaiju zhi furu 尋章摘句之腐儒
Xunzi 荀子

ya de zheme su 雅的這麼俗
ya sheng 亞聖
Yan Gongsheng 嚴貢生
Yan Liang 顏良
Yan Ruoqu 閻若璩
Yan Shigu 顏師古
Yan Yuan (Qing scholar, 1635–1704) 顏元
Yan Yuan (Confucius's disciple, 521–481 BCE) 顏淵
yan zhi da zhe ye 言之大者也
yan zhi xiao zhe ye 言之小者也
yan zhi you xiao zhe 言之尤小者
Yan Ziling 嚴子陵
Yang Minglang 楊明瑯
Yang Shen 楊慎

# Glossary of Chinese Characters

*Yang Taizhen waizhuan* 楊太真外傳
Yang Weizhen 楊維楨
Yang Wenke 楊文恪
Yang Xiu 楊修
Yang Yuhuan 楊玉環
*Yangpingguan wu ma po Cao* 陽平關五馬破曹
*Yan-Li xueshuo dui Wu Jingzi de yingxiang* 顏李學說對吳敬梓的影響
*Yanyi* 演義
Yao 堯
Yao Guangxiao 姚廣孝
*Yao Shun zhi dao* 堯舜之道
ye 野
yi guwen wei shiwen 以古文為時文
*Yi jing* 易經
yi jun wei zhu tianxia wei ke 以君為主天下為客
yi renyi fu ren 以仁義服人
yi shi wei ming, qupi xiangcheng 以事為名，取譬相成
yi shili dai zhi 以師禮待之
yi shouzu dai zhi 以手足待之
yi tianxia zhi renxin 一天下之人心
yi weizi wei gongming zhi jie 以文字為功名之階
yi wenci wei guofa 以文詞為國法
yi yi yu dayou 以昇於大猷
Yi Yin 伊尹
Yidu lu 益都路
*Yijia fu bing xu* 移家賦並序
Yilingzhou 夷陵州
yin wen jian dao 因文見道
Yin Zhi 尹直
Ying Zheng 嬴政
Yingtian fu 應天府
yingxiong 英雄

*Yingxiong pu* 英雄譜
*Yingxiong pu juanshou* 英雄譜卷首
Yingyang Gongzi 滎陽公子
*Yingying zhuan* 鶯鶯傳
yinyun 氤氳
yisheng de zhengshi 一生的正事
yisheng shiye 一生事業
yiwai zhi yi 意外之意
yiyang taiguo 抑揚太過
yiyin 意淫
Yizhou lu 益州路
yizhudan 儀註單
Yonghui 永徽
Yongle 永樂
*Yongle dadian* 永樂大典
Yongyuzi 庸愚子
Yongzheng 雍正
you 友
You Tong 尤侗
youxi bimo 遊戲筆墨
Yu (legendary ruler) 禹
Yu (ancient kingdom) 虞
Yu Kai 余愷
Yu Pingbo 俞平伯
yu shidafu zhi tianxia 與士大夫治天下
yu wei chen, jin chen dao 欲為臣，盡臣道
Yu Xiangdou 余象斗
Yu Yude 虞育德
Yu Zhengxie 俞正燮
Yuan Di 元帝
Yuan Hongdao 袁宏道
Yuan Shao 袁紹
Yuan Zhen 元稹
Yuanchun 元春
yuanse qinxian 遠色親賢
yuanshi 院試

*Yuanyang mei* 鴛鴦媒
Yue 越
Yue Fei 岳飛
Yue Lin 越麟
Yue Shi 樂史
Yue Zhongqi 岳鐘琪
yuefu 樂府
yuegui 月桂
Yunchang 雲長
yushi 御史
yuwan pa du wenzhang 愚頑怕讀文章

zaixiang 宰相
*Zaixiang xuyong dushuren* 宰相須用讀書人
*Zaiyuan zazhi* 在園雜誌
zalan 雜覽
zan 贊
zaxue 雜學
Zeng Jing 曾靜
Zeng Shen 曾參
Zha Siting 查嗣庭
Zhang Boxing 張伯行
Zhang Dai 張岱
Zhang Fei 張飛
Zhang Jun 張浚
Zhang Juzheng 張居正
Zhang Liang 張良
Zhang Shangde 張尚德
Zhang Sheng 張生
*Zhang shi yishu waibian* 章氏遺書外編
Zhang Shiqi 張時起
Zhang Tingyu 張廷玉
Zhang Wenhu 張文虎
Zhang Xin 張信
Zhang Xuecheng 章學誠
Zhang Yi 張儀

Zhang Zai 張載
Zhao Feiyan 趙飛燕
*Zhao Feiyan waizhuan* 趙飛燕外傳
Zhao Gu 趙嘏
Zhao Pu 趙普
Zhao Xuezhai 趙雪齋
Zhao Yun 趙雲
Zhao Yunke 趙雲客
*Zhaojun bianwen* 昭君變文
*Zhaojun chusai* 昭君出塞
*Zhaojun meng* 昭君夢
*Zhaojun zhuan* 昭君傳
*Zhaoshi bei* 照世杯
Zhaoti Si 朝啼司
zhe gui 折桂
zhen 真
Zhen 甄
Zhen Baoyu 甄寶玉
zhen baoyu 真寶玉
zhen cai 真才
zhen ru 真儒
Zheng Banqiao 鄭板橋
Zheng Xie 鄭燮
Zheng Xuan 鄭玄
zhengce 正冊
zhenglu 正路
zhengqi 爭氣
zhengse 正色
zhengshi 正事
zhengtong (lineage of political power) 政統
zhengtong (orthodoxy) 正統
Zhenguan 貞觀
zhengwu 正務
zhengzhi zhuti yishi 政治主體意識
Zhenru Fudi 真如福地
zhenshi yin 真事隱

# Glossary of Chinese Characters

zhenzheng zhi jia 真正之家
Zhenzong 真宗
zhexian 謫仙
Zhi bei you 知北遊
Zhi Jianfeng 支劍峰
zhi tianxia wei min yong 治天下為民用
zhide 至德
zhisheng xianshi 至聖先師
zhishidan 執事單
*Zhixin lu* 知新錄
*Zhiyanzhai* 脂硯齋
*Zhiyike suoji* 制義科瑣記
zhizhuan 志傳
zhong 忠
zhong'e 中惡
zhongdeng 中等
zhongyin 中隱
Zhou (dynasty) 周
Zhou (ancient ruler) 紂
Zhou Dunyi 周敦頤
Zhou Gong 周公
Zhou Jin 周進
Zhou Leqing 周樂清
Zhou Wu Wang 周武王
Zhou Xuan 周璇
*Zhou Yi* 周易
Zhou Yu 周瑜
*Zhouyi zhezhong* 周義折中
Zhu Di 朱棣
Zhu Pengshou 朱彭壽
Zhu Xi 朱熹
Zhu Yizun 朱彝尊

Zhu Yuanzhang 朱元璋
Zhu Yunming 祝允明
Zhuang Shaoguang 莊紹光
zhuangyuan 狀元
zhuangyuan quan 狀元拳
*Zhuangzi* 莊子
Zhuangzi 莊子
Zhuge Jin 諸葛瑾
Zhuge Jun 諸葛均
Zhuge Liang 諸葛亮
*Zhuge Liang Bowang shaotun* 諸葛亮博望燒屯
*Zhuge Liang zhuan* 諸葛亮傳
zhukao 主考
zhulin qixian 竹林七賢
Zhuo Jing 卓敬
zhusi 主司
*Zhuzi quanshu* 朱子全書
Zi Si 子思
ziyi canjun 諮議參軍
*Zizhi tongjian* 資治通鑒
*Zizhi tongjian houbian* 資治通鑑後編
Zizi kanlai jieshi xue, shinian xinku bu xunchang 字字看來皆是血, 十年辛苦不尋常
zong qi quanbu zhi ming 總其全部之名
*Zou Fengchu Pang lue si jun* 走鳳雛龐掠四郡
Zou Yang 鄒陽
zun zhi zun 尊之尊
*Zuo zhuan* 左傳

# Selected Bibliography

Aixinjueluo Xuanye 愛新覺羅. 玄燁. *Qing Shengzu Ren Huangdi yuzhi wenji* 清聖祖仁皇帝御製文集. *Siku quanshu* 四庫全書 ed.

Ames, Roger T. *The Art of Rulership: A Study of Ancient Chinese Political Thought.* Albany: State University of New York Press, 1994.

Anderson, Marston. "The Scorpion in the Scholar's Cap: Ritual, Memory, and Desire in *Rulin Waishi*." In *Culture and State in Chinese History: Conventions, Accommodations, and Critiques,* edited by Theodore Huters, R. Bin Wong, and Pauline Yu, 259–76. Stanford: Stanford University Press, 1997.

Anonymous. *Guoyu* 國語. *Siku quanshu* ed.

Anonymous. *Nükaike zhuan* 女開科傳. *Guben xiaoshuo jicheng* 古本小說集成 ed.

Aristotle. *The Poetics.* Translated by Leon Golden. Tallahassee: University Presses of Florida, 1981.

Bakhtin, M. M. *The Dialogic Imagination.* Edited by Michael Holquist. Translated by Caryl Emerson and Michael Holquist. Austin: University of Texas Press, 1981.

Ban Gu 班固. *Qian Han shu* 前漢書. *Siku quanshu* ed.

Bol, Peter K. "On the Problem of Contextualizing Ideas: Reflections on Yu Ying-shi's Approach to the Study of Song Daoxue." *Journal of Song-Yuan Studies* 34 (2004): 59–79.

Brokaw, Cynthia J. *The Ledgers of Merit and Demerit.* Princeton: Princeton University Press, 1991.

Brook, Timothy. *The Confusions of Pleasures: Commerce and Culture in Ming China*. Berkeley: University of California Press, 1998.

Cao Renhu 曹仁虎 and Ji Huang 嵇璜. *Qinding Xu wenxian tongkao* 欽定續文獻通考. Siku quanshu ed.

Cao Xueqin 曹雪芹. *Honglou meng: Qi xu ben* 紅樓夢: 戚序本. 5 vols. *Guben xiaoshuo jicheng* ed.

———. *Zhiyanzhai chongping Shitou ji: Gengchen ben* 脂硯齋重評石頭記: 庚辰本. 4 vols. *Guben xiaoshuo jicheng* ed.

———. *Zhiyanzhai chongping Shitou ji: Jiaxu ben* 脂硯齋重評石頭記: 甲戌本. *Guben xiaoshuo jicheng* ed.

Cao Xueqin 曹雪芹 and Gao E 高鶚. *Honglou meng* 紅樓夢. 4 vols. Beijing: Renmin wenxue chubanshe, 1973.

———. *The Story of the Stone*. 5 vols. Translated by David Hawkes and John Minford. London: Penguin, 1973–1986.

Cao Xuewei 曹學偉. "Daojiao yu Zhuge Liang de xingxiang suzao" 道教與諸葛亮的形象塑造. In *Sanguo yanyi yu Zhongguo wenhua*, edited by Tan Luofei et al., 169–80. Chengdu: Bashu shushe, 1992.

Chan, Albert. *The Glory and Fall of the Ming Dynasty*. Norman: University of Oklahoma Press, 1982.

Chan, Wing-tsit, ed. *Chu Hsi and Neo-Confucianism*. Honolulu: University of Hawai'i Press, 1986.

Chang, Chun-shu, and Shelley Hsueh-lun Chang. *Crisis and Transformation in Seventeenth-Century China: Society, Culture, and Modernity in Li Yü's World*. Ann Arbor: University of Michigan Press, 1992.

Chang, Shelley Hsueh-lun. *History and Legend: Ideas and Images in the Ming Historical Novels*. Ann Arbor: University of Michigan Press, 1990.

Chen Bangzhan 陳邦瞻. *Song mo jishi benmo* 宋末紀事本末. Siku quanshu ed.

Chen Dongyuan 陳東原. *Zhongguo jiaoyu shi* 中國教育史. Taibei: Shangwu yinshuguan, 1966.

Chen Jian 陳建, ed. *Huang Ming tongji jiyao* 皇明通紀集要. Reprint. 4 vols. Taibei: Wenhai chubanshe, n.d.

Chen, Li. "Legal Specialists and Judicial Administration in Late Imperial China, 1651–1911." *Late Imperial China* 33, no. 1 (June 2012): 1–54.

Chen Liangyun 陳良運, ed. *Zhongguo lidai shixue lunzhu xuan* 中國歷代詩學論著選. Nanchang: Baihuazhou wenyi chubanshe, 1995.

Chen Maotong 陳茂同. *Zhongguo lidai xuanguan zhidu* 中國歷代選官制度. Shanghai: Huadong shifandaxue chubanshe, 1994.

Chen Meilin 陳美林. *Wu Jingzi yanjiu* 吳敬梓研究. Shanghai: Shanghai guji chubanshe, 1984.

Chen Qixin 陳其欣, ed. *Mingjia jiedu* Sanguo yanyi 名家解讀《三國演義》. Jinan: Shandong renmin chubanshe, 1998.

Chen Shilong 陳世隆 and Chen Si 陳思. *Liang Song mingxian xiaoji* 兩宋名賢小集. *Siku quanshu* ed.

Chen Shou 陳壽. *Sanguo zhi* 三國志. Annotated by Pei Songzhi 裴松之. 5 vols. Beijing: Zhonghua shuju, 1959.

Chen Xizhong 陳曦鐘 et al., eds. *Shuihu zhuan huipingben* 《水滸傳》會評本. 2 vols. Beijing: Beijing daxue chubanshe, 1981.

Chen Zhouchang 陳周昌. "*Sanguozhi tongsu yanyi* xingcheng guocheng lunlue" 《三國志通俗演義》形成過程論略. In *Sanguo yanyi yanjiuji*, 306–25. Chengdu: Sichuansheng shehuikexueyuan, 1983.

Cheng Tingzuo 程廷祚. *Qingxi wenji* 青溪文集. Beijing: Beijing daxue chubanzu, 1936.

Cheng Yizhong 程一中. "Chongti jiu'an shuo Cao Cao" 重提舊案說曹操. In *Sanguo yanyi yanjiuji*, 153–73. Chengdu: Sichuansheng shehuikexueyuan, 1983.

Chow, Kai-wing. "Discourse, Examination, and Local Elite: The Invention of the T'ung-ch'eng School in Ch'ing China." In *Education and Society in Late Imperial China, 1600–1900*, edited by Benjamin A Elman and Alexander Woodside, 183–219. Berkeley: University of California Press, 1994.

———. *The Rise of Confucian Ritualism in Late Imperial China: Ethics, Classics, and Lineage Discourse*. Stanford: Stanford University Press, 1994.

Chow, Kai-wing, On-Cho Ng, and John Henderson, eds. *Imagining Boundaries: Changing Confucian Doctrines, Texts, and Hermeneutics*. Albany: State University of New York Press, 1999.

Dardess, John W. *Confucianism and Autocracy: Professional Elites in the Founding of the Ming Dynasty*. Berkeley: University of California Press, 1983.

———. *Conquerors and Confucians: Aspects of Political Change in Late Yuan China*. New York: Columbia University Press, 1973.

———. *A Ming Society: T'ai-ho County, Kiangsi, Fourteenth to Seventeenth Centuries*. Berkeley: University of California Press, 1996.

de Bary, William Theodore. "Individualism and Humanitarianism in Late Ming Thought." In William Theodore de Bary, ed., *Self and Society in Ming Thought*, 145–247.

———, ed. *Self and Society in Ming Thought*. New York: Columbia University Press, 1970.

———, ed. *The Unfolding of Neo-Confucianism*. New York: Columbia University Press, 1975.

Deng Siyu 鄧嗣禹. *Zhongguo kaoshi zhidu shi* 中國考試制度史. Taibei: Taiwan xuesheng shuju, 1967.

Ding Xigen 丁錫根, ed. *Song Yuan pinghua ji* 宋元平話集. 2 vols. Shanghai: Shanghai guji chubanshe, 1990.

Ding Yuanji 丁原基, *Qingdai Kang Yong Qian sanchao jinshu yuanyin zhi yanjiu* 清代康雍乾三朝禁書原因之研究. Taibei: Huazheng shuju, 1983.

Dongfang Shuo 東方朔. "Da ke nan" 答客難. In *Wen xuan* 文選, edited by Li Shan 李善 and Xiao Tong 蕭統, 45.2/a-6/b. *Siku quanshu* ed.

Dreyer, Edward L. *Early Ming China: A Political History 1355–1435*. Stanford: Stanford University Press, 1982.

Elman, Benjamin A. "Changes in Confucian Civil Service Examinations from the Ming to the Ch'ing Dynasty." In *Education and Society in Late Imperial China, 1600–1900*, edited by Benjamin A. Elman and Alexander Woodside, 111–49. Berkeley: University of California Press, 1994.

———. *A Cultural History of Civil Examinations in Late Imperial China*. Berkeley: University of California Press, 2000.

———. "'Where is King Ch'eng?': Civil Examinations and Confucian Ideology During the Early Ming, 1368–1415." *T'oung Pao* 79, nos. 1–3 (1993): 23–68.

Elman, Benjamin A., and Alexander Woodside, eds. *Education and Society in Late Imperial China, 1600–1900*. Berkeley: University of California Press, 1994.

Epstein, Maram. *Competing Discourses: Orthodoxy, Authenticity, and Engendered Meaning in Late Imperial Chinese Fiction*. Cambridge: Harvard University Asia Center, 2001.

Fairbank, John K., ed. *Chinese Thoughts and Institutions*. Chicago: University of Chicago Press, 1957.

Fan Wenlan 范文瀾. *Zhongguo tongshi jianbian* 中國通史簡編. 2nd ed. Beijing: Renmin chubanshe, 1964.

Fan Ye 范曄. *Hou Han shu* 後漢書. *Siku quanshu* ed.

Fan Zhongyan 范仲淹. *Fan Wenzheng ji* 范文正集. *Siku quanshu* ed.

Fei Xiaotong 費孝通. "Lun shenshi" 論紳士. In *Huangquan yu shenquan*, edited by Wu Han, Fei Xiaotong et al., 1–9. Tianjin: Tianjin renmin chubanshe, 1988.

———. "Lun shiru" 論師儒. In *Huangquan yu shenquan*, edited by Wu Han, Fei Xiaotong et al., 23–39. Tianjin: Tianjin renmin chubanshe, 1988.

Feng Menglong 馮夢龍. *Yushi mingyan* 喻世明言. Shanghai: Shanghai guji chubanshe, 1992.

Foucault, Michel. *Discipline and Punish: The Birth of the Prison*. Translated by A. M. Sheridan-Smith. Harmondsworth: Penguin, 1977.

———. *Power*. Edited by James D. Faubion. Translated by Robert Hurley et al. New York: New Press, 1994.

———. *Society Must Be Defended: Lectures at the Collège de France: 1975–1976*. Edited by Mauro Bertani and Alessandro Fontana. Translated by David Macey. New York: Picador, 2003.

Fung Yu-lan. *A History of Chinese Philosophy*. Translated by Derk Bodde. 2 vols. Princeton: Princeton University Press, 1953.

Gallagher, Catherine, and Stephen Greenblatt. *Practicing New Historicism*. Chicago: University of Chicago Press, 2000.

Gao Mingge 高明閣. *Sanguo yanyi lungao* 《三國演義》論稿. Shenyang: Liaoning daxue chubanshe, 1986.

Gao Xiaokang 高小康. *Shimin, shiren yu gushi: Zhongguo jindai shehui wenhua zhong de xushi* 市民, 士人與故事: 中國近代社會文化中的敘事. Beijing: Renmin chubanshe, 2001.

Gao You 高誘, annot. *Huainanzi* 淮南子. In *Zhuzi jicheng*, vol. 7. Beijing: Zhonghua shuju, 1954.

Ge, Liangyan. *Out of the Margins: The Rise of Chinese Vernacular Fiction*. Honolulu: University of Hawai'i Press, 2001.

Ge Quan 葛荃. *Quanli zaige lixing: Shiren, chuantong zhengzhi wenhua yu Zhongguo shehui* 權利宰割理性: 士人, 傳統政治文化與中國社會. Tianjin: Nankai daxue chubanshe, 2003.

Ge Zhaoguang 葛兆光. *Zhongguo sixiang shi* 中國思想史. Beijing: Shangwu yinshuguan, 2007.

Geng, Song. *The Fragile Scholar: Power and Masculinity in Chinese Culture*. Hong Kong: Hong Kong University Press, 2004.

Goldin, Paul Rakita. *The Culture of Sex in Ancient China*. Honolulu, University of Hawai'i Press, 2002.

Gong Wei 龔煒. *Chaolin bitan* 巢林筆談. Beijing: Zhonghua shuju, 1981.

Gramsci, Antonio. *An Antonio Gramsci Reader: Selected Readings, 1916–1935*. Edited by David Forgacs. New York: Schocken Books, 1988.

Gu Mingtang 顧鳴塘. *Rulin waishi yu jiangnan shishen shenghuo* 《儒林外史》與江南士紳生活. Beijing: Shangwu yinshuguan, 2005.

Gu Yanwu 顧炎武. *Rizhilu* 日知錄. In *Rizhilu jishi: Wai qi zhong* 日知錄集釋: 外七種. 3 vols. Shanghai: Shanghai guji chubanshe, 1985.

Gu Yingtai 古應泰. *Mingshi jishi benmo* 明史記事本末. 10 vols. Beijing: Zhonghua shuju, 1985.

Guo Kangsong 郭康松. *Qingdai kaojuxue yanjiu* 清代考據學研究. Wuhan: Hubei cishu chubanshe, 2001.

Gutang Tianfang Daoren 古棠天放道人 [pseud.]. *Xinghua tian* 杏花天. Taibei: Taiwan Daying Baike Gufen Youxian Gongsi, 1995.

Guy, R. Kent. "Fang Pao and the *Ch'in-ting Ssu-shu-wen*." In *Education and Society in Late Imperial China, 1600–1900*, edited by Benjamin A Elman and Alexander Woodside, 150–182. Berkeley: University of California Press, 1994.

Han Yu 韓愈. *Han Yu xuanji* 韓愈選集. Annotated by Sun Changwu 孫昌武. Shanghai: Shanghai guji chubanshe, 1996.

Hanan, Patrick, trans. *The Carnal Prayer Mat*. New York: Ballantine, 1990.

———. *The Chinese Vernacular Story*. Cambridge: Harvard University Press, 1981.

———. *The Invention of Li Yu*. Cambridge: Harvard University Press, 1988.

Hegel, E. Robert. *The Novel in Seventeenth-Century China*. New York: Columbia University Press, 1981.

———. *Reading Illustrated Fiction in Late Imperial China*. Stanford: Stanford University Press, 1998.

Ho, Ping-ti. *The Ladder of Success in Imperial China: Aspects of Social Mobility, 1368–1911*. New York: Columbia University Press, 1962.

Hong Mai 洪邁. *Rongzhai si bi* 容齋四筆. Siku quanshu ed.

Hou Wailu 侯外廬. *Zhongguo sixiang tongshi* 中國思想通史. 5 vols. Beijing: Renmin chubanshe, 1956.

Hsia, C. T. *The Classic Chinese Novel: A Critical Introduction*. New York: Columbia University Press, 1968.

Hu Shi 胡適. "Dai Dongyuan de zhexue" 戴東原的哲學. In *Hu Shi xuanji: Shuxue* 胡適選集: 述學, 23–79. Taibei: Wenxing shudian, 1966.

———. "*Honglou meng* kaozheng" 《紅樓夢》考證. In *Honglou meng pinglun xuan*, edited by Wang Zhiliang, 1:300–334. Beijing: Zhongguo shehui kexue chubanshe, 1998.

———. *Hu Shi gudian wenxue yanjiu lunji* 胡適古典文學研究論集. 2 vols. Shanghai: Shanghai guji chubanshe, 1988.

———. "Wu Jingzi zhuan" 吳敬梓傳. In *Hu Shi gudian wenxue yanjiu lunji*, 2:1060–64. Shanghai: Shanghai guji chubanshe, 1988.

———. "Yan-Li xuepai de Cheng Tingzuo" 顏李學派的程廷祚, in *Hu Shi xuanji: Renwu* 胡適選集: 人物, 111–58. Taibei: Wenxing shudian, 1966.

Hu Yiming 胡益明 and Zhou Yueliang 周月亮. *Rulin waishi yu Zhongguo shi wenhua* 《儒林外史》與中國士文化. Hefei: Anhui daxue chubanshe, 2005.

Huang, Martin. *Negotiating Masculinities in Late Imperial China*. Honolulu: University of Hawai'i Press, 2006.

Huang Qiang 黃強. "Lun *Jin Ping Mei* dui Ming Wuzong de yingshe" 論《金瓶梅》對明武宗的影射. *Jingsu Jiaoyu Xueyuan xuebao* 江蘇教育學院學報 3 (1995): 49–53.

———. "Rou putuan wei Li Yu suo zuo neizheng" 《肉蒲團》為李漁所作內證. *Xuchang shizhuan xuebao* 許昌師專學報 1 (1992): 62–65.

Huang Tingjian 黃庭堅. *Shangu ji waiji* 山谷集外集. Siku quanshu ed.
Huang Yuji 黃虞稷. *Qianqingtang shumu* 千頃堂書目. Taibei: Wangwen shuju, 1967.
Huang Zongxi 黃宗羲. *Ming ru xue'an* 明儒學案. 2 vols. Taibei: Guoli bianyiguan, 1968.
——. *Ming yi dai fang lu* 明夷待訪錄. Beijing: Zhonghua shuju, 1985.
Huang Zuo 黃佐. *Hanlin ji* 翰林記. 3 vols. Beijing: Zhonghua shuju, 1985.
Huters, Theodore, R. Bin Wong, and Pauline Yu, eds. *Culture and State in Chinese History: Conventions, Accommodations, and Critiques*. Stanford: Stanford University Press, 1997.
Idema, W. L. *Chinese Vernacular Fiction: The Formative Period*. Leiden: Brill, 1974.
Jameson, Fredric. *The Political Unconscious: Narrative as a Socially Symbolic Act*. Ithaca: Cornell University Press, 1981.
Ji Yun 紀昀. *Ji Xiaolan wenji* 紀曉嵐文集. 3 vols. Shijiazhuang: Hebei jiaoyu chubanshe, 1995.
——. "Ming Yi'an Huanghou waizhuan" 明懿安皇后外傳. In *Ji Xiaolan wenji*, 3:1–10. Shijiazhuang: Hebei jiaoyu chubanshe, 1995.
——. *Yuewei Caotang biji* 閱微草堂筆記. In *Ji Xiaolan wenji*, 2:1–572. Shijiazhuang: Hebei jiaoyu chubanshe, 1995.
Jia Zhongming 賈仲明. *Luguibu xubian* 錄鬼簿續編. In *Zhongguo gudian xiqu lunzhu jicheng* 中國古代戲曲論著集成, 2:277–300. Beijing: Zhongguo xiqu chubanshe, 1959–1960.
Jiang Liangqi 蔣良騏. *Donghua lu* 東華錄. Beijing: Zhonghua shuju, 1980.
Jiang Qingbo 江慶柏. *Ming Qing Sunan wangzu wenhua yanjiu* 明清蘇南望族文化研究. Nanjing: Nanjing shifan daxue chubanshe, 1999.
Jin Shengtan 金聖嘆. *Jin Shengtan quanji* 金聖嘆全集. 4 vols. Nanjing: Jiangsu guji chubanshe, 1985.
Jin Zheng 金諍. *Keju zhidu yu Zhongguo wenhua* 科舉制度與中國文化. Shanghai: Shanghai renmin chubanshe, 1990.
King, Gail. "A Few Textual Notes Regarding Guan Suo and the Sanguo yanyi." *Chinese Literature: Essays, Articles, Reviews* 9, nos .1–2 (July 1978): 89–92.
Ko, Dorothy. "The Written Word and the Bound Feet: A History of the Courtesan's Aura." In *Writing Women in Late Imperial China*, edited by Elle Widmer and Kang-I Sun Chang, 74–100. Stanford: Stanford University Press, 1997.
Kong Yingda 孔穎達. *Zhouyi zhushu* 周易注疏. Siku quanshu ed.
Kuhn, Philip A. *Soulstealers: The Chinese Sorcery Scare of 1768*. Cambridge: Harvard University Press, 1990.
Lang Ying 郎瑛. *Qixiu leigao* 七修類稿. Shanghai: Shanghai shudian, 2001.

Lanling Xiaoxiaosheng 兰陵笑笑生 [pseud.]. *Jin Ping Mei cihua* 金瓶梅詞話. Taibei: Zengnizhi wenhua shiye youxian gongci, 1980.

Lau, D. C., trans. *Mencius*. London: Penguin, 1970.

Lee, Thomas H. C. *Education in Traditional China: A History*. Leiden: Brill, 2000.

Legge, James, trans. *Confucian Analects, The Great Learning, and The Doctrine of the Mean*. New York: Dover, 1971.

Li Diaoyuan 李調元. *Dan mo lu* 淡墨錄. 2 vols. Beijing: Zhonghua shuju, 1985.

Li Gong 李塨. *Shugu hou ji* 恕谷後集. 3 vols. Beijing: Zhonghua shuju, 1985.

Li Guangdi 李光地. *Rongcun quanji* 榕村全集. Siku quanshu ed.

Li Guojun 李國鈞 ed. *Qingdai qianqi jiaoyu lunzhu xuan* 清代前期教育論著選. 3 vols. Beijing: Jiaoyu chubanshe, 1990.

Li Hanqiu 李漢秋. *Rulin waishi yanjiu* 《儒林外史》研究. Shanghai: Huadong shifandaxue chubanshe, 2001.

Li Huiming 李惠明. "Chuanshen wenbi xie Guan Yu: Guan Yu yishu xingxiang shenshenghua zhi lishi bianqian" 傳神文筆寫關羽: 關羽藝術形象神聖化之歷史變遷. *Shanghai shifan daxue xuebao* 上海師範大學學報 2 (1993): 41–47.

Li Tao 李燾. *Xu Zizhi tongjian changbian* 續資治通鑑長編. Siku quanshu ed.

Li, Wai-yee. *Enchantment and Disenchantment: Love and Illusion in Chinese Literature*. Princeton: Princeton University Press, 1993.

———. "The Late Ming Courtesan: Invention of a Cultural Ideal." In *Writing Women in Late Imperial China*, edited by Ellen Widmer and Kang-I Sun Chang, 46–73. Stanford: Stanford University Press, 1997.

Li Yu 李漁. *Li Liweng piyue Sanguo zhi* 李笠翁批閱《三國志》. In *Li Yu quanji*, vols. 5–6. Hangzhou: Zhejiang guji, 1992.

———. *Li Yu quanji* 李漁全集. 12 vols. Hangzhou: Zhejiang guji, 1992.

———. *Liancheng bi* 連城璧. In *Li Yu quanji*, vol. 4. Hangzhou: Zhejiang guji, 1992.

———. *Rou putuan* 肉蒲團. Taibei: Taiwan Da Ying baike gufen youxian gongsi, 1994.

———. *Shi'er lou* 十二樓. Shanghai: Shanghai guji chubanshe, 1992.

———. *Wusheng xi* 無聲戲. In Li Yu quanji, vol. 4. Hangzhou: Zhejiang guji, 1992.

Li Zhi 李贄. *Fen shu, Xu Fen shu* 焚書. 續焚書. Beijing: Zhonghua shuju, 1975.

Liang Gongchen 梁恭辰. *Chishang caotang biji* 池上草堂筆記. Taibei: Guangwen shuju, 1970.

Liang Qichao 梁啟超. *Zhongguo jin sanbainian xueshushi* 中國近三百年學術史. Beijing: Zhongguo shehui kexue chubanshe, 2008.

Liang Zhangju 梁章鉅. *Zhiyi conghua* 制藝叢話. Shanghai: Shanghai shudian, 2001.

Lin, Shuen-fu. "Chia Pao-yu's First Visit to the Land of Illusion: An Analysis of a

Literary Dream in Interdisciplinary Perspective." *Chinese Literature: Essays, Articles, Reviews* 14 (1992): 77–106.

———. "Ritual and Narrative structure in Ju-lin wai-shi." In *Chinese Narrative: Critical and Theoretical Essays,* edited by Andrew H. Plaks, 244–65. Princeton: Princeton University Press, 1977.

LiPuma, Edward. "Culture and the Concept of Culture in a Theory of Practice." In *Bourdieu: Critical Perspectives,* edited by Craig Calhoun et al., 14–34. Chicago: University of Chicago Press, 1993.

Liu Baonan 劉寶楠, ed. *Lunyu zhengyi* 論語正義. In *Zhuzi jicheng,* vol. 1. Beijing: Zhonghua shuju, 1954.

Liu Cunren 柳存仁 [Ts'un-yan Liu]. "Luo Guanzhong jiangshi xiaoshuo zhi zhenwei xingzhi" 羅貫中講史小說之真偽性質. In *Zhongguo gudai xiaoshuo yanjiu: Taiwan Xianggang lunwen xuanji,* edited by Liu Shide 劉世德, 74–172. Shanghai: Shanghai guji chubanshe, 1983.

Liu, James J. Y. *Chinese Theories of Literature.* Chicago: University of Chicago Press, 1975.

Liu Shide 劉世德, ed. *Zhongguo gudai xiaoshuo yanjiu: Taiwan Xianggang lunwen xuanji* 中國古代小說研究: 台灣香港論文選集. Shanghai: Shanghai guji chubanshe, 1983.

Liu Weiwei 劉蔚瑋. "Wan Ming yu Qing zhongye shanren xintai bijiao yanjiu: Yi Xu Wei he Zheng Xie wei zhongxin" 晚明與清中葉山人心態比較研究—以徐渭和鄭燮為中心. *Anhui guangbo dianshi daxue xuebao* 安徽電視廣播大學學報 1 (2001): 113–16.

Liu Xiaoyan 劉孝嚴. "Zhengtongguan yu Sanguo yanyi" 正統觀與《三國演義》. *Changbai luncong* 長白論叢 1 (1995): 81–84.

Liu Yiqing 劉義慶. *Shishuo xinyu* 世說新語. Hong Kong: Xuelin shudian, n.d.

Liu Zhaobin 劉兆璸. *Qingdai keju* 清代科舉. Taibei: Dongda tushu, 1977.

Liu Zongzhou 劉宗周. *Liuzi yishu* 劉子遺書. Siku quanshu ed.

Lo, Ping-cheung. "Zhu Xi and Confucian Sexual Ethics." *Journal of Chinese Philosophy* 20, no. 4 (December 1993): 465–77.

Louie, Kam. *Theorising Chinese Masculinity: Society and Gender in China.* Cambridge: Cambridge University Press, 2002.

Lu Xun. *A Brief History of Chinese Fiction.* Beijing: Foreign Languages Press, 1976.

Lü Kun 呂坤. *Shenyin yu* 呻吟語. Beijing: Xueyuan chubanshe, 1993.

Lü Xiangxie 呂相燮. *Guochao kechang yiwenlu* 國朝科場異聞錄. Shanghai: Shuncheng shuju, 1898.

———. *Qian Ming kechang yiwenlu* 前明科場異聞錄. Shanghai: Shuncheng shuju, 1898.

———. *Tang Song kechang yiwenlu* 唐宋科場異聞錄. Shanghai: Shuncheng shuju, 1898.

———. *Xiaoshi kechang yiwenlu* 小試科場異聞錄. Shanghai: Shuncheng shuju, 1898.

———. *Zhisheng kechang yiwenlu* 直省科場異聞錄. Shanghai: Shuncheng shuju, 1898.

Lukacs, Georg. *The Theory of the Novel: A Historico-Philosophical Essay on the Forms of Great Epic Literature*. Translated by Anna Bostock. Cambridge: MIT Press, 1971.

Luo Guanzhong 羅貫中. *Sanguozhi tongsu yanyi* 三國志通俗演義. 6 vols. Guben xiaoshuo jicheng ed.

———. *Three Kingdoms: A Historical Novel*. Translated by Moss Roberts. Berkeley: University of California Press, 1991.

Luo Kanglie 羅忼烈. "Wenxue he lishi zhong de Guan Yu" 文學和歷史中的關羽. *Shehui hexue zhanxian* 社會科學戰線 1 (1993): 235–45.

Ma Duanlin 馬端臨. *Wenxian tongkao* 文獻通考. Siku quanshu ed.

Ma, Tai-loi. "Novels Prohibited in the Literary Inquisition of Emperor Ch'ien Lung, 1722–1788." In *Critical Essays on Chinese Fiction*, edited by Winston Yang et al., 201–2. Hong Kong: Chinese University Press, 1980.

Mair, Victor H., trans. *Wandering on the Way: Early Taoist Tales and Parables of Chuang Tzu*. Honolulu: University of Hawai'i Press, 1994.

Mao, Nathan K., and Liu Ts'un-yan. *Li Yü*. Boston: Twayne, 1977.

Mao Zonggang 毛宗崗. "Du Sanguo zhi fa" 讀《三國志》法. In Zhu Yixuan and Liu Yuchen, eds. *Sanguo yanyi ziliao huibian*, 293–309.

McLaren, Anne E. "Ming Audience and Vernacular Hermeneutics: The Uses of The Romance of the Three Kingdoms." *T'oung Pao* 81 (1995): 51–80.

———. "Popularizing The Romance of the Three Kingdoms: A Study of Two Early Editions." *Journal of Oriental Studies* 33, no. 2 (1995): 165–85.

McMahon, Keith. "Eroticism in Late Ming, Early Qing Fiction: The Beauteous Realm and the Sexual Battlefield." *T'oung Pao* 73, nos. 4–5 (1987): 217–64.

———. *Misers, Shrews, and Polygamists: Sexuality and Male-Female Relations in Eighteenth-Century Chinese Fiction*. Durham: Duke University Press, 1995.

Miyazaki Ichisada. *China's Examination Hell: The Civil Service Examinations of Imperial China*. Translated by Conrade Schirokauer. New Haven: Yale University Press, 1981.

Moody, Peter R. "The Romance of the Three Kingdoms and Popular Chinese Political Thought." *Review of Politics* 37, no. 2 (April 1975): 175–99.

Naquin, Susan, and Evelyn S. Rawski. *Chinese Society in the Eighteenth Century*. New Haven: Yale University Press, 1987.

O'Farrell, Clare. *Michel Foucault*. London: Sage Publications, 2005.
Ouyang Jian 歐陽健. "Shilun Sanguozhi tongsu yanyi de chengshu niandai" 試論《三國志通俗演義》的成書年代. In *Sanguo yanyi yanjiuji,* 280–95. Chengdu: Sichuansheng shehuikexueyuan, 1983.
Ouyang Jian and Xiao Xiangkai 蕭相愷, eds. *Zhongguo tongsu xiaoshuo zongmu tiyao* 中國通俗小說總目提要. Beijing: Zhongguo wenlian chubanshe, 1990.
Pan Guangdan 潘光旦. *Ming Qing liangdai Jiaxing de wangzu* 明清兩代嘉興的望族. Shanghai: Shanghai shudian, 1991.
Pan Yongyin 潘永因. *Song bai lei chao* 宋稗類鈔. Siku quanshu ed.
Pan Zhonggui 潘重規. *Honglou meng xinjie*《紅樓夢》新解. Taibei: Sanmin shuju, 1990.
Peng Dingqiu 彭定求. *Ming xian mengzheng lu* 明賢蒙正錄. In *Mingdai zhuanji congkan* 明代傳記叢刊, edited by Zhou Junfu 周駿富, 21:667–798. Taibei: Mingwen shuju, 1991.
Peterson, William J. "Fang I-chih: Western Learning and the 'Investigation of Things.'" In *The Unfolding of Neo-Confucianism*, edited by William T. de Bary, 369–411. New York: Columbia University Press, 1975.
Plaks, Andrew H., ed. *Chinese Narrative: Critical and Theoretical Essays*. Princeton: Princeton University Press, 1977.
———. *The Four Masterworks of the Ming Novel*. Princeton: Princeton University Press, 1987.
Pu Songling 蒲松齡. *Liaozhao zhiyi* 聊齋誌異. Hangzhou: Zhejiang guji chubanshe, 1993.
Qian Mu 錢穆. *Guoxue gailun* 國學概論. Taibei: Taiwan Shangwu yinshuguan, 1993.
Qian Xuantong 錢玄同. "Rulin waishi xin xu"《儒林外史》新敘. In *Rulin waishi huijiao huiping ben,* Wu Jingzi, 2:781–93. Shanghai: Shanghai guji chubanshe, 1984.
Qian Yong 錢泳. *Lüyuan conghua* 履園叢話. 2 vols. Beijing: Zhonghua shuju, 1979.
Qian Zhongshu 錢鐘書. *Qi zhui ji* 七錐集. Shanghai: Shanghai guji, 1994.
———. *Qian Zhongshu lunxue wenxuan* 錢鐘書論學文選, vol. 3. Guangzhou: Huacheng chubanshe, 1990.
*Qing Gaozong shilu* 清高宗實錄. In *Qing shilu* 清實錄, vols. 9–12. Beijing: Zhonghua shuju, 1985.
Qishan Zuochen 歧山左臣 [pseud.]. *Nükaike zhuan* 女開科傳. Guben xiaoshuo jicheng ed.
Rawski, Evelyn S. *Education and Popular Literacy in Ch'ing China*. Ann Arbor: University of Michigan Press, 1979.

———. *The Last Emperors: A Social History of Qing Imperial Institution*. Berkeley: University of California Press, 1998.

Richards, I. A. *The Philosophy of Rhetoric*. Oxford: Oxford University Press, 1936.

Ricoeur, Paul. *The Rule of Metaphor: Multi-disciplinary Studies of the Creation of Meaning in Language*. Translated by Robert Czerny et al. Toronto: University of Toronto Press, 1977.

Roddy, Stephen J. *Literati Identity and Its Fictional Representations in Late Imperial China*. Stanford: Stanford University Press, 1998.

Rolston, David L., ed. *How to Read the Chinese Novel*. Princeton: Princeton University Press, 1990.

Ropp, Paul S. "Ambiguous Images of Courtesan Culture in Late Imperial China." In *Writing Women in Late Imperial China*, edited by Ellen Widmer and Kang-I Sun Chang, 17–45. Stanford: Stanford University Press, 1997.

———. *Dissent in Early Modern China: Ju-lin wai-shih and Ch'ing Social Criticism*. Ann Arbor: University of Michigan Press, 1981.

Roy, David T., trans. "How to Read *The Romance of the Three Kingdoms*." In *How to Read the Chinese Novel*, edited by David L. Rolston, 152–95. Princeton: Princeton University Press, 1990.

Ruan Kuisheng 阮葵生. *Chayu kehua* 茶餘客話. 2 vol. Beijing: Zhonghua shuju, 1959.

Sakai Tadao 酒井忠雄. *Chūgoku zensho no kenkyū* 中国全書の研究. Tokyo: Kōbundō, 1960.

*Sanguo yanyi yanjiuji* 三國演義研究集. Edited by Shehui kexue yanjiu congkan bianjibu 《社會科學研究叢刊》編輯部. Chengdu: Sichuansheng shehuikexueyuan, 1983.

*Sanguozhi pinghua* 三國志平話. In *Song Yuan pinghua ji* 宋元平話集, edited by Ding Xigen 丁錫根, 2:741–882. Shanghai: Shanghai guji chubanshe, 1990.

Shan Jinheng 單錦珩. *Li Yu nianpu* 李漁年譜. In *Li Yu quanji* 李漁全集, Li Yu, vol. 12. Hangzhou: Zhejiang guji, 1992.

———. *Li Yu yanjiu ziliao xuanji* 李漁研究資料選編. In *Li Yu quanji*, Li Yu, vol. 12. Hangzhou: Zhejiang guji, 1992.

———. *Li Yu zhuan* 李漁傳. Chengdu: Sichuan wenyi chubanshe, 1986.

Shang, Wei. *Rulin waishi and Cultural Transformation in Late Imperial China*. Cambridge: Harvard University Asia Center, 2003.

Shang Yanliu 商衍鎏. *Qingdai keju kaoshi shulu* 清代科舉考試述錄. Beijing: Sanlian, 1958.

Shanghai shudian chubanshe 上海書店出版社, ed. *Mingjiao zuiren tan* 《名教罪人》談. Shanghai: Shanghai shudian chubanshe, 1999.

Shen Defu 沈德符. *Wanli yehuobian* 萬曆野獲編. 3 vols. Beijing: Zhonghua shuju, 1979.

Shen Jia 沈佳. *Ming ru yanxing lu* 明儒言行錄. Siku quanshu ed.

Shinian Kanchai 十年砍柴. *Wan Ming qishi nian 1573–1644: Cong zhongxing dao fuwang* 晚明七十年1573–1644: 從中興到覆亡. Xi'an: Shaanxi shifandaxue chubanshe, 2007.

Sima Qian 司馬遷. *Shi ji* 史記. 2nd ed. 10 vols. Beijing: Zhonghua shuju, 1982.

Spence, Jonathan D. *Emperor of China: Self Portrait of K'ang Hsi*. New York: Knopf, 1974.

———. *Ts'ao Yin and the K'ang-hsi Emperor: Bondservant and Master*. New Haven: Yale University Press, 1966.

Spence, Jonathan D., and John E. Wills, Jr., eds. *From Ming to Ch'ing: Conquest, Religion, and Continuity in Seventeenth-Century China*. New Haven: Yale University Press, 1979.

Stone, Charles R. *The Fountainhead of Chinese Erotica: The Lord of Perfect Satisfaction (Ruyijun zhuan)*. Honolulu: University of Hawai'i Press, 2003.

Struve, Lynn A. "Ambivalence and Action: Some Frustrated Scholars of the K'ang-hsi Period." In *From Ming to Ch'ing: Conquest, Religion, and Continuity in Seventeenth-Century China*, edited by Jonathan D. Spence and John E. Wills, Jr., 321–56. New Haven: Yale University Press, 1979.

Su Tongbing 蘇同炳. "Mingdai xiaoquan yanjiu" 明代相權研究. In *Ming shi ou bi* 明史偶筆, Su Tongbing, 1–45. Taibei: Shangwu yinshuguan, 1970.

Su'an Zhuren 蘇庵主人 [pseud.]. *Xiu ping yuan* 繡屏緣. Guben xiaoshuo jicheng ed.

Sun Kaidi 孫楷第. *Cangzhou ji* 滄州集. 2 vols. Beijing: Zhonghua shuju, 1965.

———. "Cihua kao" 詞話考. In *Cangzhou ji*, Sun Kaidi, 1:97–108.

———. "Shuihu zhuan jiuben kao" 《水滸傳》舊本考. In *Cangzhou ji*, Sun Kaidi, 1:121–43.

Swartz, David. *Culture and Power: The Sociology of Pierre Bourdieu*. Chicago: University of Chicago Press, 1997.

Tan Luofei 譚洛非 et al., eds. *Sanguo yanyi yu Zhongguo wenhua* 《三國演義》與中國文化. Chengdu: Bashu shushe, 1992.

Tang Zhen 唐甄. *Qian shu* 潛書. Beijing: Guji chubanshe, 1955.

Tao Zongyi 陶宗儀. *Shuo fu* 說郛. Siku quanshu ed.

Tianhuzang Zhuren 天花藏主人 [pseud.]. *Ping Shan Leng Yan* 平山冷燕. Guben xiaoshuo jicheng ed.

Tsai, Shih-shan Henry. *The Eunuchs in the Ming Dynasty*. Albany: State University of New York Press, 1996.

Tu, Wei-ming. "The Sung Confucian Idea of Education: A Background Understanding." In *Neo-Confucian Education: The Formative Stage,* edited by Wm. Theodore de Mary and John W. Chaffee, 139–50. Berkeley: University of California Press, 1989.

Tuo Tuo 脫脫 et al. *Song shi* 宋史. Beijing: Zhonghua shuju, 1985.

van Gulik, R. H. *Sexual Life in Ancient China: A Preliminary Survey of Chinese Sex and Society from ca. 1500 B.C. till 1644 A.D.* Leiden: Brill, 1961.

Wan Sida 萬斯大. *Ming ru yanxinglu* 明儒言行錄. Siku quanshu ed.

Wang Daocheng 王道成. *Keju shihua* 科舉史話. Beijing: Zhonghua shuju, 1988.

Wang Debao 王德保. *Shi yu yin* 仕與隱. Beijing: Huawen chubanshe, 1997.

Wang Dezhao 王德昭. *Qingdai keju zhidu yanjiu* 清代科舉制度研究. Hong Kong: Chinese University Press, 1982.

Wang Dingbao 王定保. *Tang zhiyan* 唐摭言. 2 vols. Beijing: Zhonghua shuju, 1985.

Wang Jian 王椷. *Qiudeng conghua* 秋燈叢話. 3 vols. Taibei: Guangwen shuju, n.d.

Wang Jilie 王季烈, ed. *Guben Yuan Ming zaju* 孤本元明雜劇. Beijing: Zhongguo xiju chubanshe, 1958.

Wang Liqi 王利器. "Luo Guanzhong yu Sanguozhi tongsu yanyi" 羅貫中與《三國志通俗演義》. In *Sanguo yanyi yanjiuji,* 240–65. Chengdu: Sichuansheng shehuikexueyuan, 1983.

———, ed. *Yuan Ming Qing san dai jinhui xiaoshuo xiqu shiliao* 元明清三代禁毀小說戲曲史料. Beijing: Zuojia chubanshe, 1958.

Wang Shizhen 王士禎. *Chibei outan* 池北偶談. 2 vols. Beijing: Zhonghua shuju, 1982.

Wang Xianqian 王先謙, ed. *Xunzi jijie* 荀子集解. In *Zhuzi jicheng,* vol. 2. Beijing: Zhonghua shuju, 1954.

Wang Xuetai 王學泰. "Kang Yong Qian san chao duiyu shiren de xunhua: Zaishuo Qingdai you jingxue wu ruxue" 康雍乾三朝對於士人的馴化: 再說清代有經學無儒學. *Yu hua* 雨花 6 (2012): 33–39.

———. *Youmin wenhua yu Zhongguo shehui* 遊民文化與中國社會. Beijing: Xueyuan chubanshe, 1999.

Wang Yangming 王陽明. *Wang Wencheng quanshu* 王文成全書. Siku quanshu ed.

Wang Zhiliang 王志良, ed. *Honglou meng pinglun xuan* 《紅樓夢》評論選. 2 vols. Beijing: Zhongguo shehui kexue chubanshe, 1998.

Watt, Ian. *The Rise of the Novel: Studies in Defoe, Richardson and Fielding.* Berkeley: University of California Press, 1971.

Wei Zi'an 魏子安. *Hua yue hen* 花月痕. Guben xiaoshuo jicheng ed.

White, Hayden. "Getting Out of History." In *Contemporary Literary Criticism: Modernism through Post-Structuralism,* edited by Robert Con Davis, 146–60. New York: Longman, 1986.

Widmer, Ellen, and Kang-I Sun Chang, eds. *Writing Women in Late Imperial China*. Stanford: Stanford University Press, 1997.

Wilhelm, Hellmut. "The Scholar's Frustration: Notes on a Type of Fu." *Chinese Thoughts and Institutions*, edited by John K. Fairbank, 43–60. Chicago: University of Chicago Press, 1957.

Wong, Timothy C. *Wu Ching-Tzu*. Boston: Twayne, 1978.

Wu Enyu 吳恩裕. "Dunmin, Duncheng he Cao Xueqin" 敦敏, 敦誠和曹雪芹. In *Mingjia jiedu Honglou meng*, edited by Zhang Baokun, 2:849–57. Ji'nan: Shandong renmin chubanshe, 1998.

Wu Han 吳晗. "Lun shenquan" 論紳權. In *Huangquan yu shenquan*, edited by Wu Han, Fei Xiaotong et al., 48–54. Tianjin: Tianjin renmin chubanshe, 1988.

———. "Lun shidafu" 論士大夫. In *Huangquan yu shenquan*, edited by Wu Han, Fei Xiaotong et al., 66–73. Tianjin: Tianjin renmin chubanshe, 1988.

———. *Zhu Yuanzhang zhuan* 朱元璋傳. Hong Kong: Sanlian, 1949.

Wu Han 吳晗, Fei Xiaotong 費孝通 et al. *Huangquan yu shenquan* 皇權與紳權. Tianjin: Tianjin renmin chubanshe, 1988.

Wu Jingzi 吳敬梓. *Rulin waishi* 儒林外史. Beijing: Renmin wenxue, 1978.

———. *Rulin waishi huijiao huiping ben* 儒林外史會校會評本. Edited by Li Hanqiu 李漢秋. 2 vols. Shanghai: Shanghai guji chubanshe, 1984.

———. *The Scholars*. Translated by Yang Hsien-yi and Gladys Yang. New York: Columbia University Press, 1992.

Wu Shichang 吳世昌. *Honglou tanyuan* 紅樓探源. Beijing: Beijing chubanshe, 2000.

Wu Zuxiang 吳組緗. *Shuo Bai ji* 說稗集. Beijing: Beijing daxue chubanshe, 1987.

Xie Qing 謝青 and Tang Deyong 湯德用, eds. *Zhongguo kaoshi zhudu shi* 中國考試制度史. Hefei: Huangshan shushe, 1995.

Xiong Du 熊篤. "Zhongguo fengjian junchen guanxi de biange yanbian" 中國封建君臣關係的變革演變. In *Sanguo yanyi yu Zhongguo wenhua*, edited by Tan Luofei et al., 39–51. Chengdu: Bashu shushe, 1992.

Xu Ke 徐珂. *Qing bai lei chao* 清稗類鈔. 13 vols. Beijing: Zhonghua shuju, 1986.

Xu Song 徐松. *Dengkeji kao* 登科記攷. 3 vols. Beijing: Zhonghua shuju, 1984.

Yan Buke 閻步克. *Shidafu zhengzhi yansheng shigao* 士大夫政治演生史稿. Beijing: Beijing daxue chubanshe, 1996.

Yan Yuan 顏元. *Cun xue bian* 存學編. Beijing: Zhonghua shuju, 1985.

———. *Xizhai jiyu* 習齋記餘. 2 vols. Beijing: Zhonghua shuju, 1985.

Yang Bojun 楊伯峻. *Mengzi yizhu* 孟子譯注. 2 vols. Beijing: Zhonghua shuju, 1960.

Yang, Shuhui. *Appropriation and Representation: Feng Menglong and the Chi-*

nese Vernacular Story. Ann Arbor: University of Michigan Center for Chinese Studies, 1998.

Yang, Winston L. Y., and Curtis P. Adkins, eds. *Critical Essays on Chinese Fiction.* Hong Kong: Chinese University Press, 1980.

Yang, Xiaoshan. *Metamorphosis of the Private Sphere: Gardens and Objects in Tang-Song Poetry.* Cambridge: Harvard University Asia Center, 2003.

Yang Xuewei 楊學為 et al., eds. *Zhongguo kaoshi zhidu shi ziliao xuanbian* 中國考試制度史資料選編. Hefei: Huangshan shushe, 1992.

Yi Su 一粟, ed. *Honglou meng juan* 紅樓夢卷. Taibei: Xinwenfeng chuban gongsi, 1989.

Yin Xuanbo 尹選波. *Zhongguo Mingdai jiaoyu shi* 中國明代教育史. Beijing: Remmin chubanshe, 1994.

Yongzheng 雍正. *Dayi juemi tan* 《大義覺迷》談. Shanghai: Shanghai shudian, 1999.

Yu, Anthony C. *Rereading the Stone: Desire and the Making of Fiction in* Dream of the Red Chamber. Princeton: Princeton University Press, 1997.

Yu Chaogui 余朝貴. "Sanguo yanyi banben er ti" 《三國演義》版本二題. In *Mudanjiang Shifan Xueyuan xuebao* 牡丹江師範學院學報 1 (1992): 53-60.

Yu Jin 余金, *Xichao xinyu* 熙朝新語. Taibei: Wenhai, 1985.

Yu Jingxiang 于景祥. *Jinbang timing: Qingdai keju shuyao* 金榜題名: 清代科舉述要. Shenyang: Liaohai, 1997.

Yu Pingbo 俞平伯. "Honglou meng bian" 《紅樓夢》辯. In *Honglou meng pinglun xuan,* edited by Wang Zhiliang, 1:427-616. Beijing: Zhongguo shehui kexue chubanshe, 1998.

———. "'Honglou meng bian' de xiuzheng" 《紅樓夢辯》的修正. In *Honglou meng pinglun xuan,* edited by Wang Zhiliang, 1:617-23. Beijing: Zhongguo shehui kexue chubanshe, 1998.

———. "Honglou meng jianlun" 《紅樓夢》簡論. In *Mingjia jiedu Honglou meng,* edited by Zhang Baokun, 1:57-73. Ji'nan: Shandong renmin chubanshe, 1998.

Yu Yingshi 余英時. *Honglou meng de liangge shijie.* 紅樓夢的兩個世界. Shanghai: Shanghai shehuikexueyuan, 2002.

———. "Qian Mu yu xin rujia" 錢穆與新儒家. In *You yi feng chui shui shang lin* 猶憶風吹水上鱗, Yu Yingshi, 31-98. Taibei: Sanmin shuju, 1991.

———. *Shi yu Zhongguo wenhua* 士與中國文化. Shanghai: Shanghai renmin chubanshe, 1987.

———. *Song Ming lixue yu zhengzhi wenhua* 宋明理學與政治文化. Guilin: Guangxi Shida chubanshe, 2006.

———. *Zhu Xi de lishi shijie: Songdai shidafu zhengzhi wenhua de yanjiu* 朱熹的歷史世界: 宋代士大夫政治文化的研究. 2 vols. Beijing: Sanlian shudian, 2004.

Yuan Hongdao 袁宏道. *Yuan Hongdao jijian jiao* 袁宏道集箋校. Edited by Qian Bucheng 錢伯城. 3 vols. Shanghai: Shanghai guji chubanshe, 1979.

Yuan Shishuo 袁世碩. "Ming Jiajing ben Sanguozhi tongsu yanyi nai Yuanren Luo Guanzhong yuanzuo" 明嘉靖本《三國志通俗演義》乃元人羅貫中原作. In *Mingjia jiedu Sanguo yanyi* 名家解讀三國演義, edited by Chen Qixin 陳其欣, 425–40. Jinan: Shandong renmin chubanshe, 1998.

Yuanhu yanshui sanren 鴛湖煙水散人 [pseud.]. *Taohua ying* 桃花影. Taibei: Taiwan daying baike gufen youxian gongsi, 1994.

Yue Hengjun 樂蘅軍. "Ma Chunshang zai Xihu" 馬純上在西湖. In *Gudian xiaoshuo sanlun* 古典小說散論, 135–48. Taibei: Da'an chubanshe, 2004.

Zang Jinshu 臧晉叔. *Yuanqu xuan* 元曲選. 4 vols. Beijing: Zhonghua shuju, 1958.

Zeng Jing 曾靜. "Gui ren shuo" 歸仁說. In *Dayi juemi tan*, Yongzheng, 271–85. Shanghai: Shanghai shudian, 1999.

Zhan Changhao 詹長皓. "Shilun Ming chu daru Song Lian zhi si" 試論明初大儒宋濂之死. In *Ming shi yanjiu zhuankan* 明史研究專刊, 5:299–309. Taibei: Mingshi yanjiu xiaozu, 1982.

Zhang Baokun 張寶坤, ed. *Mingjia jiedu Honglou meng* 名家解讀《紅樓夢》. 2 vols. Jinan: Shandong renmin chubanshe, 1998.

Zhang Dai 張岱. *Langhuan wenji* 琅嬛文集. Changsha: Yuelu shushe, 1985.

———. *Taoan mangyi* 陶庵夢憶. Shanghai: Yuandong chubanshe, 1996.

Zhang Guofeng 張國風. *Rulin waishi shilun* 《儒林外史》試論. Beijing: Zhonghua shuju, 2002.

Zhang Guoguang 張國光. "Sangguozhi tongsu yanyi chengshu yu Ming zhongye bian" 三國志通俗演義成書於明中葉辯. In *Sanguo yanyi yanjiuji*, 266–79. Chengdu: Sichuansheng shehuikexueyuan, 1983.

Zhang Peiheng 章培恆. "Guanyu Jiajing ben Sanguozhi tongsu yanyi xiaozhu de zuozhe" 關於《嘉靖本三國志通俗演義》小注的作者. In *Xian yi ji*, Zhang Peiheng, 122–44. Changsha: Yuelu shushe, 1993.

———. "Guanyu Luo Guanzhong de shengzu nian" 關於羅貫中的生卒年. In *Xian yi ji*, Zhang Peiheng, 106–21. Changsha: Yuelu shushe, 1993.

———. *Xian yi ji* 獻疑集. Changsha: Yuelu shushe, 1993.

———. "Zaitan Sanguozhi tongsu yanyi de xiezuo niandai wenti" 再談《三國志通俗演義》的寫作年代問題. In *Xian yi ji*, Zhang Peiheng, 145–78. Changsha: Yuelu shushe, 1993.

Zhang Tingyu 張廷玉 et al. *Ming shi* 明史. 28 vols. Beijing: Zhonghua shuju, 1974.

Zhang Wende 張文德. *Wang Zhaojun gushi de chuancheng yu shanbian* 王昭君故事的傳承與嬗變. Beijing: Xuelin chubanshe, 2008.

Zhang Zai 張載 et al. *Zhangzi zhengmeng* 張子正蒙. Shanghai: Shanghai guji chubanshe, 2000.

Zhao, Henry Y. H. *The Uneasy Narrator: Chinese Fiction from the Traditional to the Modern*. Oxford: Oxford University Press, 1995.

Zhao Jihui 趙吉惠 et al., eds. *Zhongguo ruxueshi* 中國儒學史. Zhengzhou: Zhongzhou guji chubanshe, 1991.

Zhao Yi 趙翼. *Nian'ershi zhaji* 廿二史劄記. 10 vols. Beijing: Zhonghua shuju, 1985.

Zhao Yuan 趙園. *Ming Qing zhi ji shidafu yanjiu* 明清之際士大夫研究. Beijing: Beijing daxue chubanshe, 1999.

Zhao Zifu 趙子富. *Mingdai xuexiao yu keju zhidu yanjiu* 明代學校與科舉制度研究. Beijing: Yanshan chubanshe, 1995.

Zheng Qian 鄭騫, ed. *Jiaoding Yuan kan zaju sanshizhong* 校訂元刊雜劇三十種. Taibei: Shijie shuju, 1962.

Zheng Zhenduo 鄭振鐸. "Sanguozhi yanyi de yanhua" 《三國志演義》的演化. *Zhongguo wenxue yanjiu* 中國文學研究 1:166–239.

———. *Zhongguo wenxue yanjiu* 中國文學研究. 2 vols. Hong Kong: Guwen shuju, 1970.

Zhong Ling 鍾錂. *Yan Xizhai xiansheng yanxing lu* 顏習齋先生言行錄. Taibei: Shangwu yinshuguan, 1939.

Zhong Sicheng 鍾嗣成. *Lu gui bu* 錄鬼簿. In *Zhongguo gudian xiqu lunzhu jicheng*, 2:85–274. Beijing: Zhongguo xiqu chubanshe, 1959–60.

*Zhongguo gudian xiqu lunzhu jicheng* 中國古典戲曲論著集成. Edited by Zhongguo xiqu yanjiuyuan 中國戲曲研究院. 10 vols. Beijing: Zhongguo xiqu chubanshe, 1959–60.

Zhou Jialu 周甲祿. "Shilun Sanguozhi tongsu yanyi dui chuantong sixiang wenhua de fansi" 試論《三國志通俗演義》對傳統思想文化的反思, in *Sanguo yanyi yu Zhongguo wenhua*, edited by Tan Luofei et al., 62–70. Chengdu: Bashu shushe, 1992.

Zhou Junfu 周駿富, ed. *Mingdai zhuanji congkan* 明代傳記叢刊. Taibei: Mingwen shuju, 1991.

Zhou Lengqie 周楞伽. "Guanyu Luo Guanzhong shengping de xin shiliao" 關於羅貫中生平的新史料. In *Sanguo yanyi yu Zhongguo wenhua*, edited by Tan Luofei et al., 119–30. Chengdu: Bashu shushe, 1992.

Zhou Wuchun 周五純. "Cong Sanguo yanyi Chibi zhi zhan tan lishi he xiaoshuo de guanxi" 從《三國演義．赤壁之戰》談歷史和小說的關係. In *Manhua Ming Qing xiaoshuo* 漫話明清小說, 31–40. Beijing: Zhonghua shuju, 1991.

Zhou Zhaoxin 周兆新. *Sanguo yanyi kaoping* 《三國演義》考評. Beijing: Beijing daxue chubanshe, 1990.

Zhu Ronggui 朱榮貴. "Cong Liu Sanwu Mengzi jiewen lun junquan de xianzhi yu zhishifenzi zhi zizhuxing" 從劉三吾《孟子節文》論君權的限制與知識分子之自主性. *Zhongguo wenzhe yanjiu jikan* 中國文哲研究集刊 6 (1995): 173–98.

Zhu Xi 朱熹. *Yupi Tongjian gangmu* 御批通鑑綱目. Siku quanshu ed.

Zhu Yixuan 朱一玄, ed. *Ming Qing xiaoshuo ziliao xuanbian* 明清小說資料選編. 2 vols. Ji'nan: Qi Lu shushe, 1989.

Zhu Yixuan and Liu Yuchen 劉毓忱, eds. *Sanguo yanyi ziliao huibian* 《三國演義》資料匯編. Tianjin: Baihua wenyi chubanshe, 1983.

———, eds. *Shuihu zhuan ziliao huibian* 《水滸傳》資料彙編. Tianjin: Baihua wenyi chubanshe, 1981.

Zhu Yizun 朱彝尊. *Jingyi kao* 經義考. Siku quanshu ed.

Zhuoyuanting Zhuren 酌元亭主人 [pseud.]. *Zhao shi bei* 照世杯. Guben xiaoshuo jicheng ed.

*Zhuzi jicheng* 諸子集成. 8 vols. Beijing: Zhonghua shuju, 1954.

Zuili Yanshui Sanren 檇李煙水散人 [pseud.]. *Taohua ying* 桃花影. Taibei: Taiwan Daying Baike Gufen Youxian Gongsi, 1994.

# Index

Ames, Roger T., 181n12
An Lushan, 158
*Analects* (Lunyu), 149, 209n16, 219n24
Aristotle, 6
Aroma (Hua Xiren), 143, 163

Bai Juyi (772–846), 201n33, 212n53, 224n50
Bai Xindao (d. 1397), 40
Bakhtin, M.M., 97, 226n3
Bao Shuya, 20
Bao Zheng, 66, 197n86
Baohe Palace, 88
Beijing, 114, 115–118, 133
Bo Yi, 53, 115
*Book of Documents*, 123; Old Text portion of, 123
*boshi dizi*, 57, 195n65
Bourdieu, Pierre, 173
*boxue hongci*, 23, 152, 185n37
Brokaw, Cynthia J., 199n11
Brook, Timothy, 203n46, 226n12
Buddhism, 3, 70, 122

*butian* (mending heaven), 140, 143, 169; as metaphor for government service, 143–144, 146, 169, 218n20

Cai Qizun, 73, 93
Cao Cao, 43, 45, 46, 48, 50, 51, 60, 61, 62, 63, 193n49
Cao Huan, 62
Cao Nai, 71, 83, 199n15
Cao Pi, 62
Cao Wanshu, 86
Cao Xueqin (ca. 1715–64), 136, 138, 140, 141, 142, 167, 172, 216n1, 223n46
Cao Yin (1658–1712), 167, 225n64
*Carnal Prayer Mat, The* (Rou putuan), 13, 86–91; Li Yu's authorship of, 206n65
*chaju*, 57, 195n66
Chen Jitai, 221n36
Chen Ping, 56
Chen Que (1604–77), 122, 214n70
Cheng brothers, 30, 32, 102, 122
Cheng Tingzuo (1691–1767), 127, 128

267

Cheng Yi (1033–1107), 156, 223n47
Cheng Yizhong, 192n43
Chenghua (emperor of the Ming), 121
Chen-Zhu school, 9, 10, 23, 30, 32, 100, 122, 124, 132, 165
Chi Hengshan, 117, 129, 133
Chow, Kai-wing, 199n10
Christian church, 11
*Chronicle of the Three Kingdoms* (Sanguo zhi), 34, 44, 45, 49, 52, 58. *See also* Romance of the Three Kingdoms
*Chronicle of Zuo* (Zuo zhuan), 30
*Chunqiu*, 21
Cixi (empress dowager of the Qing), 200n29
*Classified Anecdotes of the Qing Dynasty* (Qing bai lei chao), 139, 204n50, 217n12
*Collection of Commentaries on Spring and Autumn* (Chunqiu chuanshuo huizuan), 24
*Collection of Commentaries on the Book of Poetry* (Shijing chuanshuo huizuan), 24
*Complete Collection of Writings on Nature and Principle* (Xingli Daquan), 23
*Complete Works of Master Zhu* (Zhuzi quanshu), 24
*Comprehensive Elucidations on the Book of Changes* (Zhouyi zhezhong), 24
Confucianism, 3, 10, 21, 24, 49, 57, 100–101, 107; as orthodox ideology, 21, 24, 172; attitude toward women, 96; project of, 18
Confucius, 10, 17, 19, 20, 24, 31, 41, 59, 101, 102, 122, 163, 192n33; as "commoner king," 20
Crab Flower Club (Haitang She), 153
*Creation of the Gods* (Fengshen yanyi), 66
Crimson Pearl (Jiangzhu Xiancao), 153, 157, 165

Dai Mingshi (1653–1713), 127, 214n66
Dai Zhen (1724–77), 31
*dao*, 17, 18, 32, 111–112, 119
*dao* learning (*daoxue*), 10, 17, 23, 67, 179
*dao zun yu shi*, 102
Daoism, 3, 70, 106, 122, 138
*daotong*, 8, 10, 11, 12, 14, 18, 20, 26, 28, 33, 39, 67, 97, 100, 101–103, 111, 112, 113, 118, 136, 138; decline of, 139, 174, 179; evolution of, 182n17; imperial state's appropriation of, 22–26, 172–173; partnership with *zhengtong*, 17–19, 67, 169, 171; power balance with *zhengtong*, 21, 112; rivalry with state power, 102
Daoyan (Yao Guangxiao, 1335–1418), 42
de Bary, William T., 28
*dejun xingdao*, 26, 27, 28, 172, 187n49
Deng Yu, 56
*Diagram of the Great Ultimate* (Taiji tu), 123
Divine Luminescent Page (Shengying Shizhe), 153, 157, 163, 165
*Doctrine of the Mean* (Zhongyong), 149
Dong Qichang (1555–1636), 152
Dong Zhongshu (179–104 BCE), 21
Dong Zhuo, 46

Dongfang Shuo (154–93 BCE), 21, 212n53
Dream of the Red Chamber (Honglou meng), 14, 75, 136–169, 170, 171, 172, 174, 179; alternative titles of, 219n25; *gengchen* edition of, 141, 218n15, 219nn25,27, 222n40; *jiaxu* edition of, 140, 141, 153, 166, 217n14, 219nn25,27; *Qi xu ben*, 219n25; typographic editions of, 218n15, 219n25, 222n40
Du Fu (712–770), 134
Du Shaoqing, 114, 115, 118, 123–124, 128, 129, 134, 135, 168, 174
Du Shengqing, 110
Duan Ganmu, 102, 105, 210n31
Duan Yucai (1735–1815), 31
Duke Huan of the Qi, 20, 21, 58
Duke Miao (of the Lu), 59, 102
Duke of Ningguo (Ningguo Gong), 147
Duke of Rongguo (Rongguo Gong), 147
Duke Zhou, 31, 41

eight-legged essay (*bagu wen*), 57, 90, 110, 118–122, 131, 149; as synecdoche for the examination system, 119; anthologies of, 119–121, 214n65, 214n66; form divorced from content in, 124; in the Ming, 119, 121, 196n67; in the Qing, 119–121, 124–125; prioritized over belletristic writing, 125–126, 214n79, 216n90, 220n30, 221n36; ties to other prose forms, 213n63
Elman, Benjamin A., 42, 67, 192n32, 214n66, 221n32
Emperor Wu (of the Han), 21, 57

Eptein, Maram, 221n37
eremitism, 104, 106
erotic scholar-lover, 67, 69, 70, 74, 80–82, 83, 86, 92, 93, 94, 96, 171
eroticism, fictional, 13, 198n2, 198nn3,4, 205n54
*Essential Meanings of the Works on Human Nature and Principle* (Xingli jingyi), 24
ether (*qi*), 157, 223n47
Evidential Studies (*kaojuxue*), 31, 123–124, 187n66
*Examination for Women, An* (Nükaike zhuan), 80–82, 202n42
examination, metropolitan, 40, 95, 123, 125, 207n70. See also examinations, civil service
examination, palace, 88, 90, 95, 97, 207n70, 208n86. See also examinations, civil service
examination, prefectural, 78. See also examinations, civil service
examination, provincial, 95, 109, 118, 120, 124, 125, 168. See also examinations, civil service
examinations, civil service, 3, 4, 9, 11, 16, 29, 58, 78, 94, 98, 106, 109, 125, 149, 171; and commercial market for fiction, 176–177, 226n11; as analogous to sexual act, 79; as "culture booster," 175–176; as interface between literati and state, 9, 67; as lifeline of imperial state, 94–95; as metaphor in fictional eroticism, 13, 68–79, 86, 89–97; body search in, 200n20; empowering efficacy of, 78; evolution of, 57; examiner and candidates in, 207n73; grading system in, 89,

examinations, civil service *(continued)* 207n70; in the Ming, 220n32; metaphors for success in, 205n57; moral status of, 73; simulated, 80–82. *See also* examination, metropolitan; examination, palace; examination, prefectural; examination, provincial
Exhortation to Studies (Quan xue wen), 16, 173

Fan Jin, 208, 124
Fan Zhongyan (989–1052), 112
Fang Bao (1668–1749), 120
Fang Xiaoru (1357–1402), 41, 191n32, 197n78. *See also* Jianwen martyrs
Fang Yizhi (1611–71), 30
Fanli (Statement of general principles), 14, 140, 141, 142, 144, 145, 148, 154, 155, 157, 161, 165, 218n14
Fei Xiaotong, 18, 28, 182n17
Feng Menglong, 4, 70, 174–175, 178
*fenshu kengru*, 20
filial piety, 106, 148
Five Classics (*wujing*), 23, 149
flower adjudication (*hua'an*), 80, 204n50
Flying Swallow (Zhao Feiyan), 158
Foucault, Michel, 8, 9, 11, 183n26
Four Books (*sishu*), 23, 38, 149, 150
Fourth Sister Lin (Lin Siniang), 150

Gadamer, Han Georg, 181n9
Gao Qi (1336–74), 126, 127
Ge Quan, 182n13
Geng Yan, 56
Goddess of Disenchantment (Jinghuan Xianzi), 147, 153, 157, 158, 159, 162, 164, 165, 167, 225n57

*gong*, 113
*gongming* (rank and fame), 103–104, 107, 108, 115, 120, 128, 131, 133, 134, 166
*gongming fugue*, 103
Gongyang, 21
government service, 5, 6, 14, 19, 27, 28, 32, 96, 138, 140, 153, 165, 167–169, 171–174, 176, 179; as authoritative discourse, 175–176; as Confucian ideal, 17–19, 143; privileged over other professions, 151–152. *See also* examinations, civil service
Gramsci, Antonio, 8
*Grand Announcement* (Dagao), 24
*Grand Collection of the Four Books* (Sishu Daquan), 42
Grandmother Jia, 147, 148, 158
*Great Collection of the Four Treasuries* (Siku quanshu), 23
*Great Compendium of the Yongle* (Yongle dadian), 23
*Great Learning* (Daxue), 18, 122, 149
Great Prospect Garden (Daguanyuan), 142, 150, 160, 161
Gu Yanwu, 24, 29, 31, 112, 113, 114, 117, 119, 120, 227n20
Guan Yu, 45, 50, 58, 61, 62; worship of, 199n18; Yunchang, 45
Guan Zhong (d. 645 BCE), 20
Guangwu (emperor of Eastern Han), 106
Gui Youguang (1506–71), 31
Gui Zhuang (1613–73), 175
*guo*, 112, 113
Guo Kangsong, 31
Guo Tieshan, 219

Han (dynasty), 20, 57, 125
Han (ethnic group), 23

Han Fei (d. 233 BCE), 20
Han Yu (768–824), 182n17, 213n63
Hanan, Patrick, 87, 198n8, 207n65
Hawkes, David, 154, 163
He Xinyin (1517–79), 28
Hegel, Robert, 177, 188n5, 207n65, 216n96, 227n15
Herder, 6
*History as Mirror to Aid Governance* (Zizhi tongjian), 52
Hong-niang, 158
Hongwu (emperor of the Ming), 10, 13, 39, 40, 121, 126, 127; See also Zhu Yuanzhang
Hongzhi (emperor of the Ming), 121
Hsia, C. T., 181n1, 209n2, 216n91
Hu Wei (1633–1714), 123
Hu Weiyong (?-1380), 40, 64–65
Hua Tuo, 50, 193n50
Huang Qiang, 207n65
Huang Tingjian (1045–1106), 144
Huang Zongxi (1610–95), 24, 29, 64, 79, 107, 113, 114, 117, 118, 227n20
Hui Dong (1696–1758), 31
Huizong (emperor of the Northern Song), 74

Illusory Land of Great Void (Taixu Huanjing), 156, 157, 163, 164; Jia Baoyu's dream visit to, 159–162, 162–164, 167
Imperial Academy (Guozijian), 24, 40–41, 191n27
imperial state, 8, 35, 118–128, 126; and the eight-legged essay, 118–122, 124–125; appropriation of *daotong*, 8; manipulation of examination curriculum, 35, 123. See also zhengtong

*Imperially Authorized Edition of Essays on the Four Books* (Qingding Sishuwen), 120–121

Ji Chang, 116
Ji Kang (224–263), 106
Ji Ping, 63
Ji Yun (1724–1805), 75
Jia Baoyu, 14, 75, 136, 138, 140, 143, 144, 145, 147, 170–171, 174, 180; antipathy for examination learning, 148–150; dream visit to Illusory Land of Great Void, 155–161; dream visit to Paradise of Truth, 161; dreams and illusions of, 154–155; as fiction maker, 153, 165; and the jade, 220n27, 221n40; and Jia Yucun, 146–147; qing-li conflict, influenced by, 166; scenarios of qing, exposed to, 164–166; sexual initiation of, 162–164; and Stone, 219n27, 221n40; talent for versification, 150–151, 152–153; in "triplex parallel," 148; and Zhen Baoyu, 167–169
Jia Diru, 150, 151, 166
Jia Kui (174–228), 32
Jia Yuanchun, 75
Jia Yucun, 146–147, 149
Jia Zheng, 142, 148, 150, 151, 152, 170
Jia Zhongming (b. 1343), 36, 37
Jiajing (emperor of the Ming), 24, 121
Jiang Daqi (Yongyuzi), 35, 37
Jiang Gan, 48
Jiang Ziya, 56, 66
Jiangnan, 23, 116
Jianmei, 163
Jianwen (emperor of the Ming), 41
Jianwen martyrs, 41, 191n32

Jiao Hong (1540–1620), 31
Jiaqing (emperor of the Qing) 31
Jie, 42
Jin Shengtan (1718–84), 176, 226n10
Jin Wenzheng (d. 1382), 40
Jing Lanjiang, 126
Jing Yuan, 134
*Journey to the West* (Xiyou ji), 5
Ju Xianfu, 121, 126
*juemin xingdao*, 27
Jung, C.G, 6

Kangxi (emperor of the Qing), 10, 23, 24, 25, 76, 95, 100, 124, 127, 136, 138, 167, 185n37; as "standard bearer of the *daotong*," 25
King, Gail, 190n17
King Wen (of the Zhou), 17, 21, 41, 66, 103, 117
King Wu (of the Zhou), 17, 66, 103
*King Wu's Expedition against King Zhou* (Wu Wang fa Zhou ji), 66
King Xuan (of the Qi), 38
Ko, Dorothy, 204n50
Kong Rong, 49
Kong Yingda (574–648), 156
Kuang Chaoren, 108, 111, 120, 121, 124
Kuhn, Philip, 137–138

Lady Yang (Yang Yuhuan), 158, 224n55
Latter Seven Scholars (*houqizi*), 152
*Laws of the Mind in the Sages' Learning* (Shengxue xinfa), 23, 185n32
ledgers of merits and demerits (*gongguoge*), 70–71, 72–73, 85, 96
*Ledger of Merits and Demerits Regarding the Ten Precepts* (Shi jie gongguoge), 70–71
*Ledger of Merits and Demerits to Warn the World* (Jingshi gongguoge), 70–71
Leng Zixing, 146
*li* (moral principle), 12, 29, 112; relationship to *qing*, 165, 166
Li Bai (701–762), 134, 201n33, 212n53
Li Baichuan (ca. 1720–71), 138
Li Chen, 217n13
Li Gong (1659–1733), 30, 99, 107, 128–129, 215n88; influence on Wu Jingzi, 215n86
Li Guangdi (1642–1718), 25
Li Lüyuan (1707–90), 138
Li Shanchang (1314–90), 64
Li Shizhen (1518–93), 30
Li Si (d. 208 BCE), 20
Li Wa, 74, 200n23
Li, Wai-yee, 141, 222nn41,43
Li Yu (1611–80), 13, 74–75, 78, 84–91, 176
*li yue bing nong*, 99, 129, 131, 133
Li Yuerui (1862–1927), 217n7
Li Zhi (1527–1602), 28, 57, 69, 176
Liang Qichao (1873–1929), 23, 31, 227n20
Liang Zhangju (1775–1849), 119, 213n63, 215n79
*Liangzhi*, 27
*lijia*, 22
Lin Daiyu, 148, 157, 163
Lin, Shuen-fu, 98, 159
literary inquisition, 11, 24, 31–32; during the Yongzheng reign, 215n83
literati, 8, 9, 11, 12, 13, 14, 16, 19, 25, 28, 32, 78, 103, 118, 171; in Qianlong period, 138–140; speech rights of, 12; and textual culture, 14, 99, 118–122, 128; women, compared

to, 78–79, 202nn34,35. *See also* shi
(intellectual elite)
Liu Bang (emperor of the Han), 20, 49,
184nn19,20
Liu Bei, 34, 43, 45, 50, 52, 53, 54, 56, 58,
60–63, 66; and sworn brothers,
60–63, 197n77; three visits to
Zhuge Liang, 53–54, 66; Xuande,
46
Liu Cunren (Ts'un-yan Liu), 190n17,
207n65
Liu Ji (1311–75), 105
Liu Sanwu (1319–1400), 39, 40
Liu Xiang, 158
Liu Xie, 62
Liu Zhu, 127
Liu Zongzhou (1578–1645), 22
Liuxia Hui, 115
*liyin*, 115, 212n53
Lone Peak (Gufeng Zhanglao), 87
Louie, Kam, 200n18
Lü Kun (1536–1618), 29, 112
Lü Liuliang (1629–83), 101, 102,
119–120, 214n66
Lu Su, 48
Lu Xiaojie (Miss Lu), 125
Lu Xinhou, 127
Lu Xun, 206n65
Lü Zaisheng, 85
Lu Zhishen, 130
Lukacs, Georg, 5
Luo Guanzhong, 36, 37
Lu-Wang school, 122

Ma Chunshang, 108, 110–111, 120, 121,
122, 125, 127, 133
Ma Rong (79–166), 32
McLaren, Anne E., 190n16
McMahon, Keith, 198n2, 205n54

Mair, Victor, 223n44
Male Mother Meng Thrice Changes
His Residence, A (Nan Mengmu
jiaohe sanqian), 85
Manchu, 22, 23, 25, 100, 112, 123, 125
Mao, Nathan, 207n65
Mao Yanshou, 77
Mao Zonggang (1632–1709), 43, 47, 62,
176, 193n48, 194n54, 196n76
Marquis Wen (of the Wei), 102
*Meeting in Xiangyang* (Xiangyang
hui), 52
Mencius, 10, 13, 17, 18, 19, 31, 39,
52–53, 59, 60, 101, 102, 104, 115,
163, 210n19; ideal of benevolent
governance, 42–43; ideal of
political sovereignty, 13, 35, 43, 65,
66; mother of, 206n60
*Mencius* (Mengzi), 13, 35, 38, 39, 40, 41,
42, 59, 63, 65, 104, 122, 149, 192n37;
early Ming suppression of, 13, 23,
35, 41–42; expurgated version of,
39, 42, 46; restoration of complete
version of, 42.
Ming (dynasty), 3, 7, 10, 13, 21, 23, 28,
30, 36, 38–42, 57, 58, 64, 70, 71, 95,
125, 152; downfall of, 22, 30; early
decades of, 38–42; eight-legged
essay in, 119, 121
*Ming wenhai*, 118
*Ming yi dai fang lu*, 113
Ming-Qing transition, 29, 30, 79
*mingshi*, 109
Miyazaki, Ichisada, 88
Muses, 160

Nanjing, 100, 114, 115–118, 129, 131, 133,
134, 212n57
Naquin, Susan, 139, 175, 182n16, 185n36

*nei sheng*, 18
*nei sheng wai wang*, 18, 184n10
neo-Confucianism, 12, 24, 31, 32, 70, 100, 122, 156; as foundation of examination curriculum, 24, 120; mistrust of human desires, 70; textual crisis of, 122–125
New Historicism, 6
Ni Shuangfeng, 132
Nian Gengyao (d. 1726), 100, 209n11
Niu Buyi, 110
Niu Pulang, 110, 111
Northern Song (dynasty), 7, 22, 26
Nüwa, 143, 154, 165, 169

Oboi regency, 23
O-erh-tai (1680–1745), 125, 137, 173
Ouyang Xiu (1007–72), 212n53, 213n63

Pan Pingge (1610–77), 122
Pang Tong, 50
Paradise of Truth (Zhenru Fudi), 157
Pei Songzhi (372–451), 53, 194n57
*Ping Shan Leng Yan*, 4
*ping tianxia*, 143
Ping Shaobao (Marshal Ping), 129–130, 132
Plaks, Andrew, 38, 194n58
*Plum in the Golden Vase* (Jin Ping Mei), 68
*Poetry Classic* (Shijing), 149
*Popular Stories of the Three Kingdoms* (Sanguozhi pinghua), 44, 52, 56, 58. *See also* Romance of the Three Kingdoms
Pretense Became Reality in the Seven-Pine Garden (Qisongyuan nongjia chengzhen), 152

*Previously Unrecorded Account of the Daye Reign* (Daye shiyi ji), 68, 198n3
Prince of Wu'an (Wu'an Wang), 72, 73
Pu Songling (1640–1715), 178

*qijia*, 143
Qian Daxi (1728–1804), 31
Qian Mingshi (1660–1730), 100–101, 209n11
Qian Mu (1895–1990), 32, 172, 215n88
Qian Tang (d. 1394), 39; confrontation with Zhu Yuanzhang, 191n22
Qian-Jia Han learning (*Han xue*), 31
Qianlong (emperor of the Qing), 10, 23, 24, 31, 120, 125, 138–139, 152, 173, 217n7; return to the Three Generations, 136–138
Qin (dynasty), 20,
Qin (state), 22, 102
Qin Shi (Qin Keqing), 158, 159, 164, 225n60; name of, 225n59
Qing (dynasty), 3, 7, 10, 15, 21, 24, 32, 70, 71, 76, 95, 103, 112, 119–120, 152; eight-legged essay in, 119–121, 124–125; High Qing, 23, 139
*qing*, 12, 164, 165, 166, 225n60; different scenarios of, 164–165; as fiction-making material, 165; relationship to *li*, 165, 166
Qu Yuan (340?–278 BCE), 78, 202n34

Rawski, Evelyn, 139, 175, 182n16, 185n36
*Record of Being Awakened from Befuddlement by the Cardinal Principles* (Dayi juemi lu), 101
*Record of Learning the New* (Zhixin lu), 101
Red Cliffs, 45, 48, 50, 56, 62

Red Inkstone (Zhiyanzhai), 142, 146, 159, 160, 165, 167, 217n14, 220n29, 225nn58,61
*Registers of Heroes* (Yingxiong pu), 4
*Registry of Ghosts* (Luguibu), 58
Renzong (emperor of the Song), 110, 111
Richards, I. A., 208n81
Ricoeur, Paul, 93, 97
ritualism, 99, 114
Roddy, Stephen J., 99, 119, 130, 211n33
*Romance of the Embroidered Screen* (Xiu ping yuan), 82–83, 94, 204n51
*Romance of the Three Kingdoms* (Sanguo yanyi), 4, 13, 34–66, 171, 177; 1522 edition of (*Sanguozhi tongsu yanyi*), 35–36, 188n8, 189n15, 190n17, 190nn19,20, 193nn44,48, 196n69; pro-Shu and anti-Wei stance in, 63; simplified version (*jianben*) of, 4; and Three Kingdoms variety plays (*sanguo zaju*), 55–56; Wanjuanlou edition of, 189n8; *zhizhuan* editions of, 38, 190n17. See also Chronicle of the Three Kingdoms, Popular Stories of the Three Kingdoms, Three Kingdoms variety plays
Ropp, Paul, 211n49
Ruan Ji (210–263), 106
*rushi*, 106, 117

*Sacred Edict* (Shengyu), 24
*Sacred Edict for General Admonitions* (Shengyu guangxun), 24
*Sacred Edict in Six Maxims* (Shengyu liuyan), 24
*San yan*, 4
scholar-beauty (*caizi jiaren*) fiction, 68, 203n42
scholar-courtesan romance, 80–82, 203n45
scholars, selection of, 13, 75, 171; compared with selection of women 77–78, 79, 81–82, 86, 87–88, 92–94
*Scholars, The* (Rulin waishi), 13–14, 96, 98–135, 139, 140, 152, 168, 172, 174, 179, 204n50; narrative structure of, 98–100, 216n91; Qixingtang edition of, 103, 128; Woxian Caotang edition of, 103, 114, 126
*Sequel to the Registry of Ghosts* (Luguibu xubian), 36, 37, 189nn12,13
Seven Worthies of the Bamboo Grove (*zhulin qixian*), 106
*Shadow of the Peach Blossoms* (Taohua ying), 83–84, 94, 205n53
Shang (dynasty), 26
Shang Wei, 99, 131, 132, 213n57
Shen Defu (1578–1642), 22, 79, 200n20
Shen Qiongzhi, 130
Shenzong (emperor of the Ming), 27. See also Wanli
Shenzong (emperor of the Northern Song), 26
*shi* (intellectual elite), 7, 8, 17, 18, 19, 20, 21, 28, 60, 78, 179; as upholders of the *daotong*, 20; balance of power with political state, 20–22; compared to women, 78–79; origin of the term, 7; relationship with political power, 9, 22, 172. See also literati; daotong
*shi* (political power), 7, 8, 17, 112; relationship with intellectual elite, 9, 22, 172. See also zhengtong

*shidafu* (intellectual elite), 7; origin of the term, 7
Shitou ji, 14
Shu (kingdom), 47, 60
Shu-ho-te (1711–77), 125
Shun, 17, 31, 61, 103, 137
Shunzhi (emperor of the Qing), 24
*si*, 113
Sima Yan, 62
Skybright (Qingwen), 150
Song (dynasty), 21, 57, 95, 122
Song Lian (1310–81), 40, 105; death of, 191n25
Song Na (d. 1390), 40
Song Yingxing (1587–?), 30
Southern Song (dynasty), 7, 22
Spring and Autumn period, 17, 101, 179
Stone, 14, 136, 144, 146, 148, 153–154, 157, 159, 161, 163, 165, 166, 169; and Jia Baoyu, 219n27
*Stories Old and New* (Gujin xiaoshuo), 174
*Story of the Lord of Perfect Satisfaction* (Ruyijun zhuan), 68, 198n4
Story of the Stone (Shitou ji), 145, 154, 155, 157, 159, 161, 162, 168
*Story of the Stone* (Shitou ji), 145. See also Dream of the Red Chamber
*Strange Tales from Liaozhai* (Liaozhai zhiyi), 178
Struve, Lynn A., 185n35
Sui (dynasty), 9, 95
Sun Ce, 47
Sun Kaidi, 206n65
Sun Quan, 43, 46, 47, 48, 50, 56, 60
Sun Wukong, 5, 133
symbolic order, 14, 173, 174, 175, 176, 178
symbolic violence, 173

Tai Bo, 99, 116, 118, 128, 129, 131, 215n85
*taixu* (great void), 156, 157, 223n46
Taizhou school, 28, 69, 70
Taizong (emperor of the Tang), 9, 79, 95, 137, 208n83
Taizu (emperor of the Song), 64, 197n79
Tan Shaowen, 138
Tanchun, 153
Tang, 17, 21, 22, 103
Tang (dynasty), 9, 57, 95, 122, 125
Tang Ying (1470–1523), 70
Tang Zhen (1630–1704), 29
Tang Zongzhen (General Tang), 130, 132
Tao Qian, 46, 62
Tao Yuanming (376–427), 115
Three Generations, 137, 138
Three Kingdoms period, 13, 26, 57
Three Kingdoms variety plays (*Sanguo zayu*), 55–56, 58, 195n62. See also Romance of the Three Kingdoms
Tian Feng, 47
Tianhuazang Zhuren (Owner of the Depository of Heavenly Flowers), 4
*tianxia*, 99, 112, 113, 129, 178
*tianzi*, 99, 112, 113, 178
*tingzhang*, 22
Tower for Stroking Clouds (Fu yun lou), 85
Tower of Summer Pleasure (Xia yi lou), 84–85
Tower of the Returned Crane (He gui ji), 74–75, 78, 84
Tower of Winning the Contest (Duo jin lou), 84
*Trace of the Immortals on a Green Land* (Lüye xianzong), 138

Tu Wei-ming, 8, 19
*tuoxuren*, 139
Twelve Beauties from Jinling (Jinling shi'er chai), 159

*Unofficial History of Yang Taizhen, An* (Yang Taizhen waizhuan), 68, 198n3
*Unofficial History of Zhao Feiyan, An* (Zhao Feiyan waizhuan), 68, 198n3

Vanitas (Kongkong Daoren), 145, 154, 162
vernacular fiction, 3–15; as "action," 11; as channel for venting personal grievances, 5; and exodus of literati from government service, 178–180; as late chapter of the *shi-shi* relationship, 12; preparing writers of, 177; pre-Qin *xiaoshuo*, compared to, 175; in sociopolitical reality, 7; and Western novel, 5, 174, 177, 226n4; written vernacular as literary language in, 177–178
Vesperus (Weiyang Sheng), 87–91

*wai wang*, 18, 26
Wan Sida (1633–83), 17
Wang Anshi (1021–86), 26, 27, 57, 201n33; and the eight-legged essay, 57, 196n67, 212n53, 213n63
Wang Dingbao, 183n33
Wang Fuzhi (1619–92), 107, 156, 223n48, 227n20
Wang Gen (1483–1541), 28
Wang Guangyang (?–1379)
Wang Hui, 126, 127
Wang Maitao, 71

Wang Mian, 103–107, 108, 110, 114, 134, 210n33
Wang Niansun (1744–1832), 31
Wang Shizhen (1526–90), 152, 207n73, 214n79
Wang Xuetai, 139
Wang Yangming (1472–1528), 27, 28, 29, 30, 178, 226n11, 227n20
Wang Yinzhi (1766–1834), 31
Wang Yuhui, 131–133
Wang Zhaojun, 77–78, 201nn32,33
Wang Zhu, 183n1
Wang Zi'an, 178
Wanli (emperor of the Ming), 27, 65, 134, 208n86
*Warning Light for the Wrong Path* (Qi lu deng), 138
Warring States period, 101
*Water Margins* (Shuihu zhuan), 4, 38, 118, 130, 131, 177, 216n96, 227n16; Rongyutang edition of, 3–4; simplified version (*jianben*) of, 4, 38
Watt, Ian, 177
Wei (kingdom), 47
Wei Su, 104, 105
Wei Tishan, 120, 121
Wei Yuqing, 83–84
Wen Chou, 47
Wen Ruyu, 138
Wen Yanbo (1006–97), 22
*Wenmu shanfang ji*, 116
White, Hayden, 12
Wilhelm, Hellmut, 202n34
Window Sets a Ruse to Get a Bridegroom and Several Beauties Join Their Efforts to Seize a Talented Scholar, A (Guafu sheji zhui xinlang, zhongmei qixin duo caizi), 85–86

women, selection of, 13, 75–78, 200n30; compared with selection of scholars, 77–78, 79, 81–82, 86, 87–88, 92–94
Wong, Timothy, 104, 209n3
*World-Illuminating Cup, The* (Zhaoshibei), 152
Wu (kingdom), 47, 62
Wu Han (1909–69), 21
Wu Jingzi (1701–54), 13, 98, 99, 100, 103, 104, 105, 113, 116, 120, 125, 128, 172; as influenced by Gu Yanwu and Huang Zongxi, 211n49; ties to Yan Yuan and Li Gong, 215n86
Wu Shu, 132
Wu Zetian, 68, 95, 158, 223n50
Wu Zuxiang, 188n2
Wuzong (emperor of the Ming), 27, 41

Xi Shi, 158
Xia, 26
*xianliang fangzheng*, 21
Xiao Yunxian, 129, 131, 132
*xiaoshuo*, 12, 174–175
Xie Liu, 105, 210n31
Ximen Qing, 68
Xu Chu, 49
Xu Da (1332–85), 64
Xu Guangqi (1562–1633), 30
Xu Ke (1869–1928), 139
Xu Shen (58–149), 32
Xu Shu, 50, 51, 53, 54
Xu Wei (1521–93), 217n10
Xu Xiake (1586–1641), 30
Xu You, 47, 48
*xuanxiu*, 76
Xue Aocao, 68
Xue Baochai, 143, 163
Xue Pan, 143

Xun Yu, 49
Xunzi, 19

Yan Buke, 182n13
Yan Gongsheng (Senior Licentiate Yan), 96, 109, 111
Yan Hui (521–481 BCE), 134
Yan Liang, 47
Yan Ruoqu (1638–1704), 31, 122
Yan Yuan (1635–1704), 30, 31, 99, 107, 128–129, 215n88; influence on Wu Jingzi, 215n86
Yan Ziling, 106
Yang Minglang (late Ming), 4
Yang Shen (1488–1559), 31
Yang Weizhen (1296–1370), 78
Yao, 17, 31, 62, 103, 137
Yi Yin, 56
Ying Zheng (King of the Qin), 20
Yongle (emperor of the Ming), 10, 23, 121. *See also* Zhu Di
Yongzheng (emperor of the Qing), 10, 24, 25, 26, 79, 100–103, 120, 127, 136, 138, 215n83
You Ruilang, 85
Yu, 17, 26, 62, 103, 137
Yu, Anthony, 149, 155, 220n31
Yu Chaogui, 190n17
Yu Kai (d. 1382), 40
Yu Mengbai, 80, 81
Yu Pingbo (1900–90), 218n19
Yu Xiangdou (fl. 1596), 226n12
Yu Yingshi, 11, 17, 22, 27, 111, 182n17, 184n27, 224n55, 226n11
Yu Yude, 114, 115, 117, 134
Yuan (dynasty), 9, 36
Yuan Hongdao (1568–1610), 69
Yuan Shao, 47, 48, 49, 61
Yue (state), 22

Yue Fei (1103–42), 79, 218n20
Yue Lin (d. 1394), 40
Yue Zhongqi (1686–1754), 79, 101

*zaixiang*, 64–66
Zeng Jing (1679–1735), 25, 26, 79, 101–102, 186n45, 186n47
Zeng shen (505–436 BCE), 122, 134
Zhang Dai (1597–1679), 69
Zhang Fei, 58, 61, 62
Zhang Guofeng, 212n49
Zhang Jun (1097–1164), 218n20
Zhang Juzheng (1525–82), 27, 65
Zhang Liang, 49, 56
Zhang Shangde (Xiuranzi), 35
Zhang Tingyu (1672–1755), 137
Zhang Wenhu (1808–85), 104, 108, 211n35, 211n41
Zhang Xin (d. 1397), 40
Zhang Xuecheng (1738–1801), 34
Zhang Zai (1020–77), 156, 157, 223n47
Zhao Fushan, 72
Zhao, Henry Y. H., 144
Zhao Xuezhai, 109, 126
Zhao Yi (1727–1814), 185n29
Zhao Yun, 60
Zhao Yunke, 83
Zhen Baoyu, 166; and Jia Baoyu, 167–169
Zhen Shiyin, 153, 154
Zheng Xie (1693–1765), 217n10
Zheng Xuan (127–200), 32
Zheng Zhenduo (1898–1958), 189n11, 190n16
Zhengde (emperor of the Ming), 121
*zhengqi*, 148
*zhengtong*, 10, 18, 20, 21, 33, 67; appropriation of *daotong*, 22–26; partnership with *daotong*, 17–19, 67, 169, 171; power balance with *daotong*, 21, 112; rivalry with *daotong*, 102
Zhenzong (emperor of the Song), 16,
Zhi Jianfeng, 216
*zhiguo*, 143
*zhong*, 148
Zhou (ancient tyrannical ruler), 42
Zhou (dynasty), 26
Zhou Dunyi (1017–73), 123
Zhou Jialu, 192n43
Zhou Jin, 108, 125, 152, 153
Zhou Yu, 47, 55
Zhou Zhaoxin, 188n2, 192n43, 196n74
Zhu Di, 10, 23, 63. *See also* Yongle
Zhu Xi (1130–1200), 25, 30, 32, 43, 70, 102, 122, 123–124, 156, 223n48
Zhu Yuanzhang, 13, 22, 24, 27, 38, 39, 40, 41, 53, 59, 63, 64, 78, 95, 105, 173; suppression of *Mencius*, 23, 38–40; treatment of literati, 39–41. *See also* Hongwu
Zhu Yunming (1460–1526), 39, 70
Zhuang Shaoguang, 114, 115, 117, 127, 131
*Zhuangzi*, 156, 222n44
Zhuge Liang, 26, 35, 52, 53–61, 66, 171, 186n48, 194nn57,59, 196nn74,76; in the novel and in popular three Kingdoms tradition compared, 55–56; Kongming, 45
*Zhuge Liang Attacks [Cao Cao's] Camp in Bowang with Fire* (Zhuge Liang Bowang shaotun), 55
Zi Si (483–02 BCE), 59, 102
Zou Yang (2nd cent. BCE), 78, 202n35